Lecture Notes in Computer Science 3278

Commenced Publication in 1973
Founding and Former Series Editors:
Gerhard Goos, Juris Hartmanis, and Jan van Leeuwen

T0223705

Akhil Sahai   Felix Wu (Eds.)

Utility Computing

15th IFIP/IEEE International Workshop
on Distributed Systems: Operations and Management, DSOM 2004
Davis, CA, USA, November 15-17, 2004
Proceedings

 Springer

Volume Editors

Akhil Sahai
Hewlett-Packard Labs
1501 Page Mill Road, Palo-Alto, CA 94304, USA
E-mail: akil.sahai@hp.com

Felix Wu
University of California, Department of Computer Science
One Shields Avenue, Davis, CA 95616, USA
E-mail: wu@cs.ucdavis.edu

Library of Congress Control Number: 2004113913

CR Subject Classification (1998): C.2.4, C.2, D.1.3, D.4.4, K.6, K.4.4

ISSN 0302-9743
ISBN 3-540-23631-7 Springer Berlin Heidelberg New York

Springer is a part of Springer Science+Business Media

springeronline.com

© 2004 IFIP International Federation for Information Processing, Hofstrasse 3, A-2361 Laxenburg, Austria
Printed in Germany

Typesetting: Camera-ready by author, data conversion by PTP-Berlin, Protago-TeX-Production GmbH
Printed on acid-free paper   SPIN: 11339861   06/3142   5 4 3 2 1 0

Preface

This volume of the Lecture Notes in Computer Science series contains all the papers accepted for presentation at the 13th IFIP/IEEE International Workshop on Distributed Systems: Operations and Management (DSOM 2004), which was held at the University of California, Davis during November 15–17, 2004.

DSOM 2004 was the fifteenth workshop in a series of annual workshops and it followed in the footsteps of highly successful previous meetings, the most recent of which were held in Heidelberg, Germany (DSOM 2003), Montreal, Canada (DSOM 2002), Nancy, France (DSOM 2001), and Austin, USA (DSOM 2000). The goal of the DSOM workshops is to bring together researchers in the areas of networks, systems, and services management, from both industry and academia, to discuss recent advances and foster future growth in this field. In contrast to the larger management symposia, such as IM (Integrated Management) and NOMS (Network Operations and Management Symposium), the DSOM workshops are organized as single-track programs in order to stimulate interaction among participants.

The focus of DSOM 2004 was "Management Issues in Utility Computing." Increasingly there is a trend now towards managing large infrastructures and services within utility models where resources can be obtained on demand. Such a trend is being driven by the desire to consolidate infrastructures within enterprises and across enterprises using third-party infrastructure providers and networked infrastructures like Grid and PlanetLab. The intent in these initiatives is to create systems that provide automated provisioning, configuration, and lifecycle management of a wide variety of infrastructure resources and services, on demand. The papers presented at the workshop address the underlying technologies that are key to the success of the utility computing paradigm.

This year we received about 110 high-quality papers of which 21 long papers were selected for the 7 long paper sessions and 4 short papers were selected for the short paper session. The technical sessions covered the topics "Management Architectures," "SLA and Business Objective Driven Management," "Policy-Based Management," "Automated Management," "Analysis and Reasoning in Management," "Trust and Security," and "Implementation, Instrumentation, Experience."

This workshop owed its success to all the members of the technical program committee, who did an excellent job of encouraging their colleagues in the field to submit a total of 110 high-quality papers, and who devoted a lot of their time to help create an outstanding technical program. We thank them profusely. We would like to thank Hewlett-Packard and HP Laboratories, the DSOM 2004 Corporate Patron.

September 2004

Akhil Sahai,
Felix Wu

DSOM 2004

November 15–17, 2004, Davis, California, USA

Sponsored by
Hewlett-Packard
IFIP

in cooperation with
IEEE Computer Society
Computer Science Department, University of California, Davis

Program Chairs

Akhil Sahai, Hewlett-Packard, Palo Alto, California, USA

Felix Wu, University of California at Davis, USA

Program Committee

Anerousis, Nikos .... IBM T.J. Watson Research Center, USA
Boutaba, Raouf .... University of Waterloo, Canada
Brunner, Marcus .... NEC Europe, Germany
Burgess, Mark .... University College Oslo, Norway
Cherkaoui, Omar .... Université du Québec á Montréal, Canada
Clemm, Alexander .... Cisco, California, USA
Feridun, Metin .... IBM Research, Switzerland
Festor, Olivier .... LORIA-INRIA, France
Geihs, Kurt .... TU Berlin, Germany
Gentzsch,Wolfgang .... Sun Microsystems, USA
Hegering, Heinz-Gerd .... Institut für Informatik der LMU, Germany
Hellerstein, Joseph .... IBM T.J. Watson Research Center, USA
Jakobson, Gabe .... Smart Solutions Consulting, USA
Kaiser, Gail .... Columbia University, USA
Kar, Gautam .... IBM T.J. Watson Research Center, USA
Kawamura, Ryutaro .... NTT Cyber Solutions Labs, Japan
Keller, Alexander .... IBM T.J. Watson Research Center, USA
Lala, Jaynarayan .... Raytheon, USA
Lewis, Lundy .... Lundy Lewis Associates, USA
Liotta, Antonio .... University of Surrey, UK
Lupu, Emil .... Imperial College London, UK
Lutfiyya, Hanan .... University of Western Ontario, Canada
Martin-Flatin, J.P. .... CERN, Switzerland
Maughan, Douglas .... DHS/HSARPA,USA
Mazumdar, Subrata .... Avaya Labs Research, Avaya, USA

Nogueira, Jose .... Federal University of Minas Gerais, Brazil
Pavlou, George .... University of Surrey, UK
Pras, Aiko .... University of Twente, The Netherlands
Quittek, Juergen .... NEC Europe, Germany
Raz, Danny .... Technion, Israel
Rodosek, Gabi Dreo .... Leibniz Supercomputing Center, Germany
Schoenwaelder, Juergen .... International University Bremen, Germany
Sethi, Adarshpal .... University of Delaware, USA
Singhal, Sharad .... Hewlett-Packard Labs, USA
Sloman, Morris .... Imperial College London, UK
Stadler, Rolf .... KTH, Sweden
State, Radu .... LORIA-INRIA, France
Stiller, Burkhard ..... UniBW Munich, Germany & ETH Zurich, Switzerland
Torsten, Braun .... University of Bern, Switzerland
Tutschku, Kurt .... University of Wuerzburg, Germany
Wang, Yi-Min .... Microsoft Research, USA
Becker, Carlos Westphall .... Federal University of Santa Catarina, Brazil
Yoshiaki, Kirha .... NEC, Japan

Table of Contents

Management Architecture

Requirements on Quality Specification Posed by Service Orientation   1
Markus Garschhammer, Harald Roelle

Automating the Provisioning of Application Services
with the BPEL4WS Workflow Language   15
Alexander Keller, Remi Badonnel

HiFi+: A Monitoring Virtual Machine
for Autonomic Distributed Management   28
Ehab Al-Shaer, Bin Zhang

SLA Based Management

Defining Reusable Business-Level QoS Policies for DiffServ   40
André Beller, Edgard Jamhour, Marcelo Pellenz

Policy Driven Business Performance Management   52
Jun-Jang Jeng, Henry Chang, Kumar Bhaskaran

Business Driven Prioritization of Service Incidents   64
Claudio Bartolini, Mathias Sallé

Policy Based Management

A Case-Based Reasoning Approach for Automated Management
in Policy-Based Networks   76
Nancy Samaan, Ahmed Karmouch

An Analysis Method for the Improvement of Reliability
and Performance in Policy-Based Management Systems   88
Naoto Maeda, Toshio Tonouchi

Policy-Based Resource Assignment
in Utility Computing Environments   100
*Cipriano A. Santos, Akhil Sahai, Xiaoyun Zhu, Dirk Beyer,
Vijay Machiraju, Sharad Singhal*

Automated Management

Failure Recovery in Distributed Environments
with Advance Reservation Management Systems   112
Lars-Olof Burchard, Barry Linnert

Autonomous Management of Clustered Server Systems Using JINI 124
    Chul Lee, Seung Ho Lim, Sang Soek Lim, Kyu Ho Park

Event-Driven Management Automation in the ALBM Cluster System ... 135
    Dugki Min, Eunmi Choi

Analysis and Reasoning

A Formal Validation Model for the Netconf Protocol 147
    *Sylvain Hallé, Rudy Deca, Omar Cherkaoui, Roger Villemaire,
    Daniel Puche*

Using Object-Oriented Constraint Satisfaction
for Automated Configuration Generation............................ 159
    *Tim Hinrich, Nathaniel Love, Charles Petrie, Lyle Ramshaw,
    Akhil Sahai, Sharad Singhal*

Problem Determination Using Dependency Graphs
and Run-Time Behavior Models 171
    *Manoj K. Agarwal, Karen Appleby, Manish Gupta, Gautam Kar,
    Anindya Neogi, Anca Sailer*

Trust and Security

Role-Based Access Control for XML Enabled Management Gateways 183
    V. Cridlig, O. Festor, R. State

Spotting Intrusion Scenarios from Firewall Logs
Through a Case-Based Reasoning Approach 196
    *Fábio Elias Locatelli, Luciano Paschoal Gaspary,
    Cristina Melchiors, Samir Lohmann, Fabiane Dillenburg*

A Reputation Management and Selection Advisor Schemes
for Peer-to-Peer Systems 208
    Loubna Mekouar, Youssef Iraqi, Raouf Boutaba

Implementation, Instrumentation, Experience

Using Process Restarts to Improve Dynamic Provisioning 220
  * *Raquel V. Lopes, Walfredo Cirne, Francisco V. Brasileiro*

Server Support Approach to Zero Configuration In-Home Networking.... 232
    *Kiyohito Yoshihara, Takeshi Kouyama, Masayuki Nishikawa,
    Hiroki Horiuchi*

Rule-Based CIM Query Facility for Dependency Resolution 245
    Shinji Nakadai, Masato Kudo, Koichi Konishi

Short Papers

Work in Progress: Availability-Aware Self-Configuration
in Autonomic Systems 257
David M. Chess, Vibhore Kumar, Alla Segal, Ian Whalley

ABHA: A Framework for Autonomic Job Recovery 259
Charles Earl, Emilio Remolina, Jim Ong, John Brown,
Chris Kuszmaul, Brad Stone

Can ISPs and Overlay Networks Form a Synergistic Co-existence? 263
Ram Keralapura, Nina Taft, Gianluca Iannaccone, Chen-Nee Chuah

Simplifying Correlation Rule Creation
for Effective Systems Monitoring 266
C. Araujo, A. Biazetti, A. Bussani, J. Dinger, M. Feridun,
A. Tanner

Author Index 269

Requirements on Quality Specification Posed by Service Orientation

Markus Garschhammer and Harald Roelle

Munich Network Management Team
University of Munich
Oettingenstr. 67
D-80538 Munich, Germany
{markus.garschammer,harald.roelle}@ifi.lmu.de

Abstract. As service orientation is gaining more and more momentum, the need for common concepts regarding Quality of Service (QoS) and its specification emerges. In recent years numerous approaches to specifying QoS were developed for special subjects like multimedia applications or middleware for distributed systems. However, a survey of existing approaches regarding their contribution to service oriented QoS specification is still missing.

In this paper we present a strictly service oriented, comprehensible classification scheme for QoS specification languages. The scheme is based on the MNM Service Model and the newly introduced LAL–brick which aggregates the dimensions Life cycle, Aspect and Layer of a QoS specification. Using the terminology of the MNM Service Model and the graphical notation of the LAL–brick we are able to classify existing approaches to QoS specification. Furthermore we derive requirements for future specification concepts applicable in service oriented environments.

Keywords: QoS specification, service orientation, classification scheme

1 Introduction

In recent years Telco and IT industries have been shifting their business from monolithic realizations to the composition of products by outsourcing, which results in creating business critical value chains. This trend has had its impact on IT management and paved the way for concepts subsumed under the term service (oriented) management. Now, that relations involved in providing a service are crossing organizational boundaries, unambiguous specifications of interfaces are more important than ever before. In federated environments they are a fundament for rapid and successful negotiation as well as for smooth operation. Here, not only functional aspects have to be addressed, but quality is also an important issue.

In the context of service management, the technical term Quality of Service (QoS) is now perceived in its original sense. Prior to the era of service orientation, the term QoS was mainly referred to as some more or less well defined technical criterion on the network layer. Nowadays, QoS is regaining its original meaning of describing a service's quality in terms which are intrinsic to the service itself. Furthermore, QoS now

A. Sahai and F. Wu (Eds.): DSOM 2004, LNCS 3278, pp. 1–14, 2004.

reflects the demand for customer orientation, as QoS should be expressed in a way that customers understand, and not in the way a provider's implementation dictates it.

In the past, a number of QoS specification concepts and languages have been proposed. Unfortunately, when applied to real world scenarios in a service oriented way, each shows weaknesses in different situations. For example, considering negotiations between a customer and a provider, some are well suited regarding customer orientation, as they are easily understood by the customer. But they are of only limited use for the provider's feasibility and implementation concerns. Other specification techniques suffer from the inverse problem.

Apparently there is room for improvement in service oriented specification of service quality. This paper contributes to the field by introducing a classification scheme for quality specification techniques which is strictly service oriented. This is accomplished by considering e.g. the service life cycle, different roles and types of functionality. By applying the classification scheme to representative examples of quality specification techniques, the current status in the field is outlined. To contribute to the advancement of service orientation, we derive requirements for next generation specification techniques by two ways: First we analyze today's works' flaws and second we deduce requirements from our classification scheme.

The paper is organized as follows. In the next section (Sec. 2) the classification scheme for QoS specification languages and concepts is introduced. Application to typical examples of QoS specification techniques is discussed in Sec. 3. Using these results, the following section (Sec. 4) identifies requirements for future quality specification approaches. Section 5 concludes the paper and gives an outlook on further work.

2   Classification Scheme

In this section a classification scheme for quality specification concepts and languages is developed. In doing so, the paradigm of service orientation is strictly followed. Multiple aspects of services are covered, functional aspects of a specification as well as its expressiveness in relation to service properties.

In order to develop the classification, the MNM Service Model [GHH+02,GHK+01] is used as the foundation for the classification. It is a bottom–up developed model which defines a common terminology in generic service management, specifies atomic roles and denotes the major building blocks a service is composed of. Doing so, it offers a generic view on the building blocks rather than a specification for direct implementation. As the MNM Service Model is a generic model, which is not focusing a certain scenario, it serves well as a starting point for our classification, in respect to develop a model where completeness, generic applicability and scenario independency is ensured.

The second ingredient for our classification is the set of common concepts that can be found in various quality specification schemes. This set was derived from the survey of Jin and Nahrstedt [JN04] and is an enhancement of the taxonomy presented there.

2.1   The MNM Service Model as a Map for Specification Concepts

The MNM Service Model offers two major views (Service and Realization View) which group a service's building blocks into different domains, according to their roles and related responsibilities. Figure 1 combines the two views. One major characteristic of the model is the so called *Side Independent Part*[1]. Beside the *service* itself, it depicts additional building blocks which should be specified independently from realization details on either the *provider side* and the *customer side*.

The MNM Service Model decomposes the specification of a service's quality in two parts. The first part describes quality relevant properties of a *service* (class *QoS Parameters* in Fig. 1). The second part poses constraints on those specified properties which have to be met by the provider and are agreed upon in an *service agreement*. For both parts, relevant properties of the system have to be defined in an unambiguous manner.

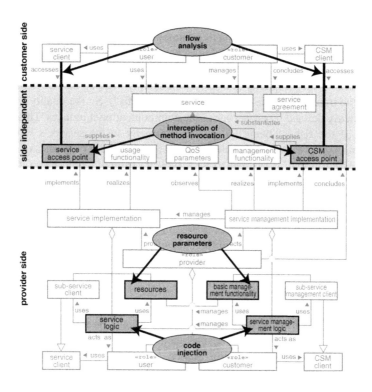

Fig. 1. Reference Points located in combined view of the MNM Service Model

QoS parameters may be specified against different reference points. Thus, even when they bear the same name, they may have different semantics. For example, a delay specification could be measured at the *user's client* or inside the *service implementation*, which results in different QoS parameters. In fact, our extension of the taxonomy presented in [JN04] describes such possible reference points for quality specification.

---

[1] In the following, parts of the model will be printed in italics

By locating the reference points in the MNM Service Model characteristics of these reference points can be identified. First of all, the model's part where the reference point is located, enables us to identify the affected roles. Furthermore, this allows us to draw conclusions on dependencies to other parts of a service. Thus we can identify typical properties of reference points, like limitations regarding portability to different realizations or the applicability in situations, when service chains come into play.

The following paragraphs first describe those reference points. In each paragraph's second part the reference point is located in the MNM Service Model as depicted in Fig. 1. By this, basic characteristics of specification techniques using the respective reference point can be pointed out later on by simply marking the corresponding reference point in the MNM Service Model.

Flow/Communication. Most of today's common QoS parameters, such as throughput or delay, are measured and thus specified from a communications point of view. Quality related properties of a service are derived from properties of a data stream or, in general, a flow. Constraints on the quality of a service are simply mapped onto constraints of the flow (e.g. "the transmission delay must not exceed 10ms"). So the quality of a service is only implicitly defined by properties of the communication it induces. This definition is therefore at the risk of being too coarse in respect to the service's functionality. However, this way of expressing quality is widespread because properties of a flow can be easily derived in real world scenarios. A typical example would be an ATM based video conferencing service where its properties are described as ATM QoS parameters.

In the MNM Service Model a communication flow in general can be observed between a client and the corresponding service access point (SAP). This relation exists between the *service client* and *service access point* (when accessing the service's *usage functionality*) as well as between the *customer service management (CSM) client* and the *customer service management (CSM) access point* (when accessing the *management functionality*). Hence, a quality specification has to be applied not only to the usage functionality but also to the management side.

As can be seen in Fig. 1, the relation between the *service client* and the *service access point* crosses the boundary between the *customer side* and the *side independent* part of the model (the same applies for the management side). Any analysis of flows depend on the service clients, thus, it cannot be implementation independent. In consequence, specifications using the technique of flow analysis depend on a client's implementation as well.

Method/API Invocation. Another technique to derive quality relevant properties of a service is motivated by object oriented (OO) design, programming and middleware architectures. Here, quality is specified as properties of a method invocation, e.g. the time it takes a method for encoding a video frame to finish. Constraints on these properties can be posed as easily as in the former case. This method of quality measurement and description requires the interception of method invocations. As this is naturally done in component oriented middleware, this technique is mostly used there.

Method invocation may occur at almost any functional component of the MNM Service Model. However, the invocation interception concept used in OO environments or middlewares can be mapped best to the service's access points where methods in the sense of service (management) functions can be invoked. The idea of interception of method invocations is therefore depicted in Fig. 1 at the *service access point* and the *customer service management (CSM) access point*. As this concept only uses blocks of the model which are located in the *side independent* part, it does not depend on any implementation, neither on the *customer* nor on the *provider side*.

Code Injection. The idea of code injection is to directly integrate constraints on quality into a service's implementation — into its executable code. Steps of execution monitored by injected code yield service properties (such as processing time or memory consumption). Constraints on these properties are inferred by directly coding conditional actions to be executed when a constraint is satisfied or violated. For example, information on memory usage during the decoding of a video stream is measured. If it exceeds a certain value, a less memory consuming but also worse performing decoding method is used. This procedure automatically assures a certain quality, in this case a guaranteed maximum amount of memory used.

The MNM Service Model divides a service's implementation into three parts: *subservice client*, *service logic* and *resources*. The *service logic* orchestrates resources and subservices to implement the service's *usage functionality* as a whole. The idea of code injection, in the sense of the service model, is to enhance the *service logic* with inserted code to automatically derive properties of the running service. Observation of these properties and reaction to changes are directly coupled. As the Service Model distinguishes between a service's *usage functionality* and its *management functionality*, this concept is shown in both the *service logic* and the *service management logic*. As one can easily see, the idea of code injection depends directly on a service's implementation by a provider. It is therefore an instrument for providers to assure a certain quality, but obviously should not be used in service negotiation when customer and provider need to establish a common understanding of a service's quality parameters.

Resource Parameters. Quality relevant properties of a service can also be derived from the parameters of resources the service is realized with. For this purpose, resource parameters can be aggregated in various ways.

However, details of the gathering and aggregation process have to be defined after service deployment, because relevant details of concrete resources used are unknown before deployment. Even worse, the specification may have to be adapted on a service instance basis because different service instances might use different resources, whose concrete characteristics might be needed for specification. Constraints on these resource oriented properties can be posed at various aggregation levels, but their derivation from constraints posed on the service itself is not a trivial task.

In the MNM Service Model, information about resources can be directly gathered from the *resources*, but can also be obtained via the class *basic management functionality*. When specifying quality aspects of the *management functionality* the *basic management functionality* itself is targeted in a QoS specification. As the location of both *resources* and *basic management functionality* inside the provider's domain illustrates, even with a suitable aggregation method, this concept of specification can only express quality that directly depends on the provider's own implementation. As most services realized today depend on subservices, this specification can be used for basic services only.

By introducing the various reference points, locating them in the MNM Service Model and by identifying their basic properties and limitations, the first part of our classification scheme is now explained. While up to here our analysis focused mostly on functional aspects of the MNM Service Model's views, additional non–functional aspects have to be regarded for a comprehensive classification of quality specification techniques. This will be carried out in the next section.

2.2   Dimensions Covered by Quality Specifications – The LAL-Brick

Apart from its decompositions into functional building blocks and related roles, as described with the MNM Service Model, a service can also be described in another view, which focuses on non–functional properties of a service. As shown in the following paragraphs, we describe this non-functional view using a three dimensional brick, depicted in Fig. 2. The brick's three dimensions are *Life cycle*, *Aspect*, *Layer* and is therefore called the LAL–brick from here on. The axes of the brick, its dimensions, can be marked with typical properties. A tiny cube is attached to each property and as the dimensions are independent from each other, all tiny cubes together form the brick. The dimensions and their properties are described in the following.

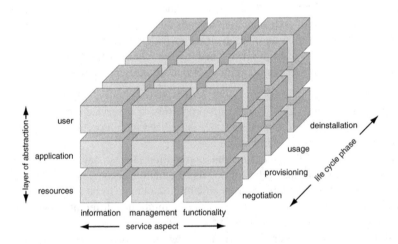

Fig. 2. Dimensions of quality specification arranged in a brick

Approaches to specify QoS can easily be depicted in the brick by simply marking the cubes corresponding to the properties this specification approach fulfills. Different "marking patterns" of different approaches explicitly visualize their classification.

Life Cycle. The process traversed by a service – when seen as an object of management – is called the life cycle. This process can be split up into different phases. According to [GHH+02] it begins with the *negotiation phase* where *customer* and *provider* determine a service's functionality, its QoS and suitable accounting schemes. In the next phase, the *provisioning phase*, the provider implements the service using its own resources and subservices he buys (then acting in the role of a *customer*). When the implementation is completed, the *usage phase* begins with *users* actually using the service. The life cycle ends with the *deinstallation* of the service.

The mapping of the reference points on the MNM Service Model already suggested that the service life cycle is a relevant dimension in quality specification. For example, as explained above, specification schemes based on *resource parameters* have a strong relation to the finalization of the *provisioning phase*, while using *method/API invocation* as reference points, quality specification could be fully done in the *negotiation phase*. Thus, concepts and methodologies dealing with service should be aware of the life cycle and ensure reusability of results they deliver to other phases. At least they should explicitly denote which phase they cover or were designed for.

Aspects of a Service. The notion of a service not only defines a set of functions accessible to a *user*. In an integrated view it also defines how the management of a service is accomplished by the *customer* (see Fig. 1). As shown above, independently from the type of reference points used in a specification mechanism, *management functionality* must be targeted as well as a service's *usage functionality*. Of course, when a service is specified, the content it delivers or the information it deals with are defined. In consequence, this information might be subject to quality considerations as well. From now on, we use the notion of aspects of a service to denote the triple of *function*, *management* and *information*.

Layer of abstraction. When concepts or methodologies dealing with services are presented, different layers of abstraction can be recognized. Some ideas focus on the *resources* that a service is built upon, some describe a service from an *application's* point of view. At last, the service can be described from an *user's* point of view (as of [JN04]).

Service orientation demands concepts spanning all three layers of abstraction denoted above, so providers, customers and users can use them. At least, mappings between the different layers should exist so that an integrated concept could be built up out of ideas only spanning one layer of abstraction.

2.3   Comprehensible, Service Oriented Classification Scheme

The set of reference points marked within the MNM Service Model in conjunction with the LAL–brick now delivers a comprehensive classification scheme for approaches specifying QoS. It should be emphasized that reference points are not exclusive to each other. This means, that a concrete quality specification mechanism might use several types of reference points. Section 3.4 shows an example for this.

The MNM Service Model and the LAL–brick offer different views on the specification of QoS. The Service Model, used as a map to visualize different reference points, focuses on functional aspects, whereas the LAL–brick gives an easy to use scheme to denote non-functional properties of specification techniques. Together, both views offer the possibility of a comprehensive classification of existing approaches in QoS specification, as will be shown in the following section.

3   The Classification Scheme Applied – State of the Art in QoS Specification by Example

After presenting a comprehensive and service oriented classification scheme in the previous section, we will now discuss typical representatives of specification languages. Each specification language realizes one of the approaches denoted in Sec. 2. We do not give a full survey on QoS specification languages and techniques here. But we demonstrate the application of our classification scheme to existing approaches in order to derive requirements on a service oriented QoS specification in the following Sec. 4.

3.1   QUAL – A Calculation Language

In her professorial dissertation [DR02a] Dreo introduces QUAL as part of "a Framework for IT Service Management". The approach of QUAL as such is also presented in [DR02b]. The key concept of QUAL is to aggregate quality parameters of devices (named as quality of device, QoD) to basic quality parameters which themselves can be aggregated to service relevant QoS parameters. The aggregation process is based upon dependency graphs which describe service and device interdependencies.

As QoD is gathered on the resource level, QUAL obviously uses *resource parameters*. Although QUAL can express higher level quality parameters at the application level, they always depend on the on the QoD gathered from the resources. Thus, *resource parameters* are the only reference point directly used in QUAL, as application level QoS is specified through aggregation.

QUAL covers a wide range of abstraction from resource to service oriented quality parameters. However, QUAL does not directly address the specification of user–oriented QoS. In our classification scheme, it therefore covers the two lower abstraction layers, *resource layer* and *application layer*. QUAL focuses on the *functionality aspect*, the *management aspect* and the *information aspect* are not explicitly mentioned.

As QUAL is based on resource parameters, its application is restricted to the *usage phase* of the life cycle where these parameters are available. Even though QUAL covers only the usage phase, it is highly dependent on specifications and decisions made in the *negotiation* and *provisioning phase*. This results from the fact, that aggregation of quality parameters is based on dependency graphs which have to be determined before QUAL is applied.

3.2   QDL – QoS Description Language

QDL [PJS+00] is an extension to the interface description language (IDL) [ITU97] which is used to specify functional interfaces in CORBA [COR04]. It is the description language used in the QuO (Quality of Service for CORBA Objects) framework introduced in

[ZBS97]. The key concept of QuO is to enhance the CORBA middleware concepts with QoS mechanisms. For this purpose, additional facilities are added to the CORBA runtime to ensure a specified quality. The desired quality is determined in QDL and its sublanguages.

Based on QDL statements, extra code is generated in the QuO framework which is joined with the functional code when the corresponding object files are linked together. Thus, QDL uses *code injection* as a reference point for the specification of QoS. By using CORBA as an implementation basis, QuO and QDL abstract from real resources and specify QoS at the *application layer* of abstraction. Naturally the CORBA based approach limits the expressiveness of QDL and prevents the specification of user–level QoS.

QDL only covers the of *aspect of functionality* and does not mention any possibilities to extend its approach to the other aspects *management* and *information*. QDL, together with the supporting framework QuO, covers the life cycle phases *provisioning* and *usage*. The reason for this is, that code executed in the usage phase is automatically generated from specifications laid down in the provisioning phase, when a service is realized according to customer's needs.

3.3   QML – Quality Modeling Language

The Quality Modeling Language QML [FK98] was developed at HP-Labs, another, quite similar approach was presented in a thesis [Aag01]. QML separates the specification of (desired) quality from its assurance or implementation respectively. As specifications are bound to abstract method definitions of the considered application, QML uses *method invocation* as the reference point. The authors of QML also propose a corresponding runtime engine that could be used to implement the specifications made in QML.

Thus, the system as a whole (QML and its runtime engine) offers support for the whole service life cycle: As specifications made in QML are independent of an implementation, they could be easily used in the *negotiation phase. Provisioning* and *usage phase* are supported by the runtime engine QRR (QoS Runtime Representation) which unfortunately has not been implemented yet.

Obviously, due to their binding to abstract methods, specifications in QML are made at the *application level* of abstraction. As long as resources are encapsulated in an (object oriented) interface, QML specifications might be used at the *resource level* as well. However, this possible extension is not mentioned by the authors of QML. A distinction of different aspects of QoS is not made either. QML, like all the other specification languages introduced so far, definitely focuses on the aspect of *functionality*.

3.4   QUAL – Quality Assurance Language

The quality assurance language was introduced in [Flo96] as part of QoSME the QoS Management Environment. Although equal in names, QUAL by Florissi and QUAL introduced at the very beginning of Sec. 3 follow quite different approaches. QoSME–QUAL specifies quality in relation to communication properties observable at a so called port. So, it uses a *flow of communication* as reference point. QoSME also provides a runtime engine to ensure the specifications made in QUAL. As this engine is directly woven into an application's executable code, QoSME uses the concept of *code injection* as well. Even though this is only done for the assurance and not for the specification of QoS, it leads to a form of specification closely related to the executable code.

QUAL statements are not very meaningful without a specific implementation in mind. Thus, QUAL cannot be used during the *negotiation* of a service, where an implementation is not yet existent. However, QUAL supports the *provisioning phase* by QoS specification directly attached to the code to be executed later. Together with the runtime system of QoSME, QUAL also supports the *usage phase*.

QUAL claims to specify QoS at the *application layer* of abstraction but does neither mention nor address the other abstraction layers (resources and user). Because QUAL analyzes communication flows, it primarily covers the *aspect of functionality*, but could in some sense also be related to the *aspect of information* when the content of flows is examined.

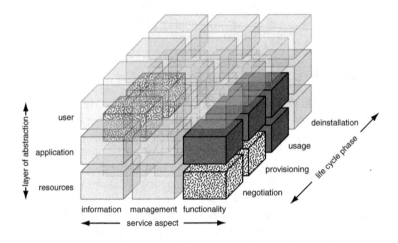

Fig. 3. Approaches marked in the LAL-brick

3.5   The Big Picture

To conclude our presentation of existing approaches we again show the LAL–brick in Fig. 3. In this figure, the parts covered by the reviewed specification languages are marked. Possible extensions of existing approaches, as mentioned above, are spotted, whereas the parts exactly matched are marked dark grey.

As one can easily observe, huge parts of the LAL–brick are not covered at all. Requirements for future specification languages resulting from this "gap" are discussed in the next section.

4 Directions and Requirements for Future Research

As the previous section shows, current work has deficiencies regarding extensive service orientation capabilities. By summing up the flaws and comparing it to the classification scheme, this identifies new requirements which should be met by the next steps in the field. The classification scheme of Sec. 2, which consists of the set of reference points on the one hand, and of the LAL–brick on the other hand, is used here again.

As a service oriented, generic and comprehensive solution for QoS specification technique is required, a full coverage of the LAL–brick should be achieved. Therefore, the still missing cubes in the LAL–brick are investigated. Additionally, in conjunction with the MNM Service Model as generic reference, the individual limitations of the reference points, induce additional requirements.

Side independency. Following the MNM Service Model, QoS should be described in a side independent manner. As already explained in Sec. 2.1, side dependency is influenced by the actual set of reference point used. A number of specification schemes suffer from the problem, that they exclusively focus on reference points which import realization dependency by design. Namely, just using *Code Injection* or *Resource Parameters* induces dependencies on the provider's realization of a service. In case of *Code Injection*, using a middleware architecture mitigates the dependencies from specific resources, but being specific on this middleware persists. Relying solely on *Resource Parameters* is even more problematic as only provider–internal resources, but not the subservices purchased by the provider are reflected. Additionally, side independency is not only desirable in the relation to customers. With quality specification being driven by a provider's implementation, when it comes to outsourcing, it will be difficult for the provider to create comprehensible bid invitations for subproviders.

Consequently, quality specification languages should support specification techniques which are independent from implementation details. As pointed out, this is not only required for customer orientation, but also aids providers in outsourcing processes. Additionally, in the LAL–brick, side independency is a first step towards the coverage of the user layer of abstraction.

Life cycle span. Regarding the LAL–brick, the previous section has shown that not all quality specification techniques are qualified to cover a service's full life cycle. As quality specification is already needed in the beginning (the *negotiation phase*), a quality description mechanism should try to cover the whole life cycle.

Especially the ability to reuse specification results should be addressed. This is desirable, as it would help providers in estimating feasibility of a customer's demands during the negotiation phase. Second, it would aid providers in realizing services, as agreed quality could be more smoothly implemented during the provisioning phase. Third, for the usage phase, a life cycle spanning approach could help in measurement of quality characteristics. As a minimum requirement, specification techniques at the very least should point out which phase of the life cycle they were designed for.

Management functionality subject to quality. As the MNM Service Model points out, *management functionality* is a vital part of any service, a point also reflected in the design of the LAL–brick. In fact, management functionality not only reports and manipulates quality aspects, but is also subject to quality considerations itself. This is even more important, as quality of management functionality can have influence on a service's usage quality.

For this, an example are situations when a main service is composed of subservices. Reporting of QoS from a subservice is part of its customer service management (CSM) functionality. When this reporting functionality has deficiencies, quality degradation from the subservice might not be determined by the main service. As a consequence its own usage functionality might be affected without being noticed, because quality degradations of the involved subservice are not noticed as the reporting functionality is degraded.

However, in current work the topic of applying quality to management functionality is not addressed. Although one can suppose that some tasks are similar to specifying quality of usage functionality, further research is needed. At least, specification techniques must be able to cope with the fact that in case of management functionality a different role (namely the *customer* instead of the *user*) is involved.

Awareness of Quality of Information (QoI). As the LAL–brick shows, a service's content may be a quality aspect, here referred to as the *information aspect*. Taking a web–based news service as an example, up–to–dateness of messages is, without a doubt, a quality criterion of the service. Dividing quality aspects of functionality (here: e.g. reachability of the service) from information quality (here: e.g. up–to–dateness and trustability of news) can aid over the whole service life cycle. During *negotiation* and *deployment*, *service agreements* with customers and subcontractors will be more accurate, outsourcing decisions gain a clearer basis. Naturally, technical infrastructure might influence the QoI. Regarding the news service, a certain up–to–dateness might require a different content management system or a faster communication infrastructure to subcontractors delivering news content. In the usage phase, e.g. in fault situations, root causes might be easier to find.

One might argue that this starts to involve high level semantics, a field which is hard to cope with. Nevertheless, separating quality aspects of a service's content from its functionality in fact already took place in some research areas. Context sensitive services are dealing with "Quality of Context" [HKLPR03,BKS03], for example the accuracy of location coordinates or temperature readings. Speaking in the terminology introduced by this paper, these are quality aspects of information. Future research in service management should be aware of this separation, should try to develop a generic approach and should try to invent techniques and mechanisms to incorporate and support Quality of Information (QoI).

It should be pointed out here that it would be unrealistic to demand or predict one single approach which is capable to span the whole LAL–brick and which can fulfill all of the requirements posed here. Instead, multiple approaches for different slices of the LAL–brick are more likely. But what should definitely be approached, is the interoperability between approaches and standards covering parts of the LAL–brick. These questions on interoperability are also subject for further research.

5   Conclusion and Outlook

In this paper a classification scheme for quality specification mechanisms and languages is presented. The classification emphasizes service orientation and consists of two parts. First a set of reference points is given, denoting the place in the MNM Service Model which is used to define quality properties of a service and on which later quality constraints are built upon. The second part of the classification scheme, called the LAL–brick, defines the dimensions along which quality description schemes can be classified. The classification scheme is applied to typical examples of current approaches in QoS specification. By this, the current state of the art in the field is outlined.

In the last part of the paper, observations of the classification scheme's application in conjunction with basic properties of the scheme itself are used to identify basic requirements and directions for future research in the field. Among others, one of the basic directions here is the awareness of the service life cycle. Additionally, a service content, or more abstract, the information it deals with, is also subject to quality (Quality of Information, QoI), which has to be separated from the quality of a service's usage and management functionality.

Further directions in our work include a specification scheme which focuses on the ability to reuse specification properties from preceding life cycle phases. Our second focus is targeted on the MNM Service Model. According to the results of this paper, it needs extensions regarding QoI, by that broadening its applicability to mobile and context aware service scenarios. Looking even further, approaches which claim the software development life cycle to be vital for quality specification (like [FK98,ZBS97]) must be investigated more precisely and eventually incorporated with the presented work.

Acknowledgment. The authors wish to thank the members of the Munich Network Management (MNM) Team for helpful discussions and valuable comments on previous versions of this paper. The MNM Team directed by Prof. Dr. Heinz-Gerd Hegering is a group of researchers of the University of Munich, the Munich University of Technology, and the Leibniz Supercomputing Center of the Bavarian Academy of Sciences. Its web–server is located at http://wwwmnmteam.ifi.lmu.de/.

References

[Aag01]   J. Ø Aagedal. *Quality of Service Support in Development of Distributed Systems.* Dr. scient. thesis, Department of Informatics, Faculty of Mathematics and Natural Sciences, University of Oslo, March 2001.

[BKS03]   T. Buchholz, A. Küpper, and M. Schiffers. Quality of Context Information: What it is and why we need it. In *Proceedings of the 10th HP–OVUA Workshop*, volume 2003, Geneva, Switzerland, July 2003.

[COR04]   Common object request broker architecture (corba/iiop). Specification version 3.0.2, OMG, March 2004.

[DR02a]   G. Dreo Rodosek. *A Framework for IT Service Management*. Habilitation, Lud-
            wig-Maximilians-Universität München, June 2002.

[DR02b]   G. Dreo Rodosek. Quality Aspects in IT Service Management. In M. Feridun,
            P. Kropf, and G. Babin, editors, *Proceedings of the 13th IFIP/IEEE International
            Workshop on Distributed Systems: Operations & Management (DSOM 2002)*, Lec-
            ture Notes in Computer Science (LNCS) 2506, pages 82–93, Montreal, Canada,
            October 2002. IFIP/IEEE, Springer.

[FK98]   Svend Frølund and Jari Koistinen. Qml: A language for quality of service spec-
            ification. Report hpl-98-10, Software Technology Laboratory, Hewlett-Packard
            Company, September 1998.

[Flo96]   Patrícia Gomes Soares Florissi. *QoSME: QoS Management Environment*. Phd
            thesis, Columbia University, 1996.

[GHH⁺ 02]   M. Garschhammer, R. Hauck, H.-G. Hegering, B. Kempter, I. Radisic, H. Roelle,
            and H. Schmidt. A Case–Driven Methodology for Applying the MNM Service
            Model. In R. Stadler and M. Ulema, editors, *Proceedings of the 8th International
            IFIP/IEEE Network Operations and Management Symposium (NOMS 2002)*, pages
            697–710, Florence, Italy, April 2002. IFIP/IEEE, IEEE Publishing.

[GHK⁺ 01]   M. Garschhammer, R. Hauck, B. Kempter, I. Radisic, H. Roelle, and H. Schmidt.
            The MNM Service Model — Refined Views on Generic Service Management.
            Journal of Communications and Networks, 3(4):297–306, December 2001.

[HAN99]   H.-G. Hegering, S. Abeck, and B. Neumair. *Integrated Management of Networked
            Systems – Concepts, Architectures and their Operational Application*. Morgan
            Kaufmann Publishers, ISBN 1-55860-571-1, 1999.

[HKLPR03]   H.-G. Hegering, A. Küpper, C. Linnhoff-Popien, and H. Reiser. Management Chal-
            lenges of Context–Aware Services in Ubiquitous Environments. In *Self–Managing
            Distributed Systems; 14th IFIP/IEEE International Workshop on Distributed Sys-
            tems: Operations and Management, DSOM 2003, Heidelberg, Germany, October
            2003, Proceedings*, number LNCS 2867, pages 246–259, Heidelberg, Germany,
            October 2003. Springer.

[ITU97]   Open Distributed Processing – Interface Definition Language. Draft Recommen-
            dation X.920, ITU, November 1997.

[JN04]   Jingwen Jin and Klara Nahrstedt. QoS Specification Languages for Distributed
            Multimedia Applications: A Survey and Taxonomy. In *IEEE Multimedia Magazine*,
            to apear 2004.

[PJS⁺ 00]   P Pal, Loyall J., R. Schantz, J. Zinky, R. Shapiro, and J. Megquier. Using QDL to
            Specify QoS Aware Distributed (QuO) Application Configuration. In *Proceedings
            of ISORC 2000, The Third IEEE International Symposium on Object-Oriented
            Real-time Distributed Computing*, Newport Beach, CA., March 2000.

[ZBS97]   J. Zinky, D. Bakken, and R. Schantz. Architectural Support for Quality of Service
            for CORBA Objects. In *Theory and Practice of Object Systems*, January 1997.

Automating the Provisioning of Application Services with the BPEL4WS Workflow Language

Alexander Keller[1] and Remi Badonnel[2][*]

[1] IBM T.J. Watson Research Center
P.O. Box 704, Yorktown Heights, NY 10598, USA
alexk@us.ibm.com
[2] LORIA-INRIA Lorraine
615, rue du Jardin Botanique - B.P. 101, 54600 Villers Les Nancy Cedex, France
remi.badonnel@loria.fr

Abstract. We describe the architecture and implementation of a novel workflow-driven provisioning system for application services, such as multi-tiered e-Commerce systems. These services need to be dynamically provisioned to accomodate rapid changes in the workload patterns. This, in turn, requires a highly automated service provisioning process, for which we were able to leverage a general-purpose workflow language and its execution engine. We have successfully integrated a workflow-based change management system with a commercial service provisioning system that allows the execution of automatically generated change plans as well as the monitoring of their execution.

1 Introduction and Problem Statement

The extremely high rate of change in emerging service provider environments based on Grid and Web Services technologies requires an increasingly automated service provisioning process. By provisioning, we mean the process of deploying, installing and configuring application services. A promising, systematic approach to this problem is based upon the adoption of Change Management [5]. An important prerequisite for automated Change Management is the ability of a service provisioning system to interpret and execute change plans (described in a general-purpose workflow language) that have been generated by a Change Management System. This requires adding new workflows "on-the-fly" to provisioning systems, i.e., without writing new program code and without human intervention. Second, the workflows should contain temporal constraints, which specify deadlines or maximum allowable durations for each of the activities within a workflow. Finally, once the workflows are executed by a provisioning system, the system should be able to check their status to determine if an activity has completed and, if yes, whether it was successful or not.

This paper describes our approach to addressing these requirements and its implementation. It enables a provisioning system to understand and execute

---

[*] Work done while the author was an intern at the IBM T.J. Watson Research Center

A. Sahai and F. Wu (Eds.): DSOM 2004, LNCS 3278, pp. 15–27, 2004.

change plans specified in the *Business Process Execution Language for Web Services (BPEL4WS)* [1], an open workflow language standard, as a means to apply change management concepts and to automate provisioning tasks significantly. In addition, our system is capable of providing feedback from the provisioning system back to the change manager, so that the latter can monitor how well the execution of the change plan proceeds, and perform adjustments if needed.

The paper is structured as follows: Section 2 gives an overview of typical service provisioning systems, such as *IBM Tivoli Intelligent Orchestrator (TIO)*, and describes related work. Our approach for integrating CHAMPS, a Change Manager developed at IBM Research, with TIO and a workflow engine capable of understanding BPEL4WS, is discussed in section 3; we present the proof-of-concept implementation in section 4. Section 5 concludes the paper and presents the lessons we learned during this work as well as issues for further research.

2   Towards Automated Service Provisioning

The importance of automating the provisioning of services is underscored by a recent study [9] showing that operator errors account for the largest fraction of failures of Internet services and hence properly managing changes is critical to availability. Today, however, service provisioning systems are isolated from the change management process: They typically come with their own, proprietary workflow/scripting language, thus making it hard for a change manager to formulate reusable change plans that can be understood by different provisioning systems. Our goal is to tie provisiong systems into the change management process. By leveraging the Web Services technology and a standardized, general-purpose workflow language for expressing change plans and demonstrating the feasibility of integrating a common-off-the-shelf workflow engine with a commercial provisioning system, our approach is applicable to a wide range of provisioning scenarios.

2.1   Provisioning Systems: State of the Art

Typical provisioning systems, such as *Tivoli Intelligent Orchestrator (TIO)* [4] provide an administrator with a runtime environment for defining and subsequently executing provisioning scripts. Figure 1 depicts the sequence of steps for provisioning a web site that uses the *IBM HTTP Server (IHS)*, a variation of the Apache Web Server. In this example, 10 actions need to be carried out by the provisioning system, which can be summarized as follows: Copying the install image of the HTTP server into a temporary directory on a target system, launching the installation, updating the httpd.conf configuration file, installing the web site content (HTML pages, pictures etc.), starting the HTTP server, and performing cleanup tasks once the installation has been completed successfully. In TIO, such a provisioning workflow consists of a sequence of operations; these are pre-defined activities that can be adapted and customized by an administrator, as well as aggregated into new workflows. For every operation, an

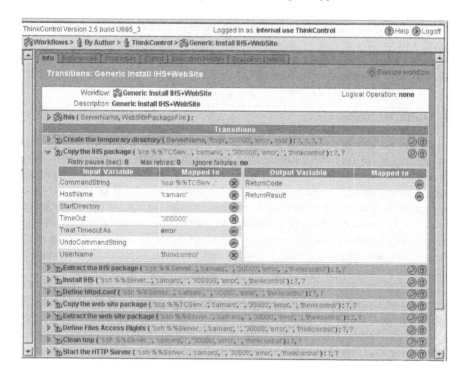

Fig. 1. Steps for Provisioning an HTTP Server from a Service Provisioning System

administrator can specify what steps need to be taken if the operation fails, such as undoing the installation or notifying the administrator. Provisioning systems that require such fine-grained definitions of provisioning workflows expect an administrator to have a detailed understanding of the steps involved in setting up the provisioning of complex, multi-tiered systems. However, the lack of knowledge about the structure of a distributed system and the dependencies between its fine-grained components often tend to make an administrator overly prudent when designing workflows, e.g., by not exploiting the potential for concurrent execution of provisioning workflows, thus resulting in inefficiencies.

Another example of a commercial service provisiong system is given in [3]. It describes a workflow-based service provisiong system for an Ethernet-to-the-Home/Business (ETTx) environment, consisting of a policy engine, a service builder, an activation engine and a workflow engine. The (proprietary) workflow engine orchestrates the execution flow of the business process, whereas the actual provisioning steps are executed by a custom-built activation engine. Our approach, in contrast, lets a common-off-the-shelf workflow engine orchestrate the actual provisioning process. Indeed, there has been interest in using workflow technologies to coordinate large scale efforts such as change management [7], and to automate the construction of a Change Plan [8]. However, no current provisioning system is able to understand change plans that leverage the full potential of typical general-purpose workflow languages, such as the concurrent execution of tasks and the evaluation of transition conditions to determine if the next task in a workflow can be started.

2.2   Related Work

In addition to the products described above, service provisioning and change management have received considerable attention in both academia and industry. A constraint satisfaction-based approach to dynamic service creation and resource provisioning in data centers is described in [10]. Whenever a policy manager finds a match between an incoming request and a set of resource type definitions, the task-to-resource assignment is treated as a constraint satisfaction problem, which takes the service classes as well as the technical capabilities of the managed resources into account, but does not perform additional optimization. The output is consumed by a deployment system.

STRIDER [12] is a change and configuration management system targeted at detecting and fixing errors in shared persistent configuration stores (such as the Windows Registry). To do so, it follows an elaborate three-step process to analyse the state of configuration parameters, finds similar, valid configurations and subsequently narrows down the range of results to the most likely configuration. Since it deals with (re)setting configuration parameters and does not perform software deployment, the system does not make assumptions about the order in which provisioning steps need to be carried out.

Finally, the Workflakes system, described in [11], provides workflow-driven orchestration of adaptation and reconfiguration tasks for a variety of managed resources. Workflakes focuses on an adaptation controller for systems and services, where workflows describe the dynamic adaptation loop. Our work supports a change management approach, where dynamically generated workflows (describing change plans) are executed by a provisioning system.

3   Integrating Change Management and Provisioning

3.1   The CHAMPS Change Manager

The CHAMPS system is a Change Manager for **CHA**nge **M**anagement with **P**lanning and **S**cheduling [6]. CHAMPS consists of two major components: The **Task Graph Builder** breaks down an incoming request for change into its elementary steps and determines the order in which they have to be carried out. This **Task Graph** is a workflow, expressed in BPEL4WS, consisting of tasks and precedence constraints that link these tasks together.

In a second step, multiple task graphs (representing the various requests for change that are serviced by the change manager at a given point in time) are consumed by the **Planner & Scheduler**. Its purpose is to assign tasks to available resources, according to additional monetary and technical constraints, such as

Service Level Agreements (SLAs) and Policies. To do so, it computes (according to various administrator-defined criteria) a **Change Plan** that includes deadlines and maximizes the degree of parallelism for tasks according to precedence and location constraints expressed in the Task Graphs. Again, the BPEL4WS workflow language is used to express the Change Plan. Figures 5, 7 and 8 in section 4 contain various examples of instructions specified in a Change Plan.

3.2   Integration Architecture

Once the Change Plan has been computed by the Planner & Scheduler, it is input to the **Provisioning System**, which retrieves the required software packages from a Package Repository, and rolls out the requested changes to the targets in the order specified in the plan. An important part of this process is the ability of the provisioning system to keep track of how well the roll-out of changes progresses on the targets, and to feed this status information back into the Planner & Scheduler. Being aware of the current status of the provisioning process enables the Planner & Scheduler to track the actual progress against the plan and perform on-line plan adjustment (by re-computing the change plan) in case the process runs behind schedule. In addition, such a feedback mechanism can be used to gain an understanding on how long it takes to complete a task.

Our architecture, depicted in figure 2, aims at integrating the provisioning system with CHAMPS to execute the change plans in a data center environment comprising resources such as server pools, servers, software products, switches, and firewalls. In section 2.1, we noted that current provisioning systems do not execute workflows in parallel and often do not take temporal and location constraints into account. The deploy-

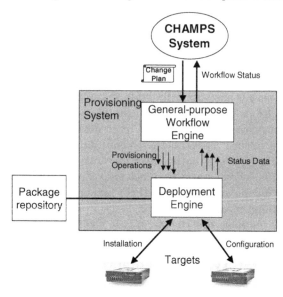

Fig. 2. Architecture for extending a Provisioning System with a Workflow Engine

ment engine of the provisioning system allows us to perform a variety of management operations on managed resources. While these operations are grouped into a single sequence on the graphical user interface (cf. figure 1), a WSDL interface exists that allows the programmatic invocation of individual operations from an application outside of the provisioning system by means of SOAP[1] messages. We exploit this feature by feeding the Change Plans created by the CHAMPS Planner & Scheduler into a general-purpose workflow engine and invoke individual operations directly from there. More specifically, we use the BPWS4J workflow engine [2] that is able to execute workflows and business processes specified using BPEL4WS. A BPEL4WS workflow describes Web Services interactions and may comprise parallel execution (so-called *flows*), sequences, conditional branching, time-out mechanisms, as well as error and compensation handling.

By doing so, we can execute provisioning tasks defined in change plans concurrently. The architecture of the extended provisioning system (depicted in figure 2) is consequently composed of two sub-systems: the BPWS4J workflow engine and the deployment engine of the provisioning system. The former interacts with the CHAMPS system (cf. section 3.1), as follows: First, the **workflow engine** inputs the change plan provided by CHAMPS and starts each provisioning operation by directly invoking the deployment engine. These invocations are performed either in parallel or sequentially, according to the change plan. In a second step, the **deployment engine** is invoked by the workflow engine and performs the provisioning operations. It reports the status of each operation execution back to the workflow engine. This status information is used by the workflow engine to check if the workflow constraints defined in the plan (such as deadlines) are met. Figure 2 also shows that status feedback happens at two stages:

First, the interactions between the deployment engine and the workflow engine (i.e., the invocations of provisioning operations and the assessment of their execution). A major advantage of using a workflow engine for our purposes is the fact that it automatically performs state-checking, i.e., it determines whether all conditions are met to move from one activity in a workflow to the next. Consequently, there is no need for us to develop additional program logic that would perform such checks, as these conditions are specified in the temporal constraints (so-called *links*) that connect the activities in a workflow.

The second status feedback loop comprises the interactions between the workflow engine and the CHAMPS Planner & Scheduler, i.e., submitting the change plan and receiving status feedback from the workflow engine. This is needed to perform plan adjustments in case the roll-out of changes runs behind schedule.

4   Prototype Implementation

The implementation of our prototype demonstrates the invocation of the TIO deployment engine from the BPWS4J engine, based on the change plans submitted by the CHAMPS system (see figure 3). More specifically, the implementation addresses the following aspects:

First, one needs to create Web Services Description Language (WSDL) [13] wrappers for the existing TIO invocation interface. Making TIO appear as a (set

---

[1] Simple Object Access Protocol.

of) Web Service(s) is a necessary step to providing a seamless integration with the BPWS4J workflow engine, as every BPEL4WS *invoke* operation refers to a Web Service. The WSDL wrappers define the allowable set of change management operations that can be used in change plans.

Once this is done, one can invoke the operations defined in the WSDL interfaces by submitting a BPEL4WS workflow (corresponding to a change plan) to the workflow engine, which allows the execution of several operations in parallel.

Third, the deployment engine needs to monitor the execution status of the change plans to determine whether they are still running, completed successfully, or completed with an error. This is important because the workflow engine depends on this information to determine if all

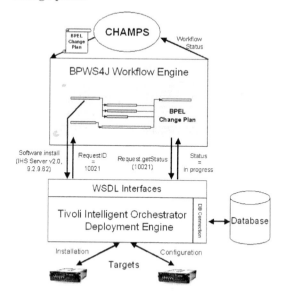

Fig. 3. Integrating the TIO Provisioning System with the CHAMPS Change Manager

the preconditions are satisfied before the next activity can be triggered.

Finally, a change plan may specify deadlines (e.g., task X must be finished by 8pm) that need to be enforced. The workflow engine must therefore be able to send an event back to the CHAMPS Planner & Scheduler if a provisioning activity takes longer than initially planned. The Planner & Scheduler would then decide if the provisioning process should be abandoned (and rolled back to a previous state), or continued despite the delay. In the following four sections, we will discuss how we addressed each of these aspects in more detail.

4.1   WSDL Wrappers for Logical Operations

To facilitate the invocation of provisioning operations from the outside, TIO can represent each individual operation or sequence of operations as a so-called *logical operation*. In TIO, each resource is treated as a component (i.e., Software, Operating Systems, Switches, Servers, etc.) that provides an (extensible) set of logical operations. Typically, the TIO component dealing with software provides logical operations such as *Software.deploy*, *Software.install*, *Software.start*, while its switch component provides *Switch.createVLAN*, *Switch.turnPortOn* etc. For example, the logical operation *Software.install* can be used to implement the IBM HTTP Server (IHS) install operation in the TIO sequence depicted in figure 1. In addition, the use of logical operations ensures that the TIO database gets updated with execution status information.

A first part of our work consists in providing WSDL interfaces to facilitate the invocation of these logical operations using server IP addresses, software identifiers, or device serial numbers as inputs. As an example, we have created the following WSDL interface to perform the logical operations (*Software.Install*, *Software.Start*, etc.) on the software component:

The listing depicted in Figure 4 shows the WSDL definition of *SoftwareComponent.install* (lines 10-17) that wraps the TIO logical operation *Software.install*. It uses the software name and server IP address as inputs (definition of the input message install-Request, lines 3-6) and returns a request ID (definition of the output message installResponse, lines 7-9). This approach can be generalized to

```
1  <?xml version="1.0" encoding="UTF-8"?>
2  <definitions name="SoftwareComponent">
3    <message name="installRequest">
4      <part name="softwareName" type="xsd:string"/>
5      <part name="deviceIP" type="xsd:string"/>
6    </message>
7    <message name="installResponse">
8      <part name="requestID" type="xsd:int"/>
9    </message>
10   <portType name="SoftwareComponent">
11     <operation name="install"
12     parameterOrder="softwareName deviceIP">
13       <input message="tns:installRequest"
14       name="installRequest"/>
15       <output message="tns:installResponse"
16       name="installResponse"/>
17     </operation>
     ...
18   </portType>
19 </definitions>
```

Fig. 4. Software Component WSDL interface

accomodate other resources, such as switches, server pools or VLANs.

4.2   Invoking Logical Operations Concurrently

The BPWS4J workflow engine [2] allows us to invoke several logical operations simultaneously through the above WSDL interfaces. As mentioned in section 3.1, the CHAMPS system uses the BPEL4WS [1] workflow language to describe change plans: the invocations of logical operations are done through our WSDL interfaces and by using the *invoke* construct of BPEL4WS; parallel and sequential execution paths map to the *flow* and *sequence* structured activities.

The deployment engine is driven by the workflow engine and thus able to execute tasks concurrently, such as the installation of the IHS server and the deployment of the web site content (HTML pages, pictures etc.). An example, briefly mentioned in section 2.1, is given in figure 5. It depicts a part of the change plan, defined in BPEL4WS and rendered in the BPWS4J workflow editor, for the simultaneous installation and configuration of two websites with different content, along with IHS servers on two different systems running Linux: The website with the name WSLA (together with the HTTP server) is to be provisioned on the system 'cuda' having the IP address 9.2.9.64 (dashed lines in the figure), while the system 'charger' with the IP address 9.2.9.63 will host another HTTP server and the website DSOM2003 (dotted lines in the figure).

One can see that using the BPEL4WS *flow* construct yields the advantage of decoupling the provisioning processes on a per-system basis: if the provisioning process on one system encounters a problem, the provisioning of the second system remains

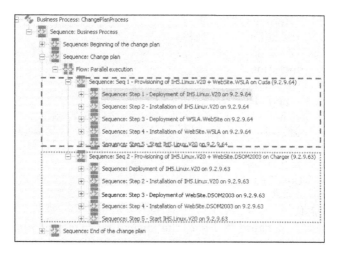

Fig. 5. Concurrent Provisioning of 2 Websites

unaffected by this and continues. Concurrent invocations of the change management operations can be carried out because the invocation of a logical operation on the provisioning system through its WSDL interface is non-blocking.

4.3   Monitoring the Execution of Change Plans

In addition to tasks that can be carried out in parallel, a Change Plan contains temporal constraints between various tasks that need to be taken into account as well. As an example, every *invoke* operation within a *sequence* can only start if its predecessor has finished. To retrieve the execution status of a logical operation from the provisioning system, we have created a second set of WSDL interfaces (listed below). This information is needed by the workflow engine to determine if a task

```
1  <?xml version="1.0" encoding="UTF-8"?>
2  <definitions name="Request">
3    <message name="getStatusRequest">
4      <part name="requestID" type="xsd:int"/>
5    </message>
6    <message name="getStatusResponse">
7      <part name="startTime" type="xsd:date"/>
8      <part name="status" type="xsd:string"/>
9    </message>
10   <portType name="Request">
11     <operation name="getStatus"
12     parameterOrder="requestID">
13       <input message="tns:getStatusRequest"
14       name="getStatusRequest"/>
15       <output message="tns:getStatusResponse"
16       name="getStatusResponse"/>
17     </operation>
18   </portType>
19 </definitions>
```

Fig. 6. WSDL interface for Status Monitoring

within a *sequence* is still running, or whether it can proceed with the execution of the next task. As an example, in figure 6, the operation *Request.getStatus* (lines 11-17) returns the start time and the status of an execution (definition of the getStatusResponse message, lines 6-8) from a request ID (definition of the getStatusRequest, lines 3-5).

To determine the execution status of a logical operation, the workflow engine periodically invokes the monitoring WSDL interface. An example of how this can be expressed in BPEL4WS is

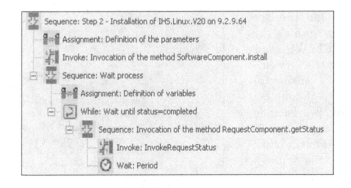

Fig. 7. Monitoring Task Execution Status

depicted in figure 7. First, the change management operation *Installation of IHS on 9.2.9.64* is invoked through the WSDL interface corresponding to the appropriate *Software.install* logical operation. In a second step, the request ID returned by the invocation is used to check periodically (through the monitoring WSDL interface implementing the method *RequestComponent.getStatus*) the status of the running logical operation, until it completes. If this is the case, the next change management operation of the workflow is started. Our implementation distinguishes between 3 states for an executing workflow: *in progress*, *completed* (with success), and *failed* (the return message includes an error code). If an error occurs during the execution of a logical operation, the workflow engine returns an error message back to the CHAMPS Planner & Scheduler, which then needs to determine how to proceed further. This may involve rolling back and subsequently retrying the operation, or bringing the target system(s) back to a well-defined state.

By using the WSDL monitoring interface, we are able to enforce temporal constraints defined in Change Plans such as: *the logical operation X must be finished before the logical operation Y can start*, or *the logical operation X must not start before the logical operation Y has started*. For a detailed discussion of the various temporal constraints in Change Plans, the reader is referrred to [6].

4.4 Enforcing Deadlines and Durations

An additional requirement is the enforcement of deadlines for change management operations that are given in a Change Plan. To do so, the workflow engine needs to understand what these deadlines are and notify the CHAMPS Planner & Scheduler in case a change management operation runs behind schedule. The Planner & Scheduler would then decide if the change management operation should be abandoned (and roll back the system to a known state), or if it should continue despite the delay.

Yet again, we are able to exploit the features of the BPEL4WS language to specify time constraints on the provisioning workflow. Activities corresponding to invocations of logical operations can be grouped together by means of the *scope* structured activity. An *event handler* is then attached to a *scope* activity, which may contain one or more alarms. Each alarm is defined by both a constraint and an escape activity, which is performed when the constraint is violated. This mechanism works for single activities as well.

We use alarms to define time constraints (the BPWS4J workflow engine comprises a timer) so that we can specify deadlines ("must be finished by 8PM") as well as impose limits on the duration of an activity

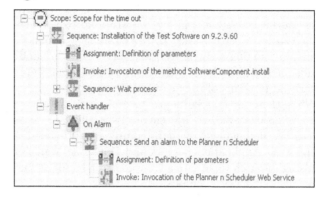

Fig. 8. Enforcing Deadlines and Durations

("must take less than 45 minutes"). The escape activities allow us to notify the CHAMPS system whenever an activity violates its time constraints. In figure 8, we place an activity (a software installation) within a *scope* and define the time constraint *duration < 5 min*. If the duration exceeds the time period defined in the change plan, the escape activity attached to the alarm invokes a WSDL method of the CHAMPS Planner & Scheduler to report the violation. Note that a notification does not mean that the change plan is automatically aborted. Instead, the Planner & Scheduler will determine how to proceed, according to the overall system state, other (competing) change plans, as well as penalties specified in Service Level Agreements or general Policies. It will then decide if the current change plan can continue, if it has to be cancelled, or if a new change plan must be generated later.

5   Conclusion and Outlook

We have presented a novel approach for integrating a change manager with a service provisioning system to facilitate the workflow-based provisioning of application services. Our work was motivated by the extremely high rate of change in emerging e-Commerce environments and the need for integrating service provisioning into the change management process. By using a standardized, general-purpose workflow language for expressing change plans and demonstrating the feasibility of integrating a common-off-the-shelf workflow engine with a commercial provisioning system, our approach is applicable to a wide range of provisioning scenarios.

Our prototype demonstrates that change plans, generated by the CHAMPS change management system, can be executed by the TIO deployment engine and that the BPEL4WS workflow language can be used effectively to describe change plans. While this advantage is likely to apply to other workflow languages as well, BPEL4WS has the additional benefit that it is specifically targeted at Web Services. Second, the use of a workflow engine yields the advantage that the task of checking the execution status of activities in a distributed system (to decide if the next activity in a workflow can start) can be completely offloaded to the workflow engine. Finally, we are able to achieve a very high degree of parallelism for a set of tasks: In the running example we used throughout this paper, provisioning a single website (server software and web content) took 185 seconds on average, whereas provisioning additional websites added less than 5% of overhead in terms of provisioning time per site.

While these initial results are encouraging, there are several areas of further work: As an example, we are currently working on extending our approach to address the deployment of more complex multi-tiered application systems involving Web Application Servers and Database Management Systems. Further promising research topics are advanced error-handling and rollback facilities, and the automated service composition and aggregation.

References

1. Business Process Execution Language for Web Services Version 1.1. Second Public Draft Release, BEA Systems, International Business Machines Corp., Microsoft Corp., SAP AG, Siebel Systems, May 2003. http://www-106.ibm.com/developerworks/library/ws-bpel/.

2. *Business Process Execution Language for Web Services JavaTM Run Time (BPWS4J)*. http://www.alphaworks.ibm.com/tech/bpws4j.

3. M. Cheung, A. Clemm, G. Lin, and A. Rayes. Applying a Service-on-Demand Policy Management Framework to an ETTx Environment. In R. Boutaba and S.-B. Kim, editors, *Proceedings of the Application Sessions of the 9th IEEE/IFIP Network Operations and Management Symposium (NOMS'2004)*, pages 101 – 114, Seoul, Korea, April 2004. IEEE Publishing.

4. E. Manoel et al. *Provisioning On Demand: Introducing IBM Tivoli Intelligent ThinkDynamic Orchestrator*. IBM Corporation, International Technical Support Organization, Research Triangle Park, NC 27709-2195, December 2003. IBM Redbook, Order Number: SG24-8888-00.

5. IT Infrastructure Library. *ITIL Service Support*, June 2000.

6. A. Keller, J.L. Hellerstein, J.L. Wolf, K.-L. Wu, and V. Krishnan. The CHAMPS System: Change Management with Planning and Scheduling. In R. Boutaba and S.-B. Kim, editors, *Proceedings of the 9th IEEE/IFIP Network Operations and Management Symposium (NOMS'2004)*, pages 395 – 408, Seoul, Korea, April 2004. IEEE Publishing.

7. F. Maurer and B. Dellen. Merging Project Planning and Web-Enabled Dynamic Workflow Technologies. *IEEE Internet Computing*, May 2000.

8. J.A. Nilsson and A.U. Ranerup. Elaborate change management: Improvisational introduction of groupware in public sector. In *Proceedings of the 34th Annual Hawaii International Conference on System Sciences*, 2001.

9. D. Oppenheimer, A. Ganapathi, and D.A. Patterson. Why do internet services fail, and what can be done about it? In *Proceedings of the 4th Usenix Symposium on Internet Technologies and Systems*, Seattle, WA, USA, March 2003. USENIX Association.

10. A. Sahai, S. Singhal, V. Machiraju, and R. Joshi. Automated Policy-Based Resource Construction in Utility Computing Environments. In R. Boutaba and S.-B. Kim, editors, *Proceedings of the 9th IEEE/IFIP Network Operations and Management Symposium (NOMS'2004)*, pages 381 – 393, Seoul, Korea, April 2004. IEEE Publishing.
11. G. Valetto and G. Kaiser. Using Process Technology to control and coordinate Software Adaptation. In L. Dillon and W. Tichy, editors, *Proceedings of the 25th International Conference of Software Engineering (ICSE 2003)*, pages 262 – 272, Portland, OR, USA, May 2003. IEEE Computer Society.
12. Y-M. Wang, C. Verbowski, J. Dunagan, Y. Chen, H.J. Wang abd C. Yuan, and Z. Zhang. STRIDER: A Black-box, State-based Approach to Change and Configuration Management and Support. In *Proceedings of the 17th Large Installation Systems Administration Conference (LISA 2003)*, pages 159 – 172, San Diego, CA, USA, October 2003. USENIX Association.
13. Web Services Description Language (WSDL) 1.1. W3C Note, Ariba, International Business Machines Corp., Microsoft Corp., March 2001. http://www.w3.org/TR/wsdl.

HiFi+: A Monitoring Virtual Machine for Autonomic Distributed Management

Ehab Al-Shaer and Bin Zhang

School of Computer Science, Telecommunications and Information Systems
DePaul University, USA
{ehab, bzhang}@cs.depaul.edu

Abstract. Autonomic distributed management enables for deploying self-directed monitoring and control tasks that track dynamic network problems such as performance degradation and security threats. In this paper, we present a monitoring virtual machine interface (HiFi+) that enables users to define and deploy distributed autonomic management tasks using simple Java programs. HiFi+ provides a generic expressive and flexible language to define distributed event monitoring and correlation tasks in large-scale networks.

1   Introduction

The continuing increase in size and complexity and dynamic state changing properties of modern enterprise network increases the challenges on network monitoring and management system. Next-generation distributed management systems need not only monitor the network events but also dynamically track the network behaviors and update the monitoring tasks accordingly at run-time. This is important to keep up with significant changes in the network and perform recovery/protection actions appropriately in order to maintain the reliability and the integrity of the network services. Traditional network monitoring and management systems lack expressive language interfaces that enable distributed monitoring, correlation and control (actions). In addition, many of the existing management systems are static and lack the ability to dynamically update the monitoring tasks based on analyzed events. In request-based monitoring systems, the managers have to initiate large number of monitoring tasks in order to track events that might overload the monitoring agents and cause events delay or dropping. Next-generation monitoring systems must allow for defining complex monitoring actions or programs, instead of monitoring requests, in order to analyze the received events and initiate customized monitoring or management programs dynamically. For example, it will be more efficient to use a general traffic monitoring task for detecting network security vulnerability and initiate customized/specialized monitoring tasks when misbehaving (suspicions) traffic exits in order to closely track particular clients.

In this paper we present a monitoring virtual machine HiFi+ that explicitly addresses these challenges and provides a generic interface for multi-purpose

A. Sahai and F. Wu (Eds.): DSOM 2004, LNCS 3278, pp. 28–39, 2004.

monitoring applications. HiFi+ system supports dynamic and automatic customization of monitoring and management operations as a response to the change in the network behavior. This is achieved though programmable monitoring interfaces (agents) that can reconfigure their monitoring tasks and execute appropriate actions on the fly based on the use's request and the information collected from the network. HiFi+ employs a hierarchical event filtering approach that distributes the monitoring load and limits event propagation. The main contribution of this work is providing a Java-based monitoring language that can be used to define a dynamic monitoring and control tasks for any distributed management application. It also incorporates many advanced monitoring techniques such as hierarchical filtering and correlation, programmable actions and imperative and declarative interfaces.

This paper is organized as follow. In section 2, we introduce our expressive monitoring language. Section 3 gives application example. In section 4, we compare our work with related works. Section 5 gives the conclusion and identifies the future work.

2   HiFi+ Expressive Language Components

In this section, we present the three components of HiFi+ monitoring language: (1) Event Interface that describes the network or system behavior, (2) Filter Interface that describes monitoring and correlation tasks, and (3) Action Interface that describes the control tasks[2,3]. HiFi+ is an object-oriented language implemented in Java. Users can use the event and filters interfaces to define the network behavior pattern to be detected and the action interface to perform the appropriate operation.

2.1   Event Definition Interface

An event is a significant occurrence in the system or network that is represented by a notification message. A notification message typically contains information that captures event characteristics such as event type, event source, event values, event generation time, and state changes. Event signaling is the process of generating and reporting an event notification. The HiFi+ Event interface allows users to use standard events like SNMP traps as well as defining a customized event specification. Figure 1 shows the class hierarchy of Event Definition Interface.

In HiFi+, although events can be in different formats, all types of events share the same interface and can be accessed and manipulated in the same way. For example, the special *SNMPTrap* event with fixed format encapsulates all the information in an SNMP trap message and these information can still be accessed by the general event function like *getAttributeValue()*. The *HiFiEvent* event format is the general event type which can be used to construct customized events. The *HiFievent* event can be divided into two parts: the event body and event id. The event id can be a string or an integer which stand for the event name or type. The event body is the container of the real information.

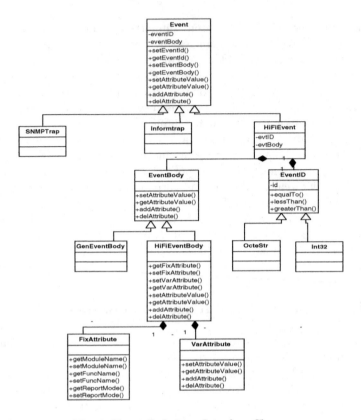

Fig. 1. Event Definition Interface Classes

Two types of event body are extended from the basic event body class: the general event body and *HiFiEvent* body. *HiFiEvent* body mainly has two parts: the fix attributes and the variable attributes. Both of these two parts are composed by a set of predicates. Each predicate has an attribute name, the value of that attribute and the relation between them. For example, $bandwidthUsage > 0.8$ is an event predicate which means the value of *bandwidthUsage* attribute is larger than 0.8. The fixed attributes define the common attributes shared by all event types. From this part, we can get the information about the event source, generated time and signaling type. When event is created, the system automatically inserts the current time in the *timestamp* attribute of the event. The variable attributes allows user to define any additional general attributes that might reveal more information. For example, suppose we want to monitor the system load of the Web server *neptune*. We can define the format of the event generated by *neptune* as follows:

```
Event systemLoad = new HiFiEvent("systemLoad, "Neptune, loadMonitor,
senderThread", "cpuUsage = Any");
```

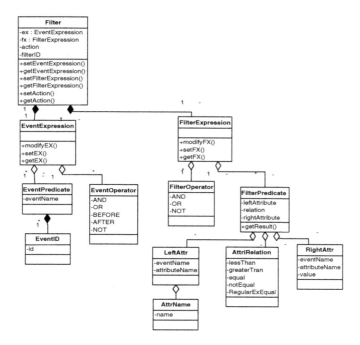

Fig. 2. Filter Definition Interface Classes

2.2   Filter Definition Interface

In HiFi+ monitoring virtual machine, users describe their monitoring demands by defining "filters" and submit them to the monitoring system at run time[2]. Figure 2 shows the filter classes hierarchy. A filter is a set of predicates where each predicate is defined as a Boolean valued expression that returns true or false. Predicates are joined by logical operators such as "AND" and "OR" to form an expression[3]. In HiFi+ language, the filter is composed by four components: filter ID, event expression which specifies the relation between the interesting events, filter expression which specifies the relations or the matching values of different attributes, and action object name. The action object will be loaded and executed by the monitoring agent if both the event and filter expressions are true. The event and filter expressions define the correlation pattern requested by consumers. Consumers may add, modify or delete filters on the fly. The filters are inserted into the monitoring system through filter subscription procedure[2]. The monitoring agent can reconfigure itself by updating their internal filtering representation. This feature is highly significant to provide dynamic features of programmable monitoring virtual machine.

Every filter has a filter id that is unique in the monitoring system. To illustrate the expressive power of the filter abstraction to define monitoring tasks, we will next show some examples. Assume we want to monitor the performance of our web server *neptune* and accept new connections only if the service time of the existing clients is acceptable. Therefore, if the simultaneous connections exceed a certain threshold and the connected clients experience unacceptable performance drop, then we need *neptune* to refuse more service requests. In this example, we need to monitor not only the system load of *neptune*, but also the performance drop in the client side. Assume *neptune* will send out *systemLoad* event periodically or when load is significantly increased as defined in the previous example. We are interested in events that reflect high increase of CPU Load (assuming 80%). The filter for this requirement can be defined like this:

```
Filter systemLoadFilter = new Filter("systemLoadFilter", "systemLoad",
"systemLoad.cpuUsage > 0.8 AND systemLoad.machine = neptune",
"systemLoadAction" )
```

The four parameters transferred to the filter constructor are filter ID, event expression, filter expression, and action class name. Suppose the web client will send out *performaceDrop* event if it experience long response time from a web server. The performaceDrop event format can be defined like this:

```
Event performaceDrop = new HiFiEvent("performaceDrop", "Any, webClient,
senderThread", "responseTime = Any, server = Any")
```

The long response time experienced by web client can be caused by network congestion and packets drop or server load exceed its capacity. If only one web client complains about the long response time, it's hard to decide it's the server or the network causes this problem. If we receive multiple *performanceDrop* events come from different web clients, we have more confidence to suspect that the long response time may be caused by server overload. So the filter should keep a counter for how many clients have sent out *performanceDrop* events. When the counter value is larger than threshold (assuming 5), the filter will send out *serverOverloadAlert* event. We can define event and filter for this task like this:

```
Event serverOverloadAlert = new HiFiEvent("serverOverloadAlert", "Any,
performanceDropFilter, Any", "server = Any")
```

```
Filter performceDropFilter = new Filter("performaceDropFilter",
"performanceDrop", performanceDrop.responseTime > 120 AND
performanceDrop.server = neptune", "performanceDropAction")
```

The counter updating and the event creation are implemented in the action and not shown in the filter definition. Suppose if we receive the *serverOverloadAlert* event in ten seconds after receive *systemLoad* event, we can get the conclusion that the server has been overloaded. The filter for this task can be defined as follow:

```
Filter serverOverloadFilter = new Filter("serverOverloadFilter",
"serverOverloadAlert AND systemLoad", "systemLoad.timeStamp -
serverOverloadAlert.timeStamp < 10000", "serverOverloadAction")
```

2.3   Action Definition Interface

Actions describe the tasks to be performed when the desired event pattern (correlation or composition) is detected. In this part, we support programmable management interface. Users can write a Java program to perform any action to respond to detected network conditions. If the event and filter expressions in filter evaluate true, the monitoring agents load and execute the corresponding action programs.

Supporting customized action is one of the major objectives of HiFi+ monitoring virtual machine. The action class allows users to define monitoring task that can dynamically be updated. It provides a set of API to allow users to create their own action implementation which extended from action abstract class. The users can also execute scripts or binary files that will be loaded on-demand into the monitoring agents. The action class supports five different action types: (1) activating/adding a new filter to the monitoring system or deactivating/removing an existing filter from the system, (2) modifying the filter expression of an existing filter to accommodate changes in the monitoring environment, (3) forwarding the receiving event to agents, (4) creating new events as a summary of previous event reports, and (5) executing a shell or binary program. The action class is actually a Java program extends "Action" abstract class, and thereby all standard Java as well as HiFi+ API can be used in an extended action class. This offers great flexibility to customize the monitoring system.

The action interface also provides "virtual registers" that the action developer can use to store event information history. The user can dynamically create and update registers in the action program, and these registers will be used locally and globally by the monitoring agents during the monitoring operations. Figure 3 shows the classes hierarchy of the action interface. To implement an action program in HiFi+ system, user defined actions must extend the action class and override the *performAction()* method to specify his action implementation. When action class is loaded and executed by the monitoring agent, the *performAction()* method will be invoked with three arguments: *EventManager, FilterManager, and ActionManager*. The *EventManager* has the methods by which the user can access and analyze the received events, create and forward events. The *FilterManager* lets the user activate (*addFilter()*) and deactivate (*delFilter()*) filters in the system or update the filter expression (*modifyFX()*). The *actionManager* allows users to execute script or binary file and create or update virtual register (*create/get/check/deleteRegister()*).

The action class provides rich event management functions that have a significant impact on the language expressiveness. Events can be retrieved based on its time-order, event type, event name, value of event attribute and so on. For Example, users can get all events sent by host *neptune* by invoking the following function: *getAnyEventQueue("machine=Neptune")*. On the other hand, we can use *getEventQueue("systemLoad", "machine=Neptune")* method to find all the *systemLoad* events sent by *neptune*. In addition, event queues can be sorted based on a specific attribute value.

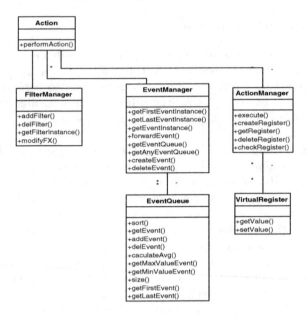

Fig. 3. Action Definition Interface Classes

Now, let's us show example of action programs using HiFi+ virtual machine language. In the web server performance monitoring example discussed in section 2.2, we didn't define the action programs for those filters. The action program for *performanceDropFilter* filter is a good example to show how to use virtual register.

```
 1 public class performanceDropAction extend Action{
 2    public void performAction(EventManager EM, FilterManager FM,
      ActionaManager AM){
 3    Register reg;
 4    if(reg = AM.createRegister("hostCounter") !=void)
 5      reg.setValue(1);
 6    else{
 7      reg = AM.getRegister("hostCounter");
 8      String host =
      EM.getLastEvent("performanceDrop").getEventAttribute("machine");
 9      if (EM.getEventQueue("systemLoad", "machine ="+host).size()==1){
10      reg.increaseValue();
11      if(reg.getValue() >=5){
12      AM.deleteRegister("hostCounter");
13      Event evt =
      EM.createEvent("serverOverloadAlert", "server =neptune");
14      EM.forwardEvent(evt);}}}
15    }
16 }
```

In this action, we extract the IP addresses of the web clients and compare it with other events and update the counter. The counter should be kept outside the action program in virtual register so it can be referenced by next round execution. When receive first *performanceDrop* event, we use the action manager to create a virtual register to store the counter (line 4). Then we initialize the counter (line 5). For the following events, we use the action manager get the register (line 7). Then in line 8, we get the IP address for the web client who sends the *performanceDrop* event. We search all the received events to find the events come from the same host with the last received event and put these events in an event queue (line 9). If the event queue size equal one, that mean this is the first time that web client send out *performanceDrop* event. Then we increase the counter (line 10). When the register value is equal or larger than 5, we delete the register and create and forward the *serverOverloadAlert* event (line 11-14).

3   Application of HiFi+ in Distributed Intrusion Detection

In this section, we will show an example of how HiFi+ can be used in intrusion detection systems (IDS) to detect DDoS attack. DDoS attacks usually launch number of aggressive traffic streams (e.g., UDP, ICMP and TCP-SYN) from different sources to a particular server. This example shows how HiFi+ can be used to support IDS devices in deploying security (signature-based or anomaly-based) monitoring tasks efficiently. In [10], a proposal for an attack signature was presented to detect DDoS by observing the number of new source IP addresses (not seen during a time window) in the traffic going to a particular server. We here will implement a variation of this technique using HiFi+ interfaces.

We will, first, monitor the load of the target servers using *systemLoadFilter* filter. If any of these filters indicates that the system load of a server goes beyond a specific threshold, then the *diffSrcCheckFilter* filter will be activated in order to monitor all new tcp connections initiated to this target server. The *diffSrc-CheckFilter* filter receives and filters all *tcpSyn* events that represent TCP-SYN packets destined (i.e., destination IP) to the target server. The *tcpSyn* events can be generated by network-based intrusion detection system (IDS). As the *diffSrcCheckFilter* filter keeps track of *tcpSyn* events, it calculates the number of different IP sources seen within a one-second time windows. If the number of different IP sources is larger than a specified threshold, then the *diffSrcChcekAction* will create *diffSrcExceedThr* event. Here we need point out the difference between our approach and the approach proposed in[10] is that we don't need keep the history of IP source for every server which makes our approach suitable for large-scale network with many target servers. Finally, we use the *DDosFilter* filter to correlate the *systemLoad* and *diffSrcExceedThr* events. Only when these two events occur within a close time window from each other and they are both related to the same server, then we can conclude the server is under DDOS attack. Let us assume that the DDOS signature will be defined like this: if the CPU usage on a server increases beyond the 0.6 and within one second we detect that there are more than 100 different IP source addresses starting tcp connections to that server, we will report DDOS attack. The events and filters used in this monitoring task can be defined as follows:

```
Event tcpSyn = new HiFiEvent("tcpSyn", "Any, Any, Any",
"sourceIP = Any, destinationIP = Any")

Event diffSrcExceedThr = new HiFiEvent("diffSrcExceedThr", " Any,
diffSrcCheckFilter, Any", "targetIP = Any")

Event systemLoad = new HiFiEvent("systemLoad", "Any, loadMonitor,
senderThread", "cpuUsage = Any, diffSrcThr = 100");

Filter systemLoadFilter = new Filter("systemLoadFilter", "systemLoad",
"systemLoad.cpuUsage > 0.6 OR systemLoad.cpuUsage <0.3",
"systemLoadAction" )

Filter diffSrcCheckFilter = new Filter("diffSrcCheckFilter", "tcpSyn",
"tcpSyn.destinationIP =Any", "diffSrcChcekAction")

Filter DDosFilter = new Filter("DDosFiler", "diffSrcExceedThr AND
systemLoad", "diffSrcExceedThr.targetIP = systemLoad.machine AND
systemLoad.timeStamp - diffSrcExceedThr.timeStamp < 1000","DDosAction")
```

Next, let us look at the action programs for *systemLoadFilter* filter. This action has three tasks: (1) activating the *diffSrcCheckFilter* filter to detect DDoS attack if the system load is beyond a threshold, (2) forward the *systemLoad* event, and (3) deactivate (or deleting) the *diffSrcChekcFilter* filter if the system load drops below the threshold because the DDoS investigation is not needed any more. In this action program we dynamically change filter expression of *diffSrcCheckFilter* filter. The original filter expression will check *tcpSyn* event for any server to find if there are more than threshold different IP want to connect to that server. After the filter expression is updated, the filter checks only the *tcpSyn* events with the destination IP of the suspect target server.

```
public class systemLoadAction extend Action {
 public void performAction(EventManager EM, FilterManager FM,
 ActionaManager AM){
   Event evt = EM.getLastEvent("systemLoad");
   float load = evt.getAttributeValue("cpuUsage");
   if (load > 0.8){
     String target = evt.getAttributeValue("machine");
     FM.modifyFX("diffSrcCheckFilter", "tcpSyn.destionationIP =" +
     target);
     FM.addFilter("diffSrcCheckFilter");
     EM.forward(ent);}
   if(load < 0.3)FM.delFilter("diffSrcCheckFilter");}
 }
```

Next, let us look at the action program of the *diffSrcCheckFilter* filter below. In line 4, we get the time stamp for last *tcpSyn* event. This event triggers the execution of action program, so the destination IP must equal the target server. We get the time t2 which is 1 second before last event in line 5. Then we delete the outdated or irrelevant events whose time stamps are less than t2 or whose IP destinations are different than the target server (line 7). We then get the rest of *tcpSyn* events and put them in an event queue (line 8) and create a set to store the source IP addresses (line 9). In lines 10-13, we go through every event in the queue and putting the source IP in source IP set. Then we get the threshold for different source IP in line 14. In lines 15-18, we check the size of the source IP set. If the size is larger than threshold, we create and forward the *diffSrcExceedThr* event.

```
1   public class diffSrcCheckFilter extend Action {
2     public void performAction(EventManager EM, FilterManager FM,
      ActionaManager AM){
3       Event evt = = EM.getLastEvent("tcpSyn");
4       int t1 = evt.getEventAttribute("timeStamp");
5       int t2 = t1 - 1000;
6       String targetIP = evt.getEventAttribute("destinationIP");
7       EM.deleteEvent("tcpSyn", "tcpSyn.timeStamp <  " + t2  + " OR
      tcpSyn.destinationIP != " + targetIP);
8       EventQueue queue= EM.getEventQueue("tcpSyn");
9       Set IpSource = new HashSet();
10      for (int i=0; i < = queue.size(); i++){
11        String sourceIP =
          (queue.getEvent(i)).getAttributeValue("sourceIP");
12        IpSource.add(sourceIP);
13      }
14      int threshold =
      EM.getLastEvent("systemLoad").getEventAttribute("diffSrcThr");
15      if (IpSource.size()> threshold){
16        Event evt = EM.createEvent("diffSrcExceedThr,", "targetIP
          =''+  targetIp );
17        EM.forwardEvent(evt);}
18  }
```

Finally, let's look at the action program for DDosFilter. It just create and forward the *DDosAlert* event.

```
public class DDosAction extend Action {
  public void performAction(EventManager EM, FilterManager FM,
  ActionaManager AM){
    EM.createEvent("DDosAlert");}
}
```

4   Related Works

Numbers of monitoring and management approaches based on event filtering have been proposed in [1,6,7,8]. Many of these approaches focus on event filtering techniques such as performance and scalability. But less attention was given to provide flexible programming interfaces as described in this paper.

Hierarchy filtering-based monitoring and management system (HiFi) was introduced in [2,3]. HiFi employs an active management framework based on programmable monitoring agents and event-filtter-action recursive model. This work is an extension of HiFi system to provide an expressive and imperative language based on Java. The user can get benefit from the new API by implementing really complex action programs using known programming language.

A general event filtering model has been discussed in [5]. But this approach can filter the primitive events based on attribute values only, thereby doesn't support event correlation. SIENA, a distributed event notification service has been described in[4]. The programming interface of SIENA mainly provides functions for the user to subscribe, unsubscribe, publish and advertise events. It doesn't provide functions for the user to aggregate and processing events.

High-level language for event management is described in READY event notification system [6]. In READY, matching expressions are used to define the event pattern. The matching expression and actions in READY have same abstraction level similarity with filter and action in HiFi+. But the action types in READY are limited, only assignment, notify and announce action are supported. HiFi+ approach allows the user define complex action to trace and analyze the event history, modify the monitoring tasks dynamically, aggregate information to generate new meaningful events or even execute scripts and binary files.

Java Management Extensions (JMX)[11] is a framework for instrumentation and management of Java based resources. JMX focuses on providing a universal management standard, so the management application will not rely on fixed information model and communication protocol. HiFi+ focuses on supplying users a flexible and expressive programming interface to define the monitoring tasks and appropriate actions.

The Meta monitoring system[9] is a collection of tools used for constructing distributed application management software. But in Meta, sensors (a function that returns program state and environment values) are static programs that are linked with the monitored application prior to its execution. This reduces the dynamism and the flexibility of the monitoring system. Unlike in HiFi+, the monitoring agent can dynamically be configured and updated.

5   Conclusion and Future Works

In this paper, we present flexible monitoring programming interfaces for distributed management systems. The presented framework, called HiFi+ virtual monitoring machine, enables users to expressively define events formats, network pattern or behaviors to be monitored and the management actions using simple Java-based filter-action programs. Filters can implement intelligent monitoring tasks that go, beyond just fetching the information, to correlate events, investigate problems, and initiate appropriate management actions. The HiFi+ virtual monitoring machine provides unified interfaces for distributed monitoring regardless of the application domain. We show examples of using HiFi+ in security and performance management applications; however, many other examples can be similarly developed.

Our future research work includes important enhancements in the language interfaces and the system architecture such as integrating more event operators, implanting safe-guard for infinite loops, improving the virtual registers abstraction, developing topology-aware agents' distribution.

References

1. S. Alexander, S. Kliger, E. Mozes, Y. Yemini, and D. Ohsie: High Speed and Robust Event Correlation. IEEE Communication Magazine, pages 433-450, May 1996.
2. Ehab Al-Shaer: Active Management Framework for Distributed Multimedia Systems. Journal of Network and Systems Management (JNSM), March 2000.
3. Ehab Al-Shaer, Hussein Abdel-Wahab, and Kurt Maly: HiFi: A New Monitoring Architecture for Distributed System Management. Proceedings of International Conference on Distributed Computing Systems (ICDCS'99), pages 171-178, Austin, TX, May1999.
4. Antonio Carzaniga, David S. Rosenblum Alexander L. Wolf: Design and evaluation of a wide-area event notification service. ACM Transactions on Computer Systems (TOCS), Volume 19, Issue 3, August 2001
5. P. Th. Eugster, P.Felber, R. Guerraoui1, S. B. Handurukande: Event Systems: How to Have Your Cake and Eat It Too. 22nd International Conference on Distributed Computing Systems Workshops (ICDCSW '02), July, 2002.
6. Robert E. Gruber, Balachander Krishnamurthy and Euthimios Panagos: High-level constructs in the READY event notification system. Proceedings of the 8th ACM SIGOPS European workshop on Support for composing distributed applications 1998, Sintra, Portugal.
7. Boris Gruschke: A New Approach for Event Correlation based on Dependency Graphs. Proceedings of the 5th Workshop of the OpenView, University Association: OVUA'98, Rennes, France, April 1998.
8. Mads Haahr and Rene Meier and Paddy Nixon and Vinny Cahill: Filtering and Scalability in the ECO Distributed Event Model. International Symposium on Software Engineering for Parallel and Distributed Systems (PDSE 2000)
9. K. Marzullo, R. Cooper, M. D. Wood, and K. P. Birman: Tools for distributed Application Management. IEEE Computer, vol. 24, August 1991.
10. Peng, C. Leckie and R. Kotagiri: Protection from Distributed Denial of Service Attack Using History-based IP Filtering. Proceedings of ICC 2003, Anchorage, Alaska, USA, May 2003.
11. Sun Microsystems: Java Management Extensions (JMX). http://java.sun.com/products/JavaManagement/index.jsp

Defining Reusable Business-Level QoS Policies for DiffServ

André Beller, Edgard Jamhour, and Marcelo Pellenz

Pontifícia Universidade Católica do Paraná – PUCPR, PPGIA
Curitiba, PR, Brazil
abeller@ig.com.br, {jamhour, marcelo}@ppgia.pucpr.br

Abstract. This paper proposes a PBNM (Policy Based Network Management) framework for automating the process of generating and distributing DiffServ configuration to network devices. The framework is based on IETF standards, and proposes a new business level policy model for simplifying the process of defining QoS policies. The framework is defined in three layers: a business level policy model (based on a IETF PCIM extension), a device independent policy model (based on a IETF QPIM extension) and a device dependent policy model (based on the IETF *diffserv* PIB definition). The paper illustrates the use of the framework by mapping the information models to XML documents. The XML mapped information model supports the reuse of rules, conditions and network information by using *XPointer* references.

1 Introduction

Policy Based Network Management (PBNM) plays an important role for managing QoS in IP-based networks. [1,2,8]. Recent IETF publications have defined the elements for building a generic, device independent framework for QoS management. An important element in this framework is QPIM (Policy QoS Information Model) [6]. QPIM is an information model that permits to describe device independent configuration policies. By defining a model that is not-device dependent, QPIM permits to "re-use" QoS configuration, i.e., configuration policy concerning similar devices can be defined only once. QPIM configuration is expressed in terms of "policies" assigned to "device interfaces", and does not take into account business level elements, such as users, applications, network topology and time constraints. The RFC 3644 that defines QPIM, points that a complete QoS management tool should include a higher level policy model that could generate the QPIM configuration based on business goals, network topology and QoS methodology (diffserv or intserv) [6].

In this context, this paper proposes a PBNM framework for automating the process of generating and distributing Differentiated Services (diffserv) configuration to network devices. The framework proposes a new business level policy model for simplifying the process of defining QoS policies. The idea of introducing a business level model for QoS management is not new [3,4,5]. However, the proposal presented in this paper differs from the similar works found in the literature because the

A. Sahai and F. Wu (Eds.): DSOM 2004, LNCS 3278, pp. 40–51, 2004.

business level polices are fully integrated with the IETF standards. By taking advantage of the recent IETF publications concerning QoS provisioning, the framework defines all the elements required for generating and distributing *diffserv* configuration to network devices.

This paper is structured as follows. Section 2 review some related works that also proposes business level models for QoS management. Section 3 presents the overview of our proposal. Section 4 presents the business level policy model, defined as a PCIM extension and fully integrated with QPIM. Section 5 describe the QPIM based configuration model, and the process adopted for transforming the business level policies into configuration policies. Section 6 presents XML mapping strategy and examples for illustrating the use of the proposed model. Finally, the conclusion resumes the important aspects of this work and points to future developments.

2 Related Works and Discussion

This section will review some important works that address the issue of defining a business level QoS policy model. Verma [3] et al. proposes a tool for managing *diffserv* configuration in enterprise networks. The work defines the elements for building a QoS management tool, permitting to transform business level policies into device configuration information. The proposal adopts the concept of translating business level policies based on SLAs (Service Level Agreements) into device configuration. Verma [4] present an extension of this work, introducing more details concerning the business level model and a configuration distributor based on the IETF framework. The business level policy is described by statements with the syntax: "a user (or group of users) accessing an application (or group of applications) in a server (or group of servers) in a specific period of time must receive a specific service class". The service class is defined in terms of "response time" (i.e., a round-trip delay of packets). An important concept developed in [4] refers to the strategy adopted for distributing the configuration to the network devices and servers. The strategy assumes a *diffserv* topology. For network devices (e.g., routers), a configuration policy is relevant only if the shortest-path between the source and destination IP includes the router. For servers, a configuration policy is relevant if the server IP is included in the source or destination IP ranges defined by the policy. As explained in the next sections, we adopt a similar strategy in our framework.

The Solaris Bandwidth Manager, implemented by Sun [7], proposes a business level QoS model for enterprise networks that closely follows the semantics of the IETF PCIM/PCIMe [12,13]. In the proposed model, a packet flow that satisfies some conditions receives a predefined service class defined in terms of bandwidth percentage and traffic priority. The Sun's approach adopts the PDP/PEP implementation framework [2], extending the enforcement points to network devices (routers and switches) and servers. The communication between the PDP and the PEP is implemented through a set of proprietary APIs.

There are also attempts of proposing a standard model for representing business level policies. According to the IETF terminology, a SLS (Service Level Specification) represents a subset of a SLA (Service Level Agreement) that refers to traffic characterization and treatment [8]. There was two attempts of defining a standard SLS model published by IETF as Internet drafts: TEQUILA [9] and AQUILA [10]. TEQUILA (Traffic Engineering for Quality of Service in the Internet, at Large Scale) define a SLS in terms of six main attributes: Scope, Flow Identifier, Performance, Traffic Conformance, Excess Treatment, Service Schedule and Reliability. AQUILA (Adaptative Resource Control for QoS Using an IP-based Layered Architecture) adopts the concept of predefined SLS types, based on the generic SLS definitions proposed by TEQUILA. A predefined SLS type fixes values (or range of values) for a subset of parameters in the generic SLS. According to [10], the mapping process between the generic SLS and the concrete QoS mechanisms can be very complex if the user can freely select and combine the parameters. Therefore, the use of predefined types simplifies the negotiation between customers and network administrators.

The proposal described in this paper has several similarities with the works reviewed in this section. However, the strategy for defining the policy model and the implementation framework differs in some important aspects. Considering the vendors efforts to follow the recent IETF standards, translating business level policies to a diffserv PIB [11], and distributing the configuration information using the COPS-PR [5] protocol is certainly a logical approach for a QoS management tool. None of the works reviewed in this section follows this approach altogether. In [3,4], even though some CIM and PCIM [8] concepts are mentioned, the proposal follows its own approach for representing policies, servers, clients and QoS configuration parameters. In [7], the policy model follows a closer PCIM extension, but the policy distribution and enforcement follows a proprietary approach where neither the PIB structure, nor the COPS protocol is adopted. The TEQUILA project offers some attempts of defining standard representations for SLS agreements. However, as pointed by AQUILA, the mapping between a generic SLS definition to QoS mechanisms can be very complex. AQUILA tries to solve the problem by proposing a set of predefined SLS types. This paper also follows the AQUILA strategy of adopting predefined SLS types. However, instead of using the generic TEQUILA template, our work represent SLS types as predefined actions described in terms of device-independent QPIM configuration policies. Because configurations described in terms of QPIM are easily translated to diffserv PIB instances, this strategy significantly simplifies the process of mapping the business level policies to QoS mechanisms in network devices.

3   Proposal

Fig. 1 presents an overview of our proposed framework (the explanation in this section follows the numbers in the arrows in the figure). The core of framework is the business level policy model (BLPM). The BLPM is defined as a PCIM extension and it is described in details in section 4. BLPM business rules semantics accommodates most of the elements proposed in [3,4 and 7], but all elements (group of users, group of applications and group of servers) are described in terms of standard CIM elements (1). Also, the service classes are defined are in terms of QPIM configuration, or more precisely, QPIM actions, as explained in the next section (2). The business level policy information (3) is "compiled" to a Configuration Level Policy Model (CLPM) information (4) by the Business Level Policy Compiler (BLPC). The CLPM and the transformations implemented by the BLPC are discussed in section 5. Note that the CLPM repository is pointed as both, input and output of the BLPC module. The CLPM is defined as a combination of QPIM and PCIM/PCIMe classes. The CLPM offers classes for describing both elements in a device configuration: conditions (traffic characterization) and actions. Actions correspond to the configuration of QoS mechanisms such as congestion control and bandwidth allocation, and correspond to predefined QPIM compound actions (i.e., a manager, when creating business level policies, assigns a service level to a SLS by pointing to a predefined group of QPIM actions). The conditions, by the other hand, are generated from the business level definitions (users, applications, and servers). Therefore, a new set of CLPM configuration is created by the BLPC module during an "off-line" compilation process.

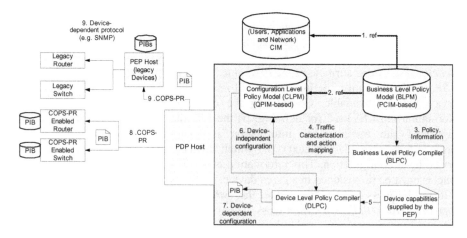

Fig. 1. Framework overview.

The CLPM device-independent configuration (6) is transformed into a device-specific configuration (7) by the Device Level Policy Compiler (DLPC). The DLPC "existence" is conceptually defined by the IETF framework, in the provisioning approach. The device-dependent configuration is expressed in terms of a diffserv PIB, which general structure is defined by the IETF [11]. Because network devices can support different mechanisms for implementing diffserv actions, the DLPC must also receive the "device capabilities" as an input parameter. Device capabilities can be "optionally" transmitted by the PEP through the COPS-PR protocol [5] when the provisioning information is requested to the PDP. The process of configuring network devices consists in transmitting the PIB using the COPS-PR protocol. Two situations can be considered. (i) COPS-PR enabled Network devices capable of directly accepting the PIB information as configuration (i.e., all necessary translation from the PIB to vendor-specific commands are implemented internally by the device). (ii) Legacy devices, where a programmable host is required to act as PEP, converting the PIB information to vendor-specific commands using a configuration protocol, such as SNMP. The DLPC module and the PIB generation is not discussed in this paper.

4 Business Level QoS Policy Model

The strategy used for describing the business level policies can be expressed as: "user (or group of users) accessing an application (or group of applications) in a server (or group of servers), in a given period of time, must receive a predefined service level". Fig. 2 presents the UML diagram of the proposed business level policy model. The policy model is derived from the PCIM/PCIMe model [12,13] by creating a new set of specialized classes. Basically, the PCIM/PCIMe model permits to create policies as a group of rules. Each rule has conditions and actions. If the conditions are satisfied, then the corresponding actions must be executed. There are many details concerning how conditions are grouped and evaluated. For a more detailed discussion about extending PCIM model, please, refer to [14].

In our proposal, the *PredefinedSLSAction* refers to a predefined QPIM compound policy action (see Fig. 3). For example, a QoS specialist can create predefined QPIM compound actions defining a Gold, Silver and Bronze service levels (this example is illustrated in the section 6). Then, in the business level policy model, the administrator only makes a reference to the predefined service description using the *PredefinedSLSName* attribute of the *PredefinedSLSAction* class. The conditions of the *SLSPolicyRule* permit to define "who" will receive the service level and "when" the service will be available. Considering the diffserv approach, the "who" policy information must be used for defining: (i) the filtering rules used by the device for classifying the traffic. This information is used for completing the QPIM configuration (as explained next). (ii) which devices must receive the pre-defined service level configuration. This information is used by the PDP for selecting which policies must be provisioned in a given device.

In the business level policy model the "who" information is represented by the *CompoundTargetPolicyCondition* class. This class defines users/applications/servers semantic and it is composed by three *CompoundPolicyCondition* extensions: *CompoundServerPolicyCondition*, *CompoundApplicationPolicyCondition* and *CompoundUserPolicyCondition*. In our model, compound conditions have been choosen for supporting information reuse. A compound condition permits defining objects in terms of logical expressions. These logical expressions are formed by *SimplePolicyConditions*, which follow the semantics "variable" match "value", defined by PCIMe. The variables refer to already defined CIM objects (*PolicyExplicitVariable*), permitting to create policies that reuse CIM information. Therefore, compound conditions can be used for representing group of users, group of applications and group of servers that can be reused in several business policies.

CompoundServerPolicyCondition   refers   to   one   or   more   CIM *UnitaryComputerSystem* objects, permitting to retrieve the correponding server IP addresses   through   the   associated   *RemoteServiceAccessPoint*   objects. *CompoundUserPolicyCondition* refers to one or more CIM *Person* objects, permitting to retrieve the correponding user's host IP addresses or host names also through the associated *RemoteServiceAccessPoint* objects. Finally, *CompoundApplicationPolicy Condition* points to one or more CIM *ApplicationSystem or InstalledProduct* objects permitting to retrieve the application's protocol and port information trough the associated *SoftwareFeatures* and *ServiceAccessPoint* objects.

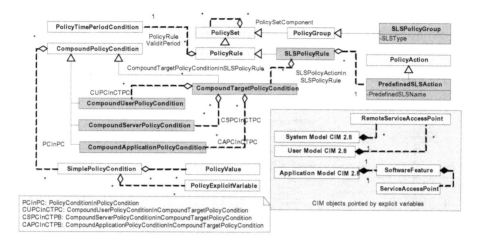

Fig. 2. The PCIM/PCIMe-based business level QoS Policy Model (extended classes are shown in gray). In the proposed model, a policy is represented by a *SLSPolicyGroup* instance. A *SLSPolicyGroup* contains one or more *SLSPolicyRule* instances (associated by the *PolicySetComponent*). When the conditions of a *SLSPolicyRule* are satisfied, then the corresponding *PredefinedSLSActions* must be executed.

5   Configuration Level QoS Policy Model

Our proposal adopts the strategy of representing SLS predefined actions using the QPIM model. The QPIM model is a PCIM/PCIMe extension, and aims to offer a device independent approach for modeling the configuration of *intserv* and *diffserv* devices. Because our work addresses only the *diffserv* methodology, only the *diffserv* elements of QPIM will be presented and discussed. For *diffserv*, QPIM should offer elements for representing both, traffic profile, used by QoS mechanisms to classify the traffic, and QoS actions, used by the QoS mechanisms to adequate the output traffic to the specified levels. In fact, the RFC 3644 [6] does not present the complete model. Instead, it presents only the new classes that are related to QoS actions. The RFC merely suggests that developers must combine the QPIM elements with PCIM/PCIMe for creating a complete configuration model. Fig. 3 presents our approach for using the QPIM extensions.

A device configuration is expressed by a *ConfigPolicyGroup* instance. Note in Fig. 3 that this class is associated to a *PolicyRole* collection. This association permits to assign "roles" for the configuration. According to IETF, roles are used by the PDP to decide which configuration must be transmitted to a given PEP (i.e., a network device interface). During the provisioning initialization, a PEP informs the roles assigned to the device interfaces, and the PDP will consider all the *ConfigPolicyGroup* instances that match these roles. In our approach a *ConfigPolicyGroup* instance is dynamically created as a result of the Business Policy Level (BPL) compilation. Therefore, the

BPL compiler must also determine which roles are assigned to the configuration. This is determined by the association between the *PolicyRoleCollection* and the CIM Network class. The BPL compiler assures that all business policies including users or servers with IP addresses belonging to the network subnet associated to a given *PolicyRoleCollection* will generate configuration policies with the same roles of this collection.

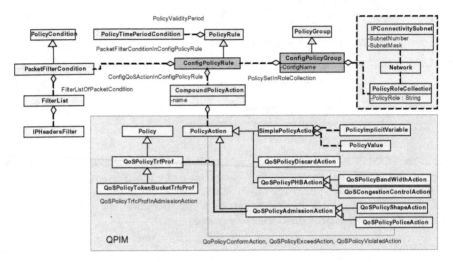

Fig. 3. The configuration policy model, including PCIM/PCIMe and QPIM classes. The QPIM classes are highlighted in the figure by a grey rectangle. We have introduced two new classes: *ConfigPolicyGroup* and *ConfigPolicyRule*. The other classes are defined by PCIM/PCIMe, CIM Policy and CIM Network.

A *ConfigPolicyGroup* instance aggregates one or more *ConfigPolicyRule* instances. In our approach, each *ConfigPolicyRule* instance is associated to *PacketFilterCondition* instances and to *CompoundPolicyAction* instances. *PacketFilterConditions* are used for defining the rules classifying the traffic that will benefit from the QoS service level defined by the *CompoundPolicyAction*. The *PacketFilterConditions* are defined by the BPL compiler considering the "who" information in the BPL model. The *CompoundPolicyAction* instance is a pre-defined SLS QoS action, which is simply pointed by the BPL compiler by matching the attribute *PredefinedSLSName* in the BPL model with the name attribute of the *CompoundPolicyAction*. The actions included in the *CompoundPolicyAction* are defined by QPIM [6]. An example of QPIM configuration is presented in the section 6.

6   XML Mapping and Examples

The proposed framework have been implemented using XML for mapping all information model related to the business level policy model, configuration policy model and CIM information. The strategy adopted for mapping the information models into XML is inspired by the LDAP mapping guidelines proposed by IETF and DTMF, and can be summarized as follows: (i) for the structural classes the mapping is one-for-one, information model classes and their properties map to XML elements and their attributes. (ii) for the relationship classes two different mappings are used: If the relationship does not involve information reuse, a superior-subordinate relationship is established by XML parent-child relationship, the association class is not represented and its attributes are included in the child element. If the relationship involves reusable information, the association class maps to a XML child node, which includes a *XPointer* reference [15] attribute that points to a specific reusable object. In this case, if the relationship is an association, the parent node corresponds to the antecedent class and the child node points to the dependent class. If the relationship is an aggregation, the parent node corresponds to the group component and the child node points to the part component class.

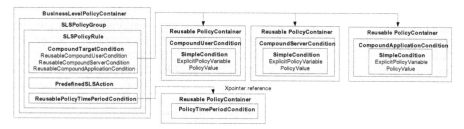

Fig. 4. Business level XML mapping structure. In the *<SLSPolicyRule>* element the conditions are defined by *<CompoundTargetPolicyCondition>* elements that point to user, application and server compositions stored in a *<ReusablePolicyContainer>*. The mapping supports the reuse of *CompoundPolicyConditions* and *PolicyTimePeriodConditions*. The simple conditions are based on the *ExplicitPolicyVariable* semantics, which permits to make references to elements described in terms of CIM objects. In our approach, simple conditions are not reusable.

In our implementation, XML was preferred as an alternative to LDAP, due to the considerable availability of development tools and recent support introduced in commercial relational databases. However, the information model discussed in this paper can also be mapped to LDAP or to a hybrid combination between LDAP and XML. Fig. 4 illustrates XML mapping structure, and the strategy adopted for supporting information reuse in the business level policy repository. Fig. 5 presents and example of a business level policy model (BLPM) mapped in XML. Fig. 6 illustrates the compound conditions representing users, applications and servers.

Fig. 7 illustrates the strategy adopted for mapping the configuration level information model. Fig. 8 illustrates an example of configuration policy generated by the BLPC. The corresponding predefined SLS compound action is illustrated in Fig. 9, and the reusable QPIM actions and associations are illustrated in Fig. 10.

```
<PolicyContainer Name="BusinessLevelPolicy">
  <SLSPolicyGroup SLSType="Olimpic" PolicyDecisionStrategy="2">
    <!--Silver Rule -->
    <SLSPolicyRule Name="SilverRule" Enabled="1" ConditionListType="1" ExecutionStrategy="2" Priority="2">
      <CompoundTargetPolicyCondition ConditionListType="1" GroupNumber="1" ConditionNegated="false">
        <CompoundUserPolicyConditionInCompoundTargetPolicyCondition GroupNumber="1
        ConditionNegated="false" PartComponent="./CompoundConditions.xml#
        xpointer(//CompoundUserPolicyCondition[@Name='CommercialManager']) " />
        <CompoundApplicationPolicyConditionInCompoundTargetPolicyCondition .../>
        <CompoundServerPolicyConditionInCompoundTargetPolicyCondition ... />
      </CompoundTargetCondition>
      <PredefinedSLSPolicyAction PredefinedSLSName="Silver" />
      <PolicyRuleValidityPeriod PartComponent="./Validity.xml#
      xpointer(//PolicyTimePeriodCondition[@Name='Period1'])" />
    </SLSPolicyRule>
    <!-- Gold Rule and Bronze Rule .... -->
  </SLSPolicyGroup>
</PolicyContainer>
```

Fig. 5. Example of business level policy in XML. The *SLSType* attribute in the *<SLSPolicyGroup>* indicates the predefined set of reusable service types adopted in the model. In this case, the "Olimpic" indicates three service levels (SLS), named "Bronze", "Silver" and "Gold". Only the service level corresponding to "Silver" is detailed in the figure by the corresponding *<SLSPolicyRule>* element. The *<CompoundTargetPolicyCondition>* defines the conditions for receiving the "Silver" pre-defined SLS action. The *XPointer* expression assigned to the *PartComponent* attributes follows the syntax "reusable-info-repository URI"#xpointer("XPath expression for selected nodes in the repository").

```
<!- CompoundConditions.xml -->
<ReusablePolicyContainer Name="CompoundUserCondition">
  <CompoundUserPolicyCondition Name="CommercialManager" ConditionListType="1">
    <SimplePolicyCondition GroupNumber="1" ConditionNegated="false">
      <PolicyExplicitVariable ModelClass="Person" ModelProperty="BusinessCategory" />
      <PolicyStringValue StringList="Manager" />
    </SimplePolicyCondition>
    <SimplePolicyCondition GroupNumber="1" ConditionNegated="false">
      <PolicyExplicitVariable ModelClass="Person" ModelProperty="OU" />
      <PolicyStringValue StringList="CommercialDepartment" />
    </SimplePolicyCondition>
  </CompoundUserPolicyCondition>
</ReusablePolicyContainer>
<ReusablePolicyContainer Name="CompoundApplicationCondition"> ...
</ReusablePolicyContainer>
<ReusablePolicyContainer Name="CompoundServerCondition"> ...
</ReusablePolicyContainer>
```

Fig. 6. Example of reusable compound conditions. The "*CommercialManager*" *<CompoundUserCondition>* selects the users matching "BusinessCategory = Manager" AND "OU = *CommercialDepartment*".

7 Conclusion

This work contributes for defining a complete framework for QoS diffserv management that is in according with recent IETF standards. This work proposes a new business level model and completes the QPIM model with classes required for defining filtering conditions for diffserv configuration. An important point with respect to the implementation of CIM/PCIM-based frameworks concerns the strategy adopted for mapping class associations to XML or LDAP. Because the directives published by IETF and DTMF offers several possibilities for mapping the information model classes, retrieving information from a repository requires a previous knowledge of how the information classes have been mapped to a specific repository schema.

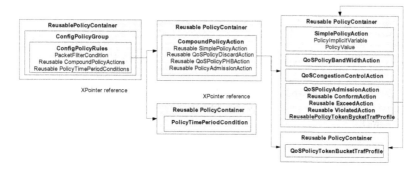

Fig. 7. Configuration Level XML Mapping Structure. A *<ConfigPolicyGroup>* groups the *<ConfigPolicyRules>* corresponding to the configuration of devices with "similar role" in the network. The *PacketFilerCondition* is generated by the BLPC, and it is not reusable. The *<CompoundPolicyActions>* and *<PolicyTimePeriodConditions>*, however, are reusable information pointed by *XPointer* references. Note the *<CompoundPolicyAction>* also points to reusable QPIM actions.

```
<PolicyContainer Name="ConfigPolicy">
   <ConfigPolicyGroup ConfigName="OlimpicConfigQoSCommercial" PolicyDecisionStrategy="1">
      <ConfigPolicyRule Enabled="1" ConditionList Type="1" Priority="2">
         <PacketFilterCondition FilterEvaluation="4" GroupNumber="2" ConditionNegated="false">
            <IPHeadersFilter IsNegated="False" HdrIPVersion="4" HdrSrcAddress="0.0.0.0" HdrSrcMask="0"
               HdrDestAddress="10.0.4.1" HdrDestMask="24" Direction="3"/>
         </PacketFilterCondition>
         <!-- ... other PacketFilterConditions -->
         <PolicyRuleValidityPeriod PartComponent="./Time.xml#
            xpointer(//PolicyTimePeriodCondition[@Name='Period1'])" />
         <ConfigQoSActionInConfigPolicyRule PartComponent="./QoSOlimpic.xml#
            xpointer(//CompoundPolicyAction[@name='SilverAction'])" />
      </ConfigPolicyRule>
   </ConfigPolicyGroup>
   <!-- ... other ConfigPolicyGroups -->
</PolicyContainer>
```

Fig. 8. Configuration policy generated by the BPL compiler. In this example, each *<ConfigPolicyGroup>* represents the configuration of the devices in a specific subnet in a enterprise *diffserv* network. Only the configuration policy corresponding to the Silver service level in the Commercial subnet is detailed in the figure.

```
<ReusablePolicyContainer Name="OlimpicQoSSpecification">
  <CompoundPolicyAction Name="BronzeAction" SequencedActions="1"
    ExecutionStrategy="2"> ... </CompoundPolicyAction>
  <CompoundPolicyAction Name="SilverAction" SequencedActions="1" ExecutionStrategy="2">
    <PolicyActionInPolicyAction ActionOrder="1" PartComponent=
      "./QPIMAction.xml#xpointer(//QoSPolicyPoliceAction[@Name=' PoliceSilverFlow '])"/>
      <PolicyActionInPolicyAction ActionOrder="2" PartComponent=
      "./QPIMAction.xml#xpointer(//QoSPolicyCongestionControlAction[@Name='SilverQueueClass'])" />
      <PolicyActionInPolicyAction ActionOrder="3" PartComponent=
      "./ QPIMAction.xml#xpointer(//QoSPolicyBandwidthAction[@Name='SilverBWClass'])" />
  </CompoundPolicyAction>
  <CompoundPolicyAction name="GoldAction" SequencedActions="1" ExecutionStrategy="2">...
  </CompoundPolicyAction>
</ReusablePolicyContainer>
```

Fig. 9. Example of reusable pre-defined QPIM compound actions. The compound "*SilverAction*" points to a set of reusable QPIM actions, which must be executed in a predefined order.

```
<ReusablePolicyContainer name="QPIMAction">
  <QoSPolicyPoliceAction Name="PoliceSilverFlow" qpAdmissionScope="0">
    <QoSPolicyTrfcProfInAdmissionAction Dependent="./QPIMAction.xml#
      xpointer(//QoSPolicyTokenBucketTrfcProf[@Name='SilverTBFlow'])" />
    <PolicyConformAction Dependent="./ QPIMAction.xml #
      xpointer(//SimplePolicyAction[@Name='SilverDSCPFlowConform'])" />
    <PolicyExceedAction ... />
    <PolicyViolateAction ... />
  </QoSPolicyPoliceAction>
  <QoSPolicyCongestionControlAction Name="SilverQueueClass" qpQueueSizeUnits="1" qpQueueSize="15"
    qpDropMethod="3" qpDropThresholdUnits="0" qpMinThresholdValue="30" qpMaxThresholdValue="45" />
  <QoSPolicyBandwidthAction Name="SilverBWClass" qpBandwidthUnits="1" qpMinBandwidth="25" />
  <SimplePolicyAction Name="SilverDSCPFlowConform">
    <PolicyDSCPVariable Name="PolicyDSCPVariable" />
    <PolicyIntegerValue IntegerList="AF21" />
  </SimplePolicyAction>
  <SimplePolicyAction Name="SilverDSCPFlowExceed">... </SimplePolicyAction>
  <SimplePolicyAction Name="SilverDSCPFlowViolate">... </SimplePolicyAction>
  ...
</ReusablePolicyContainer>

<ReusablePolicyContainer name="TokenBucket">
  <QoSPolicyTokenBucketTrfcProf Name="SilverTBFlow"
    qpTBRate="256" qpTBNormalBurst="64" qpTBExcessBurst="32" />
  <!-- other traffic profiles -->
</ReusablePolicyContainer>
```

Fig. 10. Example of reusable pre-defined QPIM actions.

That poses an important obstacle for building "out-of-the box" frameworks that could reuse existent CIM/PCIM information. This is certainly a point that should be addressed by IETF and DMTF. Future works includes extending the business level policy model for supporting more elaborated policies rules and the development of a graphical tool for generating the business level policies.

References

1. Ponnappan, A.; Yang, L.; Pillai, R.; Braun, P. "A Policy Based QoS Management System for the IntServ/DiffServ Based Internet". Proceedings of the Third International Workshop on Policies for Distributed Systems and Networks (POLICY.02). IEEE, 2002 .
2. Yavatkar, R., Pendarakis, D.; Guerin, R. A Framework for Policy-Based Admission Control, RFC2753, Jan. 2000.
3. D. Verma, M. Beigi and R. Jennings, "Policy Based SLA Management in Enterprise Networks", Proceedings of Policy WorkShop 2001.
4. D. Verma, "Simplifying Network Administration using Policy based Management", IEEE Network Magazine, March 2002.
5. Chan K.; Seligson, J.; Durham, D.; Gai, S.; McCloghrie, K.; Herzog, S.; Reichmeyer, F.; Yavatkar, R.; Smith, A.; "COPS Usage for Policy Provisioning (COPS-PR)", IETF RFC 3084, Mar. 2001.
6. Snir, Y.; Ramberg, Y.; Strassner, J.; Cohen, R.; Moore, B.; "Policy Quality of Service (QoS) Information Model", IETF RFC 3644, Nov. 2003.
7. Kakadia, D.; "Enterprise QoS Based Systems & Network Management", Sun Microsystems White Paper, Article #8934, Volume 60, Issue 1, SysAdmin Section, February 4, 2003.
8. J. Schnizlein, J. Strassner, M. Scherling, B. Quinn, S. Herzog, A. Huynh, M. Carlson, J. Perry, S. Waldbusser; "Terminology for Policy-Based Management", IETF RFC 3198, Nov. 2001.
9. D. Goderis, D. Griffin, C. Jacquenet, G. Pavlou; "Attributes of a Service Level Specification (SLS) Template", IETF draft, October 2003.
10. S. Salsano, F. Ricciato, M. Winter, G. Eichler, A. Thomas, F. Fuenfstueck, T. Ziegler, C. Brandauer; "Definition and usage of SLSs in the AQUILA consortium", IETF draft, Nov. 2000 (expired).
11. K. Chan, R. Sahita, S. Hahn, K. McCloghrie, "Differentiated Services Quality of Service Policy Information Base", IETF RFC 3317, Mar. 2003.
12. B. Moore, E. Elleson, J. Strasser, A. Weterinen: Policy Core Information Model. IETF RFC 3060, February 2001.
13. B. Moore, E. Elleson, J. Strasser, A. Weterinen: Policy Core Information Model Extensions. IETF RFC 3460, February 2001.
14. Nabhen, R., Jamhour, E., Maziero C. "Policy-Based Framework for RBAC", Proceedings for the fourteenth IFIP/IEEE International Workshop on Distributed Systems: Operations & Management, October, Germany, Feb. 2003, pg. 181-193.
15. W3C, XPointer Framework, W3C Recommendation, 25 March 2003.

Policy Driven Business Performance Management

Jun-Jang Jeng, Henry Chang, and Kumar Bhaskaran

IBM T.J. Watson Research Center
New York 10598, U.S.A.
{jjjeng,hychang,bha}@us.ibm.com

Abstract. Business performance management (BPM) has emerged as a critical discipline to enable enterprise to manage their business solutions in an on demand fashion. BPM applications promote an adaptive means by emphasizing the ability to monitor and control both business processes and IT events. However, most BPM processes and architectures are usually linear and rigid; and once done, will be very hard to change. Hence, it does not help enterprise to create adaptive monitoring and control applications for business solutions. There is an urgent need of adaptive BPM framework to be used as a platform of developing BPM applications. This paper presents a policy based BPM framework to help enterprise to achieve on demand monitoring and control framework for business solutions.

1 Introduction

Business performance management (BPM) has emerged as a critical discipline to enable enterprise to manage their business solutions in an on demand fashion. BPM applications promote an adaptive strategy by emphasizing the ability to monitor and control both business processes and IT events. By coordinating the business and IT events within an integrated framework, decision makers can quickly and efficiently align IT and human resources based on the current business climate and overall market conditions. Business executives can leverage the results of core business process execution to speed business transformation, and IT executives can leverage business views of the IT infrastructure to recommend IT-specific actions that can drive competitive advantage.

However, most BPM processes and architectures are usually linear and rigid; and once done, will be very hard to change. To change the requirements of BPM is sometimes like building a completely new application, which costs time and money. Some enterprises attempt to increase the flexibility and agility of business by introducing dynamic workflows and intelligent rules. However, this kind of **systems** is hard to be modeled, deployed and maintained. In the BPM domain, business analytics are commonly incorporated in business monitoring and management systems in order to understand the business operations in a deeper sense,. Nevertheless, most functions provided business analytics are performed in batch mode – unable to resolve business situations and exceptions in a timely fashion. How to run analytics in a continuous sense is a challenge. In general, it is extremely difficult to model, integrate and de

A. Sahai and F. Wu (Eds.): DSOM 2004, LNCS 3278, pp. 52–63, 2004.

ploy monitoring & control capabilities into larger scale business solutions such as supply chain management.

This paper presents a policy based BPM framework to address the above issues. A BPM system is a system for sensing environmental stimulus, interpreting perceived data, adjudicating the data to be business situations, and making decisions about how to respond the situations. A BPM system takes monitored data from target business solutions (e.g. business events), invokes BPM services and renders actions back to target business solutions. In general, there are five representative categories of services in a BPM system: Sense, Detect, Analyze, Decide and Effect. "Sense" is the stage when a BPM system interacts with business solutions and provides data extraction, transformation, and loading capabilities for the sake of preparing qualified data that is to be further monitored and analyzed. "Detect" is the stage of detecting business situations and/or exception occurring in the business solutions. "Analyze" is the stage when a BPM system performs business analytics such as risk-based analysis of resolving business exceptions. "Decide" is the stage when a decision maker will make decision about what to respond to business situations. A decision maker can be either human or software agent. "Effect" is the stage when a BPM system carries out actions for the purpose of enforcing the decisions made by decision makers. Actions can be of many forms. The simplest kind of action is alerting interested parties about the decisions. More complicated ones may be involved sophisticated process invocation.

As a motivating example for this paper, we want to show a BPM system for managing business solution that we built for some microelectronics manufacturer [1]. It comprises a suite of event-driven, decision management applications that enable proactive management of business disruptions in real time. The system's ability to identify potential out of tolerance situations, whether to unexpected fluctuations in supply and demand, or emerging customer, partner, and supplier needs, is enabled by analytical exception detection agents. These agents utilize standardized or configurable measurements to observe business events; for example to ensure that enterprise revenue goals are being accomplished. The BPM policies are managed pro-actively. Alert messages inform business process owners in advance if a new trend is emerging and actions must be taken. Finally, this system provides a suite of domain-dependent optimization, performance prediction, and risk assessment agents that make exception management even more effective. The agents adopt existing cost structures and business process flexibility, and recommend optimized business policies and actions that drive business performance to higher levels of productivity, efficiency, and financial predictability. The following scenario illustrates a scenario how the business line manager utilizes the BPM system.

- The BPM system receives *events* from various source systems from the supply chain. Some of these events impact the inventory levels or revenue metrics for the manufactured modules (such as "*order placed*" or "*order cancelled*" events). The BPM system continuously updates the actual revenue, the revenue outlook and inventory levels.

- Whether the progression of the accrued revenue is normal or below target is determined by the BPM system using a wineglass model [2]. In the case where the revenue is below target, the system automatically detects such a *situation* and issues an alert showing the current sales quantities of some selected saleable part numbers in the *n*th week are out of their bands.

- The BPM system recommends adjusting the planned demand quantities and safety stock requirements for the *n*th week. As next step, it invokes a demand planning module and inventory planning module to analyse demand quantities and safety stock requirements for the *n*th week.

- It further recommends altering the daily build plan in order to optimally match new daily demand statements, thus high serviceability, and minimize manufacturing and inventory costs. By doing so, it also shows the effects and risks of all suggested alternatives for changing the build plan.

- Finally, the business line manager looks at the suggestions of the BPM system and makes a final decision for improving the build plan.

- The BPM system immediately revises the actual build plan in the ERP system (*action*) and continues the monitoring of the performance indicators with the updated build plan.

This paper is organized as follows. Section 1 introduced the BPM concept and a motivating example. Section 2 describes the concepts and lifecycle of BPM policies. Section 3 presents the policy-driven architecture for BPM. The related work is given in Section 5. Finally, Section 6 concludes this paper and discusses the future endeavour.

2   Defining BPM Policies

A BPM system is meant to be a platform for adaptive enterprise information systems in that the system behavior can be altered without modifying the mechanisms of the system itself. A BPM policy aims to govern and constrain the behavior of the BPM net and its constituent services. It usually provides policy rules for how the BPM system should behave in response to emergent situations [3]. As an example, a policy of supply chain inventory may impose limits on the range of inventory levels for the manufacturing process based upon the revenue target of the enterprise. Relevant policies can be devised and applied to different aspects of business solutions. Examples include role-based authorization to manage target business solutions and resources, the scope of managed business solutions and resources, and service-level agreements. Every BPM policy has its own lifecycle. The lifecycle of a policy consists of six basic life-stages as shown in Figure 1. They are: policy definition, policy activation, policy passivation, policy deployment and configuration, policy enforcement and policy termination.

Policy Definition is the phase that a policy is created, browsed and validated. Corresponding definitional tools such as editor, browsers and policy verifiers can be used by business analysts to input the different policies that are to be effective in the BPM system. *Policy Deployment & Configuration* configures and deploys a policy into target system and configures the system correspondingly. *Policy Enforcement* is the stage when a policy is being enforced to govern and constrain the behavior of target systems. *Policy Activation* is the phase when a policy is loaded into target system and waiting for further execution. *Policy Passivation* is the phase when a policy is put to persistent storage without any active activity. *Policy Termination* is the phase when a policy ceases to exist in the system.

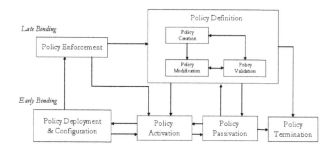

Fig. 1. Policy Lifecycle.

Potentially, a policy can be bound to BPM services at two points of its lifecycle: (1) policy deployment & configuration: this type of binding is called early binding between policy and mechanism since it is realized at the build time; and (2) policy enforcement: this type of binding is, on the other hand, called late binding between policy and mechanism since this binding is realized at the run time when policy is being executed.

The BPM policies are specified using Ponder-like expressions [11] as follows. In this syntax, every word in bold is a token in the language and optional elements are specified with square brackets [ ]. The policy with name "policyName" will be triggered when the events specified in "event-specification" are generated and captured by the BPM system. The event can be primitive event and compound event what composed from primitive event using event operator [6]. The keyword *subject* refers to the service that will act as the policy enforcer, and the *scope* phrase indicates the scope in that this policy will be applied. The "do-when" pattern signifies the actions to be enforced based on the pre-defined constraints.

```
policy policyName[(<type>argName[,<type> argName]*)]
                on event-specification;
subject [<type >] domain-Scope-Expression;
[scope [<type >] domain-Scope-Expression;]
do action-list;
[when constraint-Expression ;]
```

The following segment shows the policy of detecting the out-of-bound revenue situation based on (a) given upper- and lower-bounds; and (b) predicted revenue performance. A metric event carrying the context object of the MDBPM system (noted as MDBPMContext) acts as an input to this policy. Some of the data referred by this policy are parameterized as input parameters: (1) *upperBound* is the upper bound of the revenue performance; (2) lower*Bound* is the lower bound of the revenue performance; (3) *ActionPlanningService* indicates the service to receive the detected situation; (4) *LOBManager* is the manager who will get notified when the situation is eventually detected.

```
policy senseOutOfBoundRevenueSituation(
            int upperBound,
             int lowerBound,
             ActionPlanningService aps,
             LOBManager lob)
            on MetricEvent(MDBPMContext context);
 subject PolicyManager;            // the policy controller
 target SituationDetectionService;//the policy enforcer
 do {
      //  notify action planning service
      notify(aps, "OutOfBoundRevenueSituation",context);
      // notify LOB manager
      notify(lob, "OutOfBoundRevenueSituation",context);
 }
 // situation detection rule
 when context.revenue > upperBound \/ context.revenue <
 lowerBound ;
```

The following policy shows what needs to be actually done when the aforementioned situation occurs. This policy is triggered by a situation event carrying the MD context object *MDBPMContext*. The *do* clause defines an action by concatenating three other actions: (1) invoke the demand planning service to create a demand plan based on input situation object; (2) invoke the inventory planning service to create an inventory plan based on the demand plan; (3) notify the LOB manager about the recommended inventory plan. The execution strategy (as an input parameter) is DO_ALL_IN_SEQUENCE meaning every action indicated in *do* clause needs to be executed with indicated sequence.

```
policy respondOutOfBoundRevenueSituation(
      DemandPlanningService dps,
      InventoryPlanningService ips,
      LOBManager lob,
      ExecutionStraegy DO_ALL_IN_SEQUENCE)
      on SituationEvent(MDBPMContext context);
 subject PolicyManager;
 target ActionPlanningService;
 do {
      // invoke demand planning service
      demandPlan = invoke(dps, demandPlan, context);
      // invoke inventory planning service
      inventoryPlan = invoke(ips, demandPlan, context);
      notify(lob, inventoryPlan, context); //notify LOB
 manager
    }
```

3   Policy Architecture

This section shows a realization of policy-driven BPM architecture. Two fundamental notions are presented here: *BPM ring* and *BPM net*.

BPM Rings

The BPM cycle is realized into BPM ring. A BPM ring represents a scalable mechanism of realizing real-time BPM capabilities at various levels of granularity (e.g. business organization, enterprise, value-net). A BPM ring consists of nodes and links. A BPM node is a basic service that enables transformation from input data to output data based on its capabilities and the pre-defined policies. A BPM link transmits data with specific types from one node to another node. A BPM node can have multiple instances of input and output links. Therefore, it can process multiple input requests concurrently. The number of BPM nodes in a BPM ring is subject to the actual requirements. BPM rings are policy-driven and dynamic. The BPM policy as mentioned in previous section is used to govern the information exchange and control signaling among BPM nodes. BPM rings can be used as a simple modeling vehicle of integrating BPM capabilities at various organizational levels, e.g., strategic, operational and execution.

BPM rings provide the means of building highly configurable and adaptive integration platform for BPM solutions. In our example, we have come up with 5 typical BPM service nodes in a BPM ring: (1) event processing service that takes raw data and produce qualified data to be further processed; (2) metric generation service that receives the qualified data and produced metrics; (3) situation detection service that analyzes incoming metrics and raise situations if needed; (4) action planning service that is triggered by situations and creates an action plan in order to resolve the situation; and (5) action rendering service that takes a group of actions from action planning service and actually renders them to the target business solutions. A BPM service node can process multiple input data requests based on the functionality to which it is aimed. Each service realizes grid specification and developed upon OGSA code base.

Implementation-wise, the BPM ring architecture is a physical star and a data processing ring. The BPM ring nodes are connected to a dispatching module called a Multi Node Access Unit (MNAU). Normally several MNAUs are connected in one BPM node while BPM links connect those MNAUs to the BPM nodes. This makes up the physical star. The control flow is rendered from one BPM node to the other through the MNAUs and each connected BPM links. The control flows of BPM ring realized by control tokens. Each BPM node on a BPM ring acts as both a data transformer and a repeater, receiving a series of data from one node and passing them on to the next. During this transformation/repeating process, if a ring node notices that it is the destination of the control flow (coded in the token), each data is copied into BPM data repository and the final data stream is altered slightly to let other ring nodes know that the control token was received. The control token is sent to each ring node in a specific order, known as the ring order. This ring order never changes unless another ring node joins or leaves the ring. Once the token reaches the last node in the ring, it is sent back to the first node. This method of token passing allows each node to view the token and regenerate it along the way.

A BPM node is triggered when it receives a control token. This token gives the ring node permission to transform and transmit data. If there are more than one token residing within a BPM node. They will be queued up in local repository and will be processed in a first-come-first-serve fashion. However, some preemptive policies can be defined. One node on the network is the leader, and makes sure that the ring operates properly. This leader is called the BPM ring Leader. It performs several important functions including control token timing, making sure that control tokens and data don't circle the ring endlessly, and other maintenance duties. All nodes have the built-in capability to be the BPM ring Leader, and when there is no monitor on a ring, all the BPM nodes use special procedures to select one.

BPM Nets

Figure 2 illustrates a potential structure of BPM net formed by BPM rings and the interactions among them.

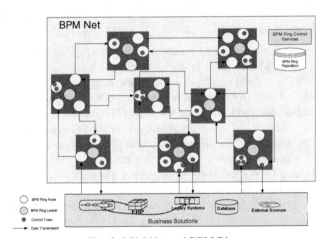

Fig. 2. BPM Net and BPM Rings.

Multiple BPM rings form a BPM net in that each BPM ring becomes a node and interactions among BPM rings constitute the links. While BPM rings capture the monitoring and control patterns of specific business situations (or exceptions), BPM net represents the pattern of communicating autonomous BPM rings in order to capture a global behavior of monitoring and control across business solution. Hence, a BPM net realizes the BPM capabilities for a business organization (enterprise). BPM rings collaborate with one another and aggregate into higher granularities. The structure of BPM nets can represent contractual bindings between business organizations (enterprises) and typically result in information exchange between business organizations (enterprises).

Formal BPM Net Model

A key goal of BPM net is to provide ubiquitous BPM services for target business solutions. Furthermore, the BPM net, is a dynamic and open environment where the availability and state of these services and resources are constantly changing. The primary focus of the BPM net model presented in this paper is to automatically create BPM policies (when possible) from the set of available services to satisfy dynamically defined monitoring and control objectives, policies and constraints. In the BPM net model, BPM services and policies can he dynamically defined. The pool of currently available BPM services is represented as a graph where the node represents services and the links, can be modeled as potential interactions.

To define BPM net, we need to define the relation, called *subsumption,* among BPM rings. For two messages M_1 and M_2, we define that M1 is subsumed by M2, (noted by $M_1 \sqsubseteq M_2$), if and only if for every argument a in the output message of M1, there is always an argument b in the input message of M2 such that either they have the same type or the type of a is the subtype of the type of b. Formally, $M_1 \sqsubseteq M_2 \Leftrightarrow \forall a \in M_1.\text{Output\_Arg}$

$$(\exists \, b \in M_2.\text{Input\_Arg s.t. } (type(a) = type(b)) \lor substype(a,b))$$.

Similarly, for two services S1 and S2, we say that S1 is subsumed by S2 if for every message M1 in S1, there is a message M2 such that M1 is subsumed by M2. Formally, $S_1 \sqsubseteq S_2 \Leftrightarrow \forall M_1 \in S_1 \, (\exists \, M_2 \in S_2 \text{ s.t. } M_1 \sqsubseteq M_2)$.

The formal definitions of BPM ring and BPM net are as follows:

1) A BPM ring $R_k = (S_k, C_k)$ where, S_k is a set of service nodes and C_k a set of service connection.

   a) Service set $S_k = \{ s_{k,1}, s_{k,2}, \dots , s_{k,nk} \}$ where n_k is the number of functional stages in the ring R_k;

   b) Connection set $C_k = \{ c_{k,1,2}, c_{k,2,3}, \dots , c_{k,nk-1,nk} \}$ where $c_{k,i-1,i}$ connects $s_{k,i-1}$ and $s_{k,i}$. The data output of $s_{k,i-1}$ is the input of $c_{k,i-1,i}$ and the input of $s_{k,i}$ is the output of $c_{k,i-1,i}$.

2) A BPM net is a structure based on a service graph $N(B, \Sigma, \Phi)$ where B is the business solution that the BPM Net monitors and controls, Σ a set of BPM rings, and Φ a set of potential interactions among rings.

   a) The target business solutions B = {P, E} where P is set of probes that emit monitored data to BPM net and E a set of effectors that received control directives from the BPM net.

   b) The set of rings $\Sigma = \{R_i\}$ where each of R_i is associated with an order set of contextual data $\{Context(R_i)\}$.

   c) The set of potential interactions among rings $\Phi = \{ L_{(i,x),(j,y)} \}$ such that R_i, $R_j \in R$ and x-th service of R_i connects to y-th service of R_j. Each connection is associated with a utility function to calculate the cost value $Cost(L_{(i,x),(j, y)})$.

3) In the net graph, $N(B, \Sigma, \Phi)$, the available services are nodes and interactions are edges. The edges $\{ L_{(i,x),(j, y)} \}$ are created at runtime when one of the following conditions hold

   a) Both $S_{(i,x)}$ and $S_{(j, y)}$ belong to the same ring, i.e., $i = j$ and $y = x+1$.

   b) $S_{(i,x)}$ is subsumed by $S_{(j, y)}$, i.e., $S_{i, x} \sqsubseteq S_{j, y}$

4) The initial service S_0 of the ultimate BPM net is the service that can consume the output generate by the probes of the business solution P, hence, $S_0 \sqsubseteq P$.

5) The final service S_f of the of the ultimate BPM net is the service that produce the output to be consumed by the effectors of the business solution E, hence, $E \sqsubseteq S_f$

6) The chosen services from BPM net at run time form an execution path $\{S_0, S'_1, S'_2, \ldots, S_f\}$ in $N(B, \Sigma, \Phi)$

7) The costs of S_0 and S_f represent the costs of instrumentation of the target business solution. Assume the total cost of monitoring and controlling business solution B is constrained by a given value $CostBound$ then we have the following relation for the final execution path:

$$Cost(S_{initial}) + Cost(S_{final}) + \sum_{i=1}^{n} Cost(S_i') \le CostBound$$

The subsumption relationships among services can be used to generate candidate BPM services for the ultimate BPM net. The constraints among services are given by the users including the total execution cost of monitoring and controlling target business solutions. We single out the cost of the instrumentation of target business solution, which make it ready to be monitored and controlled by BPM net because of the high variability of such cost for different solutions. For the BPM net, the candidate execution paths can be generated from S_0 to S_f.

BPM Capabilities

The execution paths generated from BPM net based on constrains and goals defined in the BPM requirement actually manifest the *capabilities* of a BPM system on monitoring and controlling business solutions. As described in previous section, BPM policies are applied to multiple levels of emprise abstraction: strategy, operation, execution, and implementation. Each layer consists of corresponding BPM rings that are specialized in monitoring and controlling specific layer of enterprise resources.

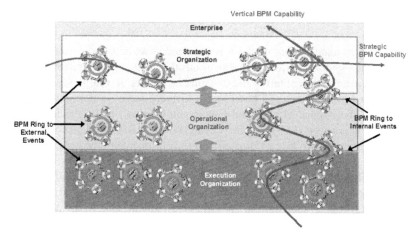

Fig. 3. BPM Capabilities.

Figure 3 illustrates the distribution of BPM rings in different enterprise layers. BPM capabilities can be defined either horizontally or vertically. Horizontal BPM capability is an execution path that consists of BPM rings exclusively of a specific layer, e.g. the strategic BPM capability. On the other hand, the vertical BPM capability is an execution path which contains the BPM rings across different layers. In the diagram, it is also indicated that some BPM rings are for processing external events and some for internal events among BPM rings.

Discussion

We have applied the concepts of BPM policies into real customer scenarios such as the one described in Section 1. A policy-driven BPM system makes it adaptive to monitor and control business solutions, which is particularly useful for the domain with high volatility of monitoring and control requirements. Crystallization of BPM policies into BPM rings and BPM net increases the modularity and reusability of BPM policies and consequently the system behavior. Formalization of BPM nets allows the dynamic formation of service execution and hence makes BPM system on demand monitoring and control system. The formal model of BPM nets also allows us to optimize the execution of BPM nets based on given constraints and cost bounds. Usually, the monitoring and control applications for specific business solution such as supply chain management systems are defined in an ad-hoc and static manner. A BPM solution is bound with a set of services at design time, which realizes the early binding of BPM policies with the underlying policy architecture. However, in an on-demand environment, the binding is not possible until the policies are discovered and enforced at run time. There are benefits and disadvantages on either approach. Early bindings facilitate the analysts to perform the policy impact at design time and hence imply an efficient implementation at run time. On the other hand, late bindings enable high flexibility of policy bindings with the policy architecture such as execution paths. Therefore, more adaptive BPM functionality can be enabled via policies.

4   Related Work

The policy-driven management model is recognized as an appropriate model for managing distributed systems [7][8]. This model has the advantages of enabling the automated management and facilitating the dynamic behaviors of a large scale distributed system. Policy works in standard bodies such as focus more on defining frameworks for traditional IT systems. Minsky and Ungureanu [9] described a mechanism called law-governed interaction (LGI), which is designed to satisfy three principles: (1) coordination policy needs to be coordinated; (2) the enforcement needs to be decentralized; and (3) coordination policies need to be formulated. LGI uses decentralized controllers co-located with agents. The framework provides a coordination and control mechanism for a heterogeneous distributed system. Verma et al. [10] proposes a policy service for resource allocation in the Grid environment. Due to the nature of Grid computing, virtualization has been greatly used for defining policy services in the paper. However, in contrast to their work, the BPM is aimed for providing policy framework for business activities instead of a service for system domain.

The Ponder Language [11] and Policy Framework for Management of Distributed Systems [12] address the implementation of managing network systems based on policies. Traditional grid based frameworks for enterprise [13] focus on distributed supercomputing, in which schedulers make decisions about where to perform computational tasks. Typically, schedulers are based on simple policies such as round-robin due to the lack of a feedback infrastructure reporting load conditions back to schedulers. However, the BPM system is governed by the BPM policies (BPM nets) that are a mode sophisticated policy than OGSA policy. ACE [14] presents a framework enabling dynamic and autonomic composition of grid services. AThe formal model of BPM nets has similar merits to their approach. However, our framework is aimed for composing monitoring and control systems for business solutions.

5   Conclusion

In this paper, we have described an approach of building an adaptive BPM policy architecture for managing business solutions. The system is designed, keeping in mind the need for multi-level of abstraction, various types of services, and different types of collaboration so that not only can BPM chores be quickly assembled and executed, but the configuration data can be deployed to the system dynamically. The dynamic interactions among services are captured in the BPM net in response to business situations that are detected from the set of observed or simulated metrics in the target business solutions. The BPM net model allows the composition of BPM services and resources using policies. We have defined a formal model for such purpose. Much more work remains to be done toward realizing complete and full implementation of BPM net. The future works include: automating the derivation of configuration model based on BPM policies, defining dynamic resource model and relations using ontological approach, applying model-driven approach into the development of BPM applications, and developing BPM policy and configuration tools.

References

1   G. Lin, S. Buckley, M.Ettl, K. Wang. Intelligent Business Activity Management – Sense and Respond Value Net Optimization. To appear in: C. An, H. Fromm (eds.) Advances in Supply Chain Management. Kluwer (2004).
2   L.S.Y. Wu, J.R.M. Hosking, and J.M. Doll, "Business Planning Under Uncertainty: Will We Attain Our Goal?," IBM Research Report RC 16120, Sep. 24, 1990, Reissued with corrections Feb. 20, 2002.
3   "Business Process Execution Language for Web Services Version 1.1," http://www-106.ibm.com/developerworks/library/ws-bpel/
4   "Web Service Notification," http://www-106.ibm.com/developerworks/library/specification/ws-notification/   March, 2004.
5   "Open Grid Services Architecture," http://www.globus.org/ogsa/
6   H. Li, J.J. Jeng, "Managing Business Relationship in E-Services Using Business Commitments", Proceedings of Third International Workshop, TES 2002, Hong Kong, China, August 23-24, 2002, LNCS 2444, pages 107-117.
7   The IETF Policy Framework Working Group: Charter available at the URL http://www.ietf.org/html.charters/policy-charter.html
8   Distributed Management Task Force Policy Working Group, Charter available at URL http://www.dmtf.org/about/working/sla.php.
9   N.H. Minsky and V. Ungureanu, "Law-Governed Interaction: A Coordination and Control Mechanism for Heterogenous Distributed Systems," ACM Transaction on Software Engineering and Methodology, Vol. 9, No. 3, July, 2000, Pages 273-305.
10   N. Damianou, N. Dulay, E. Lupu, M. and Sloman, M., "The Ponder Policy Specification Language", Proceedings of the Policy Workshop 2001, HP Labs, Bristol, UK, Springer-Verlag, 29-31 January 2001, http://www.doc.ic.ac.uk/~mss/Papers/Ponder-Policy01V5.pdf
11   N. Damianou, "A Policy Framework for Management of Distributed Systems", PhD Thesis, Faculty of Engineering of the University of London, London, England, 2002, http://www-dse.doc.ic.ac.uk/Research/policies/ponder/thesis-ncd.pdf
12   D. Verma, "A Policy Service for Grid Computing," M. Parashar (Ed.): GRID 2002, LNCS 2536, pp. 243–255, 2002.
13   Helal, S. et al, The Internet Enterprise, In Proceedings of the 2002 Symposium on Application and the Internet (SAINT2002).
14   R. Medeiros, et. al "Autonomic Service Adaptation in ICENI Using Ontological Annotation," in the Proceedings of the Fourth International Workshop on Grid Computing (GRID 2003), pages 10-17, Phoenix, Arizona, November 17, 2004.

Business Driven Prioritization of Service Incidents

Claudio Bartolini and Mathias Sallé

HP Laboratories
1501 Page Mill Rd
Palo Alto, CA 94304
USA
{claudio.bartolini, mathias.salle}@hp.com

Abstract. As a result of its increasing role in the enterprise, the Information Technology (IT) function is changing, morphing from a technology provider into a strategic partner. Key to this change is its ability to deliver business value by aligning and supporting the business objectives of the enterprise. IT Management frameworks such as ITIL (IT Infrastructure Library, [3]) provide best practices and processes that support the IT function in this transition. In this paper, we focus on one of the various cross-domain processes documented in ITIL involving the *service level, incident, problem and change management* processes and present a theoretical framework for the prioritization of service incidents based on their impact on the ability of IT to align with business objectives. We then describe the design of a prototype system that we have developed based on our theoretical framework and present how that solution for incident prioritization integrates with other IT management software products of the HP Openview™ management suite.

1   Introduction

Nowadays, organizations are continuously refocusing their strategy and operations in order to successfully face the challenges of an increasingly competitive business climate. In this context, Information Technology (IT) has become the backbone of businesses to the point where it would be impossible for many to function (let alone succeed) without it. As a result of its increasing role in the enterprise, the IT function is changing, morphing from a technology provider into a strategic partner.

To support this radical transformation, various IT frameworks have been developed to provide guidelines and best practices to the IT industry [1]. In essence, these frameworks address either the domain of IT Governance (CobiT [2]) or the domain of IT Management (ITIL [3], HP ITSM, Microsoft MOF). Whereas the domain of IT Management focuses on the efficient and effective supply of IT services and products, and the management of IT operations, IT Governance is mostly concerned setting the goals and the objectives for meeting present and future business challenges. Most importantly, the IT function needs to leverage both domains to ensure that IT decisions are made on the basis of value contribution. In other words, it is of fundamental importance that the selection among various alternative IT related management options

A. Sahai and F. Wu (Eds.): DSOM 2004, LNCS 3278, pp. 64–75, 2004.
© IFIP International Federation for Information Processing 2004

that are available to a decision maker at any point in time is made in a way that optimizes the alignment with the business objectives of the organization.

By propagating business objectives and their relative importance from the IT Governance to the IT Operations and Management as suggested in [1], it is possible to integrate them into the decision support tools used by the various IT functions involved in the different ITIL domains.

In this paper, we focus our attention on a particular process of the ITIL Service Support domain, namely *Incident Management* and we present a theoretical framework for the prioritization of service incidents based on their impact on the ability of IT to align with business objectives. We then describe the design of a prototype system that we have developed based on our theoretical framework and present how that solution for incident prioritization integrates with other IT management software products of the HP Openview™ management suite.

The structure of the paper is as follows. In section 2 we recall the definition of the ITIL reference model, with particular attention to the sub-domains of service level management and incident management. In section 3 and 4, we give a formal definition of the problem of incident prioritization driven by business objectives. In section 5, we describe the architecture of a solution for incident prioritization that integrates a prototype that we have developed with some software tools of the HP Openview™ management suite. Finally, we discuss related work and move on to the conclusion.

2   The ITIL Service, Incident, and Problem Management Sub-domain

The Information Technology Infrastructure Library (ITIL) [3] consists of an interrelated set of best practices and processes for lowering the cost, while improving the quality of IT services delivered to users. It is organized around five key domains: business perspective, application management, service delivery, service support, and infrastructure management.

The work presented in this paper focuses on one of the various cross-domain processes documented in ITIL involving the *service level, incident, problem and change management* processes. In particular, we focus on the early steps of that process linking both service level and incident management.

As defined in ITIL [3], **Service Level Management** ensures continual identification, monitoring and reviewing of the optimally agreed levels of IT services as required by the business. Most targets set in a Service Level Agreement (SLA) are subject to direct financial penalties or indirect financial repercussions if not met. It is therefore critical for this management process to flag when service levels are projected to be violated in order for an IT organization to take proactive actions to address the issue. To this extent, ITIL defines an *incident* as a deviation from the (expected) standard operation of a system or a service that causes, or may cause an interruption to, or a reduction in, the quality of the service. The objective of **Incident Management** is to provide continuity by restoring the service in the quickest way possible by whatever means necessary (temporary fixes or workarounds).

Incident priorities and escalation procedures are defined as part of the Service Level Management process and are key to ensure that the most important incident are addressed appropriately.

Example of incidents may be degradation in the quality of the service according to some measure of quality of service; unavailability of a service; a hardware failure; the detection of a virus.

3   An Approach to Incident Prioritization Driven by Business Objectives

In the incident management process it is of fundamental importance to *classify*, *prioritize* and *escalate* incidents [3]. Priority of an incident is usually calculated through evaluation of *impact* and *urgency*. However, these measures usually refer to the IT domain. The central claim of our work is that in order to achieve the strategic alignment between business and IT that is the necessary condition for IT to provide value, the enterprise needs to drive incident prioritization from its business objectives. This starts from evaluating the impact that an incident has at the business level, and its urgency in terms of the cost to the business of not dealing with it in a timely fashion.

In this section we describe the underlying method that our system follows to derive prioritization values for various incidents. In the development and the deployment of the system, we follow the principle that the *cost of modeling should be kept low*; so that it is easily offset the benefit obtained from the prioritization of the incidents. In this work we restrict the application domain of our tool, although the general techniques that we present are more widely applicable. We only consider incidents generated on detection of service level degradation or violation.

3.1 Calculating the Business Impact of Incidents

Figure 1 depicts an *impact tree* which shows how an incident can impact multiple services and in turn multiple Service Level Agreements defined over those services, hence multiple businesses, organizations, etc.

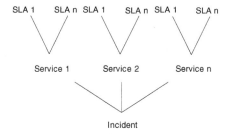

Fig. 1. Impact Tree

In order to assign a priority level to an incident, we start by computing a *business impact value* for it (which we will refer to in the following simply as *impact value*). In general, the impact value of an incident is a function of the time that it takes to get to resolution. We take into account the urgency of dealing with the incident based on how its impact is expected to vary with time. Once the impact values of the various incidents have been computed we prioritize the incidents based on their impact, urgency and on a measure of the expected time of resolution for the incidents.

Among the SLA related business indicators that we take into consideration, there are some quantitative ones such as *Projected cost of violation of the impacted SLAs, Profit Generated by Impacted Customers* and also some quantitative ones such as *Total Customer Experience* defined through the *Number of violations experienced by impacted customers,* etc. Our method requires the definition of *impact contribution maps* over business indicators. Impact contribution maps let us express how much the expected value of each indicator contributes to the total impact of an incident. Because of the assumption that we made above on the normalization of the impact values, all that matters is the shape of the function for any given indicator, regardless of affine transformations. The relative importance among the indicators is going to be adjusted with weights, as it will be clear in the following. As an aside, it should be said here that in order to work with the probabilistic nature of our decision support system, impact contribution maps need to behave like Von Neumann-Morgenstern [4] utility functions, being the calculated impact essentially a measure of the (negative) utility derived from the occurrence of the incident at the business level. Defined this way, impact contribution maps are guaranteed to preserve the preferences of the user among the expected outcomes as a consequence of the incident occurrence. Examples of impact contribution maps are presented in figure 2 and 3.

Figure 2 presents an impact contribution map for the projected cost of violation of an SLA impacted by an incident (measured in dollars, or any other currency). Its meaning is that to a higher projected cost of violation corresponds a higher contribution to the total impact for given indicator. The convexity of the curve symbolizes that the growth rate of the impact slows down as the projected cost of violation grows.

Figure 3 indicates the impact contribution of an incident on the basis of the generated profit by the impacted customers, measured in currency over a given time period (say dollars/year)[1]. It can be noted that three definite regions of profit are defined that correspond to a low, medium and high contribution to the impact. This is equivalent to classifying customers in three categories according to their historical profitability and using that information to prioritize among incidents that impact them so that most profitable customers are ultimately kept happier.

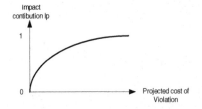
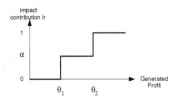

Fig. 2. Impact contribution map for the projected cost of violation of an impacted SLA

Fig. 3. Impact contribution map for the profit generated by the impacted customer

By comparing these two example indicators, we can already see that in the cost of violation example, the value of the impact exhibits a dependency on time. For example, for an SLA guaranteeing a minimum average availability, the longer a system is down, the higher is the likelihood of violating the SLA due to the incident that caused the system downtime. On the other hand, in the customer profitability, there is no such dependency on time, because the values of profitability of the customers are averaged out over a previous history time window and independent of the urgency that is assigned to the incident.

Once all the contributions to the impact are known for a given incident, the information that has been so obtained needs to be integrated over the impact tree, in order to get to an overall impact contribution for each business indicator. For example, in the case of the projected cost of violation of the SLAs, we need to navigate the impact tree and average all the contributions to the impact for all the impacted SLAs. In the next section we are going to walk the reader through an example that will make clearer how this calculation is performed.

The relative contribution of the various business indicators is taken into account by means of a weight that is associated to each business indicator. The formulation of the *incident impact* is as follows. For a set of n business indicators, we define $I_j(I, t)$, $j = 1..n$ as the contribution to the impact of the jth indicator for the incident i. ω_j is the weight representing the relative contribution of each indicator to the total impact. The total impact $I(i,t)$ is given by:

$$I(i,t) = \sum_{j=1}^{n} \omega_j . I_j(i,t) \text{ where } \sum_{j=1}^{n} \omega_j = 1 \tag{1}$$

---

[1] This measure is supposed to be available through an implemented Customer Relationship Management (CRM) system

The method described thus far has a very wide applicability. However, at this level of generality, one needs to rely on propagation of information from the operation level to the level of the business indicators, which is a difficult problem to solve in the general case.

In our prototype, the propagation of information from operational metrics to business objectives follows an impact tree similar to the one represented in Fig. 1. We first determine the services impacted by the incident; thence we collate the impacted SLAs.

3.2 Prioritization of Incidents Based on Impact and Urgency

Once the business impact of the incidents has been computed, we are faced with the problem of prioritizing them so as to minimize the total impact on the business. Our system requires the use of a *priority scheme*. Together with the definition of a set of priority levels that are used to classify the incidents (defined by the ITIL guidelines for incident management), we require the user to express constraints on what are the acceptable distributions of incidents into priority levels. For any priority level the users can either force the incidents to be classified according to some predefined distribution (e.g. 25%-30% high, 40%-50% medium, 25%-30% low), or define a minimum and maximum number of incidents to be assigned to each priority level. Our method finally requires an expected time of resolution for the incidents that are assigned to a certain priority level, necessary to cope with the business indicators whose contribution to the total impact depends on the time of resolution of the incidents.

The Incident Prioritization Problem

We here present a mathematical formulation of the incident prioritization problem as an instance of the assignment problem. The assignment problem is an integer optimization problem that is well studied in the operation research literature and for which very efficient algorithms have been developed.

Suppose we are required to prioritize between n incidents $i_1..i_n$ into m priority levels $p_1..p_m$. We introduce a variable x_{jk}, $j=1..m$, $k=1..n$ that assumes the value $x_{jk}=1$ if the kth incident is assigned to the jth priority level and $x_{jk}=0$ otherwise.

By observing that the expected impact of each incident can be calculated depending on what priority level it is assigned to, if t_j is the expected time of completion for incidents assigned to priority level j, then obviously the impact of assigning the kth incident to the jth priority level is $I(i_k, t_j)$.

The next thing to be noticed is that the constraints that the user imposes on the distribution of the incidents into priority levels can be trivially translated into minimum and maximum capacity constraints for the priority levels. For example, when dealing with $n=10$ incidents, the requirement that at least 40% of the incidents will be assigned medium priority (assume that is priority level p_2) would read: $\sum_{k=1}^{n} x_{2k} \geq 4$

In general we assign a minimum (c_j) and maximum (C_j) capacity constraint for a priority level j that are symbolized as

$$\sum_{k=1}^{n} x_{jk} \geq c_j \quad and \quad \sum_{k=1}^{n} x_{jk} \leq C_j \quad \forall j = 1..m \tag{2}$$

In order to express the importance of dealing with the most impactful incidents earlier, we introduce a time discount factor λ, $0<\lambda<1$. Introducing time discount gives the desirable property of returning a sensible prioritization of incidents even in cases where the impact of the incidents does not depend on time for any indicator.

The mathematical formulation of the incident prioritization problem (IPP) becomes:

$$(IPP) \quad \min \quad \sum_{j=1}^{m}\sum_{k=1}^{n} e^{-\lambda t_j} I(i_k, t_j) \cdot x_{jk} \tag{3}$$

$$s.t. \quad \sum_{k=1}^{n} x_{jk} \geq c_{jk} \quad and \quad \sum_{k=1}^{n} x_{jk} \leq C_{jk} \quad \forall j = 1..m \tag{4}$$

$$\sum_{j=1}^{m} x_{jk} = 1 \quad \forall k = 1..n \tag{5}$$

$$x_{jk} = 0 \ or \ 1 \quad \forall j = 1..m, k = 1..n \tag{6}$$

The solution of this problem will yield the optimal assignment of priorities to the incidents.

4   A Practical Example of Incident Management Driven by Business Objectives

We now apply the general method to an example that we have modeled in a demonstration of our prototype.

Suppose that our system is used to prioritize incidents based on three business indicators: the *projected cost of violation of the impacted SLAs*, the *profit generated by the impacted customers* and a measure of the customer experience seen through the *number of service violations experienced by the impacted customers*.

Let's explore more in detail what the definition of each business indicator means.

Projected cost of violation of the impacted SLAs

Our system computes the projected cost of violation through the likelihood of violation that the incident entails for impacted SLAs. For some SLAs there will be certainty of violation, whereas for others (such as service degradation) a value of likelihood depends on the entity of the impact of the incident on the service. In general, as we noted above, the likelihood of violation is also dependent on the time that it will take before the incident is resolved.

In the implementation of our prototype we derive the likelihood of violation from a function that is modeled a priori by looking at the historically significance of a certain value of availability to violating the SLAs in a short successive time frame. More sophisticated methods might be used here; however our system is agnostic with respect to how the likelihood is obtained.

Profit generated by the impacted customer

This is a simpler criterion that would result in prioritizing the incidents according to the relative importance that the customers have on the business, based on the profit that was generated by each customer in a given time period up to the date. If this indicator was used in isolation, it would result in dealing with incidents that impact the most profitable customers first. The value of the profit generated by each customer is supposed to be extracted by an existing CRM system, which Openview OVSD gives an opportunity to integrate with.

Number of violations experienced by the impacted customer

We use this indicator as a measure of the customer experience, which is a kind of more qualitative criterion, although our system must necessarily reduce the qualitative criteria down to measurable quantitative indicators. Therefore in our example, the third business indicator that is used is a sum of the number of violations that have been experienced by the customers with which the SLAs were contracted that are impacted by the incidents. For simplicity of expression, we will consider here all customers being equal, but weights might be added to the computation that would reflect the relative importance of each customer.

Let us now describe the impact contribution functions for an incident i

$$i_p(i, s, v(s,i,t)) = 1 - e^{(\frac{-v(s,i,t)}{\alpha})}, \forall s \in SLAs(i) \tag{7}$$

Equation (7) is the impact contribution to the incident i of the projected cost of SLA violation. $v(s,i,t)$ is the projected cost of violation for an SLA s impacted by the incident i when the incident is expected to be resolved within a time interval t. The value of the cost of violation is calculated by taking into account the likelihood of violation as described above.

$$i_r(c, p(c)) = \begin{cases} 0 & if \quad 0 \le p(c) < \beta_1 \\ \alpha & if \quad \beta_1 \le p(c) < \beta_2, \forall c \in Customers(i) \\ 1 & else \end{cases} \tag{8}$$

Equation (8) represents the contribution due to the customer generated profit. $p(c)$ is the profit that customer c yielded in the time period considered.

$$i_k(c, n(c)) = 1 - e^{(\frac{-n(c)}{\gamma})}, \forall c \in Customers(i) \tag{9}$$

Finally, equation (9) is the contribution due to the number of violation for a given customer in a given time period, represented as *n(c)*.

The equations hold for a certain choice of the parameters α, β_t and γ - obviously dimensioned in dollars, dollars and number of violations respectively – We have carried out some experiments to get to a sensible choice of parameters that we will not discuss here as they fall outside the scope of this paper.

The contribution to the total impact of an incident for a given business indicator is computed by averaging all the contributions of each impacted customer and SLA respectively. The averaging weights π express the relative importance of each customer and SLA for computing the total impact contribution of each business indicator. Without loss of generality, in this example, they might be considered uniform.

$$I_p(i,t) = \sum_{s \in SLAs(i)} \pi_{p,s} \cdot i_p(i,s,v(s,i,t)) \quad where \quad \sum_{s \in SLAs(i)} \pi_{p,s} = 1 \qquad (10)$$

$$I_r(i,t) = \sum_{c \in Customers(i)} \pi_{r,c} \cdot i_r(c,p(c)) \quad where \quad \sum_{c \in Customers(i)} \pi_{r,c} = 1 \qquad (11)$$

$$I_k(i,t) = \sum_{c \in Customers(i)} \pi_{k,c} \cdot i_c(c,n(c)) \quad where \quad \sum_{c \in Customers(i)} \pi_{k,c} = 1 \qquad (12)$$

Finally, the calculation of the total impact of an incident i necessary for assigning a priority is carried out through the formula (1), which in this case becomes:

$$I(i,t) = \omega_p I_p(i,t) + \omega_r I_r(i,t) + \omega_k I_k(i,t)$$

$$where \quad \omega_p + \omega_r + \omega_k = 1 \qquad (13)$$

for a certain choice of the relative importance given to the three business indicators, expressed through the weights ω_p, ω_r and ω_k.

5   An Incident Prioritization Solution

We have built a prototype system that embodies the method described in the previous sections, which we will refer to as the MBO prototype in the following. MBO is an acronym for Management by Business Objectives, which relates to the more general problem of taking into account business related considerations in the management of IT. In this section, we present a solution for incident prioritization that integrates our prototype with commercially available tools of the HP Openview™ management suite. We begin by briefly describing the features of the Openview components that we used in the integrated solution, and then we present the architecture of the solution, with particular regard to the modifications to the Openview incident handling mechanisms that were necessary for the solution to work.

Overview of the Openview Components Integrated in the Solution

The natural point of integration for our prototype is with the service level management capability of Openview Service Desk (OVSD). OVSD is the tool that falls more squarely in the domains of service level management, incident management and problem management. It allows a user to define a hierarchical service structure with multi-tiered SLA capabilities to describe the relationship between a higher level business service and the supporting operation management service.

OVSD was an excellent starting point for us because it provides most of the links necessary to build the impact tree that we use as the basis of our incident prioritization method. Our MBO prototype complements OVSD by helping the IT personnel faced with the incident prioritization problem with support for their decision based on data and models that are readily available through OVSD.

HP OpenView Internet Services (OVIS) provides monitoring capabilities that are necessary to service level management, as monitoring of availability and response time, along with notifications and resolutions of outages and slowdowns. It builds on a highly scalable and extensible architecture that allows programmers to build probes for a wide variety of data sources.

Architecture of the Incident Prioritization Solution

Figure 4 presents the architecture of the integration of the MBO prototype with Openview Service Desk (OVSD). OVSD receives data feeds from sources as diverse as OpenView Internet Services (OVIS), OpenView Transaction Analyzer (OVTA) and other data feeders. Aside from its reporting activity, the OVSD internal machinery that has to do with service level management -- referred to as OVSD-SLM -- can be summarized in a three step process. The first step is *compliance checking* during which OVSD-SLM seeks to assess whether current measurements comply with existing service level objectives (SLO). This compliance phase uses service level agreements contained in the Configuration Management Database (CMDB) from which are extracted SLOs. Multiple compliance thresholds can be defined for each SLO such as *violation* and *jeopardy* thresholds. This allows for proactive management of degradation of service. The second step is *Degradation and Violation Detection* during which it is detected that a particular metric associated with an SLO has either reported values that are violating that SLO or meet a jeopardy threshold. In both cases, this leads to the next phase, *Incident Generation*, which reports the violation or degradation as an incident.

At that stage, it is needed to characterize the incident from a business perspective. This is done (step 1) using the MBO prototype prioritization engine. To compute the relative importance of the incident from the business point of view and to prioritize it, the MBO engine fetches (step 2) all the open incidents from the CMDB and extracts the one that have not yet been handled, along with their related SLAs and penalties.

Finally, once the priorities are computed (step 3), the MBO engine updates (step 4) all the incidents with their new priorities.

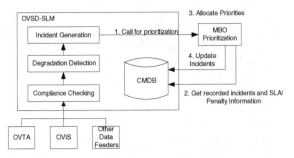

Fig. 4. Integrating SLM with MBO.

For the prioritization solution to work, we had to modify the OVSD-SLM incident handling mechanism so that the MBO prioritization engine is automatically notified on SLA compliance of jeopardy alarms.

6   Related Work

Most of the management software vendors today (such as HP, IBM, Peregrine systems to cite a few) make commercially available tools that are addressed at helping IT managers with incident prioritization. None of them however deals with the problem of driving the prioritization from the business objectives as we do in this work.

One of the few works in the IT management literature that touch on incident management is [5]. However, the aim of this work is quite different from ours, as it concentrates on the development of a specific criteria catalog for evaluating Incident Management for which it provides a methodology.

In any case, we believe that the most innovative aspect of the work here presented is driving incident prioritization from business objectives. From this point of view, among other very valuable works that we cannot review here for space reasons, the most notable in our opinion is [6]. They present a business-objectives-based utility computing SLA management system. The business objective(s) that they consider is the minimization of the exposed business impact of service level violation, for which we presented a solution in [7]. However, in this work we go far beyond just using impact of service level violations. We provide a comprehensive framework and a method for incident prioritization that takes into account strategic business objectives such as total customer experience thereby going a long way towards the much needed alignment of IT and business objectives.

7   Conclusion

We have shown in this paper that it is possible to integrate the business objectives defined by IT Governance into the decision making process that occurs within the IT Operations and Management functions. We focused our attention on *Incident Management* and we presented a theoretical framework for the prioritization of service incidents based on their business impact and urgency. We also described the design of a prototype system that we have developed based on our theoretical framework and presented how that solution for incident prioritization integrates with other IT management software products of the HP Openview™ management suite. We finally would like to thank Issam Aib for his very valuable comments.

References

1. M.Sallé, "*IT Service Management and IT Governance: Review, Comparative Analysis and their Impact on Utility Computing*", HP Labs Technical Report HPL-2004-98, 2004.
2. IT Governance Institute (ITGI), "*Control Objectives for Information and related Technology (CobiT) 3rd Edition*", 2002. Information Systems Audit and Control Association.
3. Office of Government Commerce (OGC), editor. "*The IT Infrastructure Library (ITIL)*" The Stationary Office, Norwich, UK, 2000.
4. J. Von Neumann, O. Morgenstern, "*Theory of Games and Economic Behavior*", Princeton University Press, 1944.
5. M. Brenner, I. Radisic, and M. Schollmeyer, "*A Criteria Catalog Based Methodology for Analyzing Service Management Processes*" In Proc.13th IFIP/IEEE International Workshop on Distributed Systems: Operations & Management (DSOM 2002), 2004.
6. M.J.Buco, R.N.Chang, L.Z.Luan, C.Ward, J.L.Wolf, and P.S.Yu, "Utility computing SLA management based upon business objectives", in IBM Systems Journal, Vol. 43, No. 1, 2004
7. M.Sallé and C.Bartolini , "*Management by Contract*", In Proc. 2004 IEEE/IFIP Network Operations and Management Symposium (NOMS 2004), Seoul, Korea, April 2004

A Case-Based Reasoning Approach for Automated Management in Policy-Based Networks

Nancy Samaan and Ahmed Karmouch

School of Information Technology & Engineering (SITE), University of Ottawa,
161 Louis Pasteur St. Ottawa, ON, Canada K1N-6N5
{nsamaan,karmouch}@site.uottawa.ca

Abstract. Policy-based networking technologies have been introduced as a promising solution to the problem of management of QoS-enabled networks. However, the potentials of these technologies have not been fully exploited yet. This paper proposes a novel policy-based architecture for autonomous self-adaptable network management. The proposed framework utilizes case-based reasoning (CBR) paradigms for online creation and adaptation of policies. The contribution of this work is two fold; the first is a novel guided automated derivation of network level policies from high-level business objectives. The second contribution is allowing for automated network level policy refinement to dynamically adapt the management system to changing requirements of the underlying environment while keeping with the originally imposed business objectives. We show how automated policy creation and adaptation can enhance the network services by making network components behavior more responsive and customizable to users' and applications requirements.

1 Introduction

Policies have been introduced as efficient tools for managing QoS-enabled networks. It has been widely supported by standards organizations such as the IETF and DMTF to address the needs of QoS traffic management. Policies are sets of rules that guide the behavior of network components. In current systems, policies are defined by users, administrators, or operators. Once defined, these policies are translated and stored in a policy repository. Policies are then retrieved and enforced as needed.

Despite the recent research advances in the area of policy-based network management, e.g., [1, 2, 3], existing policy frameworks are faced with various challenges. Current networking systems, characterized with increasingly growing sizes and services, are becoming extremely complex to manage. Hence, an increasing burden is put on network administrators to be able to manage such networks. Furthermore, static policy configurations built a-priori by administrators into network devices usually lack the flexibility required by wired/wireless networks environments and may not be sufficient to handle different changes in the underlying environments. On the other hand, in current systems, network

A. Sahai and F. Wu (Eds.): DSOM 2004, LNCS 3278, pp. 76–87, 2004.

reconfiguration in response to users' requests for service customization can only be performed manually by a network operator. This results in significant delays ranging from minutes to days. In summary, the traditional policy-based management approach based on *Condition-Action* notion poses a major difficulty of acquiring necessary management knowledge from administrators, while it lacks the ability to deal with unexpected faults. Further, once policies are built into the network, there is no possibility to learn from gained experience. These challenges along with current advances in hardware/software network technologies and emerging multi-services networks necessitate the existence of robust self-learning and adaptable management systems.

This paper proposes a novel approach to autonomous self-adaptable policy-based networks. The proposed work utilizes case-based reasoning (CBR) paradigms [4] for on-line selection, creation and adaptation of policies to dynamically reconfigure network components behaviors to meet immediate demands of the environment based on previously gained experiences. In general, a CBR system [4] is a system that solves current problems by adapting to or reusing the used solutions to solve past problems. It carries out the reasoning with knowledge that has been acquired by experience. This acquired experience is stored in a case-base memory and used for knowledge acquisition. The CBR systems analyze and obtain solutions through algorithms of comparison and adaptation of problems to a determined situation.

In the proposed approach, policies are presented as cases. Each case (policy) consists of policy objectives, constraints, conditions and actions. Hence, the network behavior is controlled through defining a set of applicable cases. The key idea is that the network status is maintained in terms of sets of constraints and objectives. A better network behavior can than be formed on the basis of previous experiences gained from old cases that have been applied before. The network behavior is adapted by using knowledge of the network monitored resources and users' requirements to continuously change these sets of constraints and objectives. Given these new sets, the goal is to redesign these cases such that they can operate to achieve the network desired performance. A reasoning engine uses CBR adaptation techniques, such as null adaptation, parameter substitution and transformation [4] to reach this goal.

The remainder of this paper is organized as follows. In section 2 related work and existing approaches for QoS management and policy adaptation are briefly discussed. The necessary background for case-based reasoning paradigms is introduced in Section 3. The proposed policy-based management framework is described in section 4. Finally, section 5 concludes the paper.

2   Related Work and Motivation

Existing frameworks that have been developed to support QoS management mainly fall into one of two categories [5]; reservation-based and adaptation-based Systems. Although adaptation seems to provide a more promising solution for network management, existing adaptation techniques still have certain limitations. For example, many QoS-based adaptive systems use indications of QoS failure to initiate adaptation actions. Consequently, adaptation may fail in many cases such as in the case of a QoS failure resulting from a congested link. Moreover, these techniques usually lack an essential degree of flexibility to build upon past experiences gained from the impact of previously pursued adaptation strategies on system behavior.

Policy-based network management has been introduced as a promising solution to the problem of managing QoS-enabled networks. However, static policy configurations built a-priori into network devices lack the flexibility and may not be sufficient to handle different changes in these underlying environments. Various research trends, e.g. [6], have highlighted the notion of policy adaptation and the central role that it can play in QoS management in policy-enabled networks. This notion of policy adaptation is becoming even more crucial as the managed systems become more complicated.

In [7], Granville et al. proposed an architecture to support standard policy replacement strategies on policy-based networks. They introduced the notion of policy of policies (PoP). PoPs, acting as meta-policies, are defined to coordinate the deployment of network policies. The definition of PoP requires references to every possible policy that may be deployed besides the identification of events that can trigger a policy replacement. Although their work follows the concepts of policies automation, it puts a burden on the network administrator to define both the standard policies and the PoPs. Planning policies in the existence of PoPs is a complex task. Moreover, reaching an adequate policy replacement strategy requires a complex analysis process. The administrator still has to check which policies deployment strategies were successful and which strategies failed to achieve their goals and manually update these strategies.

In [8] a genetic algorithm based architecture for QoS control in an active service network has been introduced. Users are allowed to specify their requirements in terms of loss rate and latency and then policies are used to adapt the queue length of the network routers to accommodate these requirements. The proposed work has the advantage that it is benefits from learning for adaptation.

Agents are used in [9] to represent *active policies*. The proposed architecture has a hyper-knowledge space, which is a loosely connected set of different agent groups which function as a pluggable or dynamically expandable part of the hyper-knowledge space. Active policies, which are agents themselves, can communicate with agents in the hyper-knowledge space to implement policies and retrieve information from agents. The architecture takes advantage of intelligent agents features such as the run-time negotiation of QoS requirements. However, an active policy by itself has to be created by the administrator, and once deployed to the network it remains static through its life-cycle.

In [6] a framework for adaptive management of Differentiated Services using the Ponder language [10] has been proposed. The framework provides the administrator with the flexibility to define rules at different levels. Policy adaptation is enforced by other policies, specified in the same Ponder policy notation. A goal-based approach to policy refinement has been introduced in [11] where low level actions are selected to satisfy a high-level goal using inference and event-calculus. In contrast to existing approaches, the proposed framework takes advantage of availability of previous experience gained from previously applied policies and their behavior to make decisions concerning the creation of future policies. Another approach has been presented in [12] which attach a description of the system behavior, in terms of resource utilization, such as network bandwidth and response time, to each specified rule.

3   CaseBased Reasoning Paradigms

Case-Based Reasoning (CBR) is a problem solving and learning paradigm that has received considerable attention over the last few years [4, 13]. It has been successfully applied in different domains such as e–commerce [14] and automated help desks [15]. CBR relies on experiences gained from previously solved problems to solve a new problem. In CBR past experiences are referred to as cases. A case is a contextualized piece of knowledge representing an experience that teaches a lesson fundamental to achieving the goals of the reasoner. A case is usually described by a set of attributes, also often referred to as features. Cases that are considered to be useful for future problem solving are stored in a memory-like construct called the case-base memory. In broad terms a CBR reasoning cycle consists of four basic steps; namely: case retrieval, reuse, revision and retainment. A new problem is solved by retrieving one or more previously experienced cases, reusing the case in one way or another, revising the solution based on reusing a previous case, and retaining the new experience by incorporating it into the existing case-base memory.

Compared to rule-based systems, CBR does not require causal models or a deep understanding of a domain, and therefore, it can be used in domains that are poorly defined, where information is incomplete, contradictory, or where it is difficult to get sufficient domain knowledge. Moreover, it is usually easier for experts to provide cases rather than to provide precise rules, and cases in general seem to be a rather uncomplicated and familiar problem representation scheme for domain experts. CBR can handle the incompleteness of the knowledge to which the reasoner has access by adding subsequent cases that describe situations previously unaccounted for. Furthermore, using cases helps in capturing knowledge that might be too difficult to capture in a general model, thus allowing reasoning when complete knowledge is not available. Finally, cases represent knowledge at an operational level; they explicitly state how a task was carried out or how a piece of knowledge was applied or what particular strategies for accomplishing a goal were used.

4   Case–Based Policy Management Architecture

As shown in Figure 1, the main component of the proposed architecture is the case-based policy-composer (CBPC) which is responsible for translating higher-level business policies into lower-level network policies and for continuously adapting the network behavior through the online refinement of network policies in the policy repository. The CBPC relies on two different sources of knowledge for reaching decisions concerning policies changes. It continuously receives an updated view of different business-level objectives, service-level agreements (SLAs) with customers along with the underlying network topology and constraints.

The second source of information is provided by a set of monitoring agents [16] responsible for monitoring network resources based on the monitoring policies specified by the CBPC. Once obtained, the CBPC is then responsible for analyzing these knowledge to reach decisions concerning the adaptation and creation of different sets of policies; namely: admission, provisioning, routing and monitoring policies, based on previously gained experiences. The main focus of the work presented in this paper is the automated generation and refinement of admission and provisioning policies for differentiated-services operated networks [17].

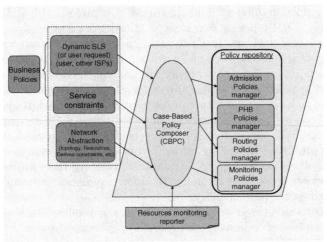

Fig. 1. Policy Management Architecture.

A detailed description of the functionalities of the CBPC is shown in Figure 2. The key idea in the proposed work is that policies are presented as cases. Hence, the terms *case* and *policy* will be used interchangeably throughout the rest of the paper. Each case (policy) consists of problem domain, describing the case's constraints and objectives, and a solution domain, describing the actions that must be taken under and which conditions to reach the specified objectives. A new policy generation/adaptation is triggered as a result of either changes in the supplied business and SLAs requirements or through objective violation indicated by information obtained from monitoring agents. The CBPC starts by deriving target objectives and constraints to represent the problem of new case. In the second step, the *retrieval step*, the CBPC uses a *similarity measure* to find previously existing cases in the policy repository with objectives and constraints that best match the target ones. Using a set of *adaptation operators*, the solutions of these retrieved cases are adapted, in the third step, to form the solution of the new target case. Once assembled, the new case (policy) is dispatched at the network level. A *refinement step* is carried-out to evaluate the behavior of dispatched policy. The case is repeatedly refined and dispatched until the target objectives are met. Finally, the new case is *retained* for future use in the case-base memory. The following sections provide a detailed description of these steps to illustrate the life cycle of policies creation and adaptation.

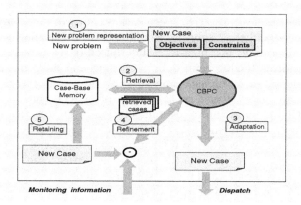

Fig. 2. Functionalities of the CBPC.

4.1   Step 1: Policy Representation and Construction

In policy-based management systems, one starts with a business-level specification of some objective (e.g., users from department A get Gold services) and ends up with a network-level mechanism that is the actual implementation of this objective (e.g., a classifier configuration for admission control and a queue configuration for per-hop-behavior treatment). The general structure of the CBPC reflects and maintains this relation between the specification of objectives and the final mechanisms passing via network-level policies through a four-level hierarchical representation of cases as shown in Figure 3. The solution of a layer i is mapped as the objectives of new subcases in the lower layer $i + 1$. For example, at the highest level, abstract cases represent different business objectives and the corresponding solution is a set of finer grain network level solutions. Each of these solutions is considered an objective for a lower level case and so forth.

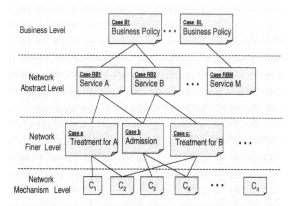

Fig. 3. General Case Hierarchy.

When a new business objective specification is posed, one or more abstract cases are retrieved and their solution is adapted to fit the specifications of the new objective. The result is a high-level description of the target solution. This high-level solution is further refined by retrieving and adapting more specific cases at each level, each solving some subproblem of the target. Eventually, concrete cases are selected and an actual set of policies can be produced. In this way, the CBPC builds up an overall solution in an iterative manner. The evolving solution forms an emergent abstraction hierarchy as high-level solution parts (from the abstract cases) are refined to produce a set of detailed policies.

Figure 4 shows a general case template, where each case Λ_i consists of a problem description part P_i and a corresponding solution S_i, i.e., $\Lambda_i = (P_i, S_i)$. Furthermore, P_i is composed of a set of objectives O_i and imposed constraints CN_i, while S_i is a set of solution steps SS_{ij}, where $SS_{ij} = (R_{ij}, C_{ij}, A_{ij}, T_{ij})$. R_{ij} is a set of roles, C_{ij} is a set of conditions, A_{ij} is the set of corresponding actions and T_{ij} is the life-time of solution step SS_{ij}.

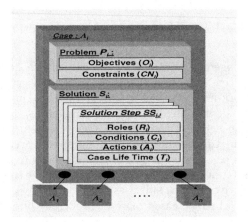

Fig. 4. Policy representation as a case.

4.2   Step 2: Policies Retrieval

During retrieval, the target objectives of the new case are matched against the described objectives of cases in the case memory and a measure of similarity is computed. The result is a ranking of cases according to their similarity to the target, allowing one or more best-matching cases to be selected. The similarity of a case Λ_i in the case-base memory to a target case $\overline{\Lambda}$ is calculated through the similarity measure defined as

$$sim(\overline{\Lambda}, \Lambda_i) = \frac{1}{\sqrt{\sum_j w_j + \sum_k cw_k}} \sqrt{\sum_j f_c(\overline{o_j}, o_{ij})w_j + \sum_k f_c(\overline{cn_k}, cn_{ik})cw_k}$$

$$(1)$$

where for each objective $o_{ij} \in O_i$, w_j is a numeric weight representing the importance of o_{ij}. Similarly, for each constraint $cn_{ik} \in CN_i$, cw_k is a numeric weight representing the influence of cn_{ik}. $f_c(x_i, y_j)$ is a local measure of similarity, defined as follows,

$$f_c(x_i, y_j) = \begin{cases} 0 & \text{if } x_i \text{ is symbolic and } x_i \neq y_i \\ 1 & \text{if } x_i \text{ is symbolic and } x_i = y_i \\ \frac{|x_i - y_i|}{range_i} & \text{if } x_i \text{ and } y_i \text{ are numeric} \end{cases} \tag{2}$$

where $range_i$ is the allowable range for x_i and y_i, used to normalize the similarity distance between the two features.

The number of retrieved cases depends on a preselected similarity threshold θ, such that a similar case Λ_i is retrieved *iff* $sim(\overline{\Lambda}, \Lambda_i) \geq \theta$.

4.3 Step 3: Policy Adaptation

Each of the retrieved cases in the previous stage undergoes a sequence of adaptation steps to meet the objectives of the target case. This stage can be referred to as *partial adaptation*. During this stage after applying a set of adaptation operators, some of the candidate cases are gradually eliminated if they failed to meet any of the target objectives. The remaining cases are then fed into the second stage for an *overall adaptation* to come up with a unified solution for the target case. Partial and overall adaptation steps are described next.

Partial adaptation. Different operators are used to adapt each of the retrieved cases separately. In the following, each of these operators is described.

- **A1: Null adaptation.** This is the simplest type of adaptation, which involves directly applying the solution from the most similar retrieved case to the target case. Null adaptation occurs when an exact match is found or when the match is not exact but the differences between the input and the target cases are known by the CBPC to be insignificant and, therefore, can be directly changed. A simple example to illustrate such a situation occurs in replacing an IP address in a classification policy, or a users' domain in a business-level policy. Figure 5 shows an example of a case adaptation using null adaptation.
- **A2: Parameter adjustment adaptation.** A structural adaptation technique that compares specified parameters of the retrieved cases and target case to modify the solution in an appropriate direction based on the parameter values in all retrieved cases. In this operator, the administrator defines a set of formulae or configuration methods according to the nature of each parameter. Figure 6 gives an example of a congestion policy adaptation using parameter adjustment operations based on two retrieved cases.
  In general, most parameters adjustments can be obtained as the average value of all recommended values from all retrieved cases as follows

$$\overline{P}_i = \frac{1}{k} \sum_{j=1}^{j=k} (P_{ji} \frac{\overline{o_l}}{o_{jl}}) \tag{3}$$

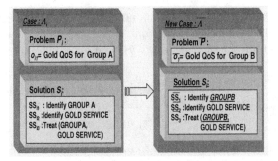

Fig. 5. An example of null adaptation.

where $\overline{P}_i$ is the new parameter value in the ith solution step $\overline{SS}_i$, in the target case. k is the number of retrieved cases, and $\overline{o_l}$ and o_{jl} are the values of related objectives in the target case, $\overline{\Lambda}$, and the retrieved case, Λ_j, respectively.

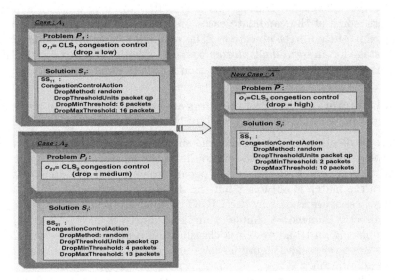

Fig. 6. Example of case adaptation using parameter Adjustment.

- **A3: Adaptation by reinstantiation.** This type of adaptation is selected when the old and new problems are structurally similar, but differ in either one or more of their constraints. In this case, reinstantiation involves replacing one or more of the old actions with a new action that is used to instantiate features of an old solution with new features.

  For example, if the retrieved and target cases differ in a constraint concerning the availability of applicable mechanisms at the lowest level of the hierarchy, then the mechanism in the old solution is replaced with an equivalent mechanism in the target case that implements the same objective.

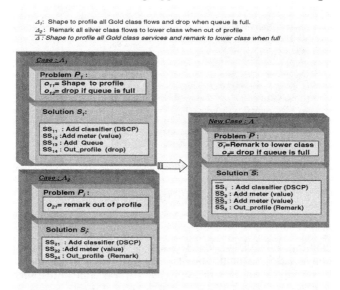

Fig. 7. A simplified example of an overall adaptation.

– **A4: Adaptation by heuristics.** This adaptation involves the utilization of a set of predefined rules set by the administrator for the purpose of case adaptation. For example, the adaptation of an admission control case can be based on the heuristic that a behavior aggregate classifier (BA) is used at edge routers connecting to other domains while a multiple field (MF) classifier is used for edge routers connected to users' hosts. Another example of a heuristic rule is that each objective in a case that includes a bandwidth allocation implies that a classifier and a queue should be allocated to the traffic class defined by the objective's conditions. Hence, once a bandwidth allocation policy is specified as a case objective, at least one classification and one scheduling action must exist as solution steps for this case.

Overall adaptation. In the case where none of the retrieved cases met the objectives of the target case after the application of one or more partial adaptation operations, an overall adaptation is performed using two or more partially adapted cases to generate the target solution. Figure 7 shows a simplified operation of an overall adaptation in response to changes in a dynamic SLA. In the Figure, two retrieved SLA policies were used to generate the required policies of a new SLA based on an overall adaptation of these two cases.

4.4   Step 4: Policy Refinement

When a new case is produced and dispatched, it has to go through a repeated cycle of evaluation and refinement before it can be finally stored in the case-base memory. As shown in Figure 8, at each refinement step i, the difference between the case's original objectives and QoS measurements obtained from the

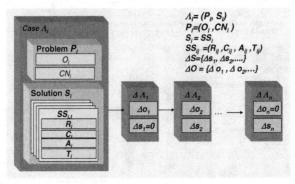

Fig. 8. Case Refinement.

monitoring agents, ΔO_i, of the leaf cases is calculated and used to perform a solution refinement ΔS_i through one or more parameter adjustment operations, described above. This cycle can be repeated several times until either the case objectives are met, i.e., $\Delta O_i = 0$, or the CBPC fails to perform any further adaptation. If the refinement is successful, the next step, case retainment, is carried out. Otherwise, if the refinement failed at the lower-level cases, it propagates to the next higher-level.

4.5   Step 5: Policy Retainment

The final step in the case life cycle is learning. Newly solved problems are learnt by packaging their objectives and solutions together as new cases, and adding them to the case memory. There are a number of issues associated with this type of learning, mainly the increasing size of the memory. However, often it is not necessary to learn an entire new case if only a small part of its solution or objectives is novel. Significant redundancy is eliminated by benefiting from the hierarchical representation of cases. Since learning can operate at a finer level of granularity as parts of different policies can be treated as separate cases.

5   Conclusions

In this paper we presented a novel framework for autonomous self- learning and adaptive policy-based network management. The proposed work utilized case-based reasoning paradigms for on-line selection, creation and adaptation of policies. The framework base policy creation and adaptation decisions on previously gained experiences of the management history. The main advantage of the proposed work is that it creates a dynamic environment where the network components are self-adaptable in response to changes in business and users' objectives. In addition, it frees up specialized administrators to other design and development tasks. In future work, we plan to evaluate our work through the implementation of the proposed architecture.

References

1. G. Valérie, D. Sandrine, K. Brigitte, D. Gladys and H. Eric, "Policy-Based Quality of Service and Security Management for Multimedia Services on IP networks in the RTIPA project", in *MMNS 2002, Santa Barbara, USA*, Oct. 2002.

2. P. Flegkas, P. Trimintzios and G. Pavlou, "A Policy-Based Qualifty of Service Management System for IP DiffServ Networks", *IEEE Network, Special Issue on Policy-Based Networking*, pp. 50–56, Mar./Apr. 2002.

3. L. Lymberopoulos, E. Lupu and M. Sloman, "QoS Policy Specification - A Mapping from Ponder to the IETF Policy Information Model", in *3rd Mexican Intl Conf in Computing Science (ENC01)*, Sept. 2001.

4. Janet Kolodner, *Case-based reasoning*, Morgan Kaufmann Publishers Inc., 1993.

5. C. Aurrecoechea, T. Campbell, A. and L. Hauw, "A Survey of QoS Architectures", *ACM/Springer Verlag Multimedia Systems Journal , Special Issue on QoS Architecture*, vol. 6, n. 3, pp. 138–151, May. 1998.

6. L. Lymberopoulos, E. Lupu and M. Sloman, "An Adaptive Policy Based Management Framework for Differentiated Services Networks", in *IEEE 3rd Intl Wrkshp on Policies for Distributed Systems and Networks (POLICY'02), Monterey, California*, pp. 147–158, Jun. 2002.

7. Z. Granville, L., A. Faraco de Sá Coelho, G., M. Almeida and L. Tarouco, "An Architecture for Automated Replacement of QoS Policies", in *7th IEEE Symp. on Comput. and Comm. (ISCC'02), Italy*, Jul. 2002.

8. I. Marshall and C. Roadknight, "Provision of Quality of Service for Active Services", *Computer Networks*, vol. 36, n. 1, pp. 75–85, Jun. 2001.

9. T. Hamada, P. Czezowski and T. Chujo, "Policy-based Management for Enterprise and Carrier IP Networking", *FUJITSU Sc and Tech Jrnl*, vol. 36, n. 2, pp. 128–139, Dec. 2000.

10. N. Damianou, E. Dulay and M. Sloman, "The Ponder Policy Specification Language", in *IEEE 2nd Intl Wrkshp on Policies for Distributed Systems and Networks (POLICY'01), Bristol, UK*, pp. 18–39, Jan. 2001.

11. A. Bandara, E. Lupu, J. Moffet and A. Russo, "A Goal-based Approach to Policy Refinement", in *Policy 2004), New York, USA*, Jun. 2004.

12. S. Uttamchandaniand, C. Talcott and D. Pease, "Eos: An Approach of Using Behavior Implications for Policy-based Self-management", in *14th IFIP/IEEE Intl Wrkshp on Distributed Systems: Operations and Management, DSOM 2003, Heidelberg, Germany, October 20-22*, pp. 16–27, 2003.

13. A. Aamodt and E. Plaza, "Case-based reasoning:Foundational issues, methodological variations and system approaches", *AI Commu.*, vol. 7, pp. 39–59, 1994.

14. R. Bergmann and P. Cunningham, "Acquiring Customers' Requirements in Electronic Commerce", *Artif. Intell. Rev.*, vol. 18, n. 3-4, pp. 163–193, 2002.

15. M. Goker and T. RothBerghofer, "Development and Utilization of a Case-Based Help-Desk Support System in a Corporate Environment", in *3rd Intl Conf on Case-Based Reasoning, ICCBR-99, Seeon Monastery, Germany, July*, 1999.

16. N. Samaan and K. Karmouch, "An Evidence-Based Mobility Prediction Agent Architecture", in *Mobile Agents for Telecommunication Applications, 5th Intl Wrkshp, MATA 2003, Marakech, Morocco*, Oct. 2003.

17. S. Blake et al., "AN Architecture for Differentiated Services", IETF RFC 2475, Dec 1998.

An Analysis Method for the Improvement of Reliability and Performance in Policy-Based Management Systems

Naoto Maeda and Toshio Tonouchi

NEC Corporation, 1753 Shimonumabe, Nakahara-ku, Kawasaki 211-8666, Japan
n-maeda@bp.jp.nec.com, tonouchi@cw.jp.nec.com

Abstract. Policy-based management shows good promise for application to semi-automated distributed systems management. It is extremely difficult, however, to create policies for controlling the behavior of managed distributed systems that are sufficiently accurate to ensure good reliability. Further, when policy-based management technology is to be applied to actual systems, performance, in addition to reliability, also becomes an important consideration. In this paper, we propose a static analysis method for improving both the reliability and the performance of policy-based management systems. With this method, all sets of policies whose actions might possibly access the same target entity simultaneously are detected. Such sets of policies could cause unexpected trouble in managed systems if their policies were to be executed concurrently. Additionally the results of the static analysis can be used in the optimization of policy processing, and we have developed an experimental system for such optimization. The results of experimental use of this system show that an optimized system is as much as 1.47 times faster than a non-optimized system.

1   Introduction

Policy-based management shows good promise for application to semi-automated distributed systems management. It enables system managers to efficiently and flexibly manage complicated distributed systems, which are composed of a large number of servers and networks. This results in dramatic reductions in system management costs.

The reliability and performance in the policy-based management systems are essential issues when applying this kind of technology to actual systems. Flaws in a management system will degrade the reliability of the managed system, and poor performance may offset the advantage initially gained by using a policy-based technology: the ability to adjust rapidly to a changing situation.

Tool support is indispensable to managers who wish to create policies that are sufficiently correct to ensure reliability. Such tools check the properties of given policies, such as type-checking equipped with programming language compilers. Recently, methods for detecting and resolving *policy conflicts* have been studied actively[2,6,8,9,11]. Policy conflicts can be categorized into a number of different types, of which there are two major groupings: *modality conflicts* and *application specific conflicts*[9,11]. Modality conflicts can be detected by purely syntactic analysis using the semantics of policy specification languages[9]. Application specific conflicts, by way of contrast, are defined by application semantics as the name suggests. As a way of providing a generic way to

A. Sahai and F. Wu (Eds.): DSOM 2004, LNCS 3278, pp. 88–99, 2004.

cope with application specific conflicts, approaches using constraint-based rules have been proposed in [2,9].

In this paper, we propose a static analysis method for detecting all sets of policies whose actions might possibly access the same target entity at the same time. We call such sets of polices *suspicious policy sets*. The exact conditions for these sets will be explained in section 3.2. A suspicious policy set could cause unexpected trouble in a managed system if a policy run-time system were to execute[1] concurrently the policies included in it. From the viewpoint of [9,11], we may regard the target of analysis as application specific (O+, O+) conflicts, where "O+" is the abbreviation for "Positive Obligation Policy".

Our analysis method can also be used to optimize policy processing. This optimization is based on the detection of suspicious policy sets. Policy processing is optimized when policies may be executed concurrently so long as they do not comprise any combination of policies found in any one of the previously detected suspicious sets. This offers great advantages in efficiency over ordinary conservative policy processing, in which individual policies are all executed sequentially, and it is just as safe.

In order to confirm the feasibility of our approach, we have also developed an experimental system to measure its performance. As an experimental policy-based management system, we employ a slightly modified PONDER[4] framework, and as the system to be managed, we use the J2EE1.4 Application Server[14] provided by Sun Microsystems. As interfaces to monitor and control the system, we use Java Management Extension (JMX) interfaces[13]. Our experiments show that an optimized system is as much as 1.47 times faster than a non-optimized system.

The contributions of the work are as follows: (1) with our analysis method, it is possible to statically detect *suspicious policy sets*, i.e., those that might cause unexpected trouble in a managed system, if their policies were to be executed concurrently, thus ensuring improved reliability; and (2) it contributes to significant performance improvement in policy systems by making it possible to optimize policy processing. The effectiveness of this second contribution is shown in our experimental results.

2   Problem Statement

Figure 1 depicts an example of a problem that could possibly be caused by concurrently executing policies contained in a suspicious policy set. In order to quickly react to problems, it is highly possible that there are multiple managers responsible for creating and modifying policies. A management system is composed of a policy repository, Policy Enforcement Point (PEP), Policy Decision Point (PDP) and an event monitor[12]. A managed system consists of servers and network devices. We assume that managers register their carelessly created policies in the policy repository, and the policies are then deployed to the PEP and enabled. If (1) policies registered by different managers were to be executed simultaneously owing to the occurrence of specified events, (2) there were to be the same action target in the policies, and (3) actions to the target were to have side-effects, that is, the actions may change the value of attributes defined in the target,

---

[1] In this paper, "execute a policy" means "execute the actions in the action clause of a policy".

then the concurrent execution of the actions might possibly lead to problems. Although problems of this kind are considered under *Multiple Managers Conflict* in [11], this work does not present a way for detecting and resolving them.

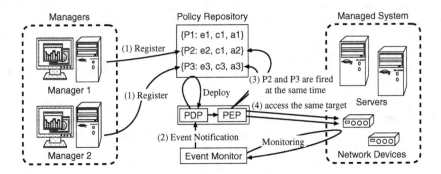

Fig. 1. Example of a problem caused by executing policies concurrently

The problems caused by the concurrent execution of policies included in a suspicious policy set are as follows: (1) if the policies were to be created without any considerations to race conditions of resources, threads executing such policies might possibly fall into deadlock; (2) if operations provided by a target were not to be implemented as thread-safe, the concurrent access to the target might possibly make states of the target inconsistent; (3) since a sequence of actions defined in a policy may be interleaved by another sequence of actions, the concurrent execution of them could cause transactional errors that might destroy the consistency of a managed system.

Our analysis introduced in the following section enables managers to ensure reliability by eliminating the potential for unexpected problems that might be caused by the concurrent execution of policies.

3   Analysis

In this section, we clarify what kind of policy specifications we assume for our analysis method and then explain the method in detail.

3.1   Target Policy Specifications

As targets of our analysis method, we assume Event-Condition-Action (ECA) policy specifications, such as PONDER[4]. An ECA policy is composed of an event clause, a condition clause and an action clause. The event clause shows events to be accepted. The condition clause is evaluated when a specified event occurs. If the condition holds, actions in the action clause will be executed.

The essential function of our method is to detect overlapped targets in policies. The accuracy of the detection depends on the characteristics of policy specifications. The most accurate information on a target is information on an instance that can be mapped to an actual device or a software entity composing a managed system. However, it is not pragmatic to expect the information on instances is available in policy definitions. Actual targets of actions are often decided at run-time, such as a target defined as the least loaded server in a managed system.

In contrast to the above case, if information on targets were not available in policy definitions, it would be impossible to apply our method to such definitions. An example of such an action clause is as follows:

```
ObjectName targetName= new ObjectName("name=logmanager,...") ;
Object[] params= makeParam("WARNING") ;
String[] signature= makeSignature(String.class.getName()) ;
mejb.invoke(targetName, "setLogLevel", params, signature) ;
```

In the above example, the action clause is written in Java programming language[1], which invokes setLogLevel provided by a managed entity in the J2EE[14] application server to change the log level to WARNING using JMX[13] interfaces. Information on the target is embedded in the parameter for the method. In general, it is impossible to analyze the exact value of parameters using program analysis techniques.

Therefore, we presume policy specifications in which targets are defined by *class* are applied to our method. The concept of class is the same as that defined in object-oriented languages, which define attributes and operations of a device or a software entity. In the network management domain, CIM[5] is the most promising model to define classes of managed entities. A rewrite of the above example using a class is as follows:

```
Target: Logmanager l ;
Action: l.setLogLevel("WARNING") ;
```

In the above example, the variable l belongs to class Logmanger and it is clear that the target of action setLogLevel is class Logmanger. While the equivalence of instances cannot be checked under our assumption, the equivalence of classes of targets can be determined.

3.2 Analysis Method

The analysis method detects all suspicious policy sets, which meet three conditions: (1) there is a shared target that appears in the action clause of policies contained in a suspicious policy set; (2) there are one or more actions that have side-effects on the shared target; (3) policies in a suspicious policy set might possibly be executed at the same time.

The method consists of two parts. One is the analysis for the action clause, corresponding to conditions 1 and 2, and the other is the analysis for the event clause and the condition clause, corresponding to condition 3. The former detects all sets of policies that are not assumed to be safe for the concurrent execution and the latter makes results of the former analysis more precise by dividing or removing the suspicious policy set containing policies that will not be executed at the same time.

The method is conservative, i.e. it detects all policy sets supposed to be unsafe, although the detected sets might possibly include the sets that are safe for the concurrent execution. Below, we will explain these two analyses.

Action Clause Analysis. In this analysis, all sets of policies meeting conditions 1 and 2 are detected. With the predicate logic, the conditions are formally defined as below:

C: set of all classes corresponding to managed entities in a managed system.
SP: set of policies (*Suspicious Policy set*).
$targets(p)$: function that returns the set of all classes appearing in policy p.
$actions(p, st)$: function that returns the set of all actions appearing in policy p and defined in class st .
$sideEffects(a)$: predicate that indicates the action a has side-effects.

$$\exists st \in C : \{\forall p \in SP : st \in targets(p)\} \wedge \{\exists p \in SP, \exists a \in actions(p, st) : sideEffects(a)\}$$

The variable st expresses the Shared Target of polices in a suspicious policy set. With this analysis, we detect all sets of the largest SP and the smallest SP for each class appearing in policies. The smallest SP is the set that contains only one policy whose actions have side-effects on the shared target. We regard the smallest set as a self conflict that a policy contained in the set should not be executed with itself concurrently, since it is possible that a policy may be executed twice at almost the same time if an event to be accepted by the policy were to be notified twice virtually simultaneously. Notice that the above logical expression is satisfied even in the case that there is only one action that has side-effects on the shared target in a suspicious policy set SP. In this case, while the race conditions of resources will not occur, the transactional errors mentioned in section 2 might possibly occur.

As mentioned before, whether targets are the same or not is determined by checking the name of classes. All sets of the smallest SP can be created by, for all policies, making a set containing only one policy whose actions have side-effects. How to obtain all sets of the largest SP is as below:

1) collect the class name of targets appearing in the action clause of all policies.
2) for each previously collected class name c, make a set of polices whose action clause contains the class name that is equal to c.
3) from the sets obtained above, remove all sets that contain only policies whose actions do not have side-effects on the shared target.

In order to decide whether an action has side-effects or not, all actions defined in classes must in advance be assigned one of 3 attributes: *Write*, *Read* and *Unknown*. *Write* is assigned to the actions that may change the target entity states, i.e. have side-effects. *Read* is assigned to the actions that do not have side-effects. Since the attributes are supposed to be assigned manually, *Unknown* is used for the actions that are not explicitly assigned an attribute. *Unknown* is treated as *Write* in this analysis.

These attributes can be included in class definitions or in other definitions separately from class definitions. For instance, using the JMX[13], which is the standard specification for monitoring and managing applications written in Java programming language, attributes of actions (or methods) can be obtained by invoking
`MBeanOperationInfo.getImpact()`.

Event and Condition Clause Analysis. The problems mentioned in section 2 occur only when multiple threads execute actions of policies concurrently. There are two issues that determine whether policies will actually be executed concurrently. One is the difference between strategies that policy run-time systems employ to execute policies and the other is how to analyze the event and the condition clause. Below, we will explain both of these.

There are several strategies for executing policies. Whether policies are concurrently executed by a policy run-time system depends on strategies. We categorized the strategies into three types:

- Conservative Strategy: All the policies executions are serialized. Although the problems mentioned in section 2 will not occur, it involves deterioration of policy processing performance. In section 4, we will introduce an application using the action clause analysis to improve the performance of systems employing the strategy.
- Serialized Event Strategy: The execution of policies for incoming events is suspended until all executions of policies triggered by the previous event have been completed. Policies triggered by the same event will be executed concurrently. With this strategy, we can detect the sets of policies that will not be executed concurrently with the analysis for the event clause and the condition clause.
- Concurrent Strategy: Policies are executed concurrently. Therefore, managers have to take into account the concurrent processing issues when writing policies. The analysis for the event clause will not make sense, since all kinds of events may possibly occur all the time. The analysis for the condition clause, however, will work effectively. For instance, a policy in which only the temporal condition 10:00-17:00 holds will not be executed with one in which the temporal condition 18:00-21:00 holds'D

Thus the effectiveness of the analysis for the event clause and the condition clause depends on strategies.

Next, we consider the analysis for the event clause. The event clause shows events to be accepted. It contains a single event or an expression of composite events. Composite events are combined by logical operators or operators that specify an order of event occurrences[3].

In the event clause analysis, we focus on the events that may directly trigger an execution of policies. Since the event clause analysis is mainly used for systems employing the serialized event strategy, whether polices can possibly be executed simultaneously can be determined by checking whether the policies have the same *direct trigger event*. Here, we will explain the direct trigger events in detail. In the case of a single event and a composite event combined by the "OR" operator, direct trigger events are all events a policy accepts, since the occurrence of these events might directly involve an execution of the policy. In the case of the composite event "$e_1 \rightarrow e_2$", which means that the event e_2 occurs after the event e_1, the direct trigger event is e_2. In the case of the "AND" operator, "e_1 AND e_2" is interpreted as "$e_1 \rightarrow e_2$ OR $e_2 \rightarrow e_1$", so the direct trigger events are both e_1 and e_2. In the other case, if we could make an automaton from the event expression we would be able to obtain direct trigger events of policies. Such an automaton may have a start state, final states, nodes to express states of the acceptance of events and transitional labels corresponding to events. Events corresponding to labels to the final states of an automaton can be regarded as direct trigger events. Thus, the policies that contain the same direct trigger event might possibly be executed concurrently.

These policy sets can be detected by a method similar to the action clause analysis. By adapting the action clause analysis to result sets detected with this analysis for the event clause, we can make suspicious policy sets more precise.

Next, we will consider the condition clause. There are two widely adopted conditions. One is the temporal constraint used for specifying the duration a policy should be enabled, such as 10:00-17:00. The other is to check whether a specified condition for a managed system holds by retrieving states of managed entites when an event occurs.

By analyzing conditions for time constraints, policies that will not be executed at the same time can be detected (only if there are no undefined variables in the condition clause). Consider an example: $\{P_1, P_2, P_3\}$ is one of suspicious policy sets detected with the action clause analysis. Then by analyzing the conditions of P_1, P_2 and P_3, we presume to obtain the result that neither P_1 and P_2 nor P_2 and P_3 will be executed at the same time. We can make suspicious policy sets obtained with the action clause analysis more precise as follows:

$$\text{We know } P_1 \text{ will not be executed with } P_2$$
$$\{P_1, P_2, P_3\} \to \{P_1, P_3\}, \{P_2, P_3\}$$
$$\text{We know } P_2 \text{ will not be executed with } P_3$$
$$\{P_1, P_3\}, \{P_2, P_3\} \to \{P_1, P_3\}, \{P_2\}, \{P_3\}$$

Since $\{P_2\}$, $\{P_3\}$ can be eliminated, we obtain the result set $\{P_1, P_3\}$. Thus we can refine results of the action clause analysis with the condition clause analysis.

In the case of conditions that check states of managed entities, it is almost impossible to determine whether the conditions will not hold at the same time. Consider a condition "x.CPU_LOAD > 90" and another condition "x.CPU_LOAD < 30". If the variable x is always bound to the same target, these conditions will not hold at the same time. In most cases, however, the variable x might possibly be bound to different target entities. Therefore, we do not deal with this kind of condition in this paper.

Thus, we have explained our analysis method that detects all suspicious policy sets. The analysis for the action clause detects all sets of policies that should not be executed concurrently, and the analysis for the event clause and the condition clause make the sets more precise using information on whether policies are actually executed concurrently.

4   Optimization for Policy Processing Using Analysis

Here, we introduce the optimization of policy processing based on the detection of suspicious policy sets and explain the implementation for the optimization.

4.1   Basic Idea

The conservative strategy mentioned in section 3.2 is highly advantageous over the concurrent strategy, in that managers are freed from complicated concurrent processing issues when writing policies. However, this strategy has a problem in terms of performance.

With our analysis, we aim to improve the performance of policy processing systems that employ the conservative strategy, retaining the advantage of the conservative strategy. We will explain this idea using Figure 2.

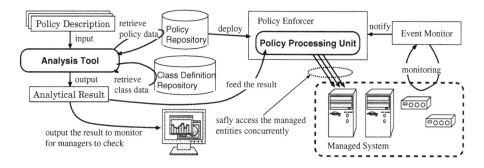

Fig. 2. Overview of the System for Policy Processing Optimization

At first, a manager applies the action clause analysis to new policy descriptions to be deployed into a policy enforcer and to deployed policies which can be retrieved from a policy repository. Then, the analytical result that indicates suspicious policy sets is reflected to a configuration of a policy processing unit in the policy enforcer. The policy processing unit controls the executions of actions and concurrently executes policies so long as they do not comprise any combination of policies found in any of the suspicious policy sets shown in the analytical result.

4.2   Implementation

We have implemented an experimental system using the PONDER[4] framework developed at Imperial College and the J2EE application server[14] provided by Sun Microsystems. The implementation of the experimental system can be divided into two parts, the policy analysis and the run-time execution control.

Policy Analysis.   Figure 3 shows the policy analysis part of the implementation. The policies written in the PONDER policy specification language are compiled into the Java classfiles and stored in an LDAP server called *Domain Storage*. The analysis component in the figure applies the action clause analysis to policies stored in the LDAP server and outputs the result into a file, which will be fed to the policy processing unit. In order to check side-effects of actions, the analysis tool retrieves information on classes of the targets and on attributes of the actions from the J2EE application server via the JMX interfaces.

While targets are expressed in *Domain Notation*[9] in the PONDER framework , we treat the domain name for targets as the name to be mapped to managed entities in a J2EE application server. For instance, a target class "/J2EE/logmanager" is mapped to the corresponding managed entity "Logmanager" in a server. The managed entities in the J2EE applications are modeled in [15].

Run-time Execution Control.   The run-time execution control is a policy run-time system based on the PONDER framework, which is intended for use in the management

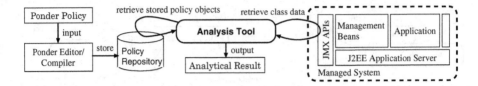

Fig. 3. Policy Analysis Part

of J2EE applications. While the framework employs the concurrent strategy, we have modified the implementation of PONDER so as to execute policies sequentially, using a waiting queue into which policies to be executed are put. This was a minor modification and we have modified less than a hundred lines of the original source code in interpreting the action clause and executing the actions defined in the clause. We have also added a few new classes for the optimization.

Figure 4 shows the internal mechanism of the run-time execution control. There are a policy enforcer that accepts events notified by a event monitor and a managed system. The policy enforcer contains a policy processing unit that controls executions of the action clause of policies with a waiting queue and a set named *active policy set*. We will explain the mechanism using the example depicted in the figure.

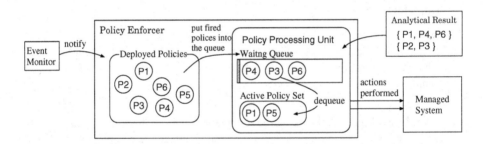

Fig. 4. Run-time Execution Control Part

The analytical result is fed to the policy processing unit beforehand, which shows that neither P1, P4 and P6 nor P2 and P3 should be executed concurrently[2]. When an event occurs and a policy is fired, the policy will be put into the waiting queue. The policy processing unit dequeues a policy in the FIFO manner and put it into the active policy set. The policy will remain in the set until the execution for it has been completed. If the analytical result shows that a policy to be dequeued conflicts with any of the policies in the active policy set, it will be skipped and the next policy will be dequeued. In the figure, P1 and P5 are in the active policy set and P4 in the waiting queue conflicts with

---

[2] The conflicts between the same policy are omitted for simplicity.

P1 and P6 as shown in the result. Thus, P4 will be skipped and P3 will be dequeued to be concurrently executed with P1 and P5 using the Java threads.

Thus, the optimized policy processing executes policies efficiently and safely using the analytical results. Using the implementation, the efficiency of optimized policy processing over the sequential processing is presented in the following section.

4.3   Experiments

We have conducted experiments for comparing performance of the sequential policy processing named the conservative strategy and the optimized policy processing. The results show the optimized one is as much as 1.47 times faster than the sequential one under the experimental environment.

We employ two PCs(CPU: Pentium4 3.0 GHz, Memory: 1.0 GBytesOS: WidnowsXP Pro). The implementation based on the latest version of the Ponder Toolkit(11 March 2003) is located at one PC. On the other PC, the J2EE1.4 Application Server Platform Edition 8 is located. The PCs are connected by a 100base-T switch.

A total of 48 polices are deployed in the implementation. The definitions of the policies are the same except the name of policy. The policy definition is as follows:

```
inst oblig /Policy/${PolicyName}{
  on EventForExperiment() ;
  subject /PMAs/PMA;
  target t= /J2EE/logmanager;
  do t.setLogLevel("","SEVERE") -> t.setLogLevel("","WARNING");
}
```

The action clause of the policy means that the operation "setLogLevel" of the managed entity "logmanager" has to be invoked twice sequentially. The operation is used for changing the grain of data to be logged.

We prepare an artificial analytical result that is only written for controlling the behavior of the optimized processing for the experiment. The result consists of 8 sets of a suspicious policy set that contains 6 name of policies that should not be executed concurrently. The name of a policy appears in the result exactly once, that is, a policy is assumed to conflict with the other 5 policies and itself.

We put the 48 polices into the waiting queue randomly at first, then measured the time to complete 100 iterations of the process that (1) make a copy of the original waiting queue and (2) process all policies in the copy. The measurement was conducted 3 times to check the variance of results. The results are shown in Table 1. The time described in the table is the average of the 100 iterations of the process. The result shows the optimized processing is as much as 1.47 times faster than the sequential one.

5   Related Work

Our analysis method is developed for detecting all sets of polices that should not be executed concurrently. This type of problem between policies is classified as *Multiple Managers Conflict* in [11], although how to detect them is not presented.

Table 1. Experimental Result

	First	Second	Third	Average
Sequential processing	951ms	944ms	944ms	946ms
Optimized processing	643ms	645ms	643ms	643ms

The way of the detection and the resolution for *Modality Conflict* is proposed in [9]. It detects sets of polices of which subjects, targets and actions are overlapped. However, it cannot detect the polices that should not be executed concurrently, since it is not necessary for actions to be overlapped, although attributes of actions should be taken into account.

In order to cope with the application specific conflicts, approaches of using constraints on polices are proposed in [2,9]. In particular [2] focuses on conflicts of actions and presents formal semantics and notation to detect and resolve such conflicts. Although they may allow managers to write constraints for the concurrent processing issues as mentioned in section 2, how to implement an interpreter for these constraints is not presented. We have focused on the concurrent processing issues and presented analysis specific to them in detail, taking into account the strategies of the policy processing. In addition to improve the reliability of the system, we have shown the analysis can be used for improving policy processing performance.

The analysis assumes the action clause is written in the typed languages. As proposed in [10], it is possible to assign type to the targets in the action clause which is written in non-typed languages, by mapping the targets to the management model, such as CIM[5] or the model of J2EE[15].

The idea of assigning attributes to operations for checking side-effects has been commonly used in distributed systems. For instance, the distributed object system "Orca" uses the attributed method of the distributed objects for keeping the consistency of replicas of objects[7]. We have applied this idea to our analysis.

6 Summary and Future Work

In this paper, we have presented an analysis method for improving both reliability and performance in policy-based management systems. It detects all set of policies whose actions might possibly access the same target entity simultaneously. This information is vital to managers, who naturally wish to ensure reliability by eliminating the potential for unexpected problems that might be caused by the concurrent execution of combinations of policies contained in any one of such *suspicious policy sets*. The same information can also be used to optimize policy processing, making it possible to execute concurrently all policy combinations not included in any detected set.

Experimental testing of our analysis method shows that it can be used to execute policies more efficiently than can be done with the conservative, sequential-execution approach, and that it can do so just as safely. Results further indicate that an optimized system is as much as 1.47 times faster than a conservative system.

In our analysis, the equivalence of targets is checked at the class level, not at the instance level. It will be a main cause of the false detection of the analysis. In order to determine whether or not this approach is both accurate and effective, we intend to continue our work by applying our analysis to use-case scenarios.

In this paper, we assume that there is one policy engine to execute policies in a policy-based management system. In the case of multiple engines, we think our method is still useful for managers to create policies, since using the method they can know whether they should consider the concurrent processing issues or not. Improvement of our method taking into account the multiple engines is also future work.

Acknowledgements. This work is supported by the Ministry of Public Management, Home Affairs, Posts and Telecommunications.

References

1. Arnold, K. and Gosling, J.: *The Java Programming Language, Second Edition*, Addison-Wesley (1998).
2. Chomicki, J., Lobo, J. and Naqvi, S.: Conflict resolusion using logic programming, IEEE Trans. on Knowledge and Data Engineering, Vol.15, pp.245–250 (2003).
3. Damianou, N.: A Policy Framework for Management of Distributed Systems, PhD Thesis, Imperial College, London, Feb (2002).
4. Damianou, N., Dulay, N., Lupu, E. and Sloman, M.: The Ponder Policy Specification Language, In Proc. of Policy2001, Jan (2001).
5. DMTF: Common Information Model Spec.v2.2, June (1999).
6. Dunlop, N., Indulska, J. and Raymond, K.: Methods for Conflict Resolution in Policy-Based Management Systems, In Proc. of EDOC2003, Sep (2003).
7. Hassen, B.S., Athanasiu, I. and Bal, H.E.: A Flexible Operation Execution Model for Shared Distributed Objects, In Proc. of OOPSLA '96, pp.30–50,(1996).
8. Fu, Z., Wu, S. F., Huang, H., Loh, K and Gong, F.: IPSec/VPN Security Policy: Correctness, Conflict Detection and Resolution, In Proc. of Policy2001, Jan (2001).
9. Lupu, E. and Sloman, M.: Conflicts in Policy-Based Distributed System Management, IEEE Trans. on SE, Vol.25, No.6, Nov (1999).
10. Lymberopoulos, L., Lupu, E. and Sloman, M: Using CIM to Realize Policy Validation within the Ponder Framework, DMTF 2003 Global Management Conference, Jun (2003).
11. Moffett, J. and Sloman, M.: Policy Conflict Analysis in Distributed System Management, Journal of Organizational Computing, Vol.4, No.1 (1994).
12. Moore, B., Ellesson, E., Strassner, J. and Westerinen A.: Policy Core Information Model - Version 1 Specification, IETF, RFC 3060, Feb (2001).
13. Sun Microsystems Inc: Java Management Extensions Instrumentation and Agent Spec.v1.2, Oct (2002).
14. Sun Microsystems Inc: Java2 Platform, Enterprise Edition Specification, v1.4 Final Release, Nov (2003).
15. Sun Microsystems Inc: Java2 Platform, Enterprise Edition Management Specification, Final Release v1.0, June (2002).

Policy-Based Resource Assignment in Utility Computing Environments

Cipriano A. Santos, Akhil Sahai, Xiaoyun Zhu, Dirk Beyer, Vijay Machiraju, and
Sharad Singhal

HP Laboratories, Palo-Alto, CA, USA
{psantos, asahai, xiaoyun, dbeyer, vijaym, sharad}@hpl.hp.com

Abstract. In utility computing environments, multiple users and applications
are served from the same resource pool. To maintain service level objectives
and maintain high levels of utilization in the resource pool, it is desirable that
resources be assigned in a manner consistent with operator policies, while
ensuring that shared resources (e.g., networks) within the pool do not become
bottlenecks. This paper addresses how operator policies (preferences) can be
included in the resource assignment problem as soft constraints. We provide the
problem formulation and use two examples of soft constraints to illustrate the
method. Experimental results demonstrate impact of policies on the solution.

1   Introduction

Resource assignment is the process of assigning specific resources from a resource
pool to applications such that their requirements can be met. This problem is
important when applications are provisioned within large resource pools (e.g. data
centers). In order to automate resource assignment, it is important to convert user
requests into specifications that detail the application requirements in terms of
resource types (e.g. servers) and the network bandwidth required between application
components. This application topology is then mapped to the physical topology of a
utility computing environment. The Resource Assignment Problem (RAP)
specification [1] describes this process. In RAP, applications are mapped to the
topology of a utility computing environment. While RAP accounts for constraints
imposed by server, storage and networking requirements during assignment, it does
not consider policies that may be desirable by operators, administrators or users. In
this paper we discuss how operator preferences (policies) may be incorporated as
logical constraints during resource assignment. We present formulations and
experimental results that deal with classes of users and resource flexing as examples
of policies that may be used during resource assignment.

Policies have been traditionally considered as event-action expressions that are
used to trigger control actions when certain events/conditions occur [2], [3]. These
policies have been applied in network and system management domain by triggering

A. Sahai and F. Wu (Eds.): DSOM 2004, LNCS 3278, pp. 100–111, 2004.

control actions as a result of threshold-based or time-based events. Sahai *et al.* [4] have formulated policies as hard constraints for automated resource construction. Other related work [5]-[8] on constraint satisfaction approaches to policy also treats policy as hard constraints.

In this paper, we describe policies as soft constraints for resource assignment. To the best of our knowledge, earlier work on resource assignment [1], [9] has not explored usage of soft constraints in resource-assignment. It is important to emphasize that the assignment system may violate soft constraints to varying degrees in order to ensure a technically feasible solution. In contrast, hard technological constraints, such as capacity limits, cannot be violated during resource assignment because their violation implies technological infeasibility.

The rest of this paper is organized as follows. In Section 2, we review the resource assignment problem, and present the mathematical optimization approach to resource assignment. Section 3 describes how policy can be incorporated in this problem as soft constraints. It also presents the formulation for incorporating class-of-user policies during resource assignment as well as for application flexing. Simulation results using this approach are described in Section 4. We conclude with some directions for future work in Section 5.

2   An Optimization Problem for Automated Resource Assignment

In [1], a resource assignment problem (RAP) for a large-scale computing utility, such as an Internet data center, was defined as follows. Given the topology of a physical network consisting of switches and servers with varying capabilities, and for a given component-based distributed application with requirements for processing and communication; decide which server from the physical network should be assigned to each application component, such that the traffic-weighted average inter-server distance is minimized, and the application's processing and communication requirements are satisfied without exceeding network capacity limits. This section briefly reviews the models used to represent computing resources and applications. The reader is referred to [1] for more details.

2.1   The RAP Models

Figure 1 shows an example of the physical network. The network consists of a set of switches and a set of servers connected in a tree topology. The root of the tree is a switching/routing device that connects the fabric to the Internet or other utility fabrics. All the internal nodes are switches, and all the leaf nodes are servers. Note that the notion of a "server" here is not restricted to a compute server. It includes other devices such as firewalls, load balancers, network attached storage (NAS), VPN gateways, or other such components. Each server is described by a set of attribute values, such as processor type, processor speed, memory size, etc. A complete list of parameters that characterize the network topology and resource capabilities is available in [1].

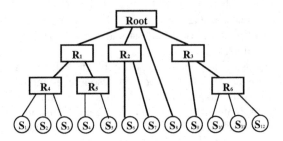

Fig. 1. Topology of a physical network

Figure 2 shows the component architecture of a distributed application, which is represented by a directed graph G(C, L). Each node $c \in C$ represents an application component, and each directed edge $l = (c, c') \in L$ is an ordered pair of component nodes, representing communication from component c to component c'. The bandwidth requirement is characterized by a traffic matrix T, where each element $T_{cc'}$ represents the amount of traffic from component c to component c'. Each component has a set of requirements on the attributes of the server that will be assigned to it.

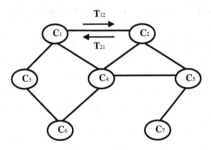

Fig. 2. A component-based distributed application architecture

2.2   A Mathematical Optimization Approach

The very large number of resources and inherent complexity of a computing utility impose the need for an automated process for dealing with RAP. Two elements make a decision problem: First there is the set of alternatives that can be followed – "like knobs that can be turned." Second, there is a description of what is "allowed", "valid", or "feasible". The task of the decision maker is to find a "setting of the knobs" that is "feasible." In many decision problems, not all feasible settings are of equal desirability. If there is a way of quantifying the desirability of a setting, one can ask to find the best of all feasible settings, which results in an optimization problem. More formally, we model the RAP optimization problem with three elements:

- *The decision variables* describe the set of choices that can be made. An assignment of values to all decision variables constitutes a candidate solution to the optimization problem. In RAP, the decision variables represent which server in the computing utility is assigned to each application component.
- *The feasible region* represents values that are allowed for the decision variables. Typically not all possible combinations of values assigned to the decision variables denote an assignment that meets all technical requirements. For example, application components may have processing or communication requirements that cannot be satisfied unless those components are assigned to specific servers. These requirements are expressed using equality or inequality constraints.
- *The objective function* is a measure of goodness of a given assignment of values to all decision variables, expressed as a parameterized function of these decision variables. In [1], we chose a specific objective function for RAP that minimizes the traffic-weighted inter-server distance. However, the formulation is flexible enough to accommodate other choices of goodness measures, such as costs, or certain utility functions.

We chose mathematical optimization as a technique to automate the resource assignment process primarily for its expressive power and efficiency in traversing a large and complex search space. Arriving at a solution that is mathematically optimal within the model specified is a welcome side effect. Therefore, RAP was formulated as a constrained optimization problem. We were not interested in developing our own optimization technology, so we chose to use off-the-shelf optimization tools. Through proper linearization of certain constraints in RAP, we derived a *mixed integer program* (MIP) [10] formulation of the problem. Our prototype solver is implemented in the GAMS language [11], which generates a MIP model that can be fed into the CPLEX solver [12]. The latter either finds an optimal/sub-optimal solution that denotes a technically feasible and desirable assignment of resources to applications, or declares the problem as infeasible, which means there is no possible assignment of resources to applications that can meet all the technical requirements.

A detailed description of the MIP formulation is presented in [1]. Note that the model in [1] also contains a storage area network (SAN) in the utility fabric and includes applications' requirements on storage. In this paper, only policies and rules that are directly related to server resources are considered. If necessary, policies for storage resources can be easily incorporated in a fashion similar to those described here.

3   Incorporating Policies in Resource Assignment

In addition to technical constraints described above, we need to include operator policies and business rules during resource assignment. For example, it may be important to consider application priority when resources are scarce, or components migration policies during application flexing.

Operator policies and business rules are often expressed as logical statements that are actually preferences. The operator would like these preferences to be true, as long as other hard constraints are not violated. The set of operator policies for an assignment itself defines a feasible region of decision variables. Replacing the feasible region of the original problem with the intersection of that region and the feasible region defined by operator policies provides the region of all feasible assignments that meet technical requirements and operator policies at the same time. Because a wide variety of operator policies can be expressed by the decision region formed by linear inequalities, they can be incorporated into the resource assignment problem during mathematical optimization.

The concept of hard and soft constraints developed in the context of mathematical programming provides a valuable tool to handle operator policies in the context of assignment. Hard constraints are stated as inequalities in an optimization problem. Any assignment that violates any of such constraints is identified as infeasible and not a viable solution. In general, we consider that constraints imposed by the technology are hard constraints that cannot be violated (i.e., their violation implies technical infeasibility of the solution). On the other hand, constraints imposed by rules, policy, or operator preferences are soft constraints that may be violated to varying degrees if a solution is otherwise not possible. This is accomplished by introducing a variable v that measures the degree of violation of a constraint. More formally, let a policy constraint be given by

$$f(x) \leq b,$$

where x is the vector of decision variables, the function $f(x)$ encapsulates the logic of the constraint and the scalar b stands for a desirable threshold. In the above formulation, the constraint is hard. Any valid assignment x must result in a function value $f(x)$ which is not larger than b. By introducing the violation variable v in the form

$$f(x) \leq b+v,$$

we see that for any choice of x, the variable v will have to take a value $v \geq f(x) - b$ which is at least as big as the amount by which the original constraint is violated. Nonetheless, whatever the particular choice of x, the soft constraint can be satisfied. This alone would render the new constraint meaningless. In order to compel the optimization algorithm to find an assignment x that violates the constraint only as much as necessary to find an otherwise feasible solution, we introduce a penalty into the objective function that is proportionate to the violation itself by subtracting[1] the term $M \cdot v$. If M is a sufficiently large number, the search for the optimal solution will attempt to minimize the violation of the constraint and only consider a violation if there is no feasible solution that satisfies all constraints.

The typical operator/customer policies related to resource assignment in a utility computing environment that can be handled by an optimization approach include the following:

- Priority policies on classes of applications.
- Migration policies during application flexing.

---

[1] This assumes that our goal is maximizing the objective. If we want to minimize the objective we simply add the same term.

- Policies for avoiding hot spots inside the resource pool, such as load balancing, or assigning/migrating servers based on local thermal conditions.
- Policies for high availability, such as dictating redundant designs, or maintaining buffer capacities in shared resources.
- Policies for improving resource utilization, such as allowing overbooking of resources.

In what follows, we use the first two policies as examples to illustrate how these policies can be incorporated into the original RAP MIP formulation. The other policies can be dealt with in a similar fashion.

3.1   Policies on Classes of Applications

In a resource constrained environment it is useful to consider different classes of applications, corresponding to different levels of service, which will be reflected in terms of priorities during resource assignment. If resources are insufficient to satisfy all applications, low priority applications are more likely to be rejected when making assignment decisions. In this paper, we consider the following priority policy:

P1. *Only assign an application with lower priority to the computing utility if its assignment does not preclude the assignment of any application of higher priority.*

While this policy has a very complex logical structure, it is easy to implement by using soft constraints. Let the binary decision variable $x_{c,s} = 1$ indicate that component c is assigned to server s, otherwise $x_{c,s} = 0$. Let $C(app)$ be the set of all components of application app with $|C(app)|$ denoting the number of components of the respective application. Then the "hard constraint"

$$\sum_{s \in S} x_{c,s} = 1 , \quad c \in C(app) \quad \text{(H1)}$$

implies that at an application component should be assigned to exactly one server. It can be relaxed as follows:

$$\sum_{s \in S} x_{c,s} \leq 1 , \quad c \in C(app) . \quad \text{(S1)}$$

The constraint (S1) means that each application component is either not assigned, or is assigned to at most one server. To disallow partial assignment (where only some of the application components are assigned) the following hard constraint is used:

$$\sum_{c \in C(app)} \sum_{s \in S} x_{c,s} = |C(app)| . \quad \text{(H2)}$$

It simply says that the number of servers assigned to an application is equal to the number of components required by the application. Now we introducing a binary violation variable v_{app} to relax the hard constraint (H2) as follows,

$$\sum_{c \in C(app)} \sum_{s \in S} x_{c,s} \geq |C(app)| * (1 - v_{app}) . \quad \text{(S2)}$$

It is easy to see from (S2) that,

$$v_{app} \geq 1 - (\sum_{c \in C(app)} \sum_{s \in S} x_{c,s}) / |C(app)| .$$

When all components of application *app* are placed on servers, $v_{app} \geq 0$. On the other hand, since v_{app} is binary, if any component of application *app* does not get a server, in which case application *app* has to be rejected, $v_{app} = 1$. If the term $M_{App} v_{App}$ is added onto the objective function, not assigning an application comes at a price of M_{App}. By choosing the magnitude of M_{App} according to the application's priority in such a way that higher priority applications have penalties that are larger than all potential penalties of lower priority applications combined, we can force the optimal solution of the modified assignment problem to conform to priority policy P1.

3.2   Migration Policies for Application Flexing

We use the term "application flexing" to refer to the process of adding additional resources to or removing resources from running applications. In this section we consider policies that are related to flexing applications. Of particular interest are policies dictating whether or not a component of an application can be migrated to accommodate changing resource requirements of the applications in the environment. Let C^{placed} be the set of components of running applications that have been placed on servers of the computing utility. Every component is currently placed on one server. This assignment can be expressed as a component-server pair. Let *ASSIGN* be the set of existing assignments, i.e.,

$$ASSIGN = \{(c, s) : \text{component } c \text{ is assigned to server } s\}.$$

We denote the set of components that can be migrated as $C^{mig} \subseteq C^{placed}$ and the set of components that cannot be migrated as $C^{nomig} = C^{placed} - C^{mig}$. Let us consider the following migration policy:

P2. *If an application component is not migratable, it should remain on the server it was placed on; if a component is migratable, migration should be avoided unless feasible assignments meeting new application requirements can not be found otherwise.*

Prohibiting migration of the components in C^{nomig} is accomplished by introducing the following additional constraints: For each assignment, $(c, s) \in ASSIGN$,

$$x_{c,s} = 1 \quad c \in C^{nomig} .$$

For components that can be migrated, P1 states that migration should be avoided unless necessary. This is incorporated by introducing a penalty π^{mig} in the objective function for changing the assignment of an existing component. Thus, we add

$$\sum_{\substack{(c,s)\in ASSIGN \\ c\in C^{mig}}} \pi^{mig}\,(1-x_{c,s})$$

to the objective function. It is easy to see that the penalty is incurred whenever a component is moved away from its current server, i.e. when $x_{c,s}=0$.

4   Simulation Results

In this section, we present simulation results of two resource assignment scenarios that required the two policies described in Section 3, respectively. The first simulation shows the use of priorities in assigning resources to applications when the available resources are insufficient to meet the demands of all applications. The second simulation demonstrates the impact of policies around mobility of application components in an application flexing scenario.

4.1   Description of the Computing Utility

The computing utility considered in our simulations is based on a 125-server utility data center [1] in HP Labs. The physical network has two layers of switches below the root switch. We refer to the one switch that is directly connected to the root switch as the edge switch ($e1$), and the four additional switches that are directly connected to the edge switch as the rack switches ($r1$-$r4$)[2]. There are no direct connections between the rack switches. All the 125 servers are either connected to the edge switch, or to a rack switch. Table 1 describes the exact network topology of the utility.

Table 1. Network topology of the computing utility

Type of switch	Edge	Rack			
Switch label	$e1$	$r1$	$r2$	$r3$	$r4$
No. of directly-connected servers	61	12	12	20	20

Among the 61 servers directly-connected to $e1$, there are 15 high-end servers in terms of their processing capacity. All the switches in the utility are non-blocking. As a result, if all traffic of an application is contained within one switch, network bandwidth is not an issue. If traffic has to traverse switches, inter-switch link capacity, as we will see, can become a scarce resource.

---

[2] Each switch has a hot standby for high availability. However, in the logical topology of the network, only the primary switch is considered.

4.2   Description of the Applications

In both simulations, we consider 10 applications that need to be hosted in the computing utility. The application topology considered is a three-tier topology typical of e-commerce applications. The resource requirements of the applications follow:

1. Application components do not share servers. Thus every application requires a separate server for each of its components.
2. Each application contains a high-end component for its back-end component (typically a database). Thus each application requires one high-end server.
3. The total amount of network bandwidth needed by each application can be classified into three categories: High, Medium, and Low.
4. Based on the criticality of meeting the application's resource demand, each application belongs to one of the three priority classes: Platinum, Gold, and Silver.

Table 2. Resource requiredments of the 10 applications

Application number	1	2	3	4	5	6	7	8	9	10
Total no. of components	8	8	10	5	7	8	6	10	5	6
High-end components	1	1	1	1	1	1	1	1	1	1
Bandwidth requirements. (Hi / Med / Low)	H	M	H	M	M	M	L	H	L	M
Application priority (Platinum/Gold/Silver)	P	P	G	P	P	P	S	P	S	P

These requirements are summarized in Table 2. Notice that, since a total of 73 servers are needed, not all applications can fit simultaneously on the 61 servers directly connected to $e1$. As a result, some applications will have to be allocated in a way that traffic traverses switches creating potential network bottlenecks.

4.3   Policies on Classes of Applications

In the first simulation, we consider the problem of assigning resources to the 10 applications simultaneously. We compare two approaches for undertaking the assignment: without any priority policies or with the priority policy P1 defined in Section 3.1. The result of the comparison is illustrated in Fig. 3.

As we can see, when no priority policies are implemented, all the applications are assigned resources from the computing utility except $App8$ – a platinum application. This result is intuitive, because when priority levels of applications are ignored, the RAP solver first tries to place the largest number of applications possible, second it chooses those applications that minimize the traffic weighted inter-server distance as described earlier. In our scenario, this results in excluding placement of $App8$ since it requires a large number of servers and high bandwidth.

As explained in Section 3.1, when application priorities are enforced, the priority policy P1 is incorporated into the RAP optimization problem using soft constraints, i.e., adding a penalty onto the objective function when the policy is violated. As indicated by the third column in Fig. 3, the resulting assignment solution is different. Now *App3* in the "Gold" class is not assigned while *App8* in the "Platinum" class is. This simulation demonstrates the impact of including the priority policy on the resulting assignment solution. It also validates the value of the soft constraint approach for incorporating priority policies into our RAP solver.

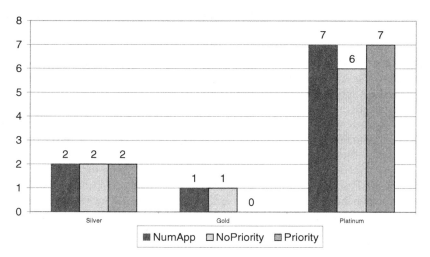

Fig. 3. Total number of applications, number of applications placed without priority, and number of applications with priority policy P1 in each priority class

4.4   Migration Policies for Flexing Applications

In this simulation, we consider an application flexing scenario and demonstrate the impact of the migration policy P2 we defined in Section 3.2. Consider the assignment obtained using the priority policy in the last section. For this assignment, all servers directly connected to the switch *e1* are assigned to applications, including the 15 high-end servers. However, the hosted nine applications together require only nine high-end servers. As a result, six high-end servers are used to host components that could have been hosted on a low-end server, and therefore, no high-end servers are currently available for assignment.

Let us now assume that after a while of running the nine applications in the computing utility, some applications' resource demands change: *App8* is requesting one additional high-end server, while *App10* is able to release three low-end components that happen to be placed on low-end servers[3]. It is obvious that if no

---

[3] The traffic requirements of the flexed applications have been adjusted accordingly in the input data. Since both applications only use servers directly connected to the edge switch *e1*, the traffic of these two applications is not affecting the assignments described below.

migration of application components is permissible, *App8*'s flexing request cannot be satisfied, because even after the release of the servers no longer needed by *App10* there are no more high-end servers available in the free pool.

On the other hand, treating all components as migratable and, in essence, solving a new initial assignment problem for all nine applications currently admitted may prescribe a new assignment that requires moving many components resulting in severe disruption of service for many of the applications.

The solution lies in specifying sensible migration policies that can be taken into account by the RAP solver. Let's consider the following migration policy on top of the formerly defined policy P2: existing low-end components can be migrated, while existing high-end components have to stay put. This is reasonable because for example, for a 3-tier Web application, the low-end components are Web servers and application servers that are more likely to be migratable, while high-end components can be database servers that are much harder to move.

As described in Section 3.2, the above migration policy was implemented by adding both hard and soft constraints to the RAP MIP formulation. Table 3 shows the resulting assignment of high-end and low-end servers to applications before and after flexing. Only the applications affected by flexing are shown. All the other assignments remain the same. As we can see, by incorporating the above migration policy, the RAP solver finds an assignment for the flexed applications, where one low-end component of *App1* previously assigned to a high-end server is migrated to a low-end server released by *App10*, and this freed high-end server is used to host the additional high-end component of *App8*.

Table 3. Server assignment to the applications affected by flexing

Applications		*App1*		*App8*		*App10*	
Servers		Low-end	Hi-end	Low-end	Hi-end	Low-end	Hi-end
Before flexing	Required	8	1	10	1	6	1
	Assigned	7	2	10	1	6	1
After flexing	Required	8	1	10	2	6	1
	Assigned	8	1	10	2	3	1

This simulation demonstrates that, by defining sensible migration policies based on properties of application components and server technologies, we are able to accommodate flexing requests that may otherwise be infeasible, thus increasing resource utilization. At the same time, we minimize the disruption to applications that are already running in the computing utility. In addition, the result verifies that using a combination of hard and soft constraints in the optimization problem can be an effective way of incorporating migration policies into the RAP optimization problem.

5   Conclusion and Future Work

In this paper, we demonstrate how operator policies can be included in a automated resource assignment using mathematical optimization techniques. Mathematical optimization is used because, as shown in [1], a simple heuristic leads to poor application placements that can create fragmented computing resources and network bottlenecks. Our simulation results on two resource assignment scenarios with common policies encountered in a utility computing environment confirm that our framework can not only address the resource assignment problem efficiently, but also offers a unified approach to tackle quantitative and rule based problems.

As a final note, observe that policies and rules need to be defined precisely in a way that helps to answer the quintessential question for resource assignment: Can resource s be assigned to component c? Consequently, we require a data model for the business rules and operator policies that allows expressing these rules and policies in terms of the parameters and decision variables of the MIP formulation of the resource assignment problem. In the future, we may develop a tool that directly writes mathematical programming code, without the need of templates and associated data models as shown in the examples of Section 3 and 4.

References

1. X. Zhu, C. Santos, J. Ward, D. Beyer and S. Singhal, "Resource assignment for large scale computing utilities using mathematical programming," *HP Labs Technical Report, HPL-2003-243*, November 2003.
   http://www.hpl.hp.com/techreports/2003/HPL-2003-243R1.html
2. N. Damianou, N. Dulay, E. Lupu, Morris Sloman, "The Ponder policy specification language," *Proceedings of IEEE/IFIP Policy 2001*, p18-38.
3. PARLAY Policy Management, http://www.parlay.org/specs
4. A. Sahai, S. Singhal, R. Joshi, V. Machiraju, "Automated policy-based resource construction in utility computing environments," *HPL-2003-176, Proceedings of IEEE/IFIP NOMS 2004.*
5. A. Sahai, S. Singhal, R. Joshi, V. Machiraju, "Automated resource configuration generation using policies," *Proceedings of IEEE/IFIP Policy 2004.*
6. P. van Hentenryck, *Constraint Satisfaction in Logic Programming*, The MIT Press, Cambridge, Mass, 1989.
7. R. Raman, M. Livny, M. Solomon, "MatchMaking: Distributed Resource Management for High Throughput Computing," *Proceedings of HPDC 98.*
8. Object Constraint Language (OCL),
   http://www-3.ibm.com/software/awdtools/library/standards/ocl.html#more
9. D. Menasce, V. Almeida, R. Riedi, R. Flavia, R. Fonseca and W. Meira Jr., "In Search of Invariants for E-Business Workloads," *Proceedings of the 2nd ACM Conference on Electronic Commerce, Minneapolis*, Oct. 2000, pp. 56-65.
10. L.A. Wolsey, *Integer Programming*, Wiley, 1998.
11. GAMS, www.gams.com
12. CPLEX, www.ilog.com

Failure Recovery in Distributed Environments with Advance Reservation Management Systems

Lars-Olof Burchard and Barry Linnert

Technische Universitaet Berlin, GERMANY {baron,linnert}@cs.tu-berlin.de

Abstract. Resource reservations in advance are a mature concept for the allocation of various resources, particularly in grid environments. Common grid toolkits such as Globus support advance reservations and assign jobs to resources at admission time. While the allocation mechanisms for advance reservations are available in current grid management systems, in case of failures the advance reservation perspective demands for strategies that support more than recovery of jobs or applications that are active at the time the resource failure occurs. Instead, also already admitted, but not yet started applications are affected by the failure and hence, need to be dealt with in an appropriate manner. In this paper, we discuss the properties of advance reservations with respect to failure recovery and outline a number of strategies applicable in such cases in order to reduce the impact of resource failures and outages. It can be shown that it pays to remap also affected but not yet started jobs to alternative resources if available. Alike reserving in advance, this can be considered as *remapping in advance*. In particular, a remapping strategy that prefers requests that were allocated a long time ago, provides a high fairness for clients as it implements similar functionality as advance reservations, while achieving the same performance as the other strategies.

1   Introduction

Advance reservations are a way of allocating resources in distributed systems before the resources are actually required, similar to flight or hotel booking. This provides many advantages, such as improved admission probability for sufficiently early reservations and reliable planning for clients and operators of the resources. Grid computing in particular uses advance reservations, which besides reliability of planning simplifies the co-allocation of very different resources and resource types in a coordinated manner. For example, the resource management integrated in the Globus toolkit [6] provides means for advance reservations on top of various local resource management systems. Currently, grid research moves its focus from the basic infrastructure that enables the allocation of resources in a dynamic and distributed environment in a transparent way to more advanced management systems that accept and process jobs consisting of numerous sub-tasks and, e.g., provide guarantees for the completion of such jobs. In this context, the introduction of service level agreements (SLA) provides flexible

A. Sahai and F. Wu (Eds.): DSOM 2004, LNCS 3278, pp. 112–123, 2004.
© IFIP International Federation for Information Processing 2004

negotiation mechanisms for various applications. This demands for control over each job and its required resources at any stage of the job's life-time from the request negotiation to the completion. An example for a resource management framework covering these aspects is the virtual resource manager architecture described in [3].

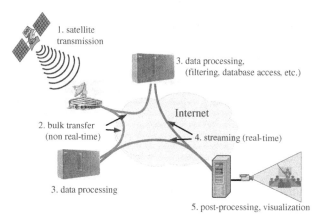

Fig. 1. Example: grid application with time-dependent tasks.

Such an application is depicted in Figure 1. The job processed in the distributed environment consists of a number of sub-tasks which are executed one after another in order to produce the final result, in this case the visualization of the data. This includes network transmissions as well as parallel computations on two cluster computers.

One important aspect in this context is the behavior of the management system in case of failures. While current research mainly focused on recovery mechanisms for those jobs that are already active, in advance reservation environments it is also necessary to examine the impact of failures onto admitted but not yet started jobs or sub-jobs. In contrast to the sophisticated and difficult mechanisms needed to deal with failures for running jobs, e.g., checkpointing and migration mechanisms, jobs not yet started can be dealt with in a transparent manner by remapping those affected jobs to alternative resources.

In this paper, a framework for dealing with those jobs is presented which includes strategies for selecting alternative resources and assigning inactive jobs. Similar to the term *reserving in advance*, we refer to this approach as *remapping in advance*, as those mechanisms perform the remapping ahead of the actual impact of the failure. Besides the description of the failure recovery framework, we show the success of our approach using simulations in a distributed environment.

The failure recovery strategies do not solely apply to actual failures of resources, e.g., hardware failures of processors or network links, but can also be used in a highly dynamic system, where resources are deliberately taken out of the distributed system for maintenance or in order to use the resource for local requests of high priority. Furthermore, the failure strategies are independent of the underlying resources, i.e., the mechanism is generic in the sense that it is not restricted to a particular resource type such as parallel computers. Instead, it is possible to apply the mechanisms to a wide range of resources as needed, e.g., in grid environments.

The remainder of this document is organized as follows: firstly, related work important for this paper is outlined. After that, the properties of the advance reservation environment are presented and the impact on the failure recovery mechanisms that must be applied. Furthermore, we introduce the notion of expected downtime which describes the estimated time of the failure and outline a number of remapping strategies for affected jobs which can be adopted in a flexible manner depending on the jobs properties. In Sec. 6, the strategies are evaluated using extensive simulations. The paper is concluded with some final remarks.

2   Related Work

Advance reservations are an important allocation strategy, widely used, e.g., in grid toolkits such as Globus [4], as they provide simple means for co-allocations of different resources. Besides flexible and easy support for co-allocations, advance reservations also have other advantages such as an increased admission probability when reserving sufficiently early, and reliable planning for users and operators. In contrast to the synchronous usage of several different resources, where also queueing approaches are conceivable [1], advance reservations have a particular advantage when time-dependent co-allocation is necessary, as shown in Fig. 1. In [3], advance reservations have been identified also as essential for a number of higher level services, such as SLAs.

In the context of grid computing, failure recovery mechanisms are particularly important as the distributed nature of the environment requires more sophisticated mechanisms than needed in a setting with only few resources that can be handled by a central management system. The focus of this paper is on the requirements for dealing with failures and outages of resources that are reserved in advance.

In general, failure detection and recovery mechanisms focus on the requirements to deal with applications that are already active. The Globus heartbeat monitor HBM [6] provides mechanisms to notify applications or users of failures occurring on the used resources. The recovery mechanisms described in this paper can be initiated by the failure detection of the HBM. In [7], a framework for handling failures in grid environments was presented, based on workflow structure. The framework allows users to select different failure recovery mechanisms, such as simply restarting jobs, or - more sophisticated - checkpointing and migration to other resources if supported by the application to be recovered.

In [2], the problem of failure recovery in advance reservation systems was addressed in a similar manner for networks. One important difference is that in contrast to the considerations in [2], jobs cannot be migrated and distributed during run-time in the same way as network transmissions, where packets can be transmitted on several paths in parallel.

Mechanisms as presented in this paper can be applied in distributed but also in centralized management systems, such as the virtual resource manager (VRM) described in [3]. Residing on top of local resource management systems, the VRM framework supports quality-of-service guarantees and SLA negotiation and with these mechanisms provides a larger variety and improved quality of the services offered for users. In particular, when SLAs were negotiated, e.g., in order to ensure job completion up to a certain deadline, failure recovery mechanisms are essential in order to avoid breaching an SLA.

3   Application Environment

Advance reservations are requests for a certain amount of resources during a specified period of time. In general, a reservation can be made for a fixed period of time in the future, called *book-ahead interval*. The time between issuing a request and the start time of the request is called *reservation time*. In contrast to immediate reservations which are usually made without specifying the duration, advance reservations require to define the stop time for a given request. This is required to reliably perform admission control, i.e., to determine whether or not sufficient resources can be guaranteed for the requested period.

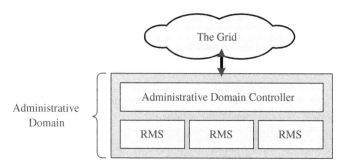

Fig. 2. Outline of the VRM Architecture

The failure recovery mechanisms described here are integrated in the VRM architecture [3] (see Fig. 2). The *administrative domain controller* (ADC) is in charge of the resource management, e.g., resource selection, scheduling, and failure recovery, of a domain consisting of one or more resource management systems. Once a failure is notified to the ADC, the failure recovery searches for alternative resources firstly within its own domain. If this is not successful, other resources available via the grid interface are contacted in order to find a suitable alternative location for a job.

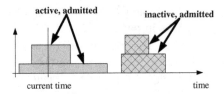

Fig. 3. Active and inactive jobs in the advance reservation environment.

4   Expected Downtime

In advance reservation environments, knowledge is available not only about jobs that are currently active, but also about those that are admitted but not yet started (see Fig. 3). While in other environments, failure recovery strategies need to be implemented only for active jobs, advance reservations require to consider also the inactive ones. For this purpose, we introduce the notion of *expected downtime*. This time represents an estimate of the actual duration of the failure and is the basis for our failure recovery strategies.

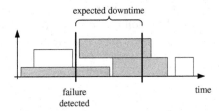

Fig. 4. Jobs within expected downtime (gray) are considered for remapping.

As depicted in Fig. 4, any job that is or becomes active during the expected downtime period is considered for remapping. In contrast to those strategies aiming at only recovering active jobs, e.g., using checkpointing and migration, remapping of inactive jobs has the advantage of requiring much less efforts, since this is done entirely within the management system. The emphasis in this paper is on remapping inactive jobs.

5   Remapping Strategies

In the context of this study, jobs running at the moment the failure occurs are considered to be not remappable. The reason is the difficulty to implement suitable recovery mechanisms, such as checkpointing and migration facilities. For many resource types, such as cluster systems or parallel computers, such functionality lacks completely or has to be implemented explicitly by the application. However, our assumption is not crucial for the evaluation of our approach or the success of the remapping strategies themselves.

Fig. 5. Timeline of the failure recovery process

In case, the failure of a specific resource system, e.g., a cluster, is notified, the management system has to face different tasks to minimize the impact of the failure, which means, as many affected jobs as possible have to be remapped to alternative resources. The amount of affected jobs to be remapped is defined by the time the failure occurred and the expected downtime. Therefore, at first it is necessary to investigate the actual allocation of the local resource system affected by the failure, which means all jobs that have a reservation for the time span between failure and end of the expected downtime have to be processed. Other jobs are not required to be taken into account. The temporal sequence of events during the recovery process is depicted in Fig. 5.

For all jobs that must be remapped, alternative resources have to be found. Hence, the resource management system must have information about all available resources which are able to run the affected jobs. Because grid environments can provide different and heterogeneous resources, the management system has to make sure that only computing systems feasible to deal with the jobs to be remapped are considered during the recovery process.

Finding the alternative resources for a set jobs is a classical bin packing problem [5]. In order to determine feasible resources, strategies such as gang-matching have been developed [10]. Once the set of feasible resources has been determined, the remapping mechanism determines the amount of unused capacity, e.g., compute nodes, on all alternative compute systems, e.g., cluster computers. Then, the task is to maximize the success of the remapping according to some optimization criterion, e.g., the amount of successfully remapped jobs. Other optimization criteria are conceivable as well although not targeted in this paper, e.g., minimizing the penalty to be paid for terminated jobs.

The bin packing problem discussed here deals with different bins of different, but fixed size, to be filled with objects of fixed size. In our case these objects are rectangles, symbolizing the reservations, fixed in height and width, and the bins are defined by the expected downtime (width) and the amount of unused resources on the potentially available alternative resource locations (height). This means, we have to deal with a special case of the multidimensional bin packing problem - a rectangle packing problem, which is NP-complete [8]. Hence, in this paper heuristics are used in order to determine how jobs are remapped onto alternative resources.

Because the reservations are fixed in time it is not possible to shift the jobs to the future on the local system or alternative resources. This differs from scheduling bin packing approaches using time as variable dimension. Thus, it is essential to find free resources during the specific downtime interval, for example, using the available resources within the grid (see Sec. 3). On the other hand, free resources on any of the alternative systems may not be available for any request.

Therefore, it the necessary to decide in which order jobs are being remapped to unused resources.

Some assumptions can be made to motivate the decision for suitable remapping heuristics, as outlined in the following.

First Come First Served (FCFS). In order to maximize the acceptance of grid environments and advance reservation systems, a predictable behavior of the system has to be assured – even in cases of failures. One opportunity is to prefer reservations allocated a long time ago. This implements a similar mechanism as advance reservations themselves, i.e., early reservations assure preferred access to the requested resources. Hence, this remapping strategy, called *first come first served*, matches best the users' expectation of the behavior of the failure recovery mechanisms. For this purpose, the reservation time, i.e., the time interval between allocation and resource usage (see Sec. 3), is stored with each request.

Earliest First (EF). Since the problem of remapping all jobs afflicted by the expected downtime is NP-complete, the search for free resources can last a significant amount of time by itself. Furthermore, in distributed management systems it is necessary to accommodate for the communication costs for status checks and remapping requests (see Fig. 2). Therefore, the termination of jobs due to the long lasting recovery process must be reduced. This is achieved by the *earliest first* strategy, which orders job according to their start time.

Smallest Job First (SJF). The *smallest job first* strategy aims at reducing the total number of terminated jobs resulting from insufficient amount of free resources. In contrast to FCFS, this strategy may be preferred by operators more than by users. This strategy orders jobs according to their total resource consumption, i.e., the product *resource usage × time*, e.g., CPU hours.

Largest Job First (LJF). The *largest job first* strategy deals with the effect of fragmentation of free resources on the grid environment. Using this strategy it is likely to optimize the utilization of the whole environment. Many small requests will not congest alternative resources.

Longest Remaining First (LRF). This strategy prefers jobs with long remaining run-time. Thus, jobs which utilize resources for a long period of time will get higher remapping probability.

Shortest Remaining First (SRF). The counterpart of LRF is *shortest remaining first*, which gives priority to jobs with low remaining run-time. Thus, more jobs are likely to be remapped successfully which may be the goal of operators.

In Fig. 6, an example of jobs to be remapped during the expected downtime is shown. Using FCFS, the jobs are prioritized according to the time intervals r_1, r_2, r_3, i.e., the remapping order is J_2, J_3, J_1, whereas when using EF, only the start time of the resource is of interest, i.e., the resulting order is J_1, J_2, J_3.

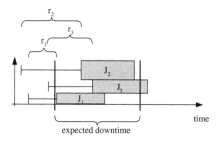

Fig. 6. Example for job ordering and remapping.

6 Evaluation

All of the strategies previously described have their advantages and may be chosen depending on the focus of operator or user perspectives. Simulations were conducted in order to show how the different strategies perform in actual grid environments.

6.1 Simulation Environment

The simulations were made assuming an infrastructure of several cluster and parallel computers with homogeneous node setting, i.e., each job is capable of running on any of the machines involved. The reason is, that although grid computing in general implies a heterogeneous infrastructure, an alternative resource used for remapping a job needs to be equipped such that the respective job is runnable. Hence, it is sensible to simplify the infrastructure.

The simulations only serve the purpose of showing the general impact of failures and since according to [9] the actual distribution of job sizes, job durations etc. do not impact the general quality of the results generated even when using simple models, the simulations were made using a simple synthetic job and failure model. Each job was assumed to be reserved in advance with the reservation time being exponentially distributed with a mean of 100 slots. Job durations were uniformly distributed in the interval $[250, 750]$ and each job demanded for a number of nodes being a power of 2, i.e., $2, 4, 8, \ldots, 256$ nodes with uniform distribution. Each time a failure occurred, a resource was chosen randomly with uniform distribution. The time between failures followed an exponential distribution with a mean of 250 slots. The hardware infrastructure consisted of different parallel computers with varying number of compute nodes, in total there were eight machines with different amount of nodes, i.e., 1024, 512, 256, 128, 96, and 16. Obviously, some jobs cannot be executed on any machine.

Each simulation run had a duration of 10,000 slots and the results presented in the following sections each represent the average of 10,000 simulation runs.

In order to assess the performance of the different strategies, two metrics were chosen that reflect both the amount of jobs that were affected but could not be successfully remapped onto alternative resources and the reduction of the utilization that resulted from terminated jobs. The first metric is the *termination ratio*, which is defined as follows:

$$\text{termination ratio} := \frac{|\bar{A}|}{|A|},$$

with A being the set of affected jobs and $\bar{A} \subset A$ being the set of terminated jobs. The second metric is called *utilization loss rate*, defined as

$$\text{utilization loss ratio} := \frac{\sum_{j \in \bar{A}} t(j)c(j)}{\sum_{j \in A} t(j)c(j)},$$

with $t(j)$ denoting the duration of job $j \in A$, and $c(j)$ denoting the extend of the resource usage of j. For example, when the resource in question is a cluster computer, the amount of CPU hours lost due to a failure is captured by the utilization loss ratio.

For the sake of simplicity, it was assumed that jobs can only be finished completely or not at all. In certain cases, users may also be satisfied with a reduced quality-of-service in the sense that even partial results or a reduced number of nodes can be tolerated. However, as the emphasis in this paper is on the general behavior of a management system using our failure recovery strategies, this was not taken into account.

6.2   Performance of the Remapping Strategies

In Fig. 7, the performance of the different strategies is depicted with respect to termination ratio and utilization loss ratio. The general result is that, the differences between the individual strategies is rather low. This means, it may be possible to select a strategy that matches the expectations of operators or users best.

While the strategies that prefer small or short jobs (SJF, SRF) achieve a low termination ratio, the strategies which give high priority to long or large jobs (LJF, LRF) achieve superior utilization loss ratio. The strategies related to the time, i.e., EF and FCFS, range between the worst and the best, with EF being near the best for both metrics.

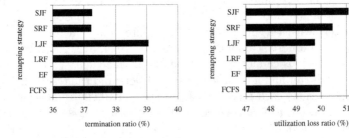

Fig. 7. Performance of the remapping strategies

6.3   Impact of the Downtime Estimation

The computation of the expected downtime is a crucial task in the whole failure recovery process. This estimation can, e.g., be based on knowledge about the type of the actual failure or statistics about previous failures. For example, replacing a failed hardware part such as a processor or interconnect can strongly depend on the time required for shipping the failed part which usually is known in advance. However, as it can not be assured that the estimation is accurate, it is important to study the impact of inaccurate downtime estimations on the termination ratio and utilization loss ratio.

Two cases must be examined: an overestimation means that the actual failure lasted shorter than expected, an underestimation means the actual failure lasted longer than originally assumed.

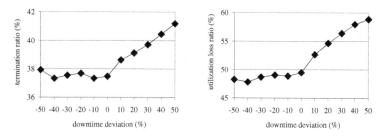

Fig. 8. Impact of inaccurate downtime estimation on the termination ratio and utilization loss ratio

In Fig. 8, the influence of over- and underestimations is depicted for the FCFS strategy as an example. It can be clearly observed, that with a positive downtime deviation, i.e., the actual failure lasted longer than expected, both the termination ratio and utilization loss ratio increase significantly. In contrast, overestimations of the actual downtime do not show significant effects with respect to both metrics.

The reason for this behavior is that with overestimations, the amount of jobs that must be terminated does not differ from the case of an exact estimation. Once the failure is removed, e.g., by replacing a failed hardware item, the management system simply changes the status to *running*. No further actions is required. In case of an underestimation, this is different. Once the end of the estimated failure period is reached and the system is still not operable, the management needs to extend the estimated downtime period and then remap the jobs within the extended downtime. Since at this time additional jobs may have arrived and assigned to the set of alternative resources, it is more likely that remapping is not successful.

While an overestimation of the actual downtime has no negative impact on the job termination ratio, this is slightly different when investigating the amount of jobs that can be accommodated by the distributed system and the

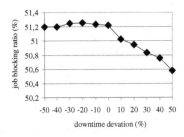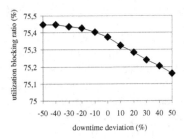

Fig. 9. Impact of inaccurate downtime estimation on the job blocking ratio and utilization blocking ratio

achievable utilization. This is depicted in Fig. 9, showing the job blocking ratio and utilization blocking ratio which capture the percentage of rejected jobs in total and the utilization these jobs would have been generated. It can be seen that both metrics decrease with increasing overestimation resulting from the assumption that the downtime lasts longer and since jobs are not admitted to a system which is failed, fewer jobs are admitted to the system. However, in this case underestimations admit more jobs at the expense that fewer jobs actually survive failures. Furthermore, the impact on the overall utilization depends on the amount of failures and their duration. As failure situations can be considered as exceptions, the actual impact of inaccurate downtime estimations remains low.

The results presented in this section show clearly, that the introduction of the expected downtime, i.e., performing remapping in advance, is an effective mean to reduce the amount of actually terminated jobs. Otherwise, the effect is similar to an underestimation, i.e., termination ratio and utilization loss ratio increase significantly. Although it is unrealistic that the actual downtime can always be accurately predicted, it is useful to have at least any rough estimate in order to increase the amount of successfully remapped jobs. Overestimations, although reducing the amount of jobs that can be accommodated, do not harm the systems performance with respect to the amount of terminated jobs. As indicated by the performance results, the estimation of the downtime is more important than the choice of the actual remapping strategy. In particular, an underestimation of the downtime by only 10 percent leads to a worse performance than selecting a different remapping algorithm.

7   Conclusion

In this paper, failure recovery strategies for advance reservation systems, e.g., several distributed parallel computers or grid environments, were presented. It could be shown, that particularly remapping in advance, i.e., remapping inactive but admitted jobs, is important to reduce the impact of failures. Furthermore, remapping of inactive jobs does not interfere with running applications but can instead be performed completely within the management system. The strategies presented in this paper are generic, i.e., they can easily be applied to almost any resource type and any resource management system, either centralized or distributed. This is particularly important for next generation grid systems, which essentially need to support higher level quality-of-service guarantees, e.g., specified by SLAs.

The results of the simulations showed, that the impact of a wrong downtime estimation is much higher than the differences between the remapping strategies. This means, the choice of the remapping strategy can be selected according to the needs of the actual environment. Concluding, the remapping of jobs in advance proved to be a useful approach for dealing with failures in advance reservation systems.

References

1. Azzedin, F., M. Maheswaran, and N. Arnason. A Synchronous Co-Allocation Mechanism for Grid Computing Systems. *Journal on Cluster Computing*, 7(1):39–49, January 2004.
2. Burchard, L.-O., and M. Droste-Franke. Fault Tolerance in Networks with an Advance Reservation Service. In *11th International Workshop on Quality of Service (IWQoS), Monterey, USA*, volume 2707 of *Lecture Notes in Computer Science (LNCS)*, pages 215–228. Springer, 2003.
3. Burchard, L.-O., M. Hovestadt, O. Kao, A. Keller, and B. Linnert. The Virtual Resource Manager: An Architecture for SLA-aware Resource Management. In *4th Intl. IEEE/ACM Intl. Symposium on Cluster Computing and the Grid (CCGrid), Chicago, USA*, 2004.
4. Foster, I., C. Kesselman, C. Lee, R. Lindell, K. Nahrstedt, and A. Roy. A Distributed Resource Management Architecture that Supports Advance Reservations and Co-Allocation. In *7th International Workshop on Quality of Service (IWQoS), London, UK*, pages 27–36, 1999.
5. Garey, M. and D. Johnson. *Computers and Intractability: A Guide to the Theory of NP-Completeness*. W. H. Freeman & Co., 1979.
6. The Globus Project. http://www.globus.org/.
7. Hwang, S. and C. Kesselman. Grid Workflow: A Flexible Failure Handling Framework for the Grid. In *12th Intl. Symposium on High Performance Distributed computing (HPDC), Seattle, USA*, pages 126–138. IEEE, 2003.
8. Karp, R., M. Luby, and A. Marchetti-Spaccamela. A Probabilistic Analysis of Multidimensional Bin Packing Problems. In *16th annual ACM Symposium on Theory of Computing (STOC)*, pages 289–298. ACM Press, 1984.
9. Lo, V., J. Mache, and K. Windisch. A Comparative Study of Real Workload Traces and Synthetic Workload Models for Parallel Job Scheduling. In *4th Workshop on Job Scheduling Strategies for Parallel Processing, Orlando, USA*, volume 1459 of *Lecture Notes in Computer Science (LNCS)*, pages 25–46. Springer, 1998.
10. Raman, R., M. Livny, and M. Solomon. Policy Driven Heterogeneous Resource Co-Allocation with Gangmatching. In *12th Intl. Symposium on High Performance Distributed Computing (HPDC), Seattle, USA*, pages 80–90. IEEE, 2003.

Autonomous Management of Clustered Server Systems Using JINI

Chul Lee, Seung Ho Lim, Sang Soek Lim, and Kyu Ho Park

Computer Engineering Research Laboratory, EECS
Korea Advnaced Institute of Science and Technology
{chullee,shlim,sslim}@core.kaist.ac.kr and kpark@ee.kaist.ac.kr

Abstract. A framework for the autonomous management of clustered server systems called LAMA[1] (Large-scale system's Autonomous Management Agent) is proposed in this paper. LAMA is based on agents, which are distributed over the nodes and built on JINI infrastructure. There are two classes of agents: a grand LAMA and ordinary LAMAs. An ordinary LAMA abstracts an individual node and performs node-wide configuration. The grand LAMA is responsible for monitoring and controlling all the ordinary ones. Using the *discovery*, *join*, *lookup*, and *distributed security* operations of JINI, a node can join the clustered system without secure administration. Also, a node's failure can be detected automatically using the *lease* interface of the JINI. Resource reallocation is performed dynamically by a reallocation engine in the grand agent. The reallocation engine gathers the status of remote nodes, predicts resource demands, and executes reallocation by accessing the ordinary agents. The proposed framework is verified on our own clustered internet servers, called the CORE-Web server, for an audio-streaming service. The nodes are dynamically reallocated satisfying the performance requirements.

1 Introduction

Server clustering techniques have been successfully used in building highly available and scalable server systems. While the clustered servers have been enlarging the scale of the service, management has become more complex, as well. It is notoriously difficult to manage all the machines, disks, and other hardware/software components in the cluster. Such management requires skilled administrators whose roles are very important to maximize the uptime of the cluster system. For instance, configurations of newly installed resources, optimization to get a well-tuned system, and recovery from any failed resources have been performed thoroughly. These days, a self-managing system is promising for its ability to automate the management of a large system, so that the scalable and reliable administration can be achieved.

We have developed our own clustered internet server, called CORE-Web server including a SAN-based shared file system[1], a volume manager[2], L-7 dispatchers[3][4], and admission controllers [5][6]. The complexity of managing the servers led us to develop a framework for autonomous management.

In order to relieve administrator's burden, GUI-based management tools [7] may be utilized. They made it easy to manage a set of clustered nodes with user-friendly

---

[1] This work is supported by NRL project, Ministry of Science and Technology, Korea

A. Sahai and F. Wu (Eds.): DSOM 2004, LNCS 3278, pp. 124–134, 2004.

interfaces; however, there are still more things to be automated, or to be more robust against failures. Many researchers have studied about self-managing systems, which includes self-configuration, self-optimization, self-healing, and self-protection [8][9]. The autonomous management will be gradually improved to help avoid manual configuration, so that humans would only be needed for physical installation or removal of hardware.

Our goal is also to develop a self-managing CORE-Web server system, while adding some attributes such as flexibility, generality, and security. To achieve our goals, we have built an agent-based infrastructure for the autonomous management, using JINI technology [10], since the JINI infrastructure provides quite useful features to build a distributed system in a secure and flexible manner. Using *discovery*, *join*, *lookup*, and *distributed security* a node can join to the clustered system without administration securely, so that another node can access the newly joined nodes without knowing specific network addresses. Also, a node's failure can be detected using the *lease* interface of the JINI. The leasing enforces each node to renew by a given expiration time, so that the failed nodes can be detected using the expiration of the lease.

We named our autonomous agent as LAMA, which stands for a Large-Scale system's Autonomous Management Agent. LAMAs are implemented on top of JINI infrastructure. Each agent, called LAMA, is spread over each node. During boot-up, the LAMA registers its capabilities to the lookup service (LUS), located in the Grand LAMA, which is the managing LAMA. Other agents might discover the LAMA simply by looking up the LUS, so as to acquire the controls over the nodes.

Next section briefly describes previous works on autonomous management. We then describe LAMA-based autonomous management for dynamic configuration in section 3. Using our CORE-Web server, we built a live audio streaming server, which provides autonomous management.

2   Background

In order to automate the management of a large system, we employed part of off-the-shelf technologies. A newly delivered bare-metal machine can be booted via remote booting like PXES[11] or Etherboot[12]. Also, the node can be booted from a SAN storage. After booting up and running a minimal set of software, we should tune and configure parameters. Individual nodes should be configured for an application service so that the node becomes a trusty component of the service. Many tools are released to enable remote configuration management of a large system, like LCFG[13] and KickStart[14].

While such tools make it easy to manage diverse systems, individual nodes must be able to optimize themselves. AutoTune agents[15] manage the performance of Apache web server by controlling configuration parameters.

The GridWeaver project is aimed to enable autonomous reconfiguration of large infrastructures, according to central policies[16]. Also, many researchers focus on the dynamic reallocation of large infrastructure based on the Service Level Agreement (SLA) like a data center[17][18].

The missing part is a methodology for a systematic development and integration of an autonomous system. Also, important points of autonomous management are run-

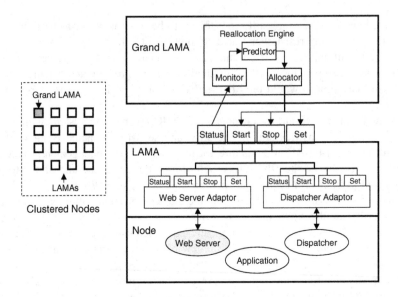

Fig. 1. LAMA architecture

time optimization and adaptation, which are too hard for humans to perform. Our work considers the issues.

3   LAMA Architecture

LAMA is an agent, which is in charge of managing each component in a system. There are two types of LAMAs; ordinary LAMAs and a Grand LAMA. The ordinary LAMAs perform node-wide configuration while residing at individual nodes. The Grand LAMA is responsible for orchestrating all the ordinary ones. As shown in Figure 1, LAMA is a kind of an adaptor that abstracts a node and provides simple control methods to the Grand LAMA. The methods include *Status*, *Start*, *Stop*, and *Set*, through that a re-allocation engine in Grand LAMA controls and monitors the nodes. LAMA abstracts detail configurations of specific applications. Inside LAMA, there are several classes of adaptors, and they enable legacy applications to be controlled by the Grand LAMA. For example, a web server adaptor is plugged in to an Apache web server, then the adaptor returns the Apache's status (status), runs up and down the processes (start/stop), or manipulates the Apache's configuration file (set). The adaptor doesn't need any modification of the Apache web server. The Grand LAMA is then able to configure the web server dynamically using four methods mentioned above.

We assumed that the management of a pool containing many nodes would be complex, since the nodes' joins and leaves (failures) might be frequent in a large scale system. In a traditional way, we would have to manually register all the nodes to the pool by specifying detailed network parameters. Also, we would required numerous manual reconfigurations, upon changing the network configuration.

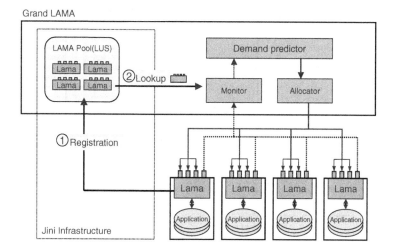

Fig. 2. LAMA pool management

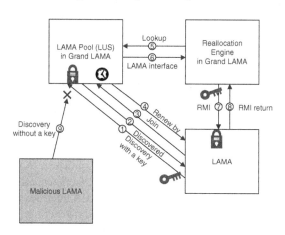

Fig. 3. LAMA in the JINI infrastructure

Our management system uses JINI infrastructure for building a pool without knowing specific network configurations. Figure 2 describes how a LAMA pool is managed. When a LAMA is booted, it discovers the pool (usually known as a Lookup Service or LUS in JINI) and registers its interface automatically. The other modules, like a monitor and an allocator of the Grand LAMA, get the interface to control and monitor the remote nodes. The detailed operations of *discovery*, *join*, *lookup*, and *distributed security* in the JINI infrastructure are described in Figure 3. A LAMA multicasts discovery messages to the network, and the LAMA pool (LUS) in the Grand LAMA responds with a discovered message only if the LAMA holds a correct key. Then, the LAMA can join the pool. The reallocation engine in the Grand LAMA can access a LAMA via RMI after looking up the LAMA. Also, the engine has to hold a correct key to invoke the LAMA methods. A

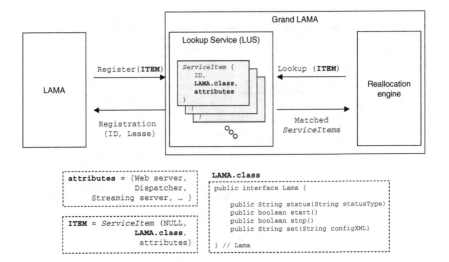

Fig. 4. Lookup Service (LUS) for the management of a LAMA pool

malicious LAMA cannot discover the pool without a correct key, so that it cannot join the pool. The key should be distributed to a identified componenet, when the component is installed firt time. JINI's *lease* interface makes the pool management robust to node failure. Leasing enables a LAMA to be listed in the pool for a given period of time; beyond that it has to renew its registration to avoid removal from the pool. JINI also provides a distributed security model, and through that the codes for the management can be distributed and executed in a secure way.

The operations of the lookup service (LUS) are shown in Figure 4. The LUS is originally from the reference implementation of JINI LUS, called REGGIE[10]. The LUS stores a set of *ServiceItem*s, which have IDs, a LAMA interface class, and attributes. A remote LAMA instantiates a *ServiceItem*, ITEM, and register it to the LUS. Then, the ID and lease duration are returned. Lookup also uses an instance of *ServiceItem*, ITEM, which specifies attributes of the needed LAMA. Attributes indicate the roles of a node; a web server, a dispatcher, or a streaming server. By specifying the attributes as a web server, a LAMA can be found, which is able to run a web server. If the attributes are not specified, all the *ServiceItem* corresponding to LAMAs will be returned.

Our CORE-Web server, which is managed by the Grand LAMA and ordinary LAMA, is shown in Figure 5. It includes a dispatcher, and back-end servers. The dispatcher distributes clients' requests over the backend servers, and then the back-end servers respond to the requests through accessing a SAN-based shared storage. The solid lines describe control paths between the Grand LAMA and LAMAs. The Grand LAMA collects the status ($L(t)$) of the back-end servers from LAMAs. $L(t)$ contains node-wide status, like CPU utilization and network bandwidth. The Grand LAMA could reallocate the nodes, by updating the control parameters of the dispatcher, D-CP, and those of servers, S-CP. Each parameter includes *start* and *stop* to initiate and destroy the server respectively. *Set* is for adjusting application specific attributes. D-CP has specific

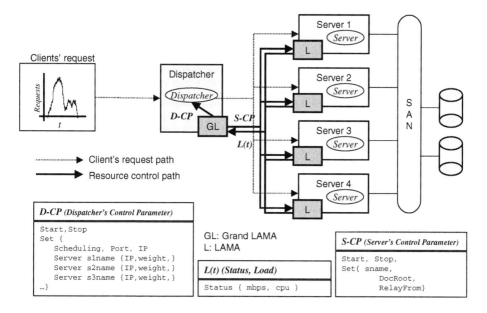

Fig. 5. CORE-Web server and LAMA

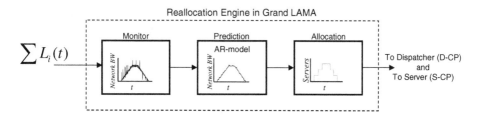

Fig. 6. Resource reallocation engine in the Grand LAMA

attributes such as a list of the back-end servers including IP addresses, host names, and weights for load-balancing. S-CP for a web server also has changeable attributes such as a hostname (sname), a root path of contents like HTML documents (DocRoot), and the address of an original source server (RelayFrom) in the case that the back-end servers relay a live media streaming.

The operation of a resource reallocation engine in the Grand LAMA is described in detail in Figure 6. The status of each node is gathered in the Grand LAMA. Therefore, the monitor module keeps overall resource usages at time t. The future resource demand is predicted using an autoregressive model. Also, the autoregressive model filters out noises in the signal of the resource usage. Based on the predicted resource demand, the allocation module adjusts the number of back-end servers in advance. This server reallocation is executed through updating D-CP and S-CP.

A goal of the resource reallocation is to save resources while meeting constraints on the application performance usually described in a Service Level Agreement (SLA).

Therefore, a proper algorithm of the demand prediction should be deployed for the most cost-effective resource allocation.

A threshold-based heuristic algorithm[18] is simple but reactive to a sudden change in resource demands; however, it may cause unstable reallocation due to the high noise of input workloads. Also, it is not easy to determine the proper upper and lower thresholds.

A forecast-based algorithm is usually based on an autoregressive model, which predicts the future resource demands. It can capture long-term trends or cyclic changes like a time-of-day effect. Short-term forecasting may handle workload surges effectively, when the time overhead of reallocation is high [17]; however, inaccuracy of forecasting causes problems. We applied and compared both algorithms for the prediction in the reallocation engine, and will present the result below.

4   Prototype: Audio Streaming Service

Our prototype system provides a live audio streaming service. At the beginning, only one back-end node might be initiated as a streaming media server, such as icecast [19]. Upon detecting load increases, more nodes should be allocated for the service. An idle node could be chosen as an additional icecast server, and configured to relay the source streams from the first initiated icecast server. In this case, the server-side control parameter (S-CP) is *RelayFrom*, which describes the address of the original source server from which the audio stream is relayed. Each LAMA registers its interface to the pool (LUS). Then, the Grand LAMA composes a set of LAMAs dedicated to the audio streaming service, by looking up LAMAs from LUS. It constantly monitors its under-managed LAMAs to detect changing resource demands.

Resources can be measured with different metrics, according to the different aspects of the specific applications. Three major aspects of resources are acceptable, such as the CPU usage, network bandwidth, and disk storage. The performance of the application is highly correlated with these three metrics. SAR [20] produces many statistics about the system including the above metrics. Our LAMA measures resource utilization using the SAR, and then sends the status to Grand LAMA.

The capacity of the live audio streaming service depends solely on a network bandwidth, since it serves multiple users with only a single stream. When the source stream is igniting at 128 kbps, our single node could serve less than 750 concurrent connections reliably. With 750 concurrent connections, network utilization reached up-to 98%. With over 750 connections, the average streaming rates decrease rapidly, and the icecast server closes many connections, since server-side queues overflow due to the severe network congestion.

We compared two prediction algorithms. In a threshold-based prediction, we simply chose 90% as the upper threshold, and 80% as the lower threshold. The algorithm is described in Algorithm 1. Even though icecast server could spend 98% of the network bandwidth, we chose 90% as the upper threshold for reliable preparation, meaning that when the overall network utilization over the distributed back-end servers exceeds 90%, an additional back-end server is supplemented. When the utilization can be lower than 80% despite excepting one of back-end servers, the victim back-end server is released. When the resource utilization decreases, excess resources should be released or yielded

Algorithm 1 Reallocation algorithm for the threshold-based and AR-based prediction

$N_A \Leftarrow$ The Number of allocated servers (1)
$C \Leftarrow$ The network capacity of a node (100Mbps)
$t \Leftarrow$ The current time (0)
$p \Leftarrow$ Sampling period (2 seconds)
$L_i(t) \Leftarrow$ Network usuage of a node i at time t in Mbps
$ut \Leftarrow$ Upper threshold (0.9)
$lt \Leftarrow$ Lower threshold (0.8)
dcp: Dispatcher's conrtrol parameters, a list of backend servers
scp: Server's conrtrol parameters, $RelayFrom$
loop
    $SUM_L \Leftarrow$ Sum of $L_i(t)$ for all i {In case of AR, SUM_L is a forecasted sum}
    $TC \Leftarrow N_A \cdot C$
    if $SUM_L > ut \cdot TC$ **then**
        Supplement an additional backend server X
        $N_A \Leftarrow N_A + 1$
        $dcp \Leftarrow dcp + X$
        $X.scp \Leftarrow$ The address of the original source server
    else if $SUM_L < lt \cdot (TC - C)$ **then**
        Release a node V
        $N_A \Leftarrow N_A - 1$
        $dcp \Leftarrow dcp - V$
    end if
    Sleep during p periods
    $t \Leftarrow t + p$
end loop

to other service in order to waste. Excess resources should be released gradually to avoid a sacrifice of service qualities by abruptly closing innocent client's open connections. In this context, it is important to choose the lowest utilized victim for release. Otherwise, some kinds of connection migration techniques should be devised. In our experiment, we simply assumed that the rejected clients would request again by client-side programs, so we did not consider the service distinction of releasing resources.

Also, we implemented a forecast-based prediction algorithm using an autoregressive model, AR(1). Even though we can see a time-of-day effect in Figure 7, the workload is more autocorrelated with short-term history within 30 minutes than the one-day-before long-term one. We saw that long-term forecasting is much less accurate than short-term forecasting. The period (around 30 minutes) that shows reasonable forecasting accuracy, is enough to handle reallocation; therefore, we used a simple short-term (20 seconds ahead) forecasting of AR(1) model with a 40 seconds history. The reallocation algorithm is similar to the threshold-based one, except using forecasted values rather than a simple sum of network usage.

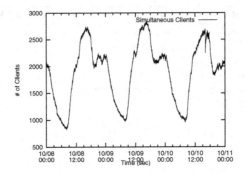

Fig. 7. Time-of-day effects in real traces from a popular audio streaming service

5   Evaluation

We have investigated real traces from a popular audio streaming service. The patterns of concurrent clients at October 9, 2003 are shown in Figure 7, and we can see the time-of-day effect. The number of listeners increased rapidly at the beginning of the day from 9 a.m.

We found that the steepest rate was 300 requests per minute, when we sampled traces every 10 seconds in October, 2003; therefore, we synthesized a workload that generates at the rate of 300 requests per minute for up to 3000 concurrent streams. The peak loads were sustained for 3 minutes, and then we removed clients' streams at 300 requests per minute as well as increasing rates. For a 128Kbps media stream, approximately 132Kbps bandwidth is required. The bandwidth includes client's TCP ACK and TCP/IP headers, so to follows the synthesized workload fully, more than 4 nodes are required, which are connected to 100Mbps network.

We observed that *discovery* takes quite a long but unpredictable time from 2 seconds to 20 seconds to discover the LAMA pool (LUS) since the JINI-based LAMA multicasts the discovery messages and waits for a few seconds until it gets discovery responses from the available LUS. However, after the discovery was completed, consequent communication did not produce latency. The discovery would be done only at the beginning, so that the unpredictable discovery time would not bother us.

The performance of the resource allocator is affected by monitoring intervals, and also by allocation overhead. In our Grand LAMA, a monitoring interval is 2 seconds. Allocation overhead was observed to be within 1 miniute.

The result of dynamic reallocation using threshold based reactive actions and prediction based proactive actions is shown in Figure 8. Since there are many noises in the monitored signal in the Figure 8-(a), the reactive reallocation shows resource cycling, in Figure 8-(c). On the other hands, the forecasted bandwidth usage in Figure 8-(d) seems to be filtered out. It shows a more stable resource reallocation than the reactive method.

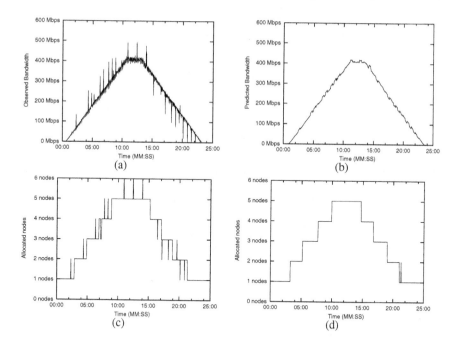

Fig. 8. Dynamic reallocation: (a) Network bandwidth usage observed by the Grand LAMA, (b) Predicted network bandwidth using AR(1) model (c) Threshold-based reactive reallocation, (d) AR(1) model based proactive reallocation

6   Conclusion

We have proposed a framework for the autonomous management of large-scale clustered internet servers. Our autonomous management is based on distributed agents known as LAMAs. We adopt JINI technology for a flexible agent, which means that static configurations of networks are removed. LAMA utilized many features provided by JINI infrastructure in building a spontaneous network securely.

Our prototype system provided autonomous management for streaming media service. In order to adapt to the changing workload patterns, LAMA sent monitored statistics on each node. The Grand LAMA gathered them, inferred resource utilization, made decisions to demand or release resources.

The live audio streaming service is a simple example in which resources are represented only with network bandwidth. In the case of complex services including a web application server, overall statistics on resource utilization would be required. One challenging problem is inferring a system's capacity without prior knowledge or human intervention. For this, it is required to estimate application performance, which is a client's perceived quality of service in the case of internet service. Also, it is highly demanded to optimize resource allocation in a shared environment by multiple services since they would compete for resources.

References

1. Joo Young Hwang, Chul Woo Ahn, Se Jeong Park, and Kyu Ho Park: A Scalable Multi-Host RAID-5 with Parity Consistency, IEICE Transactions on Information and Systems, E85-D 7 (2002) 1086-1092
2. Seung Ho Lim, et. al.: Resource Volume Management for Shared File System in SAN Environment, Proceedings of 16 th International Conference on Parallel and Distributed Computing Sytems, Reno, USA August (2003)
3. Yang Hwan Cho, Chul Lee and Kyu Ho Park: Contents-based Web Dispatcher (CBWD), Technical Report, EECS, KAIST, January (2001)
4. Chul Lee and Kyu Ho Park: Kernel-level Implementation of Layer-7 Dispatcher (KID), Technical Report, EECS, KAIST, December (2002)
5. Sang Seok Lim, Chul Lee, Chang Kyu Lee, and Kyu Ho Park: An Advanced Admission Control Mechanism for a Cluser-based Web Server System, Proceedings of IPDPS Workshop on Internet Computing and E-Commerce (2002)
6. Chul Lee, Sang Seok Lim, Joo Young Hwang, and Kyu Ho Park: A Ticket based Admission Controller(TBAC) for Users' Fairness of Web Server, Proceedings of 3rd Interneational Conference on Internet Computing (2002)
7. Redhat: Linux Advanced Server, http://www.redhat.com/
8. Jeffrey O. Kephart and David M. Chess: The Vision of Autonomic Computing, IEEE Computer, January (2003)
9. M. Parashar: AutoMate: Enabling Autonomic Applications, Technical Report Rutgers University, November (2003)
10. Sun Microsystems: JINI Network Technology, http://wwws.sun.com/software/jini/
11. PXES: Linux thin client project, http://pxes.sourceforge.net/
12. Etherboot: Remote netowrk boot project, http://www.etherboot.org/
13. Paul Anderson: LCFG A large-scale UNIX configuration system, http://www.lcfg.org/
14. Redhat: Kickstart, http://www.redhat.com/
15. Y. Diao, J. L. Hellerstein, S. Parekh, J. P. Bigus: Managing Web server performance with AutoTune agents, IBM Systems Journal Vol 42, No 1 136-149 (2003)
16. Paul Anderson and Patric Goldsack and Jim Paterson: SmartFrog meets LCFG: Autonomous Reconfiguration with Central Policy Control Proceedings of LISA XVII USENIX San Diego, USA (2003)
17. E. Lassettre, et.al.: Dynamic Surge Protection: An Approach to Handling Unexpected Workload Surges with Resource Actions that Have Lead Times, Proceedings of 14th IFIP/IEEE Disitributed Systems: Operations and Management, (2003)
18. Abhishek Chandra, Weibo Gong, and Prashant J. Shenoy: Dynamic Resource Allocation for Shared Data Centers Using Online Measurements, Proceedings of SIGMETRICS (2003)
19. icecast streaming media server: http://www.icecast.org
20. System Activity Reporter: http://perso.wanadoo.r/sebastien.godard

Event-Driven Management Automation in the ALBM Cluster System

Dugki Min[1] and Eunmi Choi[2]

[1] School of Computer Science and Engineering, Konkuk. University,
Hwayang-dong, Kwangjin-gu, Seoul, 133-701, Korea
dkmin@konkuk.ac.kr
[2] School of Business IT, Kookmin University,
Chongnung-dong, Songbuk-gu, Seoul, 136-702, Korea
emchoi@kookmin.ac.kr***

Abstract. One of major concerns on using a large-scale cluster system is manageability. The ALBM (Adaptive Load Balancing and Management) cluster system is an active cluster system that is scalable, reliable and manageable. We introduce the event-driven management automation by using the ALBM active cluster system. This architecture is based on an event management solution that is composed of event notification service, event channel service and event rule engine. Critical system state changes are generated as events and delivered to the event rule engine. According to the predefined management rules, some management actions are performed when a specific condition is satisfied. This event-driven mechanism can be used to manage the system automatically without human intervention. This event management solution can also be used for other advance management purpose, such as event correlation, root cause analysis, trend analysis or capacity planning. In order to support the management automation possibility, the experimental results are presented by comparing adaptive load balancing with non-adaptive load balancing mechanism. The adaptive scheduling algorithm that uses the event management automation results in a better performance compared to the non-adaptive ones for a realistic heavy-tailed workload.

1 Introduction

Future Internet services, such as Web Services[1] and ubiquitous services[2], become more dynamic and various in clients population size and in service pattern, due to their characteristics of dynamic integration. The unpredictable characteristic of Internet services requires their service platform architecture to be scalable and reliable. A cluster of distributed servers is a popular solution architecture that is scalable and reliable as well as cost-effective: we are able to easily add economical PC servers for more computing power and storages[3,4].

*** This work was supported by the Korea Science and Engineering Foundation (KOSEF) under Grant No. R04-2003-000-10213-0. This work was also supported by research program 2004 of Kookmin University in Korea.

A. Sahai and F. Wu (Eds.): DSOM 2004, LNCS 3278, pp. 135–146, 2004.

One of major concerns on using a large-scale cluster system is manageability[5]. Internet service providers normally have a number of clusters consisting in several tens of servers up to several hundreds of servers, which might have heterogeneous platforms. Managing a huge number of distributed servers is not an easy task. Even basic management operations such as monitoring resource status, upgrading O.S. and deploying a new service, are tasks that takes lots of efforts due to lack of global knowledge and controller, and the limitation of networked computers. Therefore, a management tool is necessary to manage a number of distributed clusters effectively.

The ALBM (Adaptive Load Balancing and Management) cluster system is an active cluster system that is scalable, reliable and manageable[6]. We developed this system for various research purposes, such as active traffic management, content-based delivery, middleware services for distributed systems, and proactive distributed system management. It is composed of L4/L7 active switches for traffic distribution and management agents and station for cluster system management. This system provides a single point of management console that shows system configuration as well as system states in real time. Using this consol, we can monitor the status of all resources and also control services on distributed nodes.

In this paper, we present an event-driven management automation architecture that is used in the ALBM cluster. This architecture is based on an event management solution that is composed of event notification service, event channel service and event rule engine. Critical system state changes are generated as events and delivered to the event rule engine. According to the predefined management rules, some management actions are performed when a specific condition is satisfied. This event-driven mechanism can be used to manage the system automatically without human intervention. This event management solution can also be used for other advance management purpose, such as event correlation, root cause analysis, trend analysis or capacity planning. In order to support the management automation possibility, the experimental results are presented by comparing adaptive load balancing with non-adaptive load balancing mechanism. The adaptive scheduling algorithm that uses the event management automation results in a better performance compared to the non-adaptive ones for a realistic heavy-tailed workload.

This paper is organized as follows. Section 2 describes the architecture of the ALBM cluster system. In the next section, we present the event management solution architecture. The event management solution is composed of three subsystems: event notification service, event channel service and event rule engine. In section 4, an experimental result of performance is given to illustrate the benefit of employing the event-drive management automation mechanism for adaptive workload scheduling. We conclude in the last section.

2   The ALBM Active Cluster Architecture

As introduced in our previous research[6], the ALBM (Adaptive Load Balancing and Management) active cluster system is composed of active switches, application servers, and the management station.

The Traffic Manager (TM) is an active switch that customizes traffic packets by controlling static or dynamic services. When client traffic arrives, the TM routes the client packet to one of the servers according to its scheduling algorithm and policy, performing network address translation on the packets flowing through them. In order to decide traffic routing, it collects the status information of collaborated servers periodically by contacting with the Node Agents from servers. Our TM provides several scheduling choices, such as Round-Robin, Least-Connected, Weighted, Response-time basis, and adaptive algorithms. Currently, our TM supports two types of L4 switching mechanisms: Direct Routing (DR) and Network Address Translation (NAT).

In a server node, a Node Agent (NA) runs as a system-level service. The NA takes two types of agent roles. First, it works as an agent for managing the managed node. It monitors and controls the system elements or the application service of the node, and collects the state and performance information on its local management information basis. It interacts with the M-Station, giving the local information and receiving administrative commands for management purposes. Second, it works as an agent for clustering. Regarding membership management, it sends heartbeat messages to one another. When there is any change in membership, the membership convergence mechanism is initiated by the master node. The master node is dynamically elected by members whenever there is no master node or there exists inconsistent master information among members. Besides, the NA provides L7 APIs to application services running on the node. Using the L7 APIs, the application service can access information of cluster configuration or the current states of cluster nodes to dynamically make a decision. Also, the NA finds the dynamic information of application states through the L7 APIs. This dynamic application information is used for system operation, such as load balancing, and for other performance management. The NA is implemented in Java to maximize portability and platform-independent characteristics.

The Management Station (M-Station) with a Web-based console provides a single point administration and the management environment of the entire ALBM active cluster system. Communicating with NAs on managed nodes, it monitors states of the system resources and application services of nodes and controls them for various management purposes, such as creating a cluster or stopping an application service. The major cluster administration task is the management tool governed by human system administrators with the help of the M-Station. By interacting with the master node of a cluster, the M-Station collects the dynamic state or performance information of the cluster system resources and application services. According to the management strategies and policies determined by the human administrator, the M-Station takes proper management actions, such as alarming events or removing failed nodes. The M-Station is implemented in Java.

2.1 Adaptive Load Balancing Mechanism

The adaptive scheduling algorithms in the ALBM active cluster system adjust their schedules, taking into accounts of dynamic state information of servers and applications collected from servers. The ALBM algorithm is as follows. By collecting appropriate information of server states, the NAs customize and store the data depending on the application architecture, machine types, and expectation of a system manager. Each NA decides if the current state is overloaded or underloaded by using upper or lower thresholds of resource utilization determined by system configuration and load balancing policies of cluster management. Each cluster has a coordinator that is in charge of any centralized task in the cluster. We call the coordinator a Master NA, and only the Master NA communicates with TM as the representative in order to control the incoming TMs traffic. After collecting state data of all NAs in a cluster, the Master NA reports the state changes to the TM. Thus, real-time performance data are transferred to the M-Station, and the state data of servers are reported to the TM. By using the state information reported by Master NAs, the TM adjusts traffics of incoming requests properly to balance server allocation. The TM does not allocate requests to overloaded servers, until the overloaded server state is back to a normal state. The scheduling algorithms are applied to the TM through the control of M-Station.

3 Event Management Solution

In this section, we introduce the overall architecture of event management solution: functionality and features of event notification service, event channel service, and event rule engine.

3.1 Event-Driven Management Automation Architecture

Event-driven management automation architecture finds the root cause of faults based on events occurred in several minutes and hours, and with the help of the event rule engine it resolves the faulty situation so that the human system administrator would not involve the system management manually. As shown in Figure 1, the management automation architecture manages the system at three levels in terms of management time: short-term, medium-term, and long term managements. Short-term management concerns real-time monitoring and immediate reaction. It monitors the system state changes, detecting system or service faults. Critical events are notified and the predefined corresponding management actions are automatically performed in real time. Event notification service and event rule engine are used at this level. Next, medium-term management concerns management intervention based on hourly information. In this level, event log accumulated in hours are analyzed to find event correlations and root causes of faults. In this analysis process, high-level events are generated and used by the event rule engine to perform management interventions automatically or human-interactively. Long-term management automation concerns analyzing and predicting the trend of system usage and capacity needed for the future. This long-term management uses the historical log data of system states and events over a couple of weeks and months.

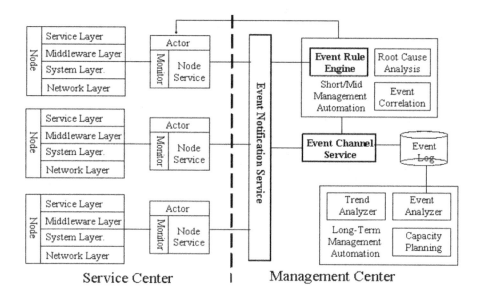

Fig. 1. Event-Based Management Automation Architecture

Figure 1 shows the system architecture of management automation. The architecture is decomposed into two subsystems. One is a service center that has a number of clusters, each of which is composed of a number of distributed servers. In each server, a NA(Node Agent) explained in Section 2 is running. It works as a management agent, monitoring and controlling system elements or application services on the node. The other is an event management center that manages the overall system. In our system, the event management center is in the M-Station. The event management center is composed of three event management solutions: Event Notification Service for event delivery, Event Channel Service for event asynchronous transmission, and Event Rule Engine for management automation. In this section, we describe the architectures of three event management services in detail.

3.2 Event Notification Service

Figure 2 shows the architecture of event notification service. It consists of three components: event communication infrastructure, event dissemination process, and event client. The event communication infrastructure is a communication infrastructure that facilitates transmitting events in various protocols and message formats. In Figure 2, the CI stands for the Communication Infrastructure. Determining a specific protocol and a message format to be used depends on the application type. In our current implementation, we provide three network protocols, i.e. TCP, UDP and a Reliable-UDP, and three message formats, i.e. a payload format, java object serialization, and a XML format. An event client is an event supplier that generates an event and sometimes becomes an event consumer that consumes an event. The event dissemination process is a service process that is shared by a number of event clients for disseminating events. The event dissemination is performed based on subject-oriented processing. In other words, an event supplier sends an event with a subject to an event dissemination process without specifying its target event consumers. The event dissemination process is responsible to deliver the subject-oriented event to appropriate target event consumers listening to the subject. By employing this shared dissemination process, individual event client can reduce a burden of disseminating tasks and thus improve the overall performance of event communication.

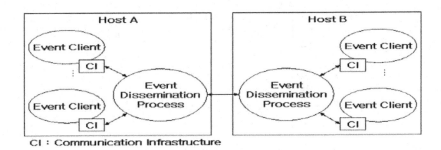

Fig. 2. Event Notification Service

Event Communication Infrastructure: Event communication infrastructure provides fundamental APIs of event transmission to event clients. Figure 3 (a) shows the structure of event communication infrastructure. Two main objects are Communication Object and DocFormat Object. *Communication Object (CO)* provides a unified communication environment that hides an underlying communication protocol and message format. The CO is implemented on top of TCP/IP protocol. Our current implementation provides communication of TCP, UDP and a reliable version of UDP. The *DocFormat Object* is used for message formatting of a CO. The DocFormat Object is in charge of converting an event object into a message format. The current version of DocFormat Object supports three kinds of message formats: a XML format, a Payload format, and an object serialization format. The lifecycle of Communication Object and DocFormat Object is managed by the *Communication Manager*. The *Configurator* is in charge of configuration management of all these components by using configuration information stored in a XML file.

Event Dissemination Process: The event dissemination process disseminates an event from an event supplier to multiple event consumers distributed in a number of hosts. Figure 3 (b) shows the structure of the event dissemination process that is composed of the following objects: Event Processor, Swappable Event Handler, Disseminator, Knowledge Manager, Dissemination Reconfigurator, Logger, Communication Infrastructure.

The *Event Processor* is the core object of the event dissemination process. It receives an event from an event supplier through the CO and activates filtering and dissemination logics. It also leaves log information. The *Swappable Event Handler* judges whether its sending event has a meaningful message. In order to judge the semantic of an event, a filtering logic is applied. A filter is implemented as a swappable component so that new filters can be added later on demand of future need. The *Disseminator* executes actual dissemination for a given event. It decides the destinations of the given event according to the event subject, and distributes the event to the target destinations. Dissemination information and rules used in the Disseminator are managed by the *Knowledge Manager*. This information can be changed by an administrator UI, or by the system environment that is dynamically changed over times. The *Dissemination Reconfigurator* is in charge of updating dissemination rules. The *Logger* records logs during processing event dissemination.

Our event dissemination process has three major characteristics. First, a supplier can disseminate events asynchronously. Asynchronous event dissemination implies that an event supplier can sends the next event without blocking as soon as it sends the previous event. It is because the event dissemination process runs on a separate proc-ess that is independent of the supplier process. The second characteristic is that a basic dissemination rule is based on the event subjects. This is, an event is transmitted without specifying its destinations. Where to be transmitted is decided by the dissemination process according to the event subject and the system environmental knowledge. The last characteristic is contents-based message filtering. During event handling, useless events can be filtered according to predefined filtering rules. This filtering process needs little computing power, but can reduce the wasted network bandwidth as well as computing resources. The rate of saving depends on the correctness of filtering rules and the situation of event generation.

3.3   Event Channel Service

The event notification service provides synchronous event communication: events are delivered to the destinations in real-time. However, this synchronous event

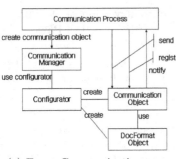

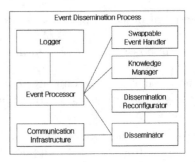

(a) Event Communication Infrastructure

(b) Event Dissemination Process

Fig. 3. Sub-components of Event Notification Service

communication is not useful when event consumers are not ready to receive. Thus, we need another communication mechanism that transmits events asynchronously. The *Event Channel Service* is such an asynchronous communication service that delivers events in a stored-and-forward mechanism. The advantage of using the event channel service is that event receivers can be decoupled from the event senders. Thus, the event receivers independently subscribe a number of event channels from which interesting events can be received. This event channel service is more valuable when the distributed servers of the cluster system are located over a number of network segments or some event receivers are available discontinuously in nature, such as mobile devices.

The event channel service has the structure as shown in Figure 4. The main components of this service are channels and its channel factory. A *channel* contains an event queue where events are stored and subscribed. The channel decouples event suppliers from event consumers, such that events can be delivered to whom subscribes the channel even though the event supplier does not know about any information of event consumers, such as their existences and locations. The *channel factory* is a factory that can create various types of channels according to QoS parameters. Each event consumer or event supplier accesses a channel through its own proxy. A proxy decides the type of event delivery: a push proxy delivers event in a push style and a pull proxy in a pull style. It also has filters inside so that an event customer can filter out a specific type of events. The proxies are created by *SupplierAdmin* or *ConsumerAdmin* according to the information of proxy QoS and management parameters.

3.4   Event Rule Engine

An event engine finds in real-time pre-defined event patterns among the generated event sequences and then it performs appropriate operations for the event patterns detected according to the event rules. Our event engine is a rule-based one that is different from the traditional rule-based engines[7] in two ways. First,

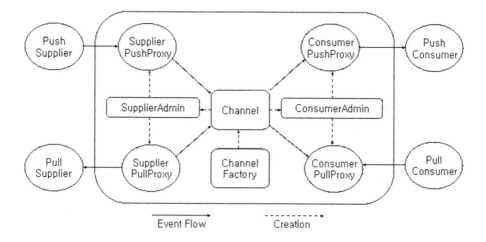

Fig. 4. Structure of Event Channel Service

its functionality can be expanded by loading hooking classes dynamically; each event condition and action is defined as a hook class that is dynamically loaded, compiled and integrated into as a part of the engine. Since we implement the engine in a high-level object-oriented language, Java, we can develop new conditions and actions easily in an object-oriented style. Another characteristic of our rule-engine is that it uses an event-token method for finding matching rules. As a conventional compiler searches a meaningful token in a collection of strings, this approach checks only pre-defined event tokens instead of searching exhaustively. An event token is specified in general BNF operators.

The event rule engine is composed of three packages: information package, engine package, and parser package. The *information package* manages the information of the engine and its rules, shown in the Figure 5 (a). The RuleInfo defines one or more rules. A rule definition has rule name, priority, event token name, condition code, and action code in Java. The rule definition is stored in a XML file. The *engine package*, shown in Figure 5 (b), is the encore part of event rule engine. The EventBuffer-Manager manages real-time events, and removes old events after the expiration date. The RuleInfoManager manages the RuleInfo explained above. The JavaCodeBuilder converts condition or action hook classes into executable java objects when the engine initially starts. The IcomparableCondition and IExeutableAction are the interfaces that the hook classes of condition and action should implement, respectively. Finally, the *parser package* organizes a parsing table by using rules defined in the information package, and finds applicable rules by searching the occurring events in real time.

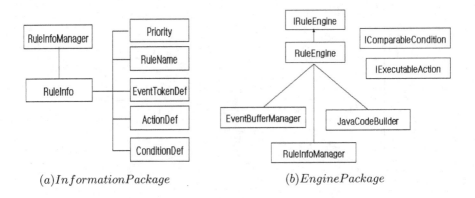

$(a) Information Package$ $(b) Engine Package$

Fig. 5. Event Rule Engine

3.5   Experimental Results

We perform experiments to illustrate the effect of applying event-driven management automation in the ALBM cluster system. In this purpose, we apply the mechanism of event-driven management automation to the workload scheduling process. In normal situation, request traffic is distributed to the servers according to a general workload scheduling algorithm, such as Round-Robin (RR) or Least Connection (LC) [8]. However, in overloaded situation NA generates an Overloaded event, and the event is delivered to the event rule engine in the M-Station through the event notification service. According to the pre-defined event rule, the overloaded server is removed from the scheduling server list. In our experiments we employ the RR as a general scheduling algorithm. The event-driven adaptive version of RR is called E-ARR (Event-driven Adaptive RR).

We make a realistic workload that is heavy-tailed. In literature, many researchers have concluded that general Internet traffics follow heavy tail distributions [9,10]. In order to make heavy-tailed e-commerce traffic, we mix an e-commerce traffic provided by Web Bench tool[11] and a memory-intensive traffic at the rate of 80% and 20%, respectively. The e-commerce traffic contains mixed requests of text pages, image files, and CGI requests. The memory-intensive traffic contains memory requests of random size and random duration. The random size of memory is randomly generated from 3M, 5MB, and 15MB and the memory holding duration is a random number between 0 to 10 seconds.

The workload requests are generated by tens of client machines, which are interconnected with a cluster of server nodes in the same network segment. Each server has PIII-866MHz and 128 MB memory. Each client has the same system configuration. The network bandwidth is 100MB. The number of connections per client thread is 4. The total running time is 2 minutes, think time between requests in a client is 10 seconds, and ramp-up time is 20 seconds.

Figure 6 and 7 show the experimental results of RR and E-ARR scheduling algorithms. The E-ARR achieved about 30 requests per second at 15 client threads; the RR achieved about 25 requests per second at 13 client threads in Figure 6. The E-ARR results in about 20% better performances than non-adaptive ones. For the same experiment, we present the throughput in Bytes per second in Figure 7. With the help of event-driven management automation, the adaptive mechanism could achieve better throughput by adjusting the load scheduling dynamically. According to the feature of Web Bench Tool, the next request from a client thread is generated after receiving the response of the previous request. That is, Web Bench Tool slows down sending requests, once the server starts to respond late. Due to this feature, all scheduling algorithms reduce their throughputs after reaching their peak performances. This makes points of results in the figure meaningless just after the peak performance points.

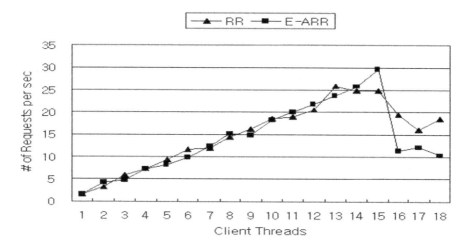

Fig. 6. Number of Requests per second of Event-driven Load Balancing

4   Conclusion

In this paper, we introduced the event-driven management automation by using the ALBM active cluster system. On top of the architecture of the ALBM cluster with its underlying components of the TM, and NAs, and M-Station introduced in Section 2, the ALBM cluster system provides the event management solution. The event-driven management automation architecture, event notification service, and event channel service, and event rule engine are introduced as the management service involved.

To support the management automation processing, the experimental results are presented by comparing adaptive load balancing with non-adaptive load balancing mechanism. The adaptive scheduling algorithm that uses the event management automation results in a better performance compared to the non-adaptive ones for a realistic heavy-tailed workload.

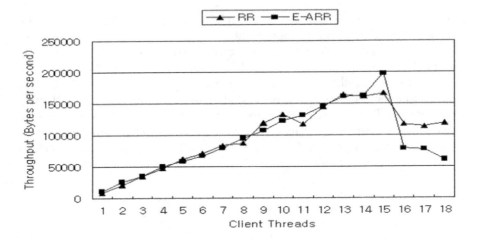

Fig. 7. Throughput (Bytes per second) of Event-driven Load Balancing

References

1. Patlak, C.; Bener, A.B.; Bingol, H.: Web service standards and real business scenario challenges, Euromicro Conference, 2003. Proceedings. 29th (2003), 421 - 424
2. YamazakiK.: Research directions for ubiquitous services, Applications and the Internet, 2004. Proceedings. 2004 International Symposium on , 26-30 Jan. (2004) 12
3. Trevor Schroeder, Steve Goddard, Byrav Tamamurthy: Scalable Web Server Clustering Technologies. IEEE Network, May/June (2000) 38-45
4. Rod Gamache, Rob Short, Mike Massa: Windows NT Clustering Service. IEEE Computer, Oct. (1988) 55-62
5. Valeria Cardellini, Emiliano Casaliccho, Michele Colajanni, Philip S. Yu: The State of the Art in Locally Distributed Web-server Systems. IBM Research Report, RC22209(W0110-048) October (2001) 1-54
6. Eunmi Choi, Dugki Min: A Proactive Management Framework in Active Clusters, LNCS on IWAN, December (2003)
7. Appleby, K., Goldszmidt, G., Steinder, M., "Yemanja - a layered event correlation engine for multi-domain server farms ", Integrated Network Management Proceedings, 2001 IEEE/IFIP International Symposium on , 2001 ,Page(s): 329 -344
8. Jeffray S. Chase: Server switching: yesterday and tomorrow. Internet Applications (2001) 114-123
9. Martin F. Arlitt, Carey L. Williamson: Internet Web Servers: Workload Characterization and Performance Implications. IEEE/ACM Transactions on Networking, Vol. 5, No. 5, October (1997) 631-645
10. Mor Harchol-Balter: Task Assignment with Unknown Duration. IEEE Distributed Computing Systems, Proceedings. (2000) 214 ?224
11. Web Bench Tool, http://www.etestinglabs.com

A Formal Validation Model for the Netconf Protocol

Sylvain Hallé[1], Rudy Deca[1], Omar Cherkaoui[1], Roger Villemaire[1], and
Daniel Puche[2]

[1] Université du Québec à Montréal
{halle,deca,cherkaoui.omar,villemaire.roger}@info.uqam.ca
[2] Cisco Systems, Inc.
dpuche@cisco.com

Abstract. Netconf is a protocol proposed by the IETF that defines a
set of operations for network configuration. One of the main issues of
Netconf is to define operations such as `validate` and `commit`, which currently lack a clear description and an information model. We propose in
this paper a model for validation based on XML schema trees. By using
an existing logical formalism called TQL, we express important dependencies between parameters that appear in those information models,
and automatically check these dependencies on sample XML trees in
reasonable time. We illustrate our claim by showing different rules and
an example of validation on a Virtual Private Network.[1]

1   Introduction

The area of network services has significantly developed over the past few years.
New and more complex services are deployed into the networks and strain the
resources. Network management capabilities have been pushed to their limits
and have consequently become more complex and error-prone. The lack of a
centralised information base, heterogeneity of all kinds (management tools, configuration modes, services, networks and devices) dependencies among service
components, increase of service complexity and undesired services interaction
are all possible causes of eventual configuration inconsistency.

Network management must constantly ensure the consistency of the network
configuration and of the deployed services. This task is difficult, since there is
no formal approach for ensuring the consistency of the network services, and
no adequate information model adapted to network configuration. Therefore,
adequate formalisms, information models and verification methods are required
that must capture the constraints and properties and ensure the integrity of the
network services.

The Netconf protocol [6] provides a framework for the network configuration
operations. Its `validate` operation checks syntactically and semantically the

---

[1] We gratefully acknowledge the support of the National Sciences and Engineering
Research Council of Canada as well as Cisco Systems for their participation on the
Meta-CLI project.

configurations. However, since the work is in progress, this operation is still too generic and not fully defined.

In this paper, we present an implementation of the Netconf `validate` capability that extends beyond simple syntax checking. From an XML Schema representing a given device configuration, we extract a tree structure and express validation rules in terms of these tree elements. By using an existing logical formalism called TQL [3], we express important, semantic dependencies between parameters that appear in those information models, and automatically check these dependencies against sample XML trees within reasonable delays. We illustrate our claim by showing different rules and and validating some of them on a sample Virtual Private Network configuration.

The network management community has proposed other approaches. Some frameworks under development consist in enriching an UML model with a set of constraints that can be resolved using policies. The *Ponder* language [9] is an example of a policy-based system for service management describing OCL constraints on a CIM model. The DMTF community as a whole is working on using OCL in conjunction with CIM. However, object-oriented concepts like class relationships are not sufficient for modelling dependencies between configuration parameters in heterogeneous topologies, technologies and device types.

On a different level, [10] defines a meta-model for management information that takes into account some basic semantic properties. [1] has also developed a formal model for studying the integrity of Virtual Private Networks. However, these approaches can be considered high-level, and ultimately need to be translated into concrete rules using device commands and parameters, in order to be effectively applied on real networks.

In section 2, we give a brief overview of the Netconf protocol and the modelling of XML configuration data in tree structures. Section 3 provides examples of different syntactical and semantic constraints of typical network services, while section 4 introduces the TQL tree logic and shows how these constraints become logical validation rules. Section 5 presents the results of the validation of several configuration rules referring to the *Virtual Private Network* service, and section 6 concludes and indicates further directions of research.

2   The Netconf Protocol

Netconf is a protocol currently under development aimed at defining a simple mechanism through which a network device can be managed [6]. It originates from the need for standardised mechanisms to manipulate the configuration of a network device. In a typical Netconf session, XML-encoded remote procedure calls (RPC) are sent by an application to a device, which in turn sends an RPC-reply giving or acknowledging reception of a full or partial XML configuration data set.

2.1   Netconf Capabilities

In order to achieve such standardised communication, the current Netconf draft defines a set of basic operations that must be supported by devices:

- get-config: Retrieves all or part of a specified configuration from a source in a given format
- edit-config: Loads all or part of a specified configuration to the specified target configuration
- copy-config: Creates or replaces an entire configuration with the contents of another configuration
- delete-config: Deletes a configuration datastore
- lock: Locks a configuration source
- unlock: Unlocks a configuration source
- get-all: Retrieves both configuration *and* device state information
- kill-session: Forces the termination of a Netconf session

Among other things, these base operations define a generic method enabling an application to retrieve an XML-encoded configuration of a Netconf-enabled device, apply modifications to it, send the updated configuration back to the device and close its session. Alternate configuration data sets can also be copied and protected from modifications. Figure 1 shows a typical RPC, and its reply by the device.

This set of basic operations can be further extended by custom, user-defined capabilities that may or may not be supported by a device. For example, version 2 of the Netconf draft proposes a command called validate, which consists in checking a candidate configuration for syntactical and semantic errors before effectively applying the configuration to the device.

The Netconf draft leaves a large margin in the definition of what validate must do. A device advertising this capability must be at least able to make simple syntax checking on the candidate configuration to be validated, thus preventing the most trivial errors to pass undetected. However, semantic validation of the configuration is left optional, but is equally important. For example, a simple syntax parser will not complain in the case of a breach of the VPNs isolation caused by address overlapping.

Moreover, although the draft currently defines the behaviour of the validation capability, it leaves open the question of the actual implementation of this capability on a network device. At the moment, there exists no systematic procedure for achieving such validation.

2.2   Modelling Configuration Data

One can remark from the example in figure 1 that the actual XML schema encoding the configuration data might depend on the device. Its format is specified by the XML namespace of the config tag in both the RPC and its reply.

```
<rpc message-id="105" xmlns="http://ietf.org/netconf/base/1.0">
  <get-config>
    <source>
      <running/>
    </source>
    <config xmlns="http://info.uqam.ca/schema/node-model"/>
    <format>xml</format>
  </get-config>
</rpc>


<rpc-reply message-id="105" xmlns="http://ietf.org/netconf/base/1.0">
  <config xmlns="http://info.uqam.ca/schema/node-model">
    <node>
      <name>ip_address</name>
      <value>10.0.0.0</value>
      <child></child>
    </node>
      ...
  </config>
</rpc-reply>
```

Fig. 1. Typical Netconf RPC and reply by the device

We briefly describe here the generic XML schema we use in our approach. All properties of a given configuration are described by hierarchically nested attribute-value pairs.

The basic element of our schema is the *configuration node*, which implements the concept of attribute-value pairs. A configuration node is in itself a small tree having a fixed shape. Its main tag is named `node`, and it must contain three children tags:

- `name`, that contains the character string of the name of the attribute
- `value`, that contains is the character string of the value of the attribute
- `child`, inside which can be nested as many other `node` structures as desired

For example, in figure 1, the boldface snippet of XML code inside the `config` tag of the `rpc-reply` shows a sample encoding of an IP address using this schema.

There is a direct correspondence between XML data and labelled trees. By viewing each XML tag as a tree node, and each nested XML tag as a descendent of the current node, we can infer a tree structure from any XML snippet. Figure 2 depicts the tree equivalent of the sample XML configuration code of figure 1.

The tree representation is a natural choice, since it reflects dependencies among components, such as the parameters, statements and features. For more information on the specific schema used in this work, we refer the reader to [8].

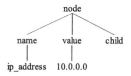

Fig. 2. A simple configuration node

3   Service Configuration Integrity

In this section, we examine the possible configuration inconsistencies that the validate capability could encounter and identify when performing verification on a device's candidate configuration. Our study is principally aimed at constraints arising from installation and management of network services.

A network service has a life cycle that starts from a customer's demand, and is followed by negotiation, provisioning and actual utilisation by the customer. Many steps of this life cycle demand that configuration information on one or more devices be manipulated. Configuration parameters can be created or removed, and their values can be changed according to a goal.

However, these manipulations must ensure that the global conditions ruling correct service operation and network integrity are fulfilled. Thus, the parameters and commands of the configuration affected by a service are in specific and precise dependencies. We present here two examples of dependencies, and deduce from each a configuration rule that formalises them.

3.1   Acces List Example

The existence or the possible state of a parameter may depend on another such parameter somewhere else in the configuration. As a simple example of this situation, consider extended IP access lists. Some network devices use these lists to match the packets that pass through an interface and decide whether to block or let them pass, according to packet information. The configuration of these extended IP access lists is variable. If the protocol used for packet matching is TCP or UDP, the port information is mandatory. If the protocol used is different, no port information is required.

Figure 3 shows two examples of access list entries, both of which are valid, although the trees that represent them do not have the same structure.

This example leads us to the formulation of a rule related to the proper use of access list entries:

Configuration Rule 1 *If the protocol used in an access list is TCP or UDP, then this access list must provide port information.*

3.2   Virtual Private Network Example

The previous example is nearest to mere syntax checking. On the other end of
the scope, there are more complex situations that can be encountered, where the
parameters of several devices supporting the same service are interdependent.
An example is provided by the configuration of a *Virtual Private Network* (VPN)
service [11], [12], [13].

VPNs must ensure the connectivity, reachability, isolation and security of customer sites over some shared public network. A VPN is a complex service that
consists of multiple sub-services and its implementation depends on the network
technology and topology. For instance, it can be provided at Layer 2 through virtual circuits (Frame Relay or ATM) or at Layer 3 using the Internet (tunnelling,
IPsec, VLAN, encryption). The MPLS VPN uses MPLS for tunnelling, an IGP
protocol (OSPF, RIP, etc.) for connectivity between the sites and the provider
backbone, and BGP for route advertisement within the backbone. The BGP process can be configured using the *direct neighbour* configuration method, which

```
<node>                                  <node>
  <name>protocol</name>                   <name>protocol</name>
  <value>tcp</value>                      <value>icmp</value>
  <child>                                 <child>
    <node>                                  <node>
      <name>source</name>                     <name>source</name>
      <value>10.0.0.1</value>                 <value>10.0.0.1</value>
      <child>                                 <child>
        <node>                                  <node>
          <name>wildcard</name>                   <name>wildcard</name>
          <value>0.0.255.255</value>              <value>0.0.255.255</value>
          <child/>                                <child/>
        </node>                                 </node>
      </child>                                 </child>
    </node>                                 </node>
    <node>                                </child>
      <name>operator</name>             </node>
      <value>eq</value>
      <child>
        <node>
          <name>port</name>
          <value>80</value>
          <child/>
        </node>
      </child>
    </node>
  </child>
</node>
```

Fig. 3. Excerpts of XML code for two access list entries

adds routing information necessary for the inter-connection on each provider edge router (PE-router).

Among other requirements of this method, an interface on each PE-router (for example, Loopback0), must have its IP address publicised into the BGP processes of all the other PE-routers' configurations using a neighbor command [11]. If one of these IP addresses changes the connectivity is lost and the VPN service functioning is jeopardised. Thus,

Configuration Rule 2 *In a VPN, the IP address of the* Loopback0 *interface of every PE-router must be publicised as a neighbour in every other PE-router.*

4   Validating Network Service Integrity

As we have shown in section 2, each XML snippet can be put in correspondence with a an equivalent labelled tree. Thus, configuration rules like those previously described can be translated into constraints on trees.

For example, Configuration Rule 2 becomes the following Tree Rule:

Tree Rule 2 *The* value *of the IP address of the interface* Loopback0 *in the PE* router_i *is equal to the IP address value of a* neighbor *component configured under the BGP process of any other PE* router_j*.*

This conversion has the advantage that many formalisms have been developed in recent years [2], [7] that allow such description. Among them, the Tree Query Logic (TQL) [3] is particularly noteworthy, as it supports both property and query descriptions. Hence one can not only check if a property is true or false, but also extract a subtree that makes that property true or false.

In the next section, we demonstrate this claim by showing how TQL can be used to perform validation on tree structures.

4.1   Expressing Configuration Rules

One can loosely define TQL as a description language for trees. Following logical conventions, we say that a tree t matches a given TQL expression e, which we write $t \models e$, when e is true when it refers to t. We also say that e *describes* t.

TQL is an extension of the traditional first-order logic suitable for description of tree-like structures. To allow branching, two operators are added: the edge ([ ]) and the composition (|).

First, the edge construct allows expression of properties in a descendent node of the current node. Thus, any TQL expression enclosed within square brackets is meant to describe the subtree of a given node. For example, the expression root[child] indicates that the root of the current tree is labelled "root", and that this root has only one child, labelled "child".

Second, the composition operator juxtaposes two tree roots; hence, the expression node[name | value] describes a tree whose root is "node", and whose two children are the nodes "name" and "value". Like other TQL operators, edge and composition are supported at any level of recursion.

The tree depicted in figure 2 is described by the following TQL expression:

$$
\begin{aligned}
&\text{node[} \\
&\quad \text{name[ip\_address]} \mid \\
&\quad \text{value[10.0.0.0]} \mid \\
&\quad \text{child} \quad]
\end{aligned}
$$

Remark the similarity between this TQL description and the XML code that actually encodes this structure in figure 1. This similarity is not fortuitous: it is in fact easy to see that edge and composition alone can describe any single XML tree.

However, interesting properties do not apply on a single tree, but rather to whole classes of trees. It is hence desirable to add the common logical operators to the syntax, whose intuitive meaning is given in table 1.

Table 1. Some of the most common TQL operators

- T: matches any tree.
- $\neg A$ (negation): if a tree does not match A, then it matches $\neg\ A$
- $A \vee B$ (disjunction): if a tree matches $A \vee B$, then either it matches A or it matches B (or both)
- $A \wedge B$ (conjunction): if a tree matches $A \wedge B$, then it must match both A and B
- % (label wildcard): % matches any label
- . (existence of a child): .x matches any tree whose root has a child labelled x
- !: (all children) : !$x[P]$ matches a tree if and only if all children labelled x verify property P

These operators allow us to express, for example, the fact that a given access list entry has a `port` node if its protocol is TCP or UDP:

```
<rule xmlns="http://info.uqam.ca/config-rules/access-list">
  node[
    name[protocol] |
    value[TCP ∨ UDP] |
    child[
        .node.child.node[.name[port]]]]]]
  ∨
  node[
    name[protocol] |
    value[¬ (TCP ∨ UDP)] |
    child]
</rule>
```

This rule stipulates that if the **node** defines a **protocol** whose **value** tag contains either TCP or UDP, then there must be a **child** tag containing a **port** node. On the contrary, if **protocol** is different from TCP and UDP, then the node has an empty **child** tag. We can check that both XML trees in table 1 verifiy the property. In the previous and all the following examples, the actual logical connectors (**and**, **or**, and the like) recognised by TQL have been replaced by their common symbols for improved clarity.

Notice that this rule is encapsulated inside an XML tag and is referenced in a global namespace, allowing for a uniform hierarchical classification of possible syntactical and semantic dependencies, and a better integration in Netconf's model. At the moment, we simply ignore this tag and submit the inside query to the standard TQL tool.

It is even possible to extract the protocol name using the query:

$$node[.value[\$P]]$$

which places into the variable $P the text inside the **value** tag for a given tree.

There are many other operators which further extend TQL's rich semantics [2], [3]. However, all of the interesting constraints we encountered in our work are expressible by means of those mentioned in this section. For more information related to TQL and its syntax, the reader is referred to [2] and [3].

4.2   The `validate` Operation

As there is a correspondence between XML and labelled trees, there is also a correspondence between tree rules and TQL queries. For example, Tree Rule 2 becomes the TQL query shown in figure 4.

The first part of the query retrieves all tuples of values of **device_name** and **ip_address** for the interface called **Loopback0**. These tuples are bound to the variables $N and $A. The second part of the query makes a further selection among these tuples, by keeping only those for which there exists a device whose name is not $N where $A is not listed as a neighbour. If the remaining set is empty, then all addresses are advertised as neighbours in all other devices, and the property is verified.

As one can see from the previous example, TQL queries can quickly become tedious to write and to manage. Fortunately, these queries can be automatically verified on any XML file by a software tool downloadable from TQL's site [15]. The tool loads an XML file and a set of TQL properties to be verified on that structure. It then makes the required validations and outputs the results of each query.

5   Results and Conclusions

As a concrete example of this method, we processed sample RPC-reply tags for multiple devices with constraints taken from the MPLS VPN service. These constraints have been checked in a different context in [8].

```
<rule xmlns="http://info.uqam.ca/config-rules/vpn/neighbours-declaration">
  network[
    .node[
      .name[device_name] |
        .value[$N] |
        .child.node[
          .name[interface_type] |
          .value[loopback] |
          .child.node[
            .name[interface_number] |
            .value[0] |
            .child.node[
              .name[ip_address] |
              .value[$A]]]]]
  ∧
  .node[
    .name[device_name] |
    .value[¬ $N]
    ∧
    ¬ .child.node[
      .name[bgp] |
      .value[%] |
      .child.node[
        .name[neighbor] |
        .child.node[
          .name[ip_address] |
          .value[$A]]]]]]
</rule>
```

Fig. 4. TQL query for Tree Rule 2

P1 If two sites belong to the same VPN, they must have similar route distinguisher and their mutually imported and exported route-targets must have corresponding numbers.

P2 The VRF name specified for the PE-CE connectivity and the VRF name configured on the PE interface for the CE link must be consistent.

P3 The VRF name used for the VPN connection to the customer site must be configured on the PE router.

P4 The interface of a PE router that is used by the BGP process for PE connectivity, must be defined as BGP process **neighbor** in all of the other PE routers of the provider.

P5 The address family vpnv4 must activate and configure all of the BGP neighbours for carrying only VPN IPv4 prefixes and advertising the extended community attribute.

All these properties were translated into TQL queries, and then verified against sample XML schema trees of sizes varying from about 400 to 40000

XML nodes. One query verified only P1 and had a size of 10 XML nodes; the second query incorporated all the previous five rules and was 81 XML nodes long. Table 2 shows validation time for these different settings.

Table 2. Validation time for different configuration and rule sizes

Configuration size	Query size	Validation time (s)
413	10	0,04
413	81	0,24
1639	10	0,06
1639	81	0,47
3681	10	0,09
3681	81	0,84
6539	10	0,12
6539	81	1,29
10213	10	0,15
10213	81	1,87
40823	10	0,52
40823	81	7,03

All queries have been validated on an AMD Athlon 1400+ system running on Red Hat Linux 9. Validation time for even the complete set of constraints is quite reasonable and does not exceed 8 seconds for a configuration of more than 40000 nodes. As an indication, a device transmitting a configuration of this size via an SSH connection in a Netconf `rpc-reply` tag would send more than 700 kilobytes of text.

For all these sets, TQL correctly validated the rules that were actually true, and identified the different parts of the configurations that made some rules false, if any.

6   Conclusions

We have shown in this paper a model for the `validate` capability proposed by the current Netconf draft. Based on an existing logical formalism called TQL that closely suits the XML nature of the protocol, this model extends beyond simple syntax checking.

We stress the fact that the validation concept must not be limited simply to mere syntax checking and should encompass semantic dependencies that express network functions and rules. Formalisms such as the Common Information Model (CIM) [5] and Directory Enabled Networking (DEN) [14] could be further exploited to this end.

The VPN case illustrated in the previous sections indicates that using a subset of a query language like TQL is sufficient to handle complex semantic dependencies between parameters on interdependent devices.

The results obtained suggest that this framework could be extended to model most, if not all, such dependencies in device configurations. It is therefore a good candidate as a template for a formal Netconf model of the `validate` capability.

References

1. Bush, R., Griffin, T.: Integrity for Virtual Private Routed Networks. Proc. IEEE INFOCOM (2003)
2. Cardelli, L.: Describing semistructured data. SIGMOD Record, 30(4) (2001) 80–85
3. Cardelli, L., Ghelli, G.: TQL: A query language for semistructured data based on the ambient logic. Mathematical Structures in Computer Science (to appear).
4. Deca, R., Cherkaoui, O., Puche, D.: A Validation Solution for Network Configuration. Communications Networks and Services Research Conference (CNSR 2004), Fredericton, N.B. (2004)
5. DSP111, DMTF white paper, Common Information Model core model, version 2.4, August 30, 2000.
6. Enns, R.: NETCONF Configuration Protocol. Internet draft, Feb. 2004. http://www.ietf.org/internet-drafts/draft-ietf-netconf-prot-02.txt
7. Gottlob G., Koch, C.: Monadic queries over tree-structured data. LICS'02 (2002) 189–202
8. Hallé, S., Deca, R., Cherkaoui, O., Villemaire, R.: Automated Validation of Service Configuration on Network Devices. Proc. MMNS 2004 (2004) (to appear).
9. Lymberopoulos, L., Lupu, E., Sloman, M.: Ponder Policy Implementation and Validation in a CIM and Differentiated Services Framework. NOMS 2004 (2004)
10. López de Vergara, J.E., Villagrá, V.A., Berrocal, J.: Semantic Management: advantages of using an ontology-based management information meta-model. HP-OVUA 2002 (2002)
11. Pepelnjak, I., Guichard, J.: MPLS VPN Architectures, Cisco Press (2001)
12. Rosen, E., Rekhter, Y.: BGP/MPLS VPNs. RFC 2547 (1999)
13. Scott, C., Wolfe, P. Erwin, M.: Virtual Private Networks, O'Reilly (1998)
14. Strassner J., Baker F.: Directory Enabled Networks, Macmillan Technical Publishing (1999)
15. TQL web site, Università di Pisa. http://tql.di.unipi.it/tql/

Using Object-Oriented Constraint Satisfaction for Automated Configuration Generation

Tim Hinrichs[1], Nathaniel Love[1], Charles Petrie[1], Lyle Ramshaw[2],
Akhil Sahai[2], and Sharad Singhal[2]

[1]Stanford University, CA, USA
[2]HP Laboratories, Palo-Alto, CA, USA
asahai@hpl.hp.com

Abstract. In this paper, we describe an approach for automatically generating configurations for complex applications. Automated generation of system configurations is required to allow large-scale deployment of custom applications within utility computing environments. Our approach models the configuration management problem as an Object-Oriented Constraint Satisfaction Problem (OOCSP) that can be solved efficiently using a resolution-based theorem-prover. We outline the approach and discuss both the benefits of the approach as well as its limitations, and highlight certain unresolved issues that require further work. We demonstrate the viability of this approach using an e-Commerce site as an example, and provide results on the complexity and time required to solve for the configuration of such an application.

1 Introduction

Automated resource configuration has gained more importance with the advent of utility computing initiatives such as HP's Utility Data Centerproduct, IBM's "on-demand" computing initiative, Sun's N1 vision, Microsoft's DSI initiative and the Grid initiative within the Global Grid Forum. All of these require large resource pools that are apportioned to users on demand. Currently, the resources that are available to these resource management systems are "raw" computing resources (servers, storage, or network capacity) or simple clusters of machines. The user still has to manually install and configure applications, or rely upon a managed service provider to obtain pre-configured systems.

Creating custom environments is usually not possible because every user has different requirements. Managed service providers rely on a small set of pre-built (and tested) application environments to meet user needs. However, this limits the ability of users to ask for applications and resources that have been specially configured for them. In our research, we are focusing on how complex application environments (for example, an e-Commerce site) can be automatically "built-to-order" for users from resources represented as hierarchies of objects. In order to create a custom solution that satisfies user requirements, many different considerations have to be taken into account. Typically, the underlying resources have technical constraints that need to be

A. Sahai and F. Wu (Eds.): DSOM 2004, LNCS 3278, pp. 159–170, 2004.
© IFIP International Federation for Information Processing 2004

met in order for valid operations—not all operating systems will run on all processors, and not all application servers will work with all databases. In addition, system operators may impose constraints on how they desire such compositions to be created. Finally, the users themselves have requirements on how they want the system to behave, and can specify these as arbitrary constraints in the same language the system operators do. These rich and diverse constraints make automating the design, deployment and configuration of such complex environments a hard problem.

In the course of investigating this problem, we encountered a powerful formalism able to model configuration management problems that are inherently object-oriented: the Object-Oriented Constraint Satisfaction Problem (OOCSP). As noted above, the utility computing environment is significantly complicated by allowing the customers to arbitrarily constrain the systems produced—there are no set number of dials they can adjust, they in fact have complete freedom to dictate all aspects of the system configuration. In the case of these arbitrary object-oriented configuration management problems, the OOCSP formalism offers a domain-independent method for producing solutions. This paper explains the result of our work on two parallel goals: solving utility computing instances with OOCSPs, and using utility computing to investigate the capabilites of the formalism.

2 Problem Definition

A number of languages/standards [1] [2] exist which can be used to describe resource configurations. Of these, the Common Information Model (CIM) of the Distributed Management Task Force (DMTF) [3] is widely used in the industry to represent resource configurations. In CIM, the type model captures the resource types, and the inheritance, aggregation, and association relationships that exist between them. A coooresponding instance model describes the Instances of the classes with the attribute values filled in. Typically, the resource types deal with a large number of classes, because the models have to describe not only the "raw" resources, but also those that can be composed out of those resource types.

When resources are combined to form other higher-level resources, a variety of rules need to be followed. For example, when operating systems are loaded on a host, it is necessary to validate that the processor architecture assumed by the operating system is indeed the architecture of the host. Similarly, when an application tier is composed from a group of servers, it may be necessary to ensure that all network interfaces are configured to be on the same subnet or that the same version of the application is loaded on all machines in the tier. To ensure correct behavior of a reasonably complex application, several hundred such rules may be necessary. This is further complicated by the fact that a large fraction of these rules are not inherent to the resources, but depend on preferences (policies) provided by the system operator or indeed, by the customer as part of the request itself.

The current CIM meta-model does not provide the capability to capture such rules. To accommodate these rules, we have extended the CIM meta-model to associate policies with the resource types. These policies capture the technical constraints and choices made by the operators or administrators that need to be obeyed by every instance of the associated class. By capturing the constraints on what is possible (or permitted) for the values of the model attributes within an instance of policy that is attached to the resource type (as opposed to within the model itself), it becomes possible to customize the configurations that are valid without constantly extending the models. The users can request customization of particular resources from the available resource types by specifying additional constraints[1] on their attribute values and on their arrangement in the system. These requests could be for instances of "raw" resources or for composite resources. Our goal is to automatically generate a system configuration by selecting the appropriate resource classes and assigning values to their attributes so that all constraints specified in the underlying resource models are satisfied.

3 A Running Example

We will start by describing a particular utility computing problem that will be used for illustration throughout the paper. We will be using a more compact representation [4] for MOF specifications and their associated constraints. In all that follows we represent a constraint on a particular MOF specification by surrounding it with the keyword *satisfy* and including it within the specification itself. The example in question models a collection of hardware and software components that can be assembled to build an e-Commerce site. The objects themselves can be defined hierarchically with e-Commerce at the top. An e-Commerce site includes three tiers of servers, including web, database, and applications servers; additional resources include a variety of operating systems, software applications, computers, and networking components. The class definitions in this environment contain the expected compositional constraints, like restricting mySQL to Linux servers. The example also contains mathematical constraints—resources have cost attributes with values constrained to be the sum of the costs of the objects contained within the resource. One portion of a class definition from this example—the DatabaseServer class—appears below. It is the compressed version of the example in Section 2.

```
class DatabaseServer
{
  type: String;
  server: Server;
  swImage: InstalledSoftware;
  satisfy (swImage.name == "Database");
  satisfy ((type == "Oracle") ∨ (type == "mySQL"));
  satisfy ((type == "Oracle") ⇒ (swImage.version == 9));
  satisfy ((type == "mySQL") ⇒ (server.osImage.name ==
"Linux"));
}
```

---

[1] The terms policy, constraint, and rule are frequently used interchangeably. From this point forward we will use only the term constraint.

User requests in our example consist of a distinguished target class usually called main, which contains a variable of type eCommercesite.␣Any␣user␣require-ments␣appear␣as␣constraints␣on␣that␣variable. For example, the request

```
main {
    ecomm: eCommercesite;
    satisfy (ecomm.tier1.numservers >= 10);
    satisfy (ecomm.tps == 5000);
}
```

asks for an instance of an e-Commerce site with at least ten servers in tier1, support-ing 5,000 transactions per second. A solution is simply an instance of an eCommerce-site object, represented just as DatabaseServer is represented above. Thus generating an e-Commerce configuration amounts to building an instance of the eCommercesite class.

The full example includes around twenty of these class definitions, ranging in com-plexity from an e-Commerce site down to specifications for a particular type of com-puter. Snippets from this problem will show up repeatedly in what follows as illustra-tion, but the principles illustrated will be applicable to a broad range of configuration management problems.

4   Configuration Management as an OOCSP

As shown above, configuration management problems such as utility computing can often be modeled as a hierarchy of class definitions with embedded constraints. Ab-stracting away from the details of any particular problem can allow a more compre-hensive understanding of not only the problem but also the possible routes for solu-tion. Paltrinieri [10] outlines the notion of an Object-Oriented Constraint Satisfaction Problem (OOCSP), which turns out to be a natural abstraction for a broad class of configuration management problems. Similarly, Alloy [6] uses an object oriented specification for describing and analyzing software models.

An OOCSP is defined by a set of class definitions, a set of enumerations, and a distinguished target class, much like main in a JAVA program. Each class definition includes an ordered set of variables, each with a declared type, and a set of constraints on those variables; each class also has a name, a set of super classes, and a function Dot (.) that gives access to its variables. An enumeration is simply a set of values; declaring a variable as an enumeration forces the variable to be assigned to one of the elements in that set. A solution to an OOCSP is an instance of the target class. In an OOCSP, the constraints are embedded hierarchically so that if an object is an instance of the target class (i.e. it satisfies all the constraints within the class) it includes in-stances of all the target's subclasses, which also satisfy all constraints within those classes. In this view of the problem, the sources of the constraints—from customers, administrators, or system designers—is no longer important, and any solution must satisfy all constraints, regardless of origin. The production of constraints forms a user interface problem that is outside the scope of this investigation.

The OOCSP for the e-Commerce example includes class definitions for eCommer-cesite, DatabaseServer, Server, and InstalledSoftware among others. The class definitions contain a set of variables, each with a declared type. DatabaseServer includes (in order) a String variable `type`, a variable `server` of type Server, and a variable `swI-mage` of type InstalledSoftware. One of the constraints requires the name component of `swImage` to be "Database". It has no superclasses, and the function Dot is defined implicitly.

While it is clear how to declare variables within a class, many options exist for how to the express constraints on those variables. In our examples we use standard logical connectives, like ∨ and ⇒, to mean exactly the same thing they do in propositional and first-order logic. We have formally defined the language chosen for representing constraints both by giving a logician a particular vocabulary and by giving a grammar; these definitions are virtually identical.

The constraint language includes all quantifier-free first-order formulas over the following vocabulary.

1. r is a relation constant iff r is the name of a class, equality or an inequality symbol
2. f is a function constant iff f is the binary Dot or a mathematical function
3. v is a variable iff v is declared as a variable or starts with a letter from the end of the alphabet, e.g. x, y, z
4. c is an object constant iff c is an atomic symbol and not one of the above

The constraints seen in the DatabaseServer example are typical and have been explained elsewhere. Two types of constraints that do not appear in our example deserve special mention. Consider the following snippet of a class definition.

```
x: DatabaseServer;
y: DatabaseServer;
x == y;
```

We define equality to be syntactic; two objects are equal exactly when all their properties are equal. That means that two objects that happen to have all the same properties are treated as essentially the same object. The exception to this interpretation of equality is arithmetic. Not only is 7==7 satisfied, but so is 2*2==4, as one would hope, even though syntactically 4 is different than 2*2.

The other type of notable constraint is more esoteric; consider the following.

```
x: Any;
y: Any;
satisfy (DatabaseServer("Oracle", x, y));
```

This constraint requires x and y to have values so that DatabaseServer("Oracle", x, y) is a valid instance of DatabaseServer. These constraints become valuable when one wants to define an object of arbitrary size, like a linked list:

```
class List {
        data: Any;
        tail: Any;
        satisfy    ((tail    ==    nil)    ∨    List(tail.data,
tail.tail));
}
```

This List class is recursively defined, with a base case given by the disjunct `tail ==` `nil`; the recursive case is the second disjunct, which requires `tail` itself to be a List object. Our constraint language allows us to define these complex objects and also write constraints on those objects.

Given what it means to satisfy a constraint we can precisely describe what it means for an object to be an instance of a particular class. An instance of a class `T is an` `ordered set of objects, one for each variable, such that` (1) the object assigned to a variable of type R is an instance of R and (2) the constraints of T are satisfied. The base case for this recursive definition is the enumerations, which are effectively objects without subcomponents. Objects are instances of an enumeration if they are one of the values listed in that enumeration.

To illustrate, an instance of a DatabaseServer is an object with three components: an instance of String, an instance of Server, and an instance of InstalledSoftware. Those components must satisfy all the constraints in the DatabaseServer class. The instance of Server must likewise include some number of components that together satisfy all the constraints within Server. The same applies to InstalledSoftware.

This section has detailed how one can formulate configuration management problems as OOCSPs[2]. The next section confronts building a system to solve these configuration management problems.

5 Solving Configuration Management Problems by Solving OOCSPs

Our approach to solving configuration management problems is based on an OOCSP solver. The two main components of the system communicate through the OOCSP formalism. The first component includes a model of the utility computing environment at hand. It allows administrators to change and expand that model, and it allows users to make requests for specific types of systems without worrying too much about that model. The second component is an OOCSP solver based on a first-order resolution-style [12] theorem prover Epilog, provided by the Stanford Logic Group. It is treated as a black box that takes an OOCSP as input and returns a solution if one exists. The rest of this paper focuses on the design and implementation of the OOCSP solver and discusses the benefits and drawbacks in the context of configuration management.

The architecture of the OOCSP solver can be broken down into four parts. Given a set of class definitions, a set of enumerations, and a target class, a set of first-order logical sentences is generated. Next, those logical sentences are converted to what is known as clausal form, a requirement for all resolution-style theorem provers. Third, a host of optimizations are run on the resulting clauses so that Epilog can more easily find a solution. Lastly, Epilog is given the result of the third step and asked to find an instantiation of the analog of the target class. If such a solution exists, Epilog returns an object that represents that instantiation, which by necessity includes instantiations

---

[2] We believe the notion of an OOCSP is equivalent to a Context Free Grammar in which each production rule includes constraints that restrict when it can be applied.

of all subcomponents of the target class, instantiations of all the subcomponents' subcomponents, and so on. Epilog also has the ability to return an arbitrary number of solutions or even all solutions. Because the conversion to clausal form is mechanical and the optimizations are Epilog-specific, we will discuss in detail only the translation of an OOCSP to first-order logic, the results of which can be used by any first-order theorem prover.

Consider the class definition for DatabaseServer. Recall we can represent an instance of a class with a term, e.g.

```
Database-
Server("Oracle",Server(...),InstalledSoftware(...))
```

Notice this is intended to be an actual instance of a DatabaseServer object. It includes a type, Oracle, and instances of the Server class and the InstalledSoftware class. To define which objects are instances of DatabaseServer given our representation for such instances we begin by requiring the arguments to the DatabaseServer term be of the correct type.

```
DatabaseServer.instance( DatabaseServer(x, y, z) ) ⇐
        String.instance(x) ∧
        Server.instance(y) ∧
        InstalledSoftware.instance(z) ∧ ...
```

But because a DatabaseServer cannot be composed of any String, any Server instance, and any InstalledSoftware instance this sentence is incomplete. The missing portion of the rule represents the constraints that appear within the DatabaseServer class definition. These constraints can almost be copied directly from the original class definition giving the sentence shown below.

```
DatabaseServer.instance( DatabaseServer(x, y, z) ) ⇐
        (String.instance(x) ∧
        Server.instance(y) ∧
        InstalledSoftware.instance(z) ∧
        z.name == "Database" ∧
        ((x == "Oracle") ∨ (x == "mySQL")) ∧
        ((x == "Oracle") ⇒ (z.version == 9)) ∧
        ((x == "mySQL") ⇒ (y.osImage.name == "Linux")) )
```

Similar translations are done for all class definitions in the OOCSP.

Once these translations have been made for all classes and enumerations in the OOCSP to first-order logic, the conversion to clausal form is entirely mechanical and a standard step in theorem-proving. For any particular class definition these first two steps operate independently of all the other class definitions; consequently, if an OOCSP has been translated once to clausal form and changes are made to a few classes, only those altered classes must undergo this transformation again.

Once the OOCSP has been converted into clausal form the result is a set of rules that look very similar to the sentence defining DatabaseServer above. Several algorithms are run on these rules as optimizations. These algorithms prune unnecessary conjuncts, discard unusable rules, and manipulate rule bodies and heads to improve efficiency in the final step. Doing all this involves reasoning about both syntactic equality and the semantics of the object-oriented Dot function. These algorithms greatly reduce the number and lengths of the rules, consequently reducing the search space without eliminating any possible solutions. Some of these optimizations are global, which means that if any changes are made to the OOCSP those algorithms must be run again. Because one of the optimizations pushes certain types of constraints down into the hierarchy, it is especially important to apply it once a new query arrives.

The final step invokes Epilog by asking for an instantiation of the (translated) target class. If the target class were DatabaseServer, the query would ask for an instance x such that DatabaseServer.instance(x) is entailed by the rules left after optimization, i.e. x must be an instance of DatabaseServer. Moreover one can ask for an arbitrary number of these instances or even all the instances.

6   Consequences of Our Approach

We have made many choices in modeling and solving problems in the configuration management domain, both in how we represent a configuration management problem as an OOCSP and in how we solve the resulting OOCSP. This section explores those choices and their consequences.

6.1 Modeling Configuration Management Problems

The choice of the object-oriented paradigm is natural for configuration management-- coupling this idea with constraint satisfaction leads to easier maintenance and adaptation of the problem so modeled. Our particular choice of language for expressing these constraints has both benefits and drawbacks and our decision to define equality syntactically may raise further questions.

Benefits

Modeling a configuration management problem as an OOCSP gives benefits similar to those gained by writing software in an object-oriented language. Class definitions encapsulate the data and the constraints on that data that must hold for an object to be an instance of the class. One class can inherit the data and constraints of another, allowing specializations of a more general class to be done efficiently. Configuration management naturally involves reasoning about these hierarchically designed objects; thus it is a natural fit with the object-oriented paradigm.

Modeling configuration management as a constraint satisfaction problem also has merits, mostly because stating a CSP is done declaratively instead of imperatively. Imperative programming requires explaining *how* a change in one of an object's fields must change the data in its other fields to ensure the object is still a valid instance. Doing this declaratively requires only explaining *what* the relationship between the fields must be for an object to be a valid instance. How those relationships are maintained is left unspecified. An imperative program describes a computational process, while the declarative version describes the results of that computational process.

Design configuration problems have previously been addressed in three primary ways. The first is as a standard CSP problem. The OOCSP has the obvious advantage that configuration problems are easier to formulate as a set of component classes and constraints among them. In particular, a CSP requires the explicit enumeration of every possible variable that could be assigned and the OOCSP does not.

Design configuration has also been attempted with expert systems [12] but domain knowledge rules are too difficult to manage because of implicit control dependencies, so the approach does not scale. The OOCSP has the advantage that the formalism is clear and the ordering of the domain knowledge has no impact on the set of possible solutions. A third approach has been to add search control as heuristics to a structure of goals and constraints [8] [9], but this approach is more complex and slower than the OOCSP approach.

Limitations

The choices outlined above do have drawbacks. In particular first-order logic is very expressive, so using it as our constraint language comes at a cost: first-order logic is fundamentally undecidable—there is no algorithm that can ensure it will always give the correct answer and at the same time halt on all inputs. If there is a solution it will be found in a finite amount of time; otherwise the algorithm may run forever. We have not yet determined the decidability and complexity of the subset of first-order logic we are using in our research. Simpler languages might lead immediately to certain complexity bounds, but as mentioned above we are interested in solving problems where we are selecting both the classes that need to be instantiated, as well as the number of instances of those classes based on arbitrary constraints. We have chosen to start with a language that is expressive enough to write such constraints and a natural fit for the utility computing problem, but as currently written it may be too expressive. We can restrict this language further if decidability or complexity become practical issues for particular applications. Certain subclasses of OOCSPs are polynomial, others are NP-Complete, and others even worse; our approach encompasses a range of results, and the right balance between expressivity and computability must be carefully considered when scaling to more complex utility computing instances.

6.2 Solving OOCSPs by Translation to First-Order Logic

Once a configuration problem has been modeled as an OOCSP, several options are available for building a configuration that meets the requirements embedded in that OOCSP. We have chosen to find such configurations by first translating the OOCSP into first-order logic sentences and then invoking a resolution-based theorem prover. To rehash the system's architecture, the input to the system is an OOCSP. That input is first translated into first-order logic, which is in turn translated to a form suitable for resolution-style theorem provers; this form is then optimized for execution in Epilog.

Benefits

Translating an OOCSP into first order logic can be done very quickly, in time linearly proportional to the number of class definitions. Both this translation and the one from first-order logic to clausal form can be performed incrementally; each class definition is translated independently of the others. The bulk of the optimization step can also be run as each class is converted, but the global optimizations can be run only once the user gives the system a particular query. These optimizations aggressively manipulate the set of constraints so it is tailored for the query at hand.

Using Epilog as the reasoning engine provides capabilities common to first-order theorem provers. Epilog can both produce one answer and all answers. More interestingly it can produce a function that with each successive call returns a new solution, giving us the ability to walk through as much or as little of the search space as needed to find the solution we desire. As we will discuss in Section 7, Epilog can at times find solutions very rapidly.

Limitations

While the translation from an OOCSP into first-order logic requires time linearly proportional to the size of the OOCSP, our use of a resolution-based theorem prover requires those first-order sentences be converted into *clausal-form.* There may be an exponential increase in the number of sentences when doing this conversion; thus not only the time but also the space requirements can become problematic.

Another source of discontent is the number of solutions found by Epilog. Many theorem provers treat basic mathematics, addition, multiplication, inequality, etc., *with* procedural attachments. This means that if one of the constraints requires $x < 5$, the theorem prover will find solutions only in those branches of the search space where x is bound to a number that happens to be less than five. If x is not assigned a value the theorem prover will not arbitrarily choose one for it. Our theorem prover, Epilog, has these same limitations.

Yet another problem with using first-order logic is derived from one of the benefits mentioned in Section 6.1. It is as expressive as any programming language, i.e. first-order logic is Turing complete. That means answering queries about a set of first-order sentences is formally undecidable; if the query can be answered positively, Epilog will halt. If the query cannot be answered positively Epilog may run forever. This problem is common to all algorithms and systems that soundly and completely answer queries about first-order sentences. But it seems undecidability may also be a property of OOCSPs; our conversion to first order logic may not be overcomplicating the problem of finding a solution at all. Theoretically our approach to solving OOCSPs may turn out to be the right one; however, from a pragmatic standpoint many OOCSPs will simply be hierarchical representations of CSPs, which means such OOCSPs are decidable.

7   Experimental Results and Future Work

The OOCSP solver architecture is a fairly simple one, and for our running example results are promising, even at this early stage. Translating the OOCSP with eighteen classes into clausal form requires four to five minutes and results in about 1150 rules. The optimization process finishes in five seconds and reduces the rule count to around 620. Those eighteen class definitions and the user request allow for roughly 150 billion solutions; in other words, our example is under-constrained. That said, Epilog finds the first solution in 0.064 seconds; it can find 39000 solutions in 147 seconds before filling 100 MB of memory, which is a rate of 1000 solutions every 3-4 seconds. If we avoid the memory problem by not storing any solutions but only walking over them, it takes 114 seconds to find those same 39000 answers--the number of answers returned by Epilog is entirely up to the user. These are results for a single example. More complicated examples are the subject of future work[3].

The limitations discussed in Section 6 present a host of problems: possible undecidability, exponential blowup when converting to clausal form, inexpressiveness of syntactic equality, incompleteness of mathematical operators. Undecidability might be dealt with by restricting the constraint language significantly. Clausal form is fundamental to using a resolution-based theorem prover; changing it to eliminate the accompanying conversion cost would require building an entirely new system. Syntactic equality, while less expressive than we might like, may be sufficient for solving the class of problems we want to solve.

The system configuration problem, however, is not the only problem to be solved when building an automatic configuration management service. In order to use one of the configurations the system has produced, that configuration must be coupled with a workflow—a structured set of activities—that will bring the configuration on line [10]. We plan to use situation calculus [11], which has been explored and expanded for 35 years. The convenient part is that an OOCSP is expressive enough to embed these carefully crafted sentences. Thus one need only write the correct OOCSP to produce both a configuration and a workflow. We are currently investigating this idea.

8   Conclusion

In this paper, we have described an approach to automated configuration management that relies on an Object-Oriented Constraint Satisfaction Problem (OOCSP) formulation. By posing the problem as an OOCSP, we can specify system configuration in a declarative form and apply well-understood techniques to rapidly search for a configuration that meets all specified constraints. We discussed both the benefits and limitations of this approach.

---

[3] These statistics are for a 500 MHz PowerPC G4 processor with 1 GB of RAM and Epilog running on MCL 5.0.

References

1. Unified Modeling Language (UML) http://www.uml.org/
2. SmartFrog http://www.smartfrog.org/
3. CIM http://www.dmtf.org/standards/cim/
4. Sahai, S. Singhal, R. Joshi, V. Machiraju, "Automated Policy-Based Resource Construction in Utility Environments" *Proceedings of the IEEE/IFIP NOMS*, Seoul, Korea, Apr. 19-23, 2004
5. M. Paltrinieri, "Some Remarks on the Design of Constraint Satisfaction Problems," *Second International Workshop on the Principles and Practice of Constraint Programming*, pp. 299-311, 1994.
6. Alloy http://sdg.lcs.mit.edu/alloy/
7. J. A. Robinson, "A machine-oriented logic based on the resolution principle," *Journal of the Association for Computing Machinery*, 12:23-41, 1965.
8. S. Mittal and A. Araya. "A Knowledge-Based Framework for Design," *Proceedings of the 5th AAAI*, 1986.
9. Petrie, "Context Maintenance," *Proceedings AAAI-91*, pp. 288-295, 1991.
10. Sahai, S. Singhal, R. Joshi, V. Machiraju, "Automated Generation of Resource Configurations through Policy," to appear in *Proceedings of the IEEE 5th International Workshop on Policies for Distributed Systems and Networks*, YorkTown Heights, NY, June 7-9, 2004
11. J. McCarthy and P. J. Hayes. Some philosophical problems from the standpoint of artificial intelligence. *Machine Intelligence 4*, pp. 463-502, 1969.
12. M. R. Hall, K. Kumaran, M. Peak, and J. S. Kaminski, "DESIGN: A Generic Configuration Shell," *Proceedings 3rd International Conference on Industrial & Engineering Applications of AI and Expert Systems*, 1990.

Problem Determination Using Dependency Graphs and Run-Time Behavior Models

Manoj K. Agarwal[1], Karen Appleby[2], Manish Gupta[1], Gautam Kar[2],
Anindya Neogi[1], and Anca Sailer[2]

[1] IBM India Research Laboratory,
New Delhi, India
{manojkag, gmanish, anindya_neogi}@in.ibm.com
[2] IBM T.J. Watson Research Center, Hawthorne, NY, USA
{gkar, applebyk, ancas}@us.ibm.com

Abstract. Key challenges in managing an I/T environment for e-business lie in the area of root cause analysis, proactive problem prediction, and automated problem remediation. Our approach as reported in this paper, utilizes two important concepts: dependency graphs and dynamic runtime performance characteristics of resources that comprise an I/T environment to design algorithms for rapid root cause identification in case of problems. In the event of a reported problem, our approach uses the dependency information and the behavior models to narrow down the root cause to a small set of resources that can be individually tested, thus facilitating quick remediation and thus leading to reduced administrative costs.

1 Introduction

A recent survey on Total Cost of Operation (TCO) for cluster-based services [1] suggests that a third to half of TCO, which in turn is 5-10 times the purchase price of the system hardware and software, is spent in fixing problems or preparing for impending problems in the system. Hence, the cost of problem determination and remediation forms a substantial part of operational costs. Being able to perform timely and efficient problem determination (PD) can contribute to a substantial reduction in system administration costs. The primary theme of this paper is to show how automatic PD can be performed using system dependency graphs and run-time performance models.

The scope of our approach is limited to typical e-business systems involving HTTP servers, application servers, messaging servers, and databases. We have experimented with benchmark storefront applications, such as TPC-W bookstore [2]. The range of problems in distributed applications is very large, from sub-optimal use of resources, violation of agreed levels of service (soft-faults), to hard failures, such as disk crash. In a traditional management system, problem determination is related to the state of components at system level (e.g., CPU, memory). Thus, a monitored system component that fails, notifies the management service, which manually or automatically detects and fixes the problem. However, when a transaction type "search for an item in an electronic store" shows a slowdown and violates user SLA (in this paper, we do

A. Sahai and F. Wu (Eds.): DSOM 2004, LNCS 3278, pp. 171–182, 2004.

not distinguish between SLA and SLO (Service Level Objective)), it is often an overwhelming and expensive task to figure out which of the many thousands of components, supporting such a transaction, should be looked at for a possible root cause. In this paper, we focus on the soft-faults within the e-business service provider domain. An approach towards tackling this complex area is combining the run-time *performance modeling* of system components with the study of their *dependencies*. The next section will provide a short summary of the notion of dependencies and dependency graphs, reported in detail in previous publications [4].

The main thesis of this paper is that PD applications can use the knowledge provided by dependency graphs and resource performance models to quickly pinpoint the root cause of SLA or performance problems that typically manifest themselves at the user transaction level. The monitoring data, say response time, is collected from individual components and compared against thresholds preset by a system administrator. Each time the monitored metric exceeds the threshold, an alert event is sent to a central problem determination engine, which correlates multiple such events to compute the likely root cause. Thresholds are hard to preset, especially in the event of sudden workload changes, and their use often results in spurious events. The primary contribution of this paper is that, we dynamically construct response time baselines for each component by observing its behavior. When an SLA monitor observes an end-to-end transaction response time violation due to some degradation inside the system, the individual components are automatically ranked in the order of the violation degree of their current response time level with their constructed good behavior baseline and of their dependency information. A system administrator can then scan the limited set of ranked components and quickly determine the actual root cause through more detailed examination of the individual components. The net gain here is that the administrator would need to examine far fewer components for the actual root cause, than conventional management approaches.

In this paper, we describe the creation of simple performance models using response time measurement data from components, end-to-end SLA limits, and component dependency graphs. We show how, given end-to-end SLA violations, these dynamic models, in combination with dependency graphs, can be used to rank the likely root cause components.

The management system has an architecture designed in three tiers, as shown in Fig. 1. The first tier consists of monitoring agents specific to server platforms. These agents can interface with the monitoring APIs of the server platforms, extract component-wise monitoring data and send them to the second tier. In the second tier, the online mining engine (OME) performs dependency extraction (if required), weighs the extracted dependencies, and stores them in a repository. The accurate dependency data may be provided through transaction correlation instrumentation, such as ARM [3]. Otherwise it is extracted by mining techniques in OME [4][5], from aggregate monitoring data. A standardized object-oriented management data modeling technology called Common Information Modeling (CIM) [6] is used when storing the dependency information in a database. The third tier comprises management applications, for example the PD application to be described in this paper, which uses the CIM dependency database.

The rest of the paper is structured as follows: Section 2 provides a short background on dependency analysis and dependency graphs. Section 3 outlines some of the more popular tools and approaches for performing PD to establish the relevance of our work to this area. In Section 4 we describe our algorithms for resource behavior modeling and we show how they can be used for PD in Section 5. Section 6 presents the prototype environment on which our PD technique is being applied and tested. We conclude the paper in Section 7 with a summary and a discussion of our on-going and future work in this domain.

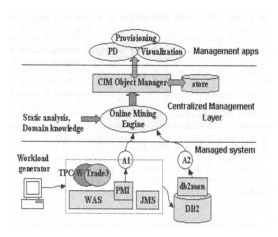

Fig. 1. Management system architecture

2 Background

This section presents an overview of the general concept of dependencies as applied to modeling relationships in a distributed environment.

Consider any two components in a distributed system, say *A* and *B*, where *A*, for example, may be an application server, and *B* a database. In the general case, *A* is said to be dependent on *B*, if *B*'s services are required for *A* to complete its own service. One of the ways to record this information is by means of a directed graph, where A and B are represented as nodes and the dependency information is represented by a directed arc, from A to B, signifying that A is dependent on B. A is referred to as the *dependent* and B as the *antecedent*. A weight may also be attached to the directed edge from *A* to *B*, which may be interpreted in various ways, such as a quantitative measure of the extent to which *A* depends on *B* or how much *A* may be affected by the non-availability or poor performance of *B*, etc. Any dependency between *A* and *B* that arises from an invocation of *B* from *A* may be synchronous or asynchronous.

There are different ways in which dependency information can be computed. Many of these techniques require invasive instrumentation, such as the use of ARM [3]. The algorithms that we have designed and implemented [5] do not require such invasive changes. Instead they infer dependency information by performing statistical correlation on run time monitored data that is typically available in a system. Of course, this approach is not as accurate as invasive techniques, but our experiments show that the level of accuracy achieved is high enough for most management applications, such as problem determination/root cause analysis, that can benefit by using the dependency data. Here, accuracy is a measure of how well an algorithm does in extracting all existing dependencies in a system. An additional consequence of a probabilistic algorithm, such as ours, is that false dependencies may be recorded which could mislead a PD application into identifying an erroneous root cause. We have devised a way of minimizing such adverse effects by ensuring that our probabilistic algorithms attach low weights to false dependencies. Thus, if all the antecedents of a dependent component were ranked in order of descending weights in the dependency graph, a PD application, while traversing this graph would be able to identify the root cause before encountering a false dependency with low weight. A measure of how disruptive false dependencies are in a weighted dependency graph is *precision* [4]. Simply stated, a dependency graph with high precision is one where the false dependencies have been assigned very low weights. In the next section we highlight some of the PD systems that are available today and point out their relevance to our work.

3 Related Work

Problem Determination (PD) is the process of detecting misbehavior in a monitored system and locating the problems responsible for the misbehavior. In the past, PD techniques have mainly concentrated on network [7], and system [9] level fault management. With the emerging Internet based service frameworks such as e-commerce sites, the PD challenge is how to pinpoint application performance root causes in large dynamic distributed systems and distinguish between faults and their consequences.

In a traditional management system, PD is related to the state of components at system level (e.g., CPU, memory, queue length) [9]. In application performance analysis, the starting point for choosing the metrics for detecting performance problems is the SLA. In our scenario, we consider a response time based SLA and characterize the system components in terms of their response time to requests triggered by user transactions. Our solution addresses the case of ARM enabled systems as well as legacy systems, and relies on agents (both, ARM agents and native agents) to collect monitoring data.

The classical approach to constructing models of the monitored components is one that requires detailed knowledge of the system [11][12]. As such models are difficult to build and validate. Most approaches use historical measurements and least-squares regression to estimate the parameters of the system components [13]. Diao *et al.* use the parameters in a linear model and the model generation is only conducted once for a representative workload, experimentally showing that there is no need to rebuild the model once the workload changes [14]. We generate the behavior characteristics of the monitored components based on historical measurements and statistical techniques, distinguishing between the good behavior model and the bad behavior model.

Furthermore, while many efforts in the literature address behavior modeling of individual components, e.g., Web Server [14], DB2 [15], we characterize the resources' behavior keeping in mind the end-to-end PD of the application environment as a whole.

Most PD techniques rely on alarms emitted by failed components to infer that a problem occurred in the system [19]. Brodie *et al.* discuss an alternate technique using synthetic transactions to probe the system for possible problems [16]. Steinder *et al.* review the existing approaches to fault localization and also presents the challenges of managing modern e-business environments [8]. The most common approaches to fault localization are AI techniques (e.g., rule-based, model-based, neural networks, decision trees), model traversing techniques (e.g., dependency-based), and fault propagation techniques (e.g., codebook-based, Bayesian networks, causality graphs). Our solution falls in the category of model traversing techniques. Bagchi *et al.* implement a PD technique based on fault injection, which may not be acceptable in most e-business environments [17]. Chen *et al.* instrument the system to trace request flows and perform data clustering to determine the root cause set [21]. Our technique uses dynamic dependencies inferred from monitored data without any extra instrumentation or fault injection.

4 Behavior Modeling Using Dependency Graphs

We assume an end-user SLA with an end-to-end response time threshold specified for each transaction type. An SLA monitor typically measures the end-to-end response time of a transaction, but it has no understanding of how the transaction is executed by the distributed application on the e-business system. Hence, when an SLA limit for a transaction type is exceeded, the monitor has no idea about the location of the bottleneck within the system. In this section, we describe how one can construct dynamic thresholds for the internal components by observing their response time behavior.

4.1 Monitoring

A threshold is an indicator of how well a resource is performing. In most management systems today, thresholds are fixed, *e.g.*, an administrator may set a threshold of x seconds for the response time of a database service, meaning that if the response is over x, it is assumed that the database has a problem and an alert should be issued. We introduce the concept of *dynamic thresholds*, which can be changed and adjusted on a regular basis through our behavior modeling, thus accommodating changes in operating conditions, such as application load. The good behavior model or dynamic threshold of a component is constructed based on two inputs: response time samples obtained through the monitoring infrastructure and a resource dependency graph. A typical real-life monitoring infrastructure provides only aggregate information, such as average response time and access counts of components etc. In our earlier work [4][5] we have shown how such aggregate monitoring information can be used to construct aggregate dependency graphs. As shown in Fig. 2, an aggregate graph captures the dependency of a transaction type on resources aggregated over multiple transaction instances.

Our technique of dynamic threshold computation uses an aggregate monitoring infrastructure and aggregate dependency graphs. Such graphs may even have imperfections, such as false and/or missing dependencies. In an extended research report, we show how our PD algorithm deals with such shortcomings [20]. Our dynamic threshold computation technique currently uses data from HTTP Server logs, WAS Performance Monitoring Infrastructure (PMI), and DB2 Snapshot API. We assume that the same aggregate monitoring APIs have also been used for dependency graph construction.

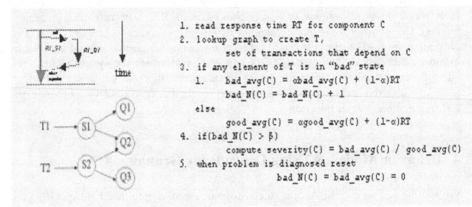

```
1. read response time RT for component C
2. lookup graph to create T,
        set of transactions that depend on C
3. if any element of T is in "bad" state
    1.    bad_avg(C) = αbad_avg(C) + (1-α)RT
          bad_N(C) = bad_N(C) + 1
    else
          good_avg(C) = αgood_avg(C) + (1-α)RT
4. if(bad_N(C) > β)
          compute severity(C) = bad_avg(C) / good_avg(C)
5. when problem is diagnosed reset
          bad_N(C) = bad_avg(C) = 0
```

Fig. 2. Aggregate graph and model-builder logic

4.2 Behavior Modeling

The goal of behavior modeling is to construct a dynamic threshold of a component, such that when an end-to-end problem is detected, the current response time samples from the component may be compared with its dynamic threshold.

A transaction type can have two states, henceforth called "good" or "bad", corresponding to when they are below or above their SLA limits, respectively. Similarly, each system component should also have a good state or a bad state depending on whether they are the cause of a problem or are affected by a problem elsewhere. In a traditional management system, a hard-coded threshold is configured on each individual component. A component is in bad state if its response time is beyond the threshold else it is in good state. Each component in bad state sends an event to a central event correlation engine, which determines the likely root cause based on some human generated script or expert rule base. This approach results in a large number of events from various components. Besides, it is very difficult and error prone for the system administrator to configure a threshold for a component without extensive benchmarking experience.

Our management system uses average response time samples from the components to build their bad or good state performance models. A key feature of our system is that it uses the dependency graph to classify response time samples from a component into bad and good state, instead of hard-coded thresholds on individual components. The classification rule states that if *any parent transaction* of a component is in bad state when the response time sample is obtained, then the sample is classified as "bad" and added to the bad behavior model of the component, otherwise it is added to its good behavior model. The good behavior model is an average of the good response time values and also serves as the dynamic threshold.

Fig. 2 shows the dependency graph of transactions T1 and T2. S1 sometimes accesses Q1 and sometimes Q2. When a response time sample from query Q2 is obtained, the model-builder logic checks the current state of T1 as well as T2. Only the SLA monitor can modify the state of T1 and T2. If T1 *and* T2 are in good state, the sample is added to the good model of Q2. If either of them is bad because the fault lies in any of the component in the sub-tree of the bad transaction, the sample is added to the bad model of Q2. The problem determination logic is invoked after a few samples of the bad model are obtained. Thereafter, the bad and good models of each component are compared and the components are ranked as described in Section 5. In our current implementation, a good or bad model is simply the average of the distribution of good or bad values, respectively. Fig. 2 shows the pseudo-code for the model-builder logic.

The good model of a component is persistent across problem phases, i.e., it is never forgotten and more samples make it more dependable for comparison against a bad model. The bad model samples are typically unique to the particular type and instance of the problem. Hence the bad models are forgotten after each problem is resolved. We assume that problems are not overlapping, i.e., there is only one problem source and independent problem phases do not overlap.

In our current implementation, the cumulative response time of a component obtained from the monitoring infrastructure is used as the model variable. This response time includes the response time of the child components. For example, the average response time of S1 includes average response times of Q1 and Q2, as illustrated in Fig. 2. Thus, if a bottleneck is created at Q1, Q1 as well as S1's response time behavior models are affected.

The cumulative time is effective in identifying a faulty path in the dependency tree, but, in many cases, is not adequate in pinpointing the root-cause resource. We are working on an enhanced approach, where the model variable can be changed to capture the local time spent at a component, excluding the response time of the children. This approach will be reported in a later paper.

5 Problem Determination

In this section we discuss how components may be ranked, so that a system administrator may investigate them in sequence to determine the actual bottleneck. In normal mode of operation each component computes a dynamic threshold or a good behavior model. When a problem occurs at a component, the dependent transactions are affected and all components that are in the transaction's sub-tree start computing a bad behavior model. The components that do not build a bad behavior model in this phase, i.e., those that do not belong to a sub-tree of any affected transaction type, are immediately filtered out. The next step is to rank all the components in the sub-tree of an affected transaction.

Each component is assigned a severity value, which captures the factor by which the bad model differs from the good behavior model or dynamic threshold of the component. Since a model in the current implementation is a simple average of the distribution of samples, a simple ratio of the bad model average to the dynamic threshold represents the severity value. Fig. 5 shows a graph with severity values computed per node when the problem is at Q2. For example, for component Q2, the bad model is 105.2 times the dynamic threshold. The un-shaded nodes are not considered because they do not have a bad model and are assigned a default severity of 0.

The shaded components are sorted based on their severity value as shown in the first ranking. Besides the root cause component, say Q2, the components that are on the path from transaction T1 to Q2, such as S1 and S2, have high severity values because we use the cumulative response time as the model variable and not the local time spent at a component. Bad models are computed for other nodes in the subtree, such as Q1 and Q3, but their bad model is very close to their good model because they do not lie on the "bottleneck path". Thus, in the first ranking we prune and order the components in the subtree so that only nodes, which are on the "bottleneck path" are clustered on top. However, this is not enough to assign the highest rank to the root cause node. There is no guarantee that a parent of a root cause node, such as S1, is not going to have higher severity value. For example, in the first ranking in Fig. 5, Q2 appears after S1.

It is possible to reorder the components further based on dependency relationship and overcome the drawback of using the cumulative response time for modeling. Given the severity values of the shaded nodes, we apply a standard 2-means clustering algorithm [18] to divide the set into "high severity set" and "low severity set". In our experience, the severity values of the affected and root cause components are much higher than the unaffected components. For example, the components in Fig. 5 are divided into high severity set: {S1, S2, Q2} and low severity set: {Q1, Q3}. In the second ranking, if a parent and child are both in the high severity set and the parent is ranked higher than the child in the first ranking, then their rankings are swapped. The assumption here is that the high severity of the parent has resulted from the high severity of the child. The assumption holds if there is a single fault in the system and the transactions are synchronous. Since S1 and Q2 are in the same set, they are reordered and Q2 is picked as the highest rank. Thus a system administrator investigating the components will first look at Q2 before any other component.   The efficiency of our technique is defined by the rank assigned to the root cause node.

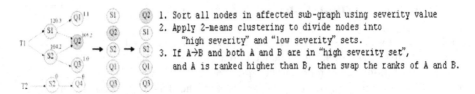

1. Sort all nodes in affected sub-graph using severity value
2. Apply 2-means clustering to divide nodes into
    "high severity" and "low severity" sets.
3. If A→B and both A and B are in "high severity set",
    and A is ranked higher than B, then swap the ranks of A and B.

Fig. 3. Ranking logic

Building performance models and subsequent PD is unaffected by the presence of the false dependencies or by the aggregate representation of dependency graphs. In the interest of space, a complete proof is presented in an extended research report [20].

6 Experimental Evaluation

In this section we present the experimental results to demonstrate the efficiency of our PD technique using behavior models and dependency graphs.

The experimental setup is shown in Fig. 1. The OME is used to extract dependencies between servlets and SQLs in the TPC-W application installed on WAS and DB2. The TPC-W bookstore application is a typical electronic storefront application [2] consisting of 14 servlets, 46 SQLs and a database of 10,000 books. The extracted dependency graph is stored in the CIM database and used by the PD application. The monitoring data is gathered through agents and used by the PD application to build performance models. An SLA monitor (not shown in the figure) intercepts all HTTP requests and responses at the HTTP server. These responses are then classified as 'good' or 'bad' based on the SLA definition. We set individual SLA thresholds for all 14 transaction types in the TPC-W application as our user level SLA definitions. Problems are injected into the system through a problem injector program (not shown in the figure), that periodically locks randomly chosen servlets on WAS or database tables on DB2 with an on-off duty cycle for the injection period, to simulate higher response times for the targeted servlets or tables. The TPC-W code is instrumented to implement the servlet level problem injection. Once we lock the table or servlet, all transactions based on that particular table or servlet slow down and we see an escalation in the response times of the corresponding transactions at the user level and thus violation of the SLAs. We have 10 tables in the DB2 holding data for the TPC-W application and 14 servlets. Thus we can inject problems at 24 different locations in the system. We log these injected problems in a separate log file as the *ground truth*. We then use this ground truth information to compute the efficiency of our PD technique. The efficiency is measured in terms of average accuracy and average rank of the root cause in the ordered list of probable components, where the averaging is performed over multiple problem injections. Accuracy is the measure of finding an injected problem in the list of probable root causes discovered by our PD algorithm. The rank measure of the root cause is the position the root cause component occupies in the ordered list of probable root causes. If the injected problem lies in the nth position from the top of listed root causes, it is assigned rank n. The success of our PD technique is determined by how close the average accuracy and the average rank of the root cause are to 100% and rank 1, respectively.

Table 1. Effect of dependency information with servlet and table level problems

Table 2. Effect of dependency information on table level problems

Load	Graph Type	Avg. Acc (%)	Avg Rank1	List Size
40	ARM	100	1.3	2.1
	Mining	100	1.1	2.7
	Instant	100	1.3	5.5
80	ARM	100	1.5	3.2
	Mining	100	1.4	4.0
	Instant	100	1.5	7.1
120	ARM	100	1.8	3.7
	Mining	100	1.6	5.0
	Instant	100	1.3	10.5

Load	Graph Type	Avg. Rank1	Avg Rank2	%age chnge
40	ARM	2.4	1.7	20
	Mining	2.1	1.6	24
	Instant	1.2	1.2	0
80	ARM	1.4	1.0	28
	Mining	1.7	1.5	15
	Instant	2.0	1.1	45
120	ARM	1.8	1.5	16
	Mining	1.2	1.2	0
	Instant	1.3	1.3	2

Dependency information used by the PD technique can be obtained by three means. An accurate and precise graph may be obtained through ARM instrumentation. A graph with some false dependencies may be obtained through the online mining techniques presented in [4][5]. We take a TPC-W bookstore graph with 100% accuracy and 82% precision extracted at a load of 100 simultaneous customers. This graph, labeled "mining" in Tables 1 and 2, is used as a more imprecise graph. Finally, we also consider a bottom-line case in which historical dependency knowledge is not used but classification is done based on instantaneous information. For example, in the TPC-W application, transactions are synchronous. Thus if a component B occurs when transaction A is active, we consider that as a dependency. This case, termed "instant" in Table 1 and Table 2, contains all the possible dependencies including much more spurious ones compared to "mined" graphs. We investigate the effect of the quality of the dependency information on the efficiency of our PD technique. We inject a set of problems sequentially over time with sufficient gaps between the problems so that the system recovers from one problem before experiencing another. We also vary the system load to observe its effect on behavior modeling and PD. Load is the number of simultaneous customers active in the system sending URL requests to the TPC-W application. At the load of 120 customers, the load generator sends around 300 URL requests/minute. We run these experiments over the duration of 2 hours each during which we inject randomly chosen 12 different problems out of set of 24 problems. Each problem is injected 5 to 10 times and the average accuracy and average rank are computed over all injected problems. Table 1 summarizes the results of our experiments.

We see that accuracy of our PD algorithm is always 100%. It means that we can always find the injected problem in our list of suspected root causes. There are total 60 different components (14 servlets and 46 SQLs). The last column "list size" shows the average number of components selected for ranking, which decreases as the quality of the dependency information increases. Thus the quality of the dependency information definitely helps in reducing the set of components that are considered (the shaded nodes in Fig. 3). However, it does not impact the ranking to a significant extent (see proof in [21]). The rank of the root cause, using this technique, in which all the components are sorted based on severity, lies between 1 and 2. This means that the root cause is almost always the first or the second component in the ordered list. Besides, the behavior modeling and PD based on the dynamic thresholds, is also not heavily impacted by load. The average rank of the root cause in this approach increases only marginally, as load increases.

We also investigate the application of dependency graph to improve the first ranking. Here we inject problems only at table level so that we can observe the effect of swapping ranks between servlets and antecedent SQLs. In Table 2, "Avg Rank2" is the average rank of the root cause after applying the dependency information on the first ranking. In most cases, the average rank of the root cause is improved in the second ranking. In the cases where the percentage improvement is not significant enough, their "Avg Rank1" is already close to the minimum possible rank. More experimentation is needed to find out the effect of load and graph type on the percentage improvement.

7 Conclusion

In this paper, we have presented our research in the area of Problem Determination for large, distributed, multi-tier, transaction based e-business systems. The novelty of our approach, as compared to others reported in the literature, is that we use a combination of resource dependency information and resource behavior models to facilitate the rapid isolation of causes when user transactions manifest unacceptably slow response time.

One of the drawbacks of our current approach is that, in some cases, when a user transaction misbehaves, we are able to narrow down the root cause to a set of resources that support the transaction, but may not be able to identify the offending resource. This is because resource behavior models are inclusive, i.e., a dependent resource's model includes the effects of its antecedents. As ongoing work we are looking at enhancing our approach to constructing models that better reflect the performance of individual resources, thus providing a better framework for root-cause analysis. One approach is to compute a resource's good behavior by capturing its individual contribution to a transaction's end-to-end response time. In addition, we are investigating how our technique can provide a reliable basis for problem prediction, through the observation of trends in the variation of resource behavior. We are extending our approach for proactive problem prediction, before the problem manifests as a user level SLA violation.

References

1.   Gillen A., Kusnetzky, McLaron S., The role of linux in reducing cost of enterprise computing, IDC white paper, January 2002.
2.   TPCW: Wisconsin University, http://www.ece.wisc.edu/~pharm/tpcw.shtml.
3.   ARM: Application Response Measurement, www.opengroup.org/zsmanagement/arm.htm

4. M. Gupta, A. Neogi, M. Agarwal, G. Kar, Discovering dynamic dependencies in enterprise environments for problem determination, Proceedings of 14th IFIP/IEEE International Workshop on Distributed Systems: Operations and Management, October 2003.

5. M. K. Agarwal, M. Gupta, G. Kar, A. Neogi, A. Sailer, Mining activity data for dynamic dependency discovery in e-business systems, under review for eTransactions on Network and Service Management (eTNSM) Journal, Fall 2004.

6. CIM: Common Information Model, http://www.dmtf.org/standards/standard_cim.php.

7. R. Boutaba, J. Xiao, network management: state of the art, IFIP World Computer Cogress2002,
    http://www.ifip.tugraz.ac.at/TC6/events/WCC/WCC2002/papers/Boutaba.pdf

8. M. Steinder, A.S. Sethi, The present and future of event correlation: A need for end-to-end service fault localization, Proc. SCI-2001, 5th World Multiconference on Systemics, Cybernetics, and Informatics, Orlando, FL (July 2001), pp. 124-129.

9. Y. Ding, C. Thornley, K. Newman, On correlating performance metrics, CMG 2001.

10. A. J. Thadhani, Interactive User Productivity, IBM System Journal, 20, p 407-423, 1981.

11. K. Ogata, Modern control engineering, Prentice Hall, 3rd Edition, 1997.

12. D. A. Menascé, D. Barbara, R. Dodge, Preserving QoS of e-commerce sites through self-tuning: a performance model approach, Proceedings of the 3rd ACM conference on Electronic Commerce, 2001.

13. S. Parekh, N. Gandhi, J. L. Hellerstein, D. Tilbury, T. S. Jayram, J. Bigus, Using control theory to achieve service level objectives in performance management, 2003.

14. Y. Diao, J. L. Hellerstein, S. Parekh, J. P. Bigus, Managing web server performance with autoTune agents, IBM Systems Journal 2003.

15. Y. Diao, F. Eskesen, S. Froehlich, J. L. Hellerstein, L. F. Spainhower, M. Surendra, Generic online optimization of multiple configuration parameters with application to a database server, DSOM 2003.

16. M. Brodie, I. Rish, S. Ma, N. Odintsova, Active probing strategies for problem diagnosis in distributed systems, in Proceedings of IJCAI 2003.

17. S. Bagchi, G. Kar, J. L. Hellerstein, Dependency analysis in distributed systems using fault injection: application to problem determination in an e-commerce environment, DSOM 2001.

18. C.M. Bishop, Neural networks for pattern recognition, Oxford, England: Oxford University Press, 1995.

19. K. Appleby, G. Goldszmidt, M. Steinder, Yemanja, A layered fault localization system for multi-domain computing utilities, in IM 2001.

20. M. Agarwal, K. Appleby, M. Gupta, G. Kar, A. Neogi, A. Sailer, Problem determination and prediction using dependency graphs and run-time behavior models, IBM Research Report, RI04004.

21. M.Y. Chen, E. Kıcıman, E. Fratkin, A. Fox, E. Brewer, Pinpoint: PD in large, dynamic internet services, International Conference on Dependable Systems and Networks (DSN'02), 2002.

Role-Based Access Control for XML Enabled Management Gateways

V. Cridlig, O. Festor, and R. State

LORIA - INRIA Lorraine
615, rue du jardin botanique
54602 Villers-les-Nancy, France
{cridligv,festor,state}@loria.fr

Abstract. While security is often supported in standard management frameworks, it has been insufficiently approached in most deployment and research initiatives. In this paper we address the provisioning of a security "continuum" for management frameworks based on XML/SNMP gateways. We provide an in depth security extension of such a gateway using the Role Based Access Control paradigm and show how to integrate our approach within a broader XML-based management framework.

Keywords: management gateways, SNMP, XML-based management, security, key management.

1 Introduction

Security needs in network management appeared when administrators realized that malicious parties can use this vector to either get confidential information like configuration and accounting data or even attack the network and the devices through management operations. Integrity, authentication, privacy, replay and access control are of major importance to the distributed management plane. Network management data is sensitive and can compromise the security of the whole network. For example, firewall tables, routing tables, routers' configuration can help attackers to discover network security holes and the network topology. This is the reason why extending management protocols with security features is crucial.

Security in distributed systems is usually built around five areas: authentication, integrity, confidentiality, availability and access control. Authentication process gives warranties that a remote principal is the one he claims to be. Integrity process assures that the transmitted data has not been altered during transmission. Confidentiality includes encryption and decryption processes to ensure that data cannot be read by a third party. Availability ensures that a service is accessible over time. Access control, which can not be performed without an authentication phase, allows to restrict access on data to some authorized principals.

A. Sahai and F. Wu (Eds.): DSOM 2004, LNCS 3278, pp. 183–195, 2004.

These issues are even more important in a utility computing type of environment. Dynamic, on-demand usage of resources provided by a third party over a well delimited time-interval requires a flexible management plane. Flexibility in this case is related to the degree of configuration accessible to a resource consumer while these resources are supporting his business.

The problem addressed in this paper is twofold: firstly, we consider how to maintain the overall security level, when migrating from SNMP-based to XML-based management. Such a migration can be assured with an XML/SNMP gateway (see [1] and [2]). The XML/SNMP gateways address the interoperability among XML managers and SNMP agents and should not introduce security holes but rather should establish a security continuum. In particular, a non-authorized principal should not be able to manage agents either directly or through the gateway. These requirements suppose a mapping and a policy coherence maintenance for the different security models involved in the whole architecture. The second issue addressed by our paper concerns the security provisioning of a management gateway required in dynamic utility computing environments, where on demand resources must allow a temporary management session by a foreign manager. A manual per device configuration is not scalable if the utilities are numerous. A more realistic solution is to use a management gateway, which mediates the access to the managed devices.

The remainder of this paper is organized as follows. In section 2, we summarize the existing XML/SNMP gateways as well as the SNMPv3 functional architecture and its security modules, namely User Security Model (USM) and View-based Access Control Model (VACM). In section 3, we propose an XML/SNMP gateway extended with the desired security features. Section 4 concludes this paper and opens perspectives to our work.

2   State of the Art

2.1   Existing XML/SNMP Gateways

Over the past few years, the eXtensible Markup Language (XML [3]) has proven to be an excellent way to build interoperable applications. Many XML standards and recommendations emerged mainly from the World Wide Web Consortium (W3C [4]) in order to avoid proprietary solutions and then improve interoperability. The advantages of XML-based techniques such as XML document transmission and processing as well as embedded security are also recognized in the management plane [2]. However, the large number of existing SNMP agents slows down the XML-based management solutions deployment. Therefore, intermediate solutions using XML/SNMP gateways are required to provide a temporary solution before a potential full and complete migration to XML-based management solution.

XML/SNMP gateways allow managers to communicate with their agents using XML technologies even if the agents are solely SNMP compliant. The managers can then benefit of XML tools to process and/or display XML documents conveniently, or to express complex relationships among managed services as in [5]. The gateway is responsible for translating XML requests coming from the managers to SNMP requests towards the agents. The mechanism is reversed for the agents responses. Mapping XML to SNMP means translating both exchange protocols and information models.

Yoon, Ju and Hong [6] proposed a full SNMP MIB (Management Information Base) to XML Schema translation algorithm. The latter is based on the following document structure conversion. A SNMP SMI (Structure of Management Information) node becomes an XML Schema element, a node name becomes an element name and clauses in node become attributes of the element. One important topic (feature, component, ...) of the proposed approach is the SMI data types translation. XML Schema provides an elegant way to define equivalent data types using default data types and patterns. Note that all XML nodes have an Object Identifier (OID) attribute corresponding to the MIB node location in order to facilitate data retrieval. For a given MIB, this translator produces both the XML Document Object Model (DOM) tree structure which is used to store management data in the gateway and also to create XML documents and the XML Schema file for validation.

Within the context of the gateway implementation, Yoon, Ju and Hong proposed three approaches for the manager/gateway communication: a DOM-based translation, an HTTP (Hypertext Transfer Protocol)-based translation and a SOAP-based translation. These approaches, their advantages and drawbacks are discussed in [1].

F. Strauss and T. Klie [2] also proposed a SMI MIB to XML Schema definitions converter. Although this converter is also based on a model-level approach (see [7]), their approach is quite different. Instead of using OIDs to process the mapping, the latter is based on namespaces: each MIB module is translated into an XML Schema and identified with a namespace to uniquely map data elements. This mapping is driven by the intention to produce an XML document close to the XML philosophy (meaning both human and machine readable). Both approaches (i.e. [6] and [2]) are elegant. A translator (mibdump) analyses a whole MIB, creates the XML Schema, generates the associated set of SNMP requests, collects the data from the agent and builds the valid (regarding the XML Schema) XML document. However, mibdump can only collect data from a single MIB.

We are working on the development of an enhanced gateway based on a role based access control paradigm. This paper describes some of its features. While being conceptually based on HTTP and XPath for manager to gateway communications and DOM for data storage, we extend this architecture with security modules to allow authentication, privacy and access control.

2.2   SNMPv3

The SNMPv3 (Simple Network Management Protocol [8,9,10]) functional architecture was designed to address potential security issues. To achieve this security challenge, this architecture integrates two subsystems. The first one, called security subsystem, consists in a privacy module, an authentication module which provides both authentication and integrity and a timeliness module. It is implemented with the User-based Security Model (USM [11]) by default. The second one, implemented with the View-based Access Control Model (VACM [12]) is an access control subsystem. These integrated security tools allow SNMP managers to perform secure requests on SNMP agents.

USM authentication and confidentiality services are based on a shared secret localized key paradigm. Each manager/agent pair uses a particular key pair (one key per service). The security level required by the manager dictates the message preparation or checking depending on whether the message is incoming or outgoing.

VACM performs access control based on different mib tables storing access policies. Authorization decision is based on input parameters like the object OID, the operation to be performed, the requesting security name, the security model and level. As every object of the MIB tree, VACM policies can be configured remotely provided that the requester has sufficient rights to modify these tables.

3   The Proposed Security Framework

3.1   Motivation

The existing XML/SNMP gateways focused mainly on the operational part of network management while security issues were not yet addressed. The application of the XML/SNMP gateway to a real network management environment requires the incorporation of additional security mechanisms, since its deployment without efficient security features provides major security breaches. The major motivation for our work is to propose a coherent security framework for SNMP/XML gateways, realizing a "security continuum", i.e. assuring that security policies are independent of the underlying used management protocol (native SNMP, SNMP/XML gateways, or native XML). We present here a security extension for the XML/SNMP gateways addressing the authentication, confidentiality and authorization issues. These security services intend to provide the ability to perform more sensitive configuration operation, which is one of the shortcomings of SNMP [2]. Such a "security continuum" is essential if a management gateway is used in a utility computing scenario. The sound configuration of many devices at once in order to temporarily serve a third party manager requires on the one hand to assure that only allowed operations are possible, and on the second hand that the security configuration be fast. We propose an access control enabled XML/SNMP gateway which meets these requirements.

3.2   Requirements

The gateway provides a unified security policy based on Role Based Access Control (RBAC [13]). The access control module must be able to create sessions for users and map the access rights of each user on the SNMP agents on the fly. This makes it possible to manage a unique centralized policy and deploy it in a transparent way for users. Moreover authoring authorization policies with RBAC is proven to be easy, scalable and less error-prone. A user creates an RBAC policy on the gateway. Since this policy is mapped on the SNMP agents VACM tables, no change is required within SNMPv3 architecture.

3.3   Functional Architecture

Our secure XML/SNMP gateway, depicted in figure 1 embeds an SSL layer to allow secure communications between the managers and the gateway. This layer is necessary to allow manager identification which is, in turn, necessary to perform access control process. First, the manager initiates an encrypted SSL session on the gateway. Then the manager is identified by filling an HTML form with his login/password credentials.

Moreover, SNMPv3 new security features are difficult to use and suffer from lack of scalability [14]. Therefore, our architecture uses an authorization model (RBAC) different and therefore independent from the SNMPv3 one. RBAC allows high level and scalable access control process and configuration. The RBAC model consists in a set of users, roles, permissions (operations on resources) and sessions. The originality of RBAC model is that permissions are not granted to users but to roles, thus allowing an easy reconfiguration when a user changes his activity. A role describes a job function within an organization. The permission to role relationships illustrates that a role can perform a set of operations on objects (privileges). In the same way, the user to role relationships describes the available function a user is allowed to endorse in the organization. Lastly, a session gathers for each user his set of currently activated role, on which behalf he can interact with the system.

In this paper, we consider the NIST (National Institute of Standards and Technologies) RBAC (Role-Based Access Control [13]) model which gathers the most commonly admitted ideas and experience of previous RBAC models. This standard provides a full description of all the features that should implement an RBAC system. RBAC model allows the description of complex authorization policies while reducing errors and costs of administration. Introduction of administrative roles and role hierarchy made it possible to reduce considerably the amount of associations representing permissions to users allocation.

Consequently, our architecture embeds an *RBAC manager* for authorization decision process consisting in an *RBAC system* and an *RBAC repository*. In order to still allow pure SNMPv3 configuration (i.e. direct manager/agent management for SNMPv3-based managers), it must be possible to push authorization policies onto the SNMP agents. Since RBAC and VACM models are different, a mapping module, *RBACToVACM translator*, is also necessary.

The *RBAC repository* owns an authorization policy. This policy describes:

- the set of users who are allowed to interact with the system,
- the set of roles that can potentially be endorsed by users,

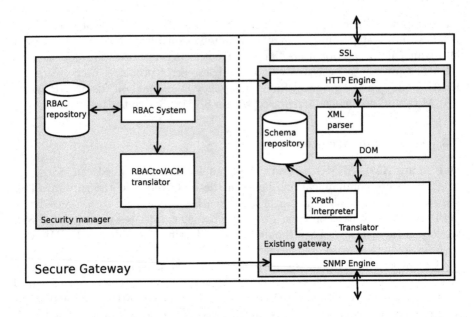

Fig. 1. Secure gateway functional architecture

- the set of scopes (objects) on which permissions are granted,
- the set of permissions which consist in an operation an a scope,
- the set of UAs (user assignment) which describe user to role association and the set of PAs (permission assignment).

An example of such a policy is depicted in figure 2.c.

The *RBAC system* implements all the features needed to handle authorization data and to process access evaluation. It is possible:

- to create, modify or delete the different RBAC elements (users, roles, permissions) in order to build policies according to our needs,
- to manage (create and close) user sessions,
- to add or remove active roles from a session,
- to evaluate the access requests regarding the policy.

Moreover when a new role becomes active, it calls the *RBACtoVACM translator* in order to update VACM policies on agents. Most of the features described here are detailed in [13].

The *RBACToVACM translator* is responsible for mapping the gateway RBAC policy on the agent VACM policy. Different XML documents are needed to perform this mapping. We describe them in the mapping section.

3.4   Authorization

Linking RBAC to management data. The XML document depicted in figure 2.c describes an RBAC policy scenario. Different existing languages such as XACML [15] Profile for RBAC or .NET MyServices Authorization language [16] can model an RBAC policy. Although the first language is acknowledged to be compliant with the NIST RBAC standard [13] and the second one is quite elegant, we propose our own language which is as close as possible to the NIST RBAC model and terminology while remaining as simple as possible for the purpose of an XML/SNMP gateway prototype. The XML representation of the RBAC model is of minor importance. We propose here to map a model, not a particular XML representation of the model.

Each RBAC element is described independently and owns an identifier (Id) attribute such that the user to role (UA) and permission to role (PA) assignments can reference them. Users (here bob and alice) consist in a login and a password. Roles are described with names. Scopes reference the XML management data of the figure 2.a using XPath. XPath is quite simple and allows to address powerfully a set of elements in an XML document. For instance, scope s1 designates all the *ifEntry* elements of the XML management data. This relationships is shown with the first arrow. Each permission has a reference to a scope and an operation. Only a subset of XPath possible expressions is allowed in our access control policies since the *vacmViewTreeFamilyTable* can only contain OIDs. For instance, an XPath expression referencing a particular attribute value can not be mapped to VACM.

Note that the XML resources depicted in figure 2.a are conforming to the XML Schema generated from the IF-MIB and partially depicted on figure 2.b. For instance, *ifPhysAddress* structure is described (see the second arrow) in the XML Schema. It is important to note that each element of the schema contains the corresponding OID for data retrieval. This will be used for the mapping of our RBAC policy on VACM tables as illustrated with the third arrow.

Mapping RBAC/VACM (one way mapping). In order to map dynamically the RBAC policy on SNMP agents, we have to translate XML RBAC policy into SNMP VACM tables. We provide, in this section an algorithm to map RBAC users on USM users, RBAC roles on VACM groups, scopes on views, and permissions to *vacmAccessTable* entries. The mapped access control has to implement the initial policy behavior. Although sessions can not be expressed in VACM, it can be simulated by mapping only the activated roles for a given user. The VACM tables reflect the activated roles, permissions and users of the RBAC model. The RBAC model is not fully mapped on the agent VACM tables, i.e. permissions are loaded on agents on demand.

The different steps of the mapping algorithm are the following: first, we create a group in the *vacmSecurityToGroupTable* for each user u; then, we add an entry in the *vacmAccessTable* associated to three views. These views are built in the *vacmViewTreeFamilyTable* and gather all objects allowed sorted by "read", "write" or "notify" access type.

Let us consider the example developed in figure 2.c. Our approach consists in collecting all permissions associated to all active roles of a given user. A user-specific group gathering all his active permissions can be created. The fourth

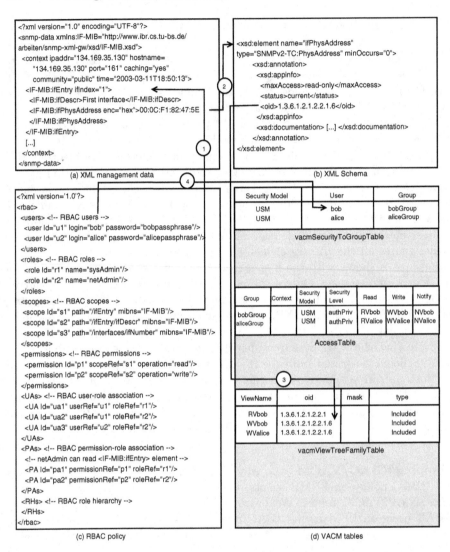

Fig. 2. RBAC/VACM mapping

arrow of figure 2.d illustrates that a new entry in the *vacmSecurityToGroupTable* is created for each RBAC user (bob for instance) with USM as default security model and a group reflecting the user SecuritName (bobGroup). Figure 3 shows the pseudo-code algorithm of a role activation immediately after the login step.

Permissions are sorted by operation, thus building available views for that user. The algorithm uses the XML Schema from the repository (figure 2.b) in order to retrieve OIDs corresponding to a scope. Note that a scope contains an XPath and *mibns* attribute bound to a particular MIB. The *vacmAccessTable*

```
addActiveRole(user u, role r){
  // Example: ("USM", "Bob", "Bobgroup")
  AddSecurityToGroupTableEntry(USM, u.securityName,
                                u.securityName+"group");

  // Example: (Bob, "", USM, authpriv, "", "RVBob", "WVBob", "NVBob")
  AddVacmAccessEntry(u.securityName, "", USM, authpriv, "",
                     "RV"+u.securityName, "WV"+u.securityName,
                     "NV"+u.securityName);

  Foreach permission p of r{
    // Example: ("R"+"V"+"Bob","1.3.6.1.2.1.2.2.1.6","FF","included");
    addVacmViewTreeFamilyEntry(p.operation+"V"+u.securityName,
                               p.getOid, mask, included);
  }
}
```

Fig. 3. RBAC to VACM mapping algorithm

depicted in figure 2.d will contain one entry for each group. For instance, in order to build the bob's read view, we have to gather all bob's active permissions whose operation is *read*, retrieve the OID using the XML schema and then add the corresponding entries in the *vacmViewTreeFamilyTable* to build a sophisticated view.

BobGroup is the union of both SysAdmin and NetAdmin roles. Roles may be associated to several shared permissions. Without separation of duty constraints, Bob can activate its two available roles at the same time in a session. Consequently, Bob can read 1.3.6.1.2.1.2.2.1 and write in 1.3.6.1.2.1.2.2.1.6 subtree. The result *vacmViewTreeFamilyTable* will have the entries shown in figure 2.d. Permissions are updated dynamically on the SNMP agents only when a user requests to add or drop an active role. It is still possible to add separation of duty constraints which are controlled on the gateway side: since the gateway is the only entity which can set permissions on SNMP agents, the gateway can deter a user from adding an active role depending on policy constraints.

This is the basic algorithm. There may be several identical entries in the *vacmViewTreeFamilyTable*. We optimize also on the number of entries in the *vacmViewTreeFamilyTable* when read access is allowed to both a tree and one of its subtrees in the same view. Note that we use only USM associated with *AuthPriv* security level because we chose the RBAC NIST standard which does not describe contexts (do not confuse RBAC context and SNMP context which is totally different). However it is possible to add new views for different security levels. This RBAC context should be first described using the RBAC model as described in [17]. This mapping algorithm serves as a base to introduce RBAC module in the XML/SNMP gateway.

In order to improve the ease of use of the RBAC manager, it is very promising to use XPath object addressing. XML DOM can then be used to translate XPath expression into OIDs and VACM views. It also makes it possible to perform XML-level access control.

Access control process. Each manager (user in RBAC terminology) owns a login / password. This login / password is a shared secret between the manager and the gateway. These credentials (in fact the password) are used to generate the SNMP keys for authentication and privacy. Consequently, both the manager and the gateway are able to perform security requests since they know the manager's password. This way, a manager can manage SNMP agents without going through the gateway provided that permissions are deployed on the managed agent.

Managers have a permanent RBAC session. A manager must explicitly close an RBAC session. When this happens, all managed agents for that manager should be reconfigured, i.e. all permissions for that manager should be deleted. A manager can log out without closing its RBAC session, because his rights are still valid on agents. Managers can activate and deactivate roles when needed. If a manager logs out of the gateway without closing its RBAC session, the gateway does not remove the access rights on the agent so that the manager can still perform SNMPv3 requests on the agent without using the gateway. In our approach, RBAC sessions are persistent. This avoids mapping RBAC on VACM or removing VACM access rights each time a manager logs on or logs out of the gateway. Hence a decreasing number of VACM requests.

When a manager activates a role on the gateway (for an agent), the gateway updates permissions available on the agent VACM tables. In order to update permissions on an agent, the RBAC system maps the RBAC permissions of all active roles of this user.

When the gateway receives a request from a manager, it uses the login / password of this manager to generate the SNMP request so that the agent can know the user performing the request and then control access. This is transparent to the agent. The login / password of each manager is stored as part of the RBAC model in the "user" object. To simplify the login / password management, the gateway uses the same login / password for manager identification on the gateway and on the agents with SNMPv3. However, this is not a strong constraint. This way, managers must remember a single login / password pair.

When a manager wants to access a new device through the gateway, the gateway creates an account for him (provided the user is in the RBAC model of that group) on the agent by cloning itself. The user activates a role on the gateway. The gateway maps the associated permissions on VACM tables of the agent. Then, the user can start performing operations on the agent either through the gateway using HTTP or directly on the agent using SNMPv3. In this way, newly arrived devices are auto-configured for access control. The only requirement is that the gateway must know a valid user login / password as a starting point on each agent.

A special user should have particular rights to modify the RBAC policies on the gateway (i.e. performing maintenance RBAC operations, like createPermission(), addUser(), assignUser() with the NIST RBAC standard model). This user defines roles, users and permissions in a high level view. Mappings from this RBAC level to the VACM level is transparent to the special user. Other users can only open and close RBAC sessions, add active roles, drop active roles.

3.5   Authentication and Confidentiality

Each manager has his own account within the gateway so that he can log on using his login/password credentials. In order to avoid sending these credentials in the clear, the gateway and a manager first establish a secure session using security mechanisms such as Secure Socket Layer (SSL [18]).

The manager password is also used to generate the SNMPv3 secret keys. Since both the manager and the gateway know this password, both can generate the keys needed to authenticate and encrypt the SNMPv3 messages. This way, both can send SNMPv3 requests to a given agent. The advantage is that a manager can still request an agent even if the gateway is down.

A bootstrap phase works as following: the gateway has a default account on all SNMPv3 agents. When a manager needs to request an agent, the gateway clones itself on the agent, thus creating a new SNMP account for this manager. In net-snmp, a new account does not inherit the access rights of the account from which it is cloned since no entry is added in the VACM tables: only the credentials are duplicated. Therefore, there is no risk that a new user can have the same permissions as the gateway. The gateway changes the remote password of the manager according to the manager's password in the local RBAC system. Then the gateway grants access rights to the manager depending on the RBAC policy and the active roles.

4   Conclusion and Future Work

The problem addressed in this paper is the lack of security introduced by the use of XML/SNMP gateways. These gateways provide powerful means to manage device and therefore should be protected with adapted security mechanisms. We proposed some security extensions to an XML/SNMP gateway in order to provide a high level of security and simplify the configuration task of SNMPv3 security managers.

The benefits of our approach are the following:

- security continuum for XML/SNMP gateways,
- uniform scalable access control policies for network management elements using the RBAC model,
- on-demand access rights distribution from the gateway to the SNMP agents using a RBAC to VACM mapping algorithm. Only needed access rights (not all the RBAC policies) are mapped on agents VACM policies,
- easy automated VACM configuration.

An early prototype has been implemented within our group. It extends the servlet based SNMP/XML gateway (SXG) implemented by Jens Mueller. We defined a simple XML Schema (http://www.loria.fr/~cridligv/download/rbac.xsd)

modeling RBAC, which is also used to automatically generate Java classes. The prototype is made of two separate parts, both secured with SSL and accessible after a login/password phase: while the first part is an web RBAC editor used by a super user to setup authorization configuration, the second part is the XML/SNMP gateway itself allowing management operation after an explicit role activation request from the manager.

In the future, there is a great interest in applying an RBAC policy on the gateway to a group of devices. Maintaining one policy for each device is not scalable. Maintaining one policy for all devices is not flexible enough because some devices are more sensitive than others and may implement different MIBs. This justifies our approach to attach an RBAC model to each group of devices. When an RBAC model changes, all devices belonging to that group are updated at the access control level (i.e. VACM tables). Although we define several RBAC models, the set of users remains the same for all of them. This way, a user managing several groups of devices owns a single password. However, roles can be different in two different models and a role can be bound to several RBAC models.

When using the gateway, we can also consider that the access control is made inside the gateway thus avoiding a request which would not be allowed. However the current permissions are still mapped on agent to keep the RBAC model state coherent with the VACM tables.

In a mobility context, we can imagine that different network domains host different XML/SNMP gateways. When a device moves from one domain to another one, the local gateway should have access rights to configure the visitor device. Inter-gateways negotiations could be envisaged to allow the local gateway to create SNMP accounts for the local managers to perform minimal operations.

References

1. Oh, Y.J., Ju, H.T., Choi, M.J., Hong, J.W.K.: Interaction Translation Methods for XML/SNMP Gateway. In Feridun, M., Kropf, P.G., Babin, G., eds.: Proceedings of the 13th IFIP/IEEE International Workshop on Distributed Systems: Operations and Management, DSOM 2002. Volume 2506 of Lecture Notes in Computer Science., Springer (2002) 54–65
2. Strauss, F., Klie, T.: Towards XML Oriented Internet Management. In Goldszmidt, G.S., Schönwälder, J., eds.: Proceedings of the Eighth IFIP/IEEE International Symposium on Integrated Network Management (IM 2003). Volume 246 of IFIP Conference Proceedings., Kluwer (2003) 505–518
3. Bray, T., Paoli, J., Sperberg-McQueen, C.M., Maler, E., Yergeau, F.: Extensible Markup Language (XML) 1.0 (Third Edition). W3C Recommendation (2004)
4. W3C: World Wide Web Consortium (W3C). (http://www.w3.org)
5. Keller, A., Kar, G.: Determining Service Dependencies in Distributed Systems. In: Proceedings of the IEEE International Conference on Communications (ICC 2001), IEEE (2001)
6. Yoon, J.H., Ju, H.T., Hong, J.W.: Development of SNMP-XML Translator and Gateway for XML-based Integrated Network Management. International Journal of Network Management **13** (2003) 259–276

7. Martin-Flatin, J.P.: Web-Based Management of IP Networks and Systems. Wiley (2003)
8. Case, J., , Mundy, R., Partain, D., Stewart, B.: Introduction and Applicability Statements for Internet Standard Management Framework. STD 62, http://www.ietf.org/rfc/rfc3410.txt (2002)
9. Stallings, W.: Network Security Essentials. Prentice Hall (2nd edition 2002)
10. Subramanian, M.: Network Management, Principle and Practice. Addison Wesley (1999)
11. Blumenthal, U., Wijnen, B.: User-based Security Model for version 3 of the Simple Network Management Protocol (SNMPv3).
    STD 62, http://www.ietf.org/rfc/rfc3414.txt (2002)
12. Blumenthal, U., Wijnen, B.: View-based Access Control Model (VACM) for the Simple Network Management Protocol (SNMP).
    STD 62, http://www.ietf.org/rfc/rfc3415.txt (2002)
13. Kuhn, R.: Role Based Access Control. NIST Standard Draft (2003)
14. Lee, H., Noh, B.: Design and Analysis of Role-Based Security Model in SNMPv3 for Policy-Based Security Management. In: Proceedings of the International Conference on Wireless Communications Technologies and Network Applications, ICOIN 2002. Volume 2344 of Lecture Notes in Computer Science., Springer (2002) 430–441
15. Anderson, A.: XACML Profile for Role Based Access Control (RBAC). OASIS Committee Draft (2004)
16. Microsoft: Ws-authorization. (http://msdn.microsoft.com/ws-security/)
17. Neumann, G., Strembeck, M.: An Approach to Engineer and Enforce Context Constraints in an RBAC Environment. In: Proceedings of the eighth ACM symposium on Access control models and technologies, ACM Press (2003) 65–79
18. Freier, A., Karlton, P., Kocher, P.: The SSL Protocol Version 3.0. Technical report, Netscape (1996)

Spotting Intrusion Scenarios from Firewall Logs Through a Case-Based Reasoning Approach

Fábio Elias Locatelli, Luciano Paschoal Gaspary, Cristina Melchiors,
Samir Lohmann, and Fabiane Dillenburg

Programa Interdisciplinar de Pós-Graduação em Computação Aplicada (PIPCA)
Universidade do Vale do Rio dos Sinos (UNISINOS)
Av. Unisinos 950 – 93.022-000 – São Leopoldo – Brazil
paschoal@exatas.unisinos.br

Abstract. Despite neglected by most security managers due to the low availability of tools, the content analysis of firewall logs is fundamental (a) to measure and identify accesses to external and private networks, (b) to access the historical growth of accesses volume and applications used, (c) to debug problems on the configuration of filtering rules and (d) to recognize suspicious event sequences that indicate strategies used by intruders in attempt to obtain non-authorized access to stations and services. This paper presents an approach to classify, characterize and analyze events generated by firewalls. The proposed approach explores the case-based reasoning technique, from the Artificial Intelligence field, to identify possible intrusion scenarios. The paper also describes the validation of our approach carried out based on real logs generated along one week by the university firewall.

1 Introduction

The strategy of using a firewall as a border security mechanism allows the centralization, in only one machine, of all the traffic coming from the Internet to the private network and vice-versa. In this control point, any packet (HTTP, FTP, SMTP, SSH, IMAP, POP3, and others) that comes in and out is inspected and can be accepted or rejected, according to the established security rules.

In this context, firewalls store – for each successful or frustrated attempt – records in log files. Some recorded data are: type of operation, source and destination network addresses, local and remote ports, among others. Depending on the network size and its traffic, the daily log can be greater than 1GB [7]. From the security management point of view, this log is rich in information because it allows: (a) to measure and identify the accesses to the private and external networks (e.g. most and least required services, stations that use more or less bandwidth, main users); (b) to historically follow the growth of the accesses and the applications used; (c) to debug problems on filtering configuration rules; and (d) to recognize suspicious event sequences that indicate strategies used by intruders trying to obtain improper access to stations and services.

A. Sahai and F. Wu (Eds.): DSOM 2004, LNCS 3278, pp. 196–207, 2004.

At the same time that the importance of these indicators is recognized, the growth of information transiting every day between the private network and the Internet has turned the manual control of the log files unviable. This paper presents an approach to classify, characterize and analyze firewall events. The paper describes, yet, the validation of the approach based on real logs generated during one week by the university firewall. The contributions of this work can be unfolded in two: (i) the approach allows identification of sequences of actions executed from or to a determined service or station through the grouping of related events; (ii) supported by the Artificial Intelligence technique called case-based reasoning, the approach provides conditions so that intrusion scenarios[1] can be modeled as cases; whenever similar sequences are repeated, the approach is able to identify them and notify the manager.

The paper is organized as follows: section 2 describes related work. Section 3 presents the proposed approach to classify and characterize the firewall events, as well as to identify automatically the intrusion scenarios. Section 4 describes the tool developed and section 5, the case study carried out to validate it. Finally, section 6 ends up the paper with the final considerations and future work perspectives.

2   Related Work

A quantitative characterization of the intrusion activities performed in the global Internet, based on firewall log analysis, was carried out by Yegneswaran in [9]. The work involved the collection, during a four month period, of more than 1.600 firewall and intrusion detection system logs distributed all over the world. The results enabled to characterize different kinds of probes and their relation to viruses and worms dissemination. It is worthwhile mentioning the fact that this work was carried out in an ad hoc way, without any tool support (this compromises a periodic, long-term analysis). Besides, the approach is exclusively quantitative, what turns difficult the comprehension of some situations in which the events need to be analyzed closely to confirm a suspicious activity.

Regarding event analysis, Artificial Intelligence techniques have been applied to relate events generated by security systems [1,4,5]. Ning presents in [4] a method that correlates prerequisites and consequences of alerts generated by intrusion detection systems in order to determine the various attack stages. The authors claim that an attack usually has different steps and it does not happen in isolation, that is, each attack stage is prerequisite to the next. The method is hard to deploy in large scale. First, prerequisites and consequences must be modeled as predicates, which is not an easy task. Second, the cases database needs to be constantly updated, which requires substantial work. Furthermore, the proposal is limited for not being effective to identify attacks where the relation of cause and consequence cannot be established. For example, two attacks (Smurf and SYN flooding) launched almost at the same time against the same target from two different locations would not be related (however there exists a strong connection between them: same instant and same target).

---

[1] In this paper an *intrusion scenario* is defined as a sequence of suspicious activities that is executed by an intruder in order to obtain non-authorized access to stations and services.

The approaches described in [1,5] analyze alerts produced by spatially distributed heterogeneous information security devices. They propose algorithms for aggregation and correlation of intrusion-detection alerts. The first defines a unified data model for intrusion-detection alerts and a set of rules to process the alerts. The detection algorithm can detect (*i*) alerts that are reported by different probes but are related to the same attack (*duplicates*) and (*ii*) alerts that are related and should occur together (*consequences*). The second approach uses strategies as topology analysis, alert priorization, and common attribute-based alert aggregation. An incident rank calculation is performed using an adaptation of Bayes framework for belief propagation in trees. These approaches tend not to cope well with the detection of intrusion scenarios that differ (even slightly) from what has been previously defined as *fusion* and *aggregation rules*.

Other Artificial Intelligence techniques have been applied to event processing, especially in the context of intrusion detection systems. One of them is the case-based reasoning paradigm (CBR). Schwartz presents in [6] a tool that applies this paradigm to a variation of the intrusion detection system Snort, where each system signature is mapped to a case. Other system that uses the CBR paradigm is presented by Esmaili in [2]. It uses CBR to detect intrusions using the audit logs produced by the operating system. The cases represent intrusion scenarios formed by operating system command sequences that result in an unauthorized access.

3 Approach to Classify, Characterize, and Analyze Firewall Events

This section describes the approach proposed to classify, characterize and analyze firewall events. It is structured in two independent and complementary parts. The first, more quantitative, allows events stored by the firewall to be grouped based on one or more aggregation elements (filters) defined by the security manager. The second part proposes to analyze these events and identify, automatically, intrusion scenarios (supported by the case-based reasoning technique).

3.1 Event Classification and Characterization

As already mentioned in the Introduction, each event generated by a firewall stores important information such as event type, source and destination addresses, local and remote ports, and others. Since some of these information are repeated in more than one type of event, it is possible to group events using one or more aggregation elements. This constitutes the central idea of the first part of the approach.

By grouping events that share common information, it becomes possible to perform a series of operations to (a) measure and identify accesses to external and private networks, including malicious actions (port scanning and attempts to access unauthorized services), (b) follow their evolution along the time, (c) debug filtering rules configuration problems, among others. Figure 1 offers many examples in this direction; some of them are commented below.

Example 1. To determine the total data sent and received to FTP connections it is necessary to group the events that belong to the statistical group (121) and that have the field protocol with the value ftp (proto=ftp). This grouping results in the events 12 and 13 (see figure 1). The accounting of the amount of exchanged data is given by the sum of the values associated to the fields sent and rcvd.

Example 2. Inconsistencies and errors in the configuration of filtering rules can be detected with similar grouping. Consider that the organization's security policy establishes that the FTP service, running in the station 10.200.160.161, must not be accessed by external hosts (IPs out of the range 10.200.160.X). The grouping presented in example 1 highlights two events, 12 and 13, which confirms the violation of such policy, since both accesses come from stations with network prefix 66.66.77.X.

Example 3. The identification of the hosts from where departed the major number of port scans is obtained by grouping 347 events, which results in the sub-group {1,2,3,4,5,6,7,8,9}. Four out of these events indicate probes departing from the station 66.66.77.77 and five from the station 66.66.77.90.

Following the same reasoning, other aggregation elements (or a combination of them) can be employed with the purpose of identifying, among the connections performed through the firewall, maximums and minimums in respect to protocols used, hosts and accessed ports, as well as quantity of hits referring to events such as port scanning and access denied, and stations that suffer and launch more port scans.

Fig. 1. Real event set extracted from a log and their relations

3.2 Automatic Event Analysis

In addition to a more quantitative analysis, where diverse accountings are possible, our approach allows the automatic identification of intrusion scenarios based on the observation of more elementary event groups. In figure 1 three suspicious behaviors can be highlighted and are detailed bellow.

Example 4. The first consists of a vertical port scanning and it is composed of events 1, 2, 3, and 4. This probe is characterized by scans coming from a single IP address to multiple ports of another IP address. Observe that four port scans were launched, in less than one second, from the host 66.66.77.77 to the host 10.200.160.161.

Example 5. The second suspicious behavior comprehends a horizontal port scanning and includes the events 5, 6, 7, 8, and 9. In this case, the probes depart from an IP address to a single port of multiple IP addresses. As it can be observed in figure 1, the probable invader 66.66.77.90 scanned port 80 of several different hosts searching for one that had an HTTP server available.

Example 6. Finally, the third intrusion scenario corresponds to a probe followed by a successful access, including the events 1, 2, 3, 4, 10, and 12. The station 10.200.160.161 suffered four scans (ports 79, 80, 81, and 82) and one unsuccessful access attempt to the port 1080. Both the port scans and the access attempt departed from the host 66.66.77.77 that, at last, obtained access to the station using the FTP protocol (event 12); the elevated number of data sent indicates an upload to the target station (10.200.160.161).

Due to the high number of firewall events, scenarios as the ones mentioned escape, many times, unnoticed by the security manager. The second part of the approach, detailed in this subsection, proposes the use of the case-based reasoning paradigm to identify intrusion scenarios in an automatic way.

Case-based reasoning (CBR) [3] is an Artificial Intelligence paradigm that uses the knowledge of previous experiences to propose a solution in new situations. The past experiences are stored in a CBR system as cases. During the reasoning process for the resolution of a new situation, it is compared to the cases stored in the knowledge base and the most similar cases are used to propose solutions to the current problem.

The CBR paradigm has some advantages to other reasoning paradigms. One of them concerns to the facility of knowledge acquisition, which is carried out searching real experiences from past situations [2]. Other advantage is the possibility of obtaining partial match between the new situation and the cases, allowing more flexibility in domains where symptoms and problem conditions can have small variation when occurring in real situations.

Case Structure. In our approach a case stored represents a possible intrusion scenario or a suspicious activity that can be identified from the firewall events stored in the log. The case structure is presented in figure 2a. As one can observe, a case is formed by: (a) *administrative part*, with fields for identification and notes that are not used during the reasoning process; (b) *classificatory part*, which contains a field used to divide the log in parts (explained later on); and (c) *descriptive part*, which contains the attributes used to match the cases.

The similarity between the events of the real log and the cases stored is calculated by the presence of events with certain characteristics in the log; we call it a *symptom*. In other words, a symptom is the representation of one or various suspicious events that should be identified in the log so that the stored case can be considered similar to the current situation.

A case can contain one or more symptoms, according to the characteristics of the intrusion scenario or the suspicious activity being described. An example of case with two symptoms is presented in figure 2b. The case modeled, simplified to facilitate the description of the approach, suggests that an alarm should be generated whenever around five scans and a successful access are observed departing from the same source station. Symptom S_1 represents PORT_SCANNING events, such as events 1 to 4 in figure 1, while symptom S_2 represents STATISTIC events, such as the event 12 in the same figure.

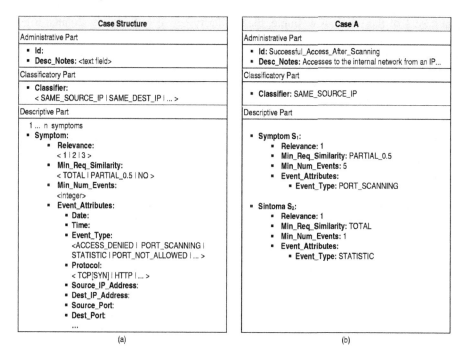

Fig. 2. Intrusion scenarios and suspicious activities modeled as cases

Parameters of the log events such as date, time, type of event, and source IP are represented in a case as attributes of the event that composes the symptom. Not all the attributes need to be defined (fulfilled); only the defined ones will be used to calculate the similarities (presented later on). Considering case A illustrated in figure 2b, only the attribute *Event_Type* is being used to identify the event that constitutes the symptom S_1. The same happens to the definition of the symptom S_2.

Reasoning Processes. The matching of log events with a stored case starts by the separation of these events in parts. The criterion to be adopted in this separation is determined by the field *Classifier* (see figure 2a). Each part is called *current case* and is compared to the stored case in a separate way. Take as example the comparison of the log events presented in figure 1 with the case A, figure 2b. Case A has as classificatory attribute the use of a same source IP address (field *Classifier* equal to SAME_SOURCE_IP). Thus, during the reasoning process the example log events are divided in two different cases, one containing the events 1 to 4 and 10 to 12 (which we will call current case 1) and the other containing events 5 to 9 (which we will call current case 2 henceforth).

After the separation of the log events in current cases, as explained above, each current case must be compared to the stored case in order to calculate its similarity, through a process called match between current case and stored case. This match is done using the similarity of the current case events regarding each symptom present in the stored case in a step called symptom matching. Back to case A and to the current case 1 of the previous example, the similarity between them is calculated using the similarity of case A symptoms, which are S_1 and S_2. At last, the similarity of a symptom is calculated based on the similarity of the current case events to the event attributes of that symptom (*Event Attributes*). In the example, the similarity of S_1 is calculated using the similarity of each event of the current case 1 (events 1 to 4 and 10 to 12) to the event attributes of that symptom (field *Event Type* equal to PORT SCANNING). These steps are explained below.

The similarity of a current case event to the event attributes of a symptom of the stored case is calculated by the total sum of each attribute similarity defined in the symptom, divided by the number of defined attributes. The approach allows the similarity of event attributes to be partial or total. In the current version, only similarities of event attributes that assume total (1) or no (0) match have been initially modeled. Resuming the example of the current case 1 and case A, in the event similarity calculation regarding symptom S_1, there is only one defined attribute, which is the *Event_Type*. The similarity of the events 1 to 4 results in 1 (100%), since these events are of the PORT_SCANNING type, which is the same event type defined in the attribute *Event_Type*. On the other hand, the similarity of the events 10 to 12 results in 0, because these events are not of PORT_SCANNING type. Considering now the similarity of the symptom S_2, there is also only one attribute defined (type of event). In the calculation of similarity of each event of the current case 1 in respect to the symptom S_2, the events 1 to 4, 10 and 11 result in 0, while the similarity of event 12 results in 1 (field *Event_Type* equal to STATISTIC).

After the calculation of the events similarity in respect to a symptom, they are ordered by their similarity. The n events with higher similarity are then used to match the symptom, where n indicates the minimum number of events needed to have total similarity to that symptom (modeled in the case as *Min_Num_Events*). The similarity of the symptom is calculated by the sum of the similarity of these n events divided by n. If the resulting similarity for a symptom is under the minimum similarity defined for that symptom in the stored case (modeled by *Min_Req_Similarity*), the comparison of that current case with the stored case is interrupted, and the current case is discarded. Recalling the previous example, the event ordering for symptom S_1 results in {1, 2, 3, 4, 10, 12}. As for this symptom the minimum number of events to total match is 5, its similarity will be calculated by $(1 + 1 + 1 + 1 + 0)/5 = 0.8$. Since the minimum similarity defined in the case for symptom S_1 is 0.5, this symptom is accepted and the process continues, calculating the similarity of the other symptoms in the case (S_2 in the example). Considering now symptom S_2 that has *Min_Num_Events* equals to 1, the similarity is calculated by $(1)/1 = 1$. With similarity 1, S_2 is also accepted.

Finally, after matching all the symptoms in the stored case, the match of the current case and the stored case is performed. This calculation is done considering the symptom similarity and its relevance using the formula bellow; ns is the number of symptoms of the stored case, r_i is the relevance of symptom i and *symptom_sim$_i$* is the similarity of symptom i. Referring once more the current case 1 and case A, the final match degree will be $((1 \times 0.8) + (1 \times 1))/2 = 0.9$, 90%. In this example, both symptoms have the same importance (*Relevance*), but assigning different weights can be necessary in other situations.

$$\frac{\sum_{i=1}^{ns} r_i \times symptom\_sim_i}{\sum_{1}^{ns} r_i}$$

When the similarity degree between the current case and a stored case is higher than a predefined value, the current case is selected as suspicious, indicating a situation that should be reported to the security manager. When a case is selected, some additional parameters are instantiated with data of the current case, in an adaptation process, in order to be possible to provide the manager with a detailed view of the identified problem. An example is the instantiation of the attribute source IP address for the cases in which the classifier corresponds to SAME_SOURCE_IP, as in case A. Using this instantiation, in the example of current case 1 commented during this section, the suspicious attitude could be presented as *Successful_Access_After_Scanning* detected to the source IP address 66.66.77.77.

In addition to the example described above we have modeled several other intrusion scenarios, including *horizontal, vertical, coordinated,* and *stealth* scans [9], IP spoofing, suspect data uploads, web server attacks, and long-term suspect TCP connections, to mention just a few. These scenarios enabled us to explore more functionalities of the case structure such as alternatives, non-ordered lists of symptoms, and time correlation between symptoms.

4 The SEFLA Tool

To validate the approach we have developed SEFLA (Symantec Enterprise Firewall Log Analysis) tool. It was developed under GNU/Linux environment, using Perl and PHP programming languages, the Apache web server and the MySQL database. Figure 3 illustrates the SEFLA architecture including its components and the interactions among them. The parser module is responsible for processing the log files (1) and inserting the main attributes of each event (e.g. type of operation, source and destination network addresses, local and remote ports, among others) in the database (2). From any web browser the security manager interacts with the core of the tool that was implemented in a set of PHP scripts (3, 4). This interaction allows (a) defining processing configurations (e.g. history size in days and types of events to be analyzed), (b) retrieving reports, (c) querying and visualizing results, (d) watching alerts for intrusion scenarios or suspicious activities and (e) verifying specific event details. For such, the database is always queried or updated (5).

Each type of event is stored in a distinct table. Some attributes, for being common for two or more events, are repeated in the corresponding tables. This scheme was adopted in detriment of a normalized one because in the latter it would require an average of six queries and seven insertions for each event to be inserted in the database (compromising the performance of the processing phase).

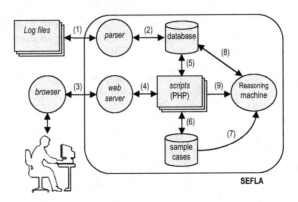

Fig. 3. SEFLA internal components

Through the web browser the security manager also includes, removes and updates cases in the cases database (3, 4, 6), as well as configures functioning parameters for the reasoning machine (3, 4, 9). The identification of intrusion scenarios is done automatically after the tool populates the database with the current day log events (parser module). The reasoning machine then searches in the database for events of interest (8) and confronts them with the sample cases (7). Whenever a new suspicious behavior is identified, the module includes an alarm in the database (8), which will become visible to the security manager.

5 Case Study

The academic network of Universidade do Vale do Rio dos Sinos was used as a case study, whose infrastructure has approximately 4.100 computers connected to it and with Internet access. Log files were collected during a one week period from the firewall located in the border of this network. SEFLA was populated with these logs and through the analysis of the obtained reports it was possible to classify, characterize and analyze the events in order to determine the network use and identify intrusion scenarios and suspicious activities. The tool was installed in an IBM NetVista station, with a 1.8GHz Intel Pentium4 processor, 256MB of RAM and GNU/Linux operating system (Red Hat Linux 9.0 distribution) with a Linux kernel version 2.4.20.

Table 1 describes the profile of each log and its processing characteristics. The largest logs are the ones generated between Monday and Friday. Given the total sum of the size of all log files (13.05GB) and considering that from this volume 52.2% of the events were processed, one can verify that the size of the log file was very reduced when inserted into the database (resulted in 22.4% of the original size). Besides, the time needed to process the 13.05GB of log data was of 144.5 minutes (2 hours, 24 minutes and 30 seconds).

Table 1. Log file sizes and processing time

	LS	**PE**	**PT**	**ADS**
28/09	0,69	1,30	8,1	0,15
29/09	2,53	3,84	28,7	0,72
30/09	2,55	3,79	28,4	1,27
01/10	2,37	3,52	24,0	1,82
02/10	2,28	3,58	23,6	2,31
03/10	1,93	3,10	22,6	2,75
04/10	0,70	1,40	9,1	2,92
Totals	13,05	20,53	144,5	2,92

LS: Log Size (GB), PE: Processed Events (millions),
PT: Processing Time (minutes), ADS: Accumulated Database Size (GB)

Figure 4 illustrates some discoveries, more of quantitative nature, carried out with SEFLA support. In (a) it is presented the data flow through the private and external networks. As it is possible to observe, the HTTP protocol was the most used, followed by TCP/1500 (used by a backup tool), FTP, SMTP, and HTTPS. The total bytes transferred through the networks of more than 30GB from Monday to Friday is another information that deserves to be emphasized. Regarding port scans, data from the day with most occurrences of this event have been processed – in this case, Sunday (see figure 4b). The five stations from where departed the major number of probes have the same network prefix (200.188.175.X). When such a hostile behavior is identified, requests coming from this network addresses should be carefully analyzed (or blocked by the firewall). Figure 4c, in counterpart, highlights stations that were most targeted for port scanning in the analyzed week. Still on the port scan analysis, figure 4d illustrates the history of the most probed port. According to the study performed about the logs, the destination port 135 represented 90% of the total probes in the period of seven days. This port is commonly used under Windows platform to start an RPC (Remote Procedure Call) connection with a remote computer. The port scans observed are probably due to the worms W32.Blaster.Worm and W32.Welchia.Worm released, respectively, in 11/Aug/2003 and 18/Aug/2003. These worms are characterized for exploring an RPC vulnerability in the DCOM (Distributed Component Object Model) acting through the TCP port 135 to launch DoS attacks [8].

Besides the analysis described above, the events collected by the firewall during the week have also been analyzed from the point of view of automatic detection of intrusion scenarios. One of the identified scenarios was the port scan (with similar behavior to the examples 4 and 5), which repeated several times in the log. One instance of this scenario corresponds to the probe represented by 24 port scan events departing from the same source IP 200.226.212.151 to the same destination IP 200.188.160.130 observed on Sunday, 1:48am. This scenario was considered 100% similar to the case *Port_Scan*, as its occurrence involved more than five events of the port scan type originating from the same source IP address (symptom defined for this case). Another scenario recognized in many occasions was the one which comprises port scans and a successful access departing from the same source station as specified in case *Successful_Access_After_Scanning* (figure 2b).

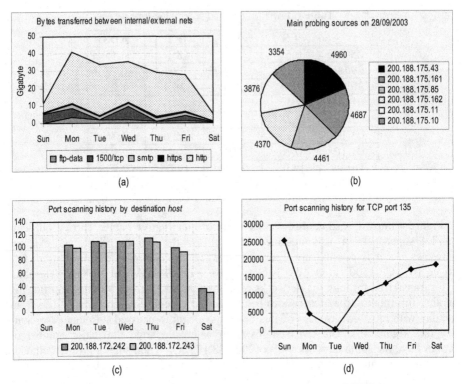

Fig. 4. Some of the information retrieved with the use of SEFLA

6 Conclusions and Future Work

Ensuring the safety of information kept by organizations is a basic requirement for their operation, since the number of security incidents grows exponentially every year. However, to protect organizations considering the quantity and the growing complexity of the executed attacks, it is needed to provide the security manager with techniques and tools that support the analysis of the evidences and, furthermore, allow the automatic identification of intrusion scenarios or suspicious activities. In this context, we presented an approach, accompanied by a tool, for classification, characterization and analysis of events generated by firewalls. It is worth mentioning that our approach does not replace other tools, as the intrusion detection systems, and must be used in conjunction with them.

The organization of the approach in two parts allows handling, in a satisfactory way, both quantitative and qualitative information. On one side, the event grouping mechanism based on one or more aggregation elements reveals network usage characteristics and malicious activities. These can be used (a) to evaluate the accomplishment of the security policy, (b) to control resource usage (reviewing current filtering rules) and (c) to recognize sources and targets of hostile behaviors (aiming at their protection). On the other side, the second part of the approach - supported by the case-based reasoning technique - provides the automatic recognition of event sequences that represent intrusion scenarios or suspicious activities. Here, more than identifying and quantifying actions, one pursuits to recognize the strategies adopted by intruders to obtain unauthorized access to stations, services and applications.

As it could be observed in section 5, even after the processing and storage of the events in the database, the resulting base size is large (considering that it contains events from only seven days). In order to obtain long-term statistics, the synthesis of essential information about the older events is proposed as a future work (at the cost of losing the possibility of detailing these events). Currently, we are working on the evaluation of how much choices on values for *Relevance* and *Min_Req_Similarity*, for example, influence the generation of high-level alerts. From this investigation we expect to learn how to better determine weights for the different parameters in the model.

References

1. Debar, H. and Wespi, A. (2001). Aggregation and correlation of intrusion-detection alerts. Recent Advances in Intrusion Detection, 2212:85-103.
2. Esmaili, M. and et al (1996). Case-Based Reasoning for Intrusion Detection. Computer Security Applications Conference, p. 214-223.
3. Kolodner, J. (1993). Case-Based Reasoning. Morgan Kaufmann.
4. Ning, P., Cui, Y., and Reeves, D. (2002). Analyzing Intensive Intrusion Alerts via Correlation. Recent Advances in Intrusion Detection, 2516:74-94.
5. Porras, P. A. , Fong, M. W. , and Valdes, A. (2002). A Mission-Impact-Based Approach to INFOSEC Alarm Correlation. Recent Advances in Intrusion Detection, 2516:95-114.
6. Schwartz, D., Stoecklin, S., and Yilmaz, E. (2002). A Case-Based Approach to Network Intrusion Detection. Internacional Conference on Information Fusion, p. 1084-1089.
7. Symantec (2001). Symantec Enterprise Firewall, Symantec Enterprise VPN, and Veloci-Raptor Firewall Appliance Reference Guide. Symantec.
8. Symantec (2003). Symantec Security Response.
9. Yegneswaran, V., Barford, P., and Ulrich, J. (2003). Internet Intrusions: Global Characteristics and Prevalence. ACM SIGMETRICS Performance Evaluation Review, 31(1):138-147.

A Reputation Management and Selection Advisor Schemes for Peer-to-Peer Systems

Loubna Mekouar, Youssef Iraqi, and Raouf Boutaba

University of Waterloo, Waterloo, Canada
{lmekouar, iraqi, rboutaba}@bbcr.uwaterloo.ca

Abstract. In this paper we propose a new and efficient reputation management scheme for partially decentralized peer-to-peer systems. The reputation scheme helps to build trust between peers based on their past experiences and the feedback from other peers. We also propose two selection advisor algorithms for helping peers select the right peer to download from. The simulation results show that the proposed schemes are able to detect malicious peers and isolate them from the system, hence reducing the amount of inauthentic uploads. Our approach also allows to uniformly distribute the load between non malicious peers.

1 Introduction

1.1 Background

In a Peer-to-Peer (P2P) file sharing system, peers communicate directly with each other to exchange information and share files. P2P systems can be divided into several categories. Centralized P2P systems (e.g. Napster [1]), use a centralized control server to manage the system. These systems suffer from the single point of failure, scalability and censorship problems. Decentralized P2P systems try to distribute the control over several peers. They can be divided into completely-decentralized and partially-decentralized systems. Completely-decentralized systems (e.g. Gnutella [2]) have absolutely no hierarchical structure between the peers. In other words, all peers have exactly the same role. In partially-decentralized systems (e.g. KaZaa [3], Morpheus [4] and Gnutella2 [5]), peers can have different roles. Some of the peers act as local central indexes for files shared by local peers. These special peers are called "supernodes" or "ultrapeers" and are assigned dynamically [6]. They can be replaced in case of failure or malicious attack. Supernodes index the files shared by peers connected to them, and proxy search requests on behalf of these peers. Queries are therefore sent to supernodes, not other peers. A supernode typically supports 300 to 500 peers depending on available resources [5]. Partially-decentralized systems are the most popular in P2P systems.

In traditional P2P systems (i.e. without any reputation mechanism), the user is given a list of peers that can provide the requested file. The user has then to choose one peer from which the download will be performed. This process is frustrating to the user as this later struggles to choose the right peer. After

A. Sahai and F. Wu (Eds.): DSOM 2004, LNCS 3278, pp. 208–219, 2004.

the download has finished, the user has to check the received file for malicious content (e.g. viruses[1]) and that it actually corresponds to the requested file (i.e. the requested content). If the file is not good, the user has to start the process again. In traditional P2P systems, little information is given to the user to help in the selection process.

In [8] it is stated that most of the shared content is provided by only 30% of the peers. There should be a mechanism to reward these peers and encourage other peers to share their content. At the same time, there should be a mechanism to punish peers with malicious behavior (i.e. those that provide malicious content or misleading filenames) or at least isolate them from the system.

Reputation-based P2P systems [9,10,11,12,13] were introduced to solve these problems. These systems try to provide a reputation management system that will evaluate the transactions performed by the peers and associate a reputation value to these peers. The reputation values will be used as a selection criteria between peers. These systems differ in the way they compute the reputation values, and in the way they use these values. The following is the life cycle of a peer in a reputation-based P2P system:

1. Send a request for a file
2. Receive a list of candidate peers that have the requested file
3. Select a peer or a set of peers based on a reputation metric
4. Download the file
5. Send a feedback and update the reputation data

1.2 Motivation and Contribution

Several reputation management systems have been proposed in the literature (cf. Section 5). All of these have focused on the completely-decentralized P2P systems. Only KaZaa, a proprietary partially-decentralized P2P system, has introduced basic reputation metric (called "participation level") for rating peers. Note that the proposed reputation management schemes for completely-decentralized P2P systems cannot be applied in the case of partially-decentralized system as this later relies on the supernodes for control messages exchange (i.e. no direct management messages are allowed between peers.)

In this paper, we propose a reputation management system for partially-decentralized P2P systems. This reputation mechanism will allow a more clear-sighted management of peers and files. Our contribution is in step 3 and 5 of the life cycle of a peer in a reputation-based P2P system (cf. section 1). The reputation considered in this paper, is for trust (i.e. maliciousness of peers), based on the accuracy and quality of the file received. Good reputation is obtained by having consistent good behavior through several transactions. The reputation criteria is used to distinguish between peers. The goal is to maximize the user satisfaction and decrease the sharing of corrupted files.

The paper is organized as follows. In Section 2, we introduce the new reputation management schemes proposed in this paper. Section 3, describes the

---

[1] such as the VBS.Gnutella Worm [7]

proposed selection advisor mechanisms. Section 4 presents the performance evaluation of the proposed schemes while Section 5 presents the related works. Finally, Section 6 concludes the paper.

2 Reputation Management

In this section, we introduce the new reputation management schemes. The following notations will be used.

2.1 Notations and Assumptions

- Let P_i denotes peer i
- Let $D_{i,j}$ be the units of downloads performed from peer P_j by peer P_i
- Let $D_{i,*}$ denotes the units of downloads performed by peer P_i
- Let $D_{*,j}$ denotes the units of uploads by peer P_j
- Let $A_{i,j}^F$ be the appreciation of peer P_i for downloading the file F from P_j.
- Let $Sup(i)$ denotes the supernode of peer i

In this paper, we assume that supernodes are selected from a set of trusted peers. This means that supernodes are trusted to manipulate the reputation data. The mechanism used to do so is outside the scope of this paper and will be addressed in the future. We also assume that the supernodes share a secret key that will be used to digitally sign data. The reader is referred to [14] for a survey on key management for secure group communication. We also assume the use of public key encryption to provide integrity and confidentiality of message exchanges.

2.2 The Reputation Management Scheme

After downloading a file F from peer P_j, peer P_i will value this download. If the file received corresponds to the requested file and has good quality, then we set $A_{i,j}^F = 1$. If not, we set $A_{i,j}^F = -1$. In this case, either the file has the same title as the requested file but different content, or that its quality is not acceptable. Note that if we want to support different levels of appreciation, we can set the appreciation as a real number between -1 and 1. Note also that a null appreciation can be used, for example, if a faulty communication occurred during the file transfer.

Each peer P_i in the system has four values, called *reputation data* (REP_{P_i}), stored by its supernode $Sup(i)$:

1. $D_{i,*}^+$: Appreciated downloads of peer P_i from other peers,
2. $D_{i,*}^-$: Non-appreciated downloads of peer P_i from other peers,
3. $D_{*,i}^+$: Successful downloads by other peers from peer P_i,
4. $D_{*,i}^-$: Failed downloads by other peers from peer P_i

$D_{i,*}^+$ and $D_{i,*}^-$ provide an idea about the health of the system (i.e. satisfaction of the peers). $D_{*,i}^+$ and $D_{*,i}^-$ provide an idea about the amount of uploads provided by the peer. They can for example help detect *free riders*. Keeping track of $D_{*,i}^-$ will also help detecting malicious peers (i.e. those peers who are providing corrupted files or misleading filenames). Note that we have the following relationships:

$$D_{i,*}^+ + D_{i,*}^- = D_{i,*} \ \forall i$$
$$D_{*,i}^+ + D_{*,i}^- = D_{*,i} \ \forall i \tag{1}$$

Keeping track of these values is important. They will be used as an indication of the reputation and the satisfaction of the peers. Figure 1 depicts the steps performed after receiving a file.

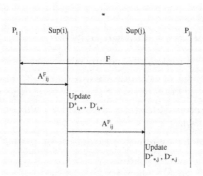

Fig. 1. Reputation update steps

When receiving the appreciation (i.e. $A_{i,j}^F$) of peer P_i, its supernode $Sup(i)$ will update the values of $D_{i,*}^+$ and $D_{i,*}^-$. The appreciation is then sent to the supernode of peer P_j to update the values of $D_{*,j}^+$ and $D_{*,j}^-$. The way these values are updated is explained in the following two subsections 2.3 and 2.4.

When a peer P_i joins the system for the first time, all values of its *reputation data* REP_{P_i} are initialized to zero[2]. Based on the peer transactions of uploads and downloads, these values are updated. Periodically, the supernode of peer P_i sends REP_{P_i} to the peer. The frequency is not too low to preserve accuracy and not too high to avoid extra overhead. The peer will keep a copy of REP_{P_i} to be used the next time the peer joins the system or if its supernode changes. To prevent tempering with REP_{P_i}, the supernode digitally signs REP_{P_i}. The *reputation data* can be used to compute important reputation parameters as presented in section 3.

2.3   The Number Based Appreciation Scheme

In this first scheme, we will use the number of downloads as an indication of the amount downloaded. This means that $D_{*,j}$ will indicate the number of uploads

---

[2] i.e. neutral reputation

by peer P_j. In this case, after each download transaction by peer P_i from peer P_j, $Sup(i)$ will perform the following operation:

If $A^F_{i,j} = 1$ then $D^+_{i,*} + +$, else $D^-_{i,*} + +$.

and $Sup(j)$ will perform the following operation:

If $A^F_{i,j} = 1$ then $D^+_{*,j} + +$, else $D^-_{*,j} + +$.

This scheme allows to rate peers according to the number of transactions performed. However, since it does not take into consideration the size of the downloads, this scheme makes no difference between peers who are uploading large files and those who are uploading small files. This may rise a fairness issue between the peers as uploading large files necessitates the dedication of more resources. Also, some malicious peers may artificially increase their reputation by uploading a large number of small files to a malicious partner.

2.4   The Size Based Appreciation Scheme

An alternative for the proposed algorithm is to take into consideration the size of the download. Once the peer sends its appreciation, the size of the download $Size(F)$ (the amount, in Megabytes, downloaded by the peer P_i from the peer P_j) is also sent[3]. The reputation data of P_i and P_j will be updated based on the amount of data downloaded.

In this case, after each download transaction by peer P_i from peer P_j, $Sup(i)$ will perform the following operation:

If $A^F_{i,j} = 1$ then $D^+_{i,*} = D^+_{i,*} + Size(F)$,

else $D^-_{i,*} = D^-_{i,*} + Size(F)$.

and $Sup(j)$ will perform the following operation:

If $A^F_{i,j} = 1$ then $D^+_{*,j} = D^+_{*,j} + Size(F)$,

else $D^-_{*,j} = D^-_{*,j} + Size(F)$.

If we want to include the content of files in the rating, it is possible to attribute a coefficient for each file. For example, in the case that the file is rare, the uploading peer could be rewarded by increasing its successful uploads with more than just the size of the file. Eventually, instead of using the size of the download, we can use the amount of resources dedicated by the uploading peer to this download operation.

3   The Selection Advisor Algorithms

In this section we assume that peer P_i has received a list of peers P_j that have the requested file. Peer P_i has to use the reputation data of these peers to choose the right peer to download from. Note that the selection operation can be performed at the level of the supernode, i.e. the supernode can, for example, filter malicious peers from the list given to peer P_i.

The following is the life cycle of a peer P_i in the proposed reputation-based P2P system:

---

[3] Alternatively the supernode can know the size of the file from the information received as a response to the peer's request.

1. Send a request for a file F to the supernode $Sup(i)$
2. Receive a list of candidate peers that have the requested file
3. Select a peer or a set of peers P_j based on a reputation metric (The reputation algorithms are presented in the following subsections 3.1 and 3.2)
4. Download the file F
5. Send the feedback $A_{i,j}^F$. $Sup(i)$ and $Sup(j)$ will update the reputation data REP_{P_i} and REP_{P_j} respectively

The following subsections describe two alternative selection algorithms. Anyone of these algorithms can be based on one of the appreciation schemes presented in section 2.3 and 2.4.

3.1 The Difference Based Algorithm

In this scheme, we compute the Difference-Based (DB) behavior of a peer P_j as:

$$DB_j = D_{*,j}^+ - D_{*,j}^- \tag{2}$$

This value gives an idea about the aggregate behavior of the peer. Note that the reputation as defined in equation 2 can be negative. This reputation value gives preference to peers who did more good uploads than bad ones.

3.2 The Real Behavior Based Algorithm

In the previous scheme, only the difference between $D_{*,j}^+$ and $D_{*,j}^-$ is considered. This may not be able to give a real idea about the behavior of the peers.

Example If peer P_1 and peer P_2 have the reputation data as follows: $D_{*,1}^+ = 40$, $D_{*,1}^- = 20$, $D_{*,2}^+ = 20$ and $D_{*,2}^- = 0$. Then according to Difference-Based reputation (cf. equation 2) and the Number-Based Appreciation scheme (cf. section 2.3), we have $DB_1 = 40 - 20 = 20$ and $DB_2 = 20 - 0 = 20$. In this case, both peers have the same reputation. However, from the user's perspective, peer P_2 is more preferable than peer P_1. Indeed, peer P_2 has not uploaded any malicious files.

To solve this problem, we propose to take into consideration not only the difference between $D_{*,j}^+$ and $D_{*,j}^-$ but also the sum of these values. In this scheme, we compute the real behavior of a peer P_j as:

$$RB_j = \frac{D_{*,j}^+ - D_{*,j}^-}{D_{*,j}^+ + D_{*,j}^-} = \frac{D_{*,j}^+ - D_{*,j}^-}{D_{*,j}} \text{ if } D_{*,j} \neq 0$$
$$RB_j = 0 \qquad\qquad\qquad\qquad\quad \text{otherwise} \tag{3}$$

Note that the reputation as defined in equation 3 can vary from -1 to 1. If we go back to the example, then we have $RB_1 = (40 - 20)/60 = 1/3$ and $RB_2 = (20 - 0)/20 = 1$. The Real Behavior Based scheme will choose peer P_2.

When using this reputation scheme, the peer can choose the peer P_j with the maximum value of RB_j.

In addition of being used as a selection criteria, the reputation data can be used by the supernode to perform service differentiation. Periodically, the supernode can check the reputation data of its peers and assign priorities to them. Peers with high reputation will receive high priority while those with lower reputation will receive a low priority. For example, by comparing the values of $D_{*,i}$ and $D_{i,*}$ one can have a real characterization of the peer's behavior. If $D_{i,*} >> D_{*,i}$, then this peer can be considered as a *free rider*. Its supernode can reduce or stop providing services to this peer. This will encourage and motivate *free riders* to share more with others. In addition, the supernode can enforce additional management policies to protect the system from malicious peers. It is also possible to implement mechanisms to prevent malicious peers from downloading in addition to prevent them from uploading.

4   Performance Evaluation

4.1   Simulated Algorithms

We will simulate the two selection advisor algorithms proposed in this paper (cf. section 3.1 and 3.2) namely, the Difference-Based (DB) algorithm and the Real-Behavior-Based (RB) algorithm. Both schemes will use the Size-Based Appreciation Scheme proposed in section 2.4. We will compare the performance of these two algorithms with the following two schemes.

In KaZaa [3], the peer participation level is computed as follows:

($uploaded/downloaded$) × 100, i.e. using our notation (cf. section 2.1) the participation level is $(D_{*,j}/D_{j,*}) \times 100$. We will consider the scheme where each peer uses the participation level of other peers as a selection criteria and we will refer to it as the KaZaa-Based algorithm (KB).

We will also simulate a system without reputation management. This means that the selection is done in a random way. We will refer to this algorithm as the Random Way algorithm (RW). Table 1 presents the list of considered algorithms.

Table 1.

Algorithm	Acronym
Difference-Based algorithm	DB
Real-Behavior-Based algorithm	RB
KaZaa-Based algorithm	KB
Random Way algorithm	RW

4.2   Simulation Parameters

We use the following simulation parameters:

- We simulate a system with 1000 peers.
- The number of files is 1000.
- File sizes are uniformly distributed between 10MB and 150MB.
- At the beginning of the simulation, each peer has one of the files randomly and each file has one owner.
- As observed by [15], KaZaa files' requests do not follow the Zipf's law distribution. In our simulations, file requests follow the real life distribution observed in [15]. This means that each peer can ask for a file with a Zipf distribution over all the files that the peer does not already have. The Zipf distribution parameter is chosen close to 1 as assumed in [15]
- The probability of malicious peers is 50%. Recall that our goal is to assess the capability of the selection algorithms to isolate the malicious peers.
- The probability of a malicious peer to upload an inauthentic file is 80%
- Only 80% of all peers with the requested file are found in each request.
- We simulate 30000 requests. This means that each peer performs an average of 30 requests. For this reason we do not specify a storage capacity limit.
- The simulations were repeated 10 times over which the results are averaged.

4.3   Performance Parameters

In our simulations we will mainly focus on the following performance parameters:

1. The peer satisfaction: computed as the difference of non-malicious downloads and malicious ones over the sum of all the downloads performed by the peer. Using our notation (cf. section 2.2) the peer satisfaction is: $(D_{i,*}^{+} - D_{i,*}^{-})/(D_{i,*}^{+} + D_{i,*}^{-})$. The peer satisfaction is averaged over all peers.
2. The size of malicious uploads: computed as the sum of the size of all malicious uploads performed by all peers during the simulation. Using our notation this can be computed as: $\sum_j D_{*,j}^{-}$.
3. Peer load share: we would like to know the impact of the selection advisor algorithm on the load distribution among the peers. The peer load share is computed as the normalized load supported by the peer. This is computed as the sum of all uploads performed by the peer over all the uploads in the system.

4.4   Simulation Results

Figure 2 (a) depicts the peer satisfaction achieved by the four considered schemes. The X axis represents the number of requests while the Y axis represents the peer satisfaction. Note that the maximum peer satisfaction that can be achieved is 1. Note also that the peer satisfaction can be negative. According to the figure, it is clear that the DB and RB schemes outperform the RW and KB schemes in terms of peer satisfaction. The bad performance of KB can be

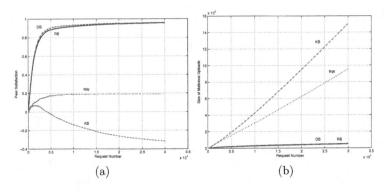

Fig. 2. (a) Peer Satisfaction, (b) Size of malicious uploads

explained by the fact that it does not distinguish between malicious and non-malicious peers. As long as the peer has the highest participation level, it is chosen regardless of its behavior. Our schemes (*DB* and *RB*) make the distinction and do not choose a peer if it is detected as malicious. The *RW* scheme chooses peers randomly and hence the results observed from the simulations (i.e. 20% satisfaction) can be explained as follows. With 50% malicious peers and 80% probability to upload an inauthentic file, we can expect to have 60% of authentic uploads and 40% inauthentic uploads in average. As the peer satisfaction is computed as the difference of non-malicious downloads and malicious ones over the sum of all the downloads performed by the peer. We can expect a peer satisfaction of $(60 - 40)/(60 + 40) = 20\%$.

Figure 2 (b) shows the size of malicious uploads, i.e. the size of inauthentic file uploads. As in *RW* scheme peers are chosen randomly, we can expect to see a steady increase of the size of malicious uploads. On the other hand, our proposed schemes *DB* and *RB* can quickly detect malicious peers and avoid choosing them for uploads. This isolates the malicious peers and controls the size of malicious uploads. This, of course, results in using the network bandwidth more efficiently and higher peer satisfaction as shown in figure 2 (a). In *KB* scheme, the peer with the highest participation level is chosen. The chosen peer will see its participation level increases according to the amount of the requested upload. This will further increase the probability of being chosen again in the future. If the chosen peer happens to be malicious, the size of malicious uploads will increase dramatically as malicious peers are chosen again and again. This is reflected in figure 2 (b) where *KB* has worse results than *RW*.

To investigate the distribution of loads between the peers for the considered schemes, we plotted the normalized load supported by each peer in the simulation. Figure 3 and 4 depict the results. Note that we organized the peers into two categories, malicious peers from 1 to 500 and non malicious peers from 501 to 1000. As expected, the *RW* scheme distributes the load uniformly among the peers (malicious and non malicious). The *KB* scheme does not distribute the load uniformly. Instead, few peers are always chosen to upload the requested files. In addition, the *KB* scheme cannot distinguish between malicious and non malicious peers, and in this particular case, the malicious peer number 280 has been chosen to perform most of the requested uploads.

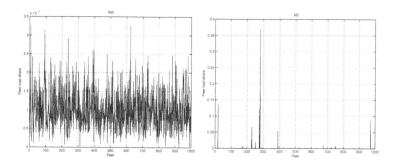

Fig. 3. Peer load share for RW and KB

In figure 4 the results for the proposed schemes are presented. We can note that in both schemes malicious peers are isolated from the system by not being requested to perform uploads. This explains the fact that the normalized loads of malicious peers (peers from 1 to 500) is very small. This also explains why the load supported by non malicious peers is higher than the one in the *RW* and *KB* scenarios. Indeed, since none of the malicious peers is involved in uploading the requested files[4], almost all the load (of the 30000 requests) is supported by the non malicious peers.

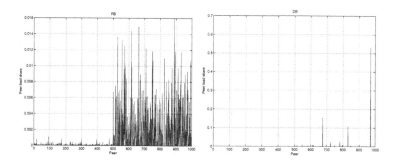

Fig. 4. Peer load share for RB and DB

---

[4] after that these malicious peers are detected by the proposed schemes

According to the figure, we can observe that even if the two proposed schemes DB and RB are able to detect malicious peers and isolate them from the system, they do not distribute the load among non malicious peers in the same manner. Indeed, the RB scheme distributes the load more uniformly among the non malicious peers than the DB scheme. The DB scheme tends to concentrate the load on a small number of peers. This can be explained by the way each scheme computes the reputation of the peers. As explained in sections 3.1 and 3.2, the DB scheme computes the reputation of a peer P_j as shown in equation 2 based on a difference between non malicious uploads and malicious ones. The RB scheme, on the other hand, computes a ratio as shown in equation 3. The fact that DB is based on a difference, makes it choose the peer with the highest difference. This in turn will make this peer more likely to be chosen again in the future. This is why, in figure 4, the load is not distributed uniformly.

The RB scheme, focuses on the ratio of the difference between non malicious uploads and malicious ones over the sum of all uploads performed by the peer (cf. eq. 3). This does not give any preference to peers with higher difference. Since in our simulations we did not consider any free riders, we can expect to have a uniform load distribution between the peers as depicted by figure 4. If free riders are considered, the reputation mechanisms will not be affected since reputation data is based on the uploads of peers. Obviously, the load distribution will be different.

5   Related Works

eBay [16] uses the feedback profile for rating their members and establishing the members' reputation. Members rate their trading partners with a positive, negative or neutral feedback, and explain briefly why. eBay suffers from the single point of failure problem as it is based on a centralized server for reputation management.

In [10], a distributed polling algorithm is used to allow a peer looking for a resource to enquire about the reputation of offerers by polling other peers. The polling is performed by broadcasting a message asking all other peers to give their opinion about the reputation of the servants. In [11], the EigenTrust algorithm assigns to each peer in the system a trust value. This value is based on its past uploads and reflects the experiences of all peers with the peer.

The two previous schemes are reactive, They require reputations to be computed *on-demand* which requires cooperation from a large number of peers in performing computations. As this is performed for each peer having the requested file with the cooperation of all other peers, this will introduce additional latency and overhead. Most of the proposed reputation management schemes for completely decentralized P2P systems suffer from these drawbacks.

6   Conclusion

In this paper, we proposed a new reputation management scheme for partially decentralized P2P systems. Our scheme is based on four simple values associated to each peer and stored at the supernode level. We also propose two selection advisor algorithms for assisting peers in selecting the right peer to download from. Performance evaluation shows that our schemes are able to detect and isolate malicious peers from the system. Our reputation management scheme is proactive and has minimal overhead in terms of computation, infrastructure, storage and message complexity. Furthermore, it does not require any synchronization between the peers and no global voting is required. Our scheme is designed to reward those who are practicing good P2P behavior, and punish those who are not. Important aspects that we will investigate in future work include mechanisms to give incentives for peers to provide appreciations after performing downloads, and countermeasures for peers who provide faked values for appreciations.

References

1. A.Oram. In: Peer-to-Peer: Harnessing the Power of Disruptive Technologies. O'Reilly Books (2001) 21–37
2. http://www9.limewire.com/developer/gnutella_protocol_0.4.pdf.
3. http://www.kazaa.com/us/help/glossary.htm.
4. http://www.morphus.com/morphus.htm.
5. http://www.gnutella2.com/.
6. Androutsellis-Theotokis, S.: A Survey of Peer-to-Peer File Sharing Technologies. Technical report, ELTRUN (2002)
7. http://www.commandsoftware.com/virus/gnutella.html.
8. Adar, E., Huberman, B.A.: Free Riding on Gnutella. Technical report, HP (2000) http://www.hpl.hp.com/research/idl/papers/gnutella/.
9. Aberer, K., Despotovic, Z.: Managing Trust in a Peer-to-Peer Information System. In: International Conference on Information and Knowledge Management. (2001)
10. Cornelli, F., Damiani, E., di Vimercati, S.D.C., Paraboschi, S., Samarati, P.: Choosing Reputable Servents in a P2P Network. In: The Eleventh International World Wide Web Conference, Honolulu, Hawaii, USA (2002)
11. Kamvar, S.D., Schlosser, M.T., Garcia-Molina, H.: The EigenTrust Algorithm for Reputation Management in P2P Networks. In: the Twelfth International World Wide Web Conference, Budapest, Hungary (2003)
12. Gupta, M., Judge, P., Ammar, M.: A Reputation System for Peer-to-Peer Networks. In: ACM 13th International Workshop on Network and Operating Systems Support for Digital Audio and Video, Monterey, California, USA (2003)
13. Xiong, L., Liu, L.: PeerTrust: Supporting Reputation-Based Trust for Peer-to-Peer Electronic Communities. IEEE Transactions on Knowledge and Data Engineering, Special Issue on Peer-to-Peer Based Data Management (2004)
14. Rafaeli, S., Hutchison, D.: A Survey of Key Management for Secure Group Communication. ACM Computing Surveys **35** (2003) 309–329
15. Gummadi, K., Dunn, R.J., Saroiu, S., Gribble, S.D., Levy, H.M., Zahorjan, J.: Measurement, Modeling, and analysis of a Peer-to-Peer File Sharing Workload. In: ACM Symposium on Operating Systems Principles, New York, USA (2003)
16. http://pages.ebay.com/help/feedback/reputation-ov.html.

Using Process Restarts to Improve Dynamic Provisioning

Raquel V. Lopes, Walfredo Cirne, and Francisco V. Brasileiro

Universidade Federal de Campina Grande,
Coordenação de Pós-graduação em Engenharia Elétrica
Departamento de Sistemas e Computação
Av. Aprígio Veloso, 882 - 58.109-970, Campina Grande, PB, Brazil
Phone: +55 83 310 1433
{raquel,walfredo,fubica}@dsc.ufcg.edu.br

Abstract. Load variations are unexpected perturbations that can degrade performance or even cause unavailability of a system. There are efforts that attempt to dynamically provide resources to accommodate load fluctuations during the execution of applications. However, these efforts do not consider the existence of software faults, whose effects can influence the application behavior and its quality of service, and may mislead a dynamic provisioning system. When trying to tackle both problems simultaneously the fundamental issue to be addressed is how to differentiate a saturated application from a faulty one. The contributions of this paper are threefold. Firstly, we introduce the idea of taking software faults into account when specifying a dynamic provisioning scheme. Secondly, we define a simple algorithm that can be used to distinguish saturated from faulty software. By implementing this algorithm one is able to realize dynamic provisioning with restarts into a full server infrastructure data center. Finally, we implement this algorithm and experimentally demonstrate its efficacy.

Keywords: dynamic provisioning, software faults, restart, n-tier applications.

1   Introduction

The desire to accommodate load variations of long running applications is not new. Traditionally, it has been made by overprovisioning the system [1,2]. Recently, dynamic provisioning has emerged, suggesting that resources can be provided to an application on an on-demand basis [3,4,5,6,7,8,9,10,11]. Dynamic provisioning is particularly relevant to applications whose workload vary widely over time (i.e. where the cost of overprovisioning is greater). This is the case of e-commerce applications, which typically are n-tier, long running applications that cater for a large user community.

We have experimented with a dynamic provisioning scheme that targeted a simple 2-tier application. To our surprise, we noticed that even when more

A. Sahai and F. Wu (Eds.): DSOM 2004, LNCS 3278, pp. 220–231, 2004.
© IFIP International Federation for Information Processing 2004

resources had been provided, application quality of service (QoS) had still remained low. Investigating further, we found out that the application failed due to hard-to-fix software bugs such as Heisenbugs [12] and aging related bugs [13]. Thus, the real problem was that dynamic provisioning systems use functions that relate system metrics (load, resource consumption, etc.) to the number of machines to be provided to the application [5,6,14]. However, when software faults occur, these functions may not reflect the reality anymore, since there are components of the application that are up, consuming resources, processing requests, but not performing according to their specifications anymore.

In fact, there is a close relationship between load and software faults. Saturated[1] applications are more prone to failures [1]. They are more susceptible to race conditions, garbage collector misbehavior, and so on, increasing the probability of occurrence of non-deterministic bugs, such as Heisenbugs. Because of this close relationship, we argue that a management system must deal with both of them in a combined fashion. This dual goal system must be able to decide between add/release resources (dynamic allocation actions) and restart software (software fault recovery).

The contributions of this paper are threefold. First, we introduce the importance of taking software faults into account when conceiving a dynamic provisioning scheme. Second, we define a simple algorithm that can be used to differentiate saturated from faulty software. Third, we implement this algorithm to experimentally evaluate its efficacy in the context of a full server infrastructure data center. Our results indicate that by taking into account both load variability and software faults, we can improve the quality of service (QoS) and yet reduce the resource consumption, compared to doing solely dynamic provisioning.

The remaining of the paper is structured in the following way. In the next section we discuss related work. Next, in Section 3, we show a control system that makes decision in order to identify the application status (saturated, faulty, optimal or underutilized) and act over an n-tier application. This system is named Dynamic Allocation with Software Restart (DynAlloc-SR). Then, in Section 4, we present some preliminary results obtained from experiments carried out to measure DynAlloc-SR efficacy. Finally, we conclude the paper and point future research directions in Section 5.

2   Related Work

Our research is related to two important areas: dynamic provisioning of resources and usage of software reboots as a remedy for soft software bugs. In the following we discuss related works in these areas and point out the novelty of our approach.

2.1   Autonomic Data Centers

Many research groups have been studying the issue of dynamic provisioning of resources in data centers (DCs). For an autonomic DC to come to reality,

---

[1] The words saturated and overloaded are used interchangeably in this paper.

some problems must be solved. One of them is to know the optimal amount of resources to give to an application on demand [3,5,6,14], which is our focus. Other issues involve DC level decisions such as whether agents requests for resources are going to be accepted, whether new applications are going to be accepted by the DC and whether DC capacity is appropriate [3,8,9,10]. Finally, technologies that enable rapid topology reconfiguration of virtual domains are needed [4,11].

In [5] authors present an algorithm that indicates the amount of machines a clustered application needs to accommodate the current load. The algorithm makes decisions based on CPU consumption and load. That work considers a full server infrastructure, where each server runs the application of only one customer at each time. A market-based approach that deals with the allocation of CPU cycles among client applications in a DC is presented in [3]. CPU consumption in servers is the monitored metric that must be maintained around a set point. A dynamic provisioning mechanism based on applications models is proposed in [6]. Application performance models relate application metrics to resource metrics and can be used to predict the effect of allotments on the application. Both [3] and [6] consider a shared server data center infrastructure, in which different applications may share the same server. An approach for dynamic surge protection is proposed in [14] to handle unexpected load surges. Resource provisioning actions are based on short and long term load predictions. The authors argue that this approach is more efficient than a control system based in thresholds. Clearly, both have advantages and disadvantages. A dynamic surge protection system is as good as the predictions it does. A threshold-based system is as good as the threshold values configured. Finally, other researchers proposed frameworks to help developers to write scalable clustered services [7,15]. Only applications in development can benefit from these frameworks.

As [5] we consider a full server infrastructure. However, we monitor application performance metrics instead of system consumption metrics, and act over the system as soon as possible in order to maintain the average availability and response times of the application around a set point. Our provisioning system is based only on QoS threshold values. Load tendency is taken into account only to reinforce a resource provisioning decision. Our approach needs neither application performance models nor specific knowledge about the implementation of the application. We also do not require modification in the application code nor in the middleware. Finally, our provisioning approach is able to detect when the degraded performance is due to data layer problems, in which case, actions in the application or presentation layers do not take effect.

2.2   Recovering from Software Faults

Some software bugs can escape from all tests and may manifest themselves during the application execution. Typically, they are Heisenbugs and aging related bugs. Both are activated under certain conditions which are not easily reproducible.

Software rejuvenation has been proposed as a remedy against the software aging phenomenon [16]. Rejuvenation is the proactive rollback of an application to a clean status. Software aging can give signs before causing a failure. As a result, they can be treated proactively. A similar mechanism named restart has been prescribed for Heisenbugs recovery, however, on a reactive basis [17,18].

Rejuvenation can be scheduled based on time (eg every Monday, at 4 a.m.), on application metrics (eg memory utilization) or on the amount of work done (eg after n requests processed) [16]. [19] and [20], for instance, try to define the best moment to rejuvenate long running systems based on memory consumption. [19] defines multiple levels of rejuvenation to cope with different levels of degradation. [21] formally describes a framework that estimates epochs of rejuvenation. They distinguish memory leakage and genuine increase on the level of memory used by a leak function (each application may have its function) that models the leaking process. The amount of leaked memory of some application can be studied by using tools to detect application program errors [22]. However, these tools are not able to detect leaks automatically during the execution of the application. Methods to detect memory leaks still require human intervention.

The execution of micro-reboots is one technique proposed in [18] to improve the availability of J2EE (Java 2 Platform, Enterprise Edition) applications by reducing the recovering time. Candea et al consider any transient software fault, not only Heisenbugs or aging related bugs. Their technique is application-agnostic, however, it requires changes in the J2EE middleware.

Our restart approach is a simplification of the one presented in [18]. We perform reactive restarts when the application exhibits bad behavior. Our restarts are always at the middleware level. We try to differentiate saturation and software faults without requiring any knowledge of the application being managed neither modification in the middleware that supports its execution. We name our recovery method restart, not rejuvenation, because of its reactive nature.

3   Dynamic Provisioning with Software Restart

DynAlloc-SR is a closed-loop control system that controls n-tier applications through dynamic provisioning and process restart. Its main components are showed in Figure 1. The managed application is an n-tier Web based application. Typically, an n-tier application is compounded of layers of machines (workers). A worker of a layer executes specific pieces of the application. For a 3-tier application, for example, there is the load balancer and workers that execute presentation, application and data layer logic. A Service Level Agreement (SLA) specifies high level QoS requirements that should be delivered to the users of the application. It defines, for instance, response time and availability thresholds. The decision layer is aware of the whole application health status. Thus, it is the one who makes decisions and executes them by actuating over the execution environment of the application. It can choose among four different actions to execute: i) add workers; ii) remove workers; iii) restart a worker software, and iv) do nothing. At the monitoring layer there are the components that produce management information to the decision layer.

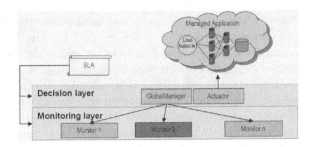

Fig. 1. DynAlloc-SR architecture

3.1   The Monitoring Layer

Monitoring components collect information from each active worker of the application. Monitoring information collected from the load balancer (LB) is related to the application as a whole because the LB is a central point on which the application depends. We call it application level monitoring information. For the other workers, monitoring information is called worker level information. These two levels of information give insight about the health status of the application and allow the detection of workers that are degrading the application QoS.

DynAlloc-SR gets monitoring information in two ways: (i) submitting probe requests, and (ii) analyzing application logs. Probe requests are used to capture the quality of the user experience. Success responses occur when the response time is less than a threshold (specified in the SLA) and does not represent an error. Logs provide information on load, response times and availability. Logs can also be processed to obtain tendencies of such metrics.

Both ways of gathering information have pros and cons. Application logs contain average response times and availability offered to the stream of real users. Moreover, they are available for free, since they are produced regardless of DynAlloc-SR and do not require modifications in the applications. However, logs may miss certain failures. For example, opening TCP connections to a busy server may fail, but the server will never know about it (and thus will not log any event). This problem does not affect probe requests, since they are treated by the application as a regular user request. On the other hand, probe requests bring intrusiveness because they add to the application load. Hence, to be as close as possible to the real user experience, and at the same time to be as unintrusive as possible, we combine both methods to infer the quality of user experience.

Each probe sends requests to a specific worker (WorkerProbe - WP) or to the load balancer (ApplicationProbe - AP) periodically. Some of these requests depend only on the services of the layer of the worker in question and others depend on services offered by other layers. Probes analyze the responses received and suggest actions to the decision layer instead of sending raw monitoring data.

WPs can suggest actions such as doNothing, addWorkers, otherLayerProblem and restart. The action doNothing means that all responses received did not exceeded the SLA threshold for response times and do not represent errors.

HTTP (Hyper Text Transfer Protocol) probes, for instance, consider good responses those who carry response code 2xx. A probe proposes addWorkers when at least one of the responses for the requests that do not depend on other layers' services do not represent errors but are exceeding the response time threshold specified in the SLA. A WP suggests restart when responses that represent errors are received even for the requests that do not depend on another layers. Finally, otherLayerProblem is proposed when all responses exceeding the SLA response time threshold or representing errors depend on other layers services.

The AP sends requests to the LB. If all responses received do not represent errors it proposes doNothing. Otherwise, it suggests addWorkers. The AP does not suggest restart actions nor otherLayerProblem because it has no idea about which worker may be degrading the QoS.

DynAlloc-SR also monitors other application metrics in the LB: availability and response times offered to the real users and load tendency. All of them are computed by processing logs. Availability and response times are well known metrics that do not need extra explanations. The tendency metric informs if the application is more or less loaded during a given monitoring interval in comparison with the previous one.

3.2   The Decision Layer

The GlobalManager (GM) is the decision layer component that periodically collects probes' suggestions and other metrics (availability, idleness, etc.) from monitoring layer components. Eventually, the GM can try to collect monitoring information while probes/monitors are still collecting new information. In this case, GM will use the last information collected. It correlates the information received, makes decisions and actuates over the application. More specifically, it correlates all monitoring metrics received and decides if the probes' suggestions must be applied.

In a first step, GM uses the application response times and availability computed by analyzing logs and the WPs suggestions to discover if the LB is a source of performance degradation. If response times or availability violates the SLA thresholds and all WPs suggest doNothing then GM restarts the LB software.

Next, the GM separates WPs' suggestions as well as the AP suggestion by layer into sets. There are 4 sets for each layer: doNothing, addWorkers, restart and otherLayerProblem. Probes' suggestions are organized as elements of these sets. A layer is considered overloaded if the cardinality of its addWorkers set is greater than a minimum quorum. One layer receives resources only if it is overloaded. We consider load balancing is fair among workers, thus, saturation happens to a set of workers at the same time. The minimal quorum is a mechanism to distinguish scenarios in which an increasing in capacity is actually needed and scenarios in which some pieces of the application are degraded. If less than the quorum has proposed an increase in capacity, the GM will restart the workers that proposed addWorkers instead of increasing the layer capacity. To give some time for the load to be rebalanced, the GM waits for some time before adding new workers, even if all conditions for a new increasing are satisfied.

The status of a layer could be degraded due to problems in other layers. The GM does not act over a layer if the cardinality of the otherLayerProblem set is greater than a quorum. It follows the same minimal quorum reasoning as for capacity increasing. If less than the quorum has proposed otherLayerProblem the GM decides to restart the software of those who suggested otherLayerProblem.

The restart process does not depend on the layer status, but on individual status of each worker. Thus, all restart suggestions are implemented by the GM as soon as possible to avoid the worker to degrade even more along the time.

Workers of the data layer do not depend on services of other layers. If problems in this layer are detected the GM forwards monitoring information to a database agent that can act over the database. A lot of new challenges are involved in the dynamic provisioning of the data layer and some systems are concerned with the load variability problem [23].

A worker is removed if DynAlloc-SR remains some period without the need to act over the application and the majority of the load tendencies collected during this period indicates load reduction. In this case, the load balancing stops sending requests to the oldest worker and when this worker has no requests to process it returns to the pool of free servers, as proposed in [5].

4   DynAlloc-SR Experimental Analysis

A prototype of DynAlloc-SR was implemented as well as a system named DynAlloc, which does not perform restarts. It increments the application capacity as soon as any signal of QoS degradation is seen. We compared the average availability and response times of the managed application as well as the number of machines used by each system in order to measure the efficacy of DynAlloc-SR.

4.1   DynAlloc-SR and DynAlloc Prototypes

Our prototypes were conceived to manage 2-tier applications. HTTP is used between the client and the presentation layer. There is a WP sending requests to each active worker of the presentation layer and an AP sending requests to the LB. All probes analyze the responses received as described in 3.1. Following the HTTP specification [24], only HTTP response codes 2xx are considered success.

A WP can suggest otherLayerProblem when it detects that the responses were unsuccessful due to poor QoS of data layer components. Each WP sends different kinds of requests to the probed worker: some that require data layer access and others that do not require[2]. If only the DB queries have delivered bad QoS, then the probe suggests otherLayerProblem.

The minimum quorum used by DynAlloc-SR is "majority". We could have used "all", but reach unanimity in such an asynchronous distributed environment is very unlikely. When one probe suggests addWorkers, others may be still waiting the workers' replies.

---

[2] We plan to send requests directly to DB workers using Java Database Connectivity.

Currently, the database agent of the DynAlloc-SR prototype does nothing. Thus we are not acting over the data layer for now.

DynAlloc-SR knows a pool of machines it can use. Each of these machines is either an idle machine or is an active worker running pieces of the application. When restarting a worker, DynAlloc-SR first verifies if there is an idle machine. In this case it prepares one of them with the appropriate software, adds it to the pool of active workers and only then stops the faulty worker and returns it to the pool of idle machines. When the pool of idle machines is empty, the rejuvenation action stops the faulty software and then restarts it in the same machine. Since this operation takes some seconds, the number of active workers is temporarily reduced by one during restart. Clearly, the first way of restart is more efficient than the second. This is yet another advantage of combining dynamic provisioning with software restart in the same system.

DynAlloc has the same monitors as DynAlloc-SR, however, its GM does not take into account the minimal quorum. It increases the application capacity as soon as some QoS degradation is perceived and ignores suggestions of restart.

4.2   Testbed

The managed application is a mock-up e-commerce application named xPet-store[3]. In our experiments, after sometime running, we observed one of the following flaws (in order of frequency of occurrence): EJBException, ApplicationDeadlockException or OutOfMemoryError.

The testbed consists of 5 application servers running JBoss 3.0.7 with Tomcat 4.29, one database server running MySQL, one LB running Apache 2.0.48 with mod_jk, 3 load generators and a manager that executes either DynAlloc-SR or DynAlloc. We start an experiment using 2 workers.

Obtaining actual logs from e-commerce companies is difficult because they consider them sensitive data. Thus, we use synthetic e-commerce workloads generated by GEIST [25]. Three workload intensities have been used: the low load, with 120 requests per minute (rpm) in average, the medium load with 320 rpm and the high load with 520 rpm. Each workload lasts for around an hour and presents one peak. Based on the study reported in [26] we assume that the average number of requests per minute doubles during peaks.

DynAlloc-SR and DynAlloc availability and response times thresholds are 97% and 3 seconds respectively.

4.3   Experimental Results

We here present results obtained by running each experiment ten times. Average values of availability and response times measured during all experiments are presented in Table 1. DynAlloc-SR yielded better average application availability and response times than DynAlloc. This is an indication that although

---

[3] xPetstore is a re-implementation of Sun Microsystem PetStore, and can be found in http://xpetstore.sourceforge.net/. Version 3.1.1 was used in our experiments.

very simple, DynAlloc-SR is able to make good choices when adding/releasing
resources and restarting software.

Table 1. Average availability and response times of xPetstore

	DynAlloc-SR	DynAlloc
Availability	88.04%	77.99%
Response times	49.65 sec.	136.37 sec.

Next we compare DynAlloc-SR and DynAlloc considering each load intensity
individually. These results are illustrated in Figures 2 and 3.

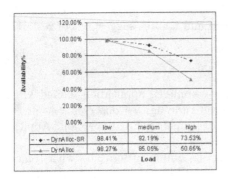

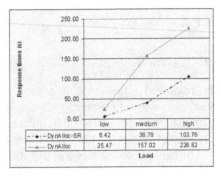

Fig. 2. Average availability   **Fig. 3.** Average response times

In average, DynAlloc-SR yielded 0.13%, 7.14% and 22.9% better availability
than DynAlloc during the low, medium and high load experiments respectively.
As we can see, the availability gain increases considerably when the load increases. The more intense is the load and the more saturated is the software,
the greater is the probability of failures due to software faults. This is because,
when load increases, the probability of race conditions, garbage collector misbehavior, acceleration of process aging, etc., also increases. This correlation makes
the differentiation between faulty and overloaded software difficult.

Response time gains did not follow the same crescent pattern. For low and
medium loads the gains were around 75%. For the higher load this gain was
smaller (54%). Investigating further, we found out that the LB reached its maximum allowed number of clients and became a bottleneck during high load experiments. The Apache MaxClients directive limits the number of child processes
that can be created to serve requests. Any connection attempt over this limit is
queued, up to a number based on the ListenBacklog directive. Since DynAlloc-
SR cannot actuate over the capacity of the LB, the response times increased
and, thus, the gain around 75% was not achieved.

These high gains may be an indicative of the fragility of the application and its execution environment. It is likely that applications in production are more robust than the one we used here and thus these gains may be overestimated. However, applications will fail someday, and when this happens, a dynamic provisioning with software restart will deliver better results than a dynamic provisioning system that does not take software faults into account.

DynAlloc-SR also used less resources than DynAlloc. The mean number of machines used by DynAlloc was 14.6% greater than the mean number of machines used by DynAlloc-SR. This is due to the fact that workers that needed rejuvenation contributed very little to the application QoS, yet kept consuming resources. When looking at the load variation, the mean number of machines used by DynAlloc was 5.3%, 15.0% and 20.5% greater than the mean number of machines used by DynAlloc-SR, for low, medium and higher loads, respectively. We believe the raise from 5.3% to 15.0% in "resource saving" is due to the greater number of software failures generated by a greater load. Interestingly, however, this phenomena does not appear when we go from medium to high load: the increase in "resource saving" is of five percent points (from 15% to 20%). We believe that this is due to the maximum number of machines used. The maximum number of machines used (5) is more than enough to process the low load. However, when load increases DynAlloc tries to correct the degraded performance of the application by adding more machines, always reaching the maximum number of machines. If more machines were available, more machines would be allocated to the application. If the total number of machines was higher than 5, the "resource saving" for high load would likely be greater.

5   Conclusions and Future Works

We have shown that a dynamic provisioning system that takes into account software faults is able to deliver better application QoS using less resources than a similar dynamic allocation system that does not consider software faults. One of the most complex duties of such a dual goal management system is to differentiate saturated and faulty software. This is because aging related bugs produce effects in the application and the execution environment that are similar to those produced by load surges. Moreover, the probability of failure is proportional to the load intensity being hold by the application, turning the relationship between load and bugs still narrower. We here propose DynAlloc-SR, a control system that copes not only with capacity adjustment, but also with software faults of n-tier applications. DynAlloc-SR assumes that saturation is something that always happens simultaneously to a minimal quorum of workers of the same layer while software faults do not follow this clustered pattern.

Our experimental results indicate the efficacy of DynAlloc-SR decision algorithms. By combining a restart scheme with our dynamic allocation scheme, we could increase the average application availability from 78% to 88%. Maybe this improvement is overestimated due to the fragility of our demo application. However, even n-tier applications in production fail. When applications fail, dynamic provisioning with software restart will deliver better results than a dynamic provisioning system that does not take software faults into account. The dual goal system also uses less resources than the dynamic allocation only system. DynAlloc used in average 15% more resources than DynAlloc-SR.

Our main goal here is not to propose a perfect dynamic provisioning algorithm but to demonstrate the importance of treating software faults in conjunction with dynamic provisioning. However, we emphasize two important features of our dynamic allocation scheme that, as far as we know, had not been applied by other schemes. Firstly, we consider dependency relationships among n-tier application layers. For instance, DynAlloc-SR does not try to add more machines in a layer L if another layer L' on which layer L depends presents poor performance. Secondly, DynAlloc-SR uses probes to infer the application health and do not depend on correct behavior of the application, since we do not use specific functions that relates QoS metrics with number of machines.

Before we proceed with the study of a combined solution to the problems of load variability and software faults, we plan to study deeper the interactions among dynamic provisioning systems, rejuvenation schemes and degradation/failure phenomena due to transient software faults. Based on the interactions discovered we hope to define new techniques in both areas (software faults recovery and dynamic provisioning), which maximize/create positive interactions or minimize/eliminate negative ones.

Acknowledgments. This work was (partially) developed in collaboration with HP Brazil R&D and partially funded by CNPq/Brazil (grants 141655/2002-0, 302317/2003-1 and 300646/1996-8).

References

1. Gribble, S.D.: Robustness in complex systems. In: Proceedings of the Eighth Workshop on Hot Topics in Operating Systems. (2001) 21–26
2. Ejasent: Utility computing: Solutions for the next generation IT infrastructure. Technical report, Ejasent (2001)
3. Chase, J.S., Anderson, D.C., Thakar, P.N., Vahdat, A., Doyle, R.P.: Managing energy and server resources in hosting centres. In: Symposium on Operating Systems Principles. (2001) 103–116
4. Appleby, K., et al: Oceano - sla based management of a computing utility. In: 7th IFIP/IEEE International Symposium on Integrated Network Management. (2001) 855 –868
5. Ranjan, S., Rolia, J., Fu, H., Knightly, E.: Qos-driven server migration for internet data centers. In: Proceedings of the International Workshop on Quality of Service. (2002)
6. Doyle, R., Chase, J., Asad, O., Jen, W., Vahdat, A.: Model-based resource provisioning in a web service utility. In: Proceedings of the USENIX Symposium on Internet Technologies and Systems USITS 2003. (2003)
7. Fox, A., Gribble, S.D., Chawathe, Y., Brewer, E.A., Gauthier, P.: Cluster-based scalable network services. In: Proceedings of the 6th ACM Symposium on Operating Systems Principles, ACM Press (1997) 78–91

8. Rolia, J., Zhu, X., Arlitt, M.F.: Resource access management for a utility hosting enterprise applications. In: Proceeding of the 2003 International Symposium on Integrgated Management. (2003) 549–562

9. Rolia, J., Arlitt, M., Andrzejak, A., Zhu, X.: Statistical service assurancecs for applications in utility grid environments. In: Proceedings of the Tenth IEEE/ACM International Symposium on Modeling, Analysis and Simulation of Computer and Telcommunication Systems. (2003) 247–256

10. Rolia, J., et al: Grids for enterprise applications. In Feitelson, D.G., Rudolph, L., Schwiegelshohn, U., eds.: Job Scheduling Strategies for Parallel Processing. Springer Verlag (2003) 129–147 Lect. Notes Comput. Sci. vol. 2862.

11. Rolia, J., Singhal, S., Friedrich, R.: Adaptive internet data centers. In: In SS-GRR'00 Conference. (2000)

12. Gray, J.: Why do computers stop and what can be done about it? In: Symposium on Reliability in Distributed Software and Database Systems. (1986)

13. Vaidyanathan, K., Trivedi, K.S.: Extended classification of software faults based on aging. In: Proceedings of the 12th International Symposium on Software Reliability Engineering. (2001)

14. Lassettre, E., et al: Dynamic surge protection: An approach to handling unexpected workload surges with resource actions that have dead times. In: 14th IFIP/IEEE International Workshop on Distributed Systems: Operations and Management. Volume 2867 of Lecture Notes in Computer Science., Springer (2003) 82–92

15. Welsh, M., Culler, D., Brewer, E.: Seda: an architecture for well-conditioned, scalable internet services. In: Proceedings of the 8th ACM Symposium on Operating Systems Principles, ACM Press (2001) 230–243

16. Huang, Y., Kintala, C., Kolettis, N., Fulton, N.D.: Software rejuvenation: Analysis, module and applications. In: Proceedings of the Twenty-Fifth International Symposium on Fault-Tolerant Computing, IEEE Computer Society (1995) 381–390

17. Candea, G., Fox, A.: Recursive restartability: Turning the reboot sledgehammer into a scalpel. In: Proceedings of the Eighth Workshop on Hot Topics in Operating Systems. (2001) 125–132

18. Candea, G., Keyani, P., Kiciman, E., Zhang, S., Fox, A.: Jagr: An autonomous self-recovering application server. In: 5th International Workshop on Active Middleware Services. (2003)

19. Hong, Y., Chen, D., Li, L., Trivedi, K.: Closed loop design for software rejuvenation. In: Workshop on Self-Healing, Adaptive, and Self-Managed Systems. (2002)

20. Li, L., Vaidyanathan, K., Trivedi, K.S.: An approach for estimation of software aging in a web server. In: International Symposium on Empirical Software Engineering. (2002)

21. Bao, Y., Sun, X., Trivedi, K.S.: Adaptive software rejuvenation: Degradation model and rejuvenation scheme. In: Proceedings of the 2003 International Conference on Dependable Systems and Networks, IEEE Computer Society (2003) 241–248

22. Erickson, C.: Memory leak detection in embedded systems. Linux Lournal (2002)

23. Oracle: Oracle database 10g: A revolution in database technology. Technical report, Oracle (2003)

24. Fielding, R., et al: Hypertext transfer protocol – http/1.1. Technical report, RFC 2616 (1999)

25. Kant, K., Tewari, V., Iyer, R.: Geist: A generator of e-commerce and internet server traffic. In: Proceedings of the 2001 IEEE International Symposium on Performance Analysis of Systems and Software, IEEE Computer Society (2001) 49–56

26. Arlitt, M., Krishnamurthy, D., Rolia, J.: Characterizing the scalability of a large web-based shopping system. ACM Trans. Inter. Tech. **1** (2001) 44–69

Server Support Approach to Zero Configuration In-Home Networking

Kiyohito Yoshihara[1], Takeshi Kouyama[2], Masayuki Nishikawa[2],
and Hiroki Horiuchi[1]

[1] KDDI R&D Laboratories Inc., 2-1-15 Ohara Kamifukuoka-shi
Saitama 356-8502, JAPAN
{yosshy hr-horiuchi}@kddilabs.jp
[2] KDDI Corporation, 3-10-10 Iidabashi Chiyoda-ku
Tokyo 102-8460, JAPAN
{ta-kouyama masa-n}@kddi.com

Abstract. This paper proposes a new server support approach to zero configuration in-home networking. We show three technical issues for zero configuration. Lack of a protocol or technique addressing all issues simultaneously motivated us to design a new approach based on (1) a two-stage autoconfiguration, (2) a UPnP and HTTP-based autoconfiguration, and (3) extended UPnP services. An elaborated flow for the global Internet connection from scratch will be presented. The proposed approach can obtain software and settings from remote servers, and updates/configures for devices. We implemented a system based on the proposed approach, and evaluated its total autoconfiguration time, and the number of technical calls to a help desk during a field trial for five months. We delivered a user-side configuration tool and an all-in-one modem to approximately 230,000 new aDSL subscribers as part of the trial system. Over 40 settings are properly configured for diverse devices in 14 minutes and 10 seconds, while the ratio of the number of calls to the number of new subscribers per month decreased from 14.9% to 8.2%.

1 Introduction

As seen in the number of Internet access subscribers via x Digital Subscriber Line (xDSL) across the globe exceeding 6.3 million by the end of 2003, we can have an always-on broadband Internet connection at home and office as well as at traditionally limited universities or research institutes.

A typical home network for xDSL Internet access is composed of Customer Premises Equipment (CPE) devices including an xDSL modem, residential gateway, and PCs. Before we use Internet applications such as e-mail and Voice over IP (VoIP), it is necessary to configure application and user-specific settings associated with the applications as well as IP network settings, for diverse devices. An e-mail account and Session Initiation Protocol (SIP) server address are examples of such settings. Media-specific settings including an Extended Service Set Identifier (ESSID) and an encryption key must be configured if we use applications

A. Sahai and F. Wu (Eds.): DSOM 2004, LNCS 3278, pp. 232–244, 2004.
© IFIP International Federation for Information Processing 2004

via IEEE802.11b[1] Wireless Local Area Network (WLAN) communications. Additionally, software updates are prerequisite for the configuration, for such new software as firmware on an xDSL modem and device driver of a WLAN card may be released for bug fixes or upgrades even after the shipping.

In contrast, the configuration and software update together require a highly skilled and experienced user with technical knowledge of the Internet, as it was initially created for academic purposes. This poses a barrier to Internet novices and raises technical issues. In order to break down this barrier, some protocols and techniques for zero configuration networking [2,3,4,5,6,7,8,9,10,11,12,13,14] have been developed; however, almost all existing protocols and techniques could not fully address this issue: some are only for single and specific devices or applications, and others are restricted to IP network settings, omitting applications and user-specific settings.

This paper proposes a new server support approach to zero configuration in-home networking to solve this issue. The proposed approach allows us to update software on diverse devices and to configure all settings: application and user-specific settings together with IP network settings, required to make available Internet applications. The proposed approach consists of two stages: the former is a Local stage in which a home network is isolated and has only local connectivity, and the latter is a Global stage in which the home network has global Internet connectivity after Local stage. In the Local stage, the proposed approach can discover all devices based on Universal Plug and Play (UPnP) [14] and configure local settings for the devices. In the Global stage, the proposed approach obtains software and settings from servers and customer information systems managed by an Internet Service Provider (ISP) then it updates the software and configures the settings instead of the user. New application and user-specific UPnP actions with the associated state variables are defined and together used in both stages in a secure manner, to cover the shortcomings of the UPnP specifications, which only provided general-purpose items at the development phase.

The emphasis of this paper lies not only in prototyping a system, but also in deploying this system to demonstrate its proven practicality. We implemented a system based on the proposed approach and yet conducted a field trial in which we offer an all-in-one asymmetric Digital Subscriber Line (aDSL) modems with IP router, VoIP, and WLAN access point capabilities to new subscribers, together with a CD-ROM that stores user-side autoconfiguration tools. The tool will automatically configure all required settings for the PC and the aDSL modem with minimum user intervention once a user inserts the CD-ROM into a PC in the home network and clicks the start button. Even an Internet novice can easily have browser access and use e-mail through WLAN communication as well as VoIP with the proposed approach, while an ISP can reduce operation costs through decreasing number of technical calls to the help desk. For proven practicality, we evaluated the proposed approach based on the total processing time of the system, including some software updates, and the number of technical calls to a help desk that were empirically collected during the field trial.

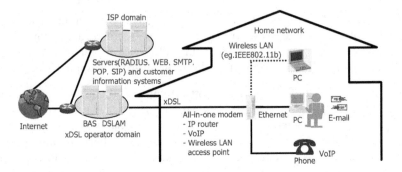

Fig. 1. Typical Home Network with xDSL Connections

This paper is organized as follows: In Sect.2, we present an overview of a typical home network with xDSL connections and address technical issues for zero configuration. We review recent related work in Sect.3. In Sect.4, we propose a new server support approach to zero configuration in-home networking. In Sect.5, we implement a system and evaluate it through a field trial.

2   Typical Home Network with xDSL Connections and Technical Issues for Zero Configuration In-Home Networking

2.1   Typical Home Network with xDSL Connections

Figure 1 shows a typical home network for Internet access via xDSL, with xDSL operator and ISP domains. The CPE devices including an all-in-one xDSL modem, PCs, and phone are connected in a tree with the modem as its root. Each home network is connected to an ISP domain, in which Remote Authentication Dial-In User Service (RADIUS), World Wide Web (WEB), Simple Mail Transfer Protocol (SMTP), Post Office Protocol (POP), and SIP servers are operated to serve such Internet applications as e-mail and VoIP via Digital Subscriber Line Access Multiplexer (DSLAM) and Broadband Access Server (BAS) installed at an xDSL operator domain. In addition to the servers, customer information systems maintain user account information, and the information should be configured for CEP devices as the application and user-specific settings.

The user must take care of software updates at present. The user voluntarily performs manual updates when they learn of new software releases.

2.2   Technical Issues for Zero Configuration In-Home Networking

The following technical issues should be addressed to achieve zero configuration in-home networking by studying typical home networks in Sect.2.1.

1. All diverse CEP devices shown in Fig.1 should be autoconfigured with minimum user intervention, to release users from the complicated and labor-intensive configuration task (Issue 1).
2. Application and user-specific settings maintained by the servers and customer information systems in a remote ISP domain should be obtained and configured for local CPE devices, to make Internet applications such as e-mail and VoIP available in a simple and easy way (Issue 2).
3. Software updates of CPE devices including firmware on an xDSL modem and device driver of a WLAN card should be performed fully within the auto-configuration whenever applicable, to run applications as reliably as possible without abnormal terminations of devices due to software bugs (Issue 3).

3   Related Work

Research and development work on the zero configuration networking have been conducted. We summarize recent related work below and show that none of them alone addresses all issues in Sect.2.2 simultaneously.

Dynamic Host Configuration Protocol (DHCP)[2] is a well-known practical protocol. It partially meets Issue 1 in Sect.2.2, in that a DHCP server centrally configures an IP address for diverse IP devices. The server can configure other IP and Domain Name System (DNS) settings; however, neither Issue 2 nor 3 could be addressed only with DHCP as they are restricted to link-local settings while software updates are out of scope.

The Internet Engineering Task Force (IETF) Zero Configuration Networking (zeroconf) working group was standardizing a distributed protocol[3] for dynamic configuration of link-local IPv4 addresses. The IETF Mobile Ad-hoc Networks (manet) working group has also standardized a distributed autoconfiguration protocol[4] for the manet. Although the protocol has inspired subsequent research efforts[5,6,7,8], they are still the same as DHCP for the three issues.

DOCSIS[9] and PacketCable[10] provide similar protocols based on DHCP and Trivial File Transfer Protocol (TFTP) for cable modems. They configure downstream frequency, Class of Service (CoS), etc. for modems. Software updates are also available for DOCSIS protocol. The protocols may meet Issue 3; however, they cannot address Issue 1 and 2 alone, as the intended device of the protocols is a single cable modem, while the configuration is limited to cable and IP-specific settings. This is also true for other effort[11] with Cisco CPE devices.

In terms of media-specific settings, Co-Link configuration technique[12] for wireless links such as IEEE802.11b and Bluetooth has been developed. This technique may meet Issue 1 partially as it introduces configuration point hardware, from which diverse devices can obtain the media-specific settings including an ESSID and encryption key. The technique integrated with the protocols[2,3,4] may achieve autoconfiguration of WLAN communication in a home network; however, even this integration addresses neither Issue 2 nor Issue 3, due to its locality and the lack of the communication software installation and update.

UPnP[14] is designed to support zero configuration networking as devices can join a network dynamically, obtain IP addresses typically with DHCP, and exchange its presence and capabilities with other devices with Simple Service Discovery Protocol (SSDP)[15]. A service interface defined as an action with state variables is described in XML and is conveyed by Simple Object Access Protocol (SOAP)[16], for controllers or control points to control and transfer data among networked devices. General Event Notification Architecture (GENA)[17] supports eventing, through which control points listen to state changes in devices after subscriptions. Although UPnP may address Issue 1, its service interfaces and typical scope restricted to proximity networking require more work to address Issue 2 and 3. Jini[13] is the same as UPnP for the three issues.

4   Server Support Approach to Zero Configuration In-Home Networking

The findings in Sect.3 motivated us to propose a new server support approach to zero configuration in-home networking to meet all issues in Sect.2.2, which will be presented in the following sections.

4.1   Design Principles and Assumptions

Design Principles. The proposed approach is designed based on the three principles as shown in Fig.2.

1. Two-stage autoconfiguration: Local and Global stages
   a) **Local stage**: In this first stage, the proposed approach configures all required settings: media, IP network, application, and user-specific settings for diverse CPE devices in a carefully-designed flow in order to address Issue 1. The successful completion of this stage enables an intended home network to have global Internet connectivity.
   b) **Global stage**: In this succeeding stage, which is the heart of the proposed approach to address Issue 2 and 3, the approach obtains software and settings from remote servers and customer information systems in an ISP domain after user authentication then it updates software and configures settings for devices.
2. UPnP and HTTP-based autoconfiguration
   The proposed approach leverages UPnP and Hyper Text Transfer Protocol (HTTP), the de-facto standards for the device configuration, to autoconfigure multi-vendor devices comprising a home network for xDSL connection, meeting Issue 1. In particular, we introduce a user-side autoconfiguration tool running on a single device, typically a PC. The device performs as a UPnP control point and autoconfigure itself and all other devices in the intended home network.
3. Extended UPnP services
   Autoconfiguring all required settings only with UPnP standard service interfaces[18] is insufficient as they are given in a generic form and are not

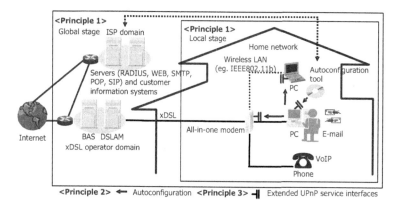

Fig. 2. Principles of Proposed Approach

ready for application and user-specific settings for e-mail and VoIP. We cannot configure all IP network settings with them. We extend UPnP services and define service interfaces so that the proposed approach may autoconfigure all the necessary settings together with the standard ones in order to meet Issue 1 and 2. See Sect.4.3 for details.

Assumptions. We assume the following before and during use of the proposed approach.

1. Application, user-specific settings and new software for updates are registered with servers and customer information systems in an ISP domain.
2. An all-in-one modem and the user-side autoconfiguration tool in removable media are delivered to a user. A password for the modem configuration is preset. The tool recognizes it, but it is treated opaquely.
3. Hardware installation of all intended CPE devices including power and Ethernet cable connections is performed properly.
4. Users initially turn on device power.
5. There are devices that can execute user-side autoconfiguration tools and perform as a UPnP control point in a home network.
6. A DHCP server works in the home network and it configures link-local IP settings containing an IP address, IP subnet mask, default gateway IP address, and DNS server IP address for devices. Recent all-in-one modems normally support a DHCP server and enables it after startup.
7. A WLAN access point conforms to IEEE802.11b/g and broadcasts a beacon including an ESSID periodically if the modem supports WLAN access point capability. The access point permits only authorized access from a device with proper encryption keys.

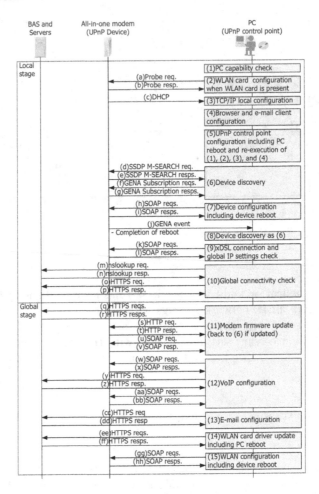

Fig. 3. Autoconfiguration Flow of Proposed Approach

8. A user manually configures an xDSL subscriber account and password, used as a key to associate applications and user-specific settings for modems. An alliance between device vendors and ISP permits modems to be shipped with preset accounts and passwords, thus the user may skip manual configuration.

4.2   Autoconfiguration Flow

Figure 3 shows autoconfiguration flow of the proposed approach. For simplicity, we suppose a typical home network shown in Fig.1 except that a single PC, an all-in-one modem, and phone constitute the network for an aDSL connection. The flow description assuming the alliance in Sect.4.1 is provided below.

Local Stage. A PC capability check (Fig.3(1)) should be performed first. The autoconfiguration tool checks the OS type and version, login users and their authority, PC hardware specs, HDD free space size, other programs running, active network interface card and/or WLAN card, TCP/IP protocol stacks, and browsers with an e-mail client and the version. The tool exits if any of these are inappropriate or insufficient.

The tool configures the card when an active WLAN card is attached to the PC (Fig.3(2)). It probes an ESSID from the modem. An encryption key is derived from the ESSID with a predefined algorithm. The tool configures these for the card to establish a peer-to-peer link. After that or when the PC is wired, the tool configures link-local IP settings obtained from the DHCP server supported by the modem (Fig.3(3)). In addition, the tool checks and configures dial-up, proxy, and SSL settings for the browser (Fig.3(4)). With the UPnP control point flagged on, the tool reboots the PC to re-execute Fig.3(1) thru (4) to check if the PC has booted and is operating properly (Fig.3(5)).

The tool tries to discover a device or modem (Fig.3(6)) by sending an SSDP M-SEARCH request as a UPnP control point. Then the tool sends GENA subscriptions to the modem to know the completion of the modem reboot required for subsequent new settings. The tool configures aDSL-specific settings: the operation mode (Point to Point Protocol over ATM (PPPoA) or PPP over Ethernet (PPPoE)), the PPPoE bridge option, the connection mode (always-on or on-demand), the encapsulation type (Logical Link Control Encapsulation (LLC) or Virtual Connection (VC)), the pair of Virtual Connection Identifier (VCI) and Virtual Path Identifier (VPI), the encryption method, the PPP keep-alive option, and the PPP retry timer, for the modem for global connectivity (Fig.3(7)). The tool leverages SOAP during configuration. The tool discovers the modem (Fig.3(8)) again then checks if the modem has an expected aDSL connection and obtains global IP settings from a BAS (Fig.3(9)), after modem reboot enabling the above settings is completed. The tool communicates with remote DNS and WEB servers to ensure the global connectivity at the end of the stage (Fig.3(10)).

Global Stage. The tool attempts to update firmware on the modem (Fig.3(11)). The tool asks the remote servers the newest version of the firmware and determines availability. The tool downloads it from the servers and updates it for the modem if the latest firmware is available. Then the tool reboots the modem and goes back to Fig.3(6) after receiving a GENA event describing the completion of modem reboot for the reconfiguration on the most recent firmware. The tool proceeds to the VoIP configuration when the firmware is the latest (Fig.3(12)). The tool checks whether the modem has VoIP capabilities. If it does, the tool downloads VoIP-specific settings from remote servers, and configures them for the modem. The settings contain SIP server address, user name and password for the SIP server, SIP URL, area code, and phone number. The tool goes on to the e-mail configuration (Fig.3(13)). The tool downloads the application-specific settings, and configures them for the e-mail client on the PC as with the VoIP configuration. The settings contain an SMTP server name,

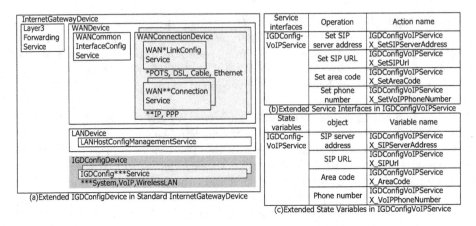

Fig. 4. Extended UPnP Services, Interfaces, and State Variables for All-In-One Modem

POP server name, e-mail account, password, user name, e-mail address, and user identifier.

Finally, the tool attempts to update a WLAN card driver (Fig.3(14)), and configures the WLAN-specific settings for the card (Fig.3(15)). The tool obtains the corresponding driver from remote servers, installs the driver including uninstalling the older version, and reboots the PC if the driver update is applicable. The tool configures for the card as appropriate after reboot, assuming a new WLAN card attachment after Fig.3(2).

Although the above flow may somewhat have redundant parts and be still optimized, the highest priority is given to the dependability for more practicality. For example, the second device discovery (Fig.3(8)) is for preventing loss of the event telling the completion of the modem reboot.

4.3   Extended UPnP Services

We extend the standard UPnP services, to achieve the autoconfiguration of all required settings as described in Sect.4.2. As shown in Fig.4 (a), we define an IGDConfigDevice (grayed out area in Fig.4) as a container of the extended three UPnP services: IGDConfigSystem Service, IGDConfigVoIPService, and IGD-ConfigWirelessLAN Service in the standard InternetGatewayDevice for a typical all-in-one modem. Each of them includes 32, 26, and 19 service interfaces for the configuration of the entire modem, VoIP-specific, and WLAN-specific settings. Note that we can now locate standard service interfaces for the configuration of WLAN-specific settings, while undefined at our development phase.

Figure 4 (b) and (c) shows some service interfaces and state variables of IGDConfigVoIPService. For example, the tool leverages X_SetSIPServerAddress service interface with the state variable X_SIPServerAddress using the desired value as the input argument in order to configure a SIP server address.

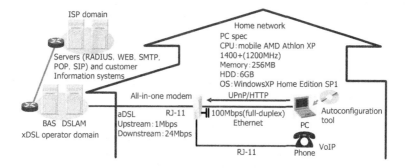

Fig. 5. Evaluation Conditions

5   Implementation and Evaluations

5.1   Implementation

We implement a system based on the proposed approach and describe a brief overview of the system below.

1. We offer the user-side autoconfiguration tool implementing the flow in Sect.4.2 in the CD-ROM as part of the proposed approach.
2. The runtime environment of the tool is WindowsXP. The tool leverages UPnP control point software on WindowsXP installed as default.
3. We embed extended UPnP services in Sect.4.3 and standard ones in the InternetGatewayDevice to a commercially available all-in-one modem. We can configure this modem via UPnP interfaces together with HTTP ones that the modem originally supports.
4. We install a server for the software update in an ISP domain.
5. The tool collects all configuration logs and uploads them to a server after successful completion of the flow in Sect.4.2 (Hereafter referred to as logging). The logs will be used to track future problems and make diagnoses.
6. The tool indicates each process. A user can gain insight into problems even when the user is unable to correct them with the tool. A help desk operator will give advice when the user indicates the problem being experienced.

5.2   Evaluations

The total processing time of the system in Sect.5.1 including all software updates will be evaluated first. After showing our promising results, we deployed the system in Sect.5.1 and deliver the tool and all-in-one modem to new aDSL subscribers in order to empirically verify its real practicality. Then the number of technical calls to a help desk that were collected for five months will be shown.

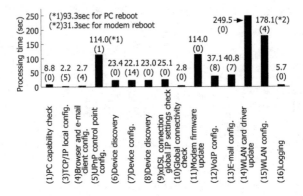

Fig. 6. Processing Time of Proposed Approach

Performance Evaluation. We evaluate the total processing time along the flow in Sect.4.2. Figure 5 shows the evaluation conditions. Note that all steps but (2) in Fig.3 will be performed. Figure 6 shows the results, where the processing time and parenthetic number of settings configured by the tool are shown over the bar for each step.

The 43 settings are properly configured for diverse devices and applications in 14 minutes and 10 seconds. This will be reduced to 8 minutes and 6 seconds if none of the software updates is required. This implies that the proposed approach is suitable for practical use, when we recall that such configuration tasks are error-prone and will generally take more time even for professionals.

Empirical Evaluation. We deployed the system in Sect5.1 and delivered the tool and all-in-one modems to approximately $230,000$ new aDSL subscribers in a field trial for five months. Note that we did not have software updates as the software was the latest version throughout the trial.

The ratio of the number of technical calls to the number of new subscribers per month decreased from 14.9% (November 2003) to 8.2% (March 2004). The decrease in the absolute number of calls and in their total time to the help desk was estimated at $48,600$ and $24,300$ (hours). These were factored from the increase in the number of new aDSL subscribers for the five months and the number of the calls observed just before the trial, assuming no deployment.

The decrease shows that the proposed approach provides both user and provider benefits in that Internet novices can also easily connect and use typical applications, while ISP can reduce operation costs.

6   Conclusions

This paper proposed a new server support approach to zero configuration in-home networking. We showed three technical issues and indicated that none of related work alone addressed all issues simultaneously. To address these issues, we designed a new approach based on: (1) a two-stage autoconfiguration, (2) a UPnP and HTTP-based autoconfiguration, and (3) extended UPnP services.

To verify practicality, we implemented a system based on the proposed approach and evaluated the total processing time of autoconfiguration including software updates, and the number of technical calls to a help desk that were collected during a filed trial for five months. We delivered the user-side configuration tool and all-in-one modems to new aDSL subscribers as part of the system in the trial. Over 40 settings were properly configured for diverse devices and applications including software updates in 14 minutes and 10 seconds. The ratio of the number of calls to the number of new subscribers per month decreased from 14.9% to 8.2%. These results suggest that the proposed approach is suitable for practical use when we recall that such configuration tasks are error-prone and will generally take more time even for professionals. It provides both user and provider benefits in that Internet novices can also easily connect, while ISP can reduce operation costs via this decrease.

The proposed approach may apply to IPv6 and the cable-based network. Further studies including interworking with other in-home technologies such as HAVi, OGSi or Bluetooth, as well as Web service technologies emerging with UPnP 2.0 are now underway.

Acknowledgment. We are indebted to Mr. Tohru Asami, President & CEO of KDDI R&D Laboratories Inc., for his continuous encouragement for this research.

References

1. IEEE: IEEE Std 802.11: Wireless LAN Medium Access Control (MAC) and Physical Layer (PHY) Specifications. 1999 ed. (1999)
2. Droms, R.: Dynamic Host Configuration Protocol. IETF, RFC 2131. (1997)
3. Cheshire, S., Aboba, B., Guttman, E.: Dynamic Configuration of Link-Local IPv4 Addresses. IETF draft-ietf-zeroconf-ipv4-linklocal-14.txt. (2004)
4. Perkins, C., Malinen, J., Wakikawa, R., Belding-Royer, E., Sun, Y.: IP Address Autoconfiguration for Ad Hoc Networks. IETF draft-ietf-manet-autoconf-01.txt. (2001)
5. Misra, A., Das, S., McAuley, A.: Autoconfiguration, Registration, and Mobility Management for Pervasive Computing. IEEE Personal Commun. 8 (2001) 24–31
6. Weniger, K., Zitterbart, M.: IPv6 Autoconfiguration in Large Scale Mobile Ad-Hoc Networks. In: Proc. of European Wireless 2002. (2002) 142–148
7. Nesargi, Prakash, R.: MANETconf: Configuration of Hosts in a Mobile Ad Hoc Network. In: Proc. of IEEE INFOCOM 2002. (2002) 1059–1068
8. Zhou, H., Ni, L.M., Mutka, M.W.: Prophet Address Allocation for Large Scale MANETs. In: Proc. of IEEE INFOCOM 2003. (2003) 1304–1311
9. CableLabs: DOCSIS 2.0 Specifications: Operations Support System Interface Specification. (2004)
10. PacketCable^{TM}: CMS Subscriber Provisioning Specification. (2002)

11. Shen, F., Clemm, A.: Profile-Based Subscriber Service Provisioning. In: Proc. of IEEE/IFIP NOMS2002. (2002)
12. Tourrilhes, J., Krishnan, V.: Co-link configuration : Using wireless diversity for more than just connectivity. Technical Report HPL-2002-258, HP Labs. (2002)
13. SUN Microsystems: Jini^{TM} Architecture Specification Version 2.0. (2003)
14. UPnP Forum: Universal Plug and Play^{TM} Device Architecture. (2000)
15. Goland, Y., Cai, T., Leach, P., Gu, Y., Albright, S.: Simple Service Discovery Protocol/1.0 Operating without an Arbiter. IETF draft-cai-ssdp-v1-03.txt. (1999)
16. World Wide Web Consortium: SOAP Version 1.2. (2003)
17. Cohen, J., Aggarwal, S., Goland, Y.: General Event Notification Architecture Base: Client to Arbiter. IETF draft-cohen-gena-p-base-01.txt. (2000)
18. UPnP Forum: Internet Gateway Device (IGD) Standardized Device Control Protocol V1.0. (2001)

Rule-Based CIM Query Facility for Dependency Resolution

Shinji Nakadai, Masato Kudo, and Koichi Konishi

NEC Corporation
s-nakadai@az.jp.nec.com

Abstract. A distributed system is composed of various resources which have mutually complicated dependencies. The fact increases an importance of the dependency resolution facility which makes it possible to check if there is given dependency between resources such as a router, and to determine which resources have given dependencies with other resources. This paper addresses a CIM query facility for dependency resolution. Its main features are ease of query description, bi-directional query execution, and completeness of query capability to CIM. These features are performed by a rule-based language that enables interesting predicates to be defined declaratively, unification and backtracking, and the preparation of predicates corresponding to CIM metamodel elements. To validate this facility, it was applied in servers dynamically allocated to service providers in a data center. The basic behavior of the query facility and the dynamic server allocation was illustrated.

1 Introduction

Today's computer network systems have become huge and heterogeneous, and the situation has induced operational mistakes from system administrators and increased operational costs. To solve these problems, the interest in autonomic computing has been growing. From the users' viewpoint, a fixed investment in servers and networks increases management risk and total cost, because the depreciation cost is a fixed cost, even though the business environment is dynamic. To solve these problems, several studies have been made on utility computing.

In this study, we focus on a dependency resolution facility [1,2] as one of the important functions in autonomic computing and utility computing. This dependency resolution facility is a facility that makes it possible to check if there is a given dependency between resources and to determine which resources have given dependencies with other resources. As for dependencies, the authors regard that some dependencies are directed and others are undirected. For example, in the case of an online bookstore, this service is hosted on a server, and the dependency *hosted* is thought to be directed. If the server has a connection with one switch, the dependency *having-connection* is thought to be undirected. It is noticeable that the dependencies such as *hosted* and *having-connection* can be combined into another dependency, an example of which is the dependency *Bookstore-Switch*. From the viewpoint of the

A. Sahai and F. Wu (Eds.): DSOM 2004, LNCS 3278, pp. 245–256, 2004.

ease of query description, this is the key-point in this study. The details of the ease of query description are described in Section 3.1.

The reason such a dependency resolution facility is important for autonomic computing is explained as follows. Suppose that under the circumstances of the above-mentioned bookstore service, some trouble occurs on three services simultaneously. Discovering a switch that has the dependency *Bookstore-Switch* with all three services may be useful for root cause analysis. The discovered switch can thus be regarded as a possible root cause. At the time of the recovery from the switch failure, an impact analysis is required, because separation of the switch may affect other irrelevant services. This analysis is realized by finding other services that have the above-mentioned dependencies with the switch. It is noticeable that service identifications should be retrieved from a switch identification in impact analysis, but vice versa in the case of root cause analysis. The capability to query bi-directionally thus enhance a reusability of query descriptions. As for utility computing, the dependency resolution facility makes it possible to match resource requests. In the following, we take the example of a service provider such as an online bookstore that is utilizing several servers provided by a data center (DC) and requests an additional server in the face of a workload increase. When a DC receives a request from a service provider, the dependency resolution facility makes it possible for the DC to resolve complicated requirements for a server, which include complicated dependencies with other resources.

Our approach to the dependency resolution is an association traversal on an information model representing dependencies between system components. The query description for the dependency resolution is realized by the declaration of what kind of dependency is to be traversed. In this paper, we adopt a Common Information Model (CIM) [5] as a target information model. The overview of CIM are described in Section 2.1.

Ease of query description, reusability of described query, and the completeness of capability are all required for retrieving data represented in CIM. To put it more concretely, ease of query description means that the description must be similar to the system administrator's concept that an interesting dependency (e.g., *Bookstore-Switch*) is composed of pre-known dependency (e.g., *hosted* and *having-connection*). In addition, the capability to query CIM without being aware of the CIM schema also contributes to the ease of query description, because the schema is strictly defined by Distributed Management Task Force, Inc. (DMTF) and is less readable. Reusability of a query means that an information retrieval is possible in both ways, even if it is composed of directed dependencies. It is desired, for example, that the same query can be used by root cause analysis and impact analysis. Completeness means that the query language should have sufficient capability to retrieve data of CIM. Our approach meets these requirements with the following features: use of a rule-based language, unification, backtracking, and unique built-in predicates.

The rest of the paper is organized as follows. In Section 2, we present backgrounds of the discussion and review related works. Section 3 describes the features and the architecture of our work. Section 4 shows the implementation applying utility computing. Finally, we conclude our paper in Section 5.

2   Background and Related Work

This section presents the backgrounds: CIM and Meta-level. CIM is a information model and Meta-level is an analysis framework for an information model. Related works are also described in this section.

2.1   CIM

DMTF is an industry organization that has provided a conceptual information model called CIM [5] in order to promote management interoperability among management-solution providers. The heterogeneity of the present management repositories makes it hard for system administrators to coordinate management information [3]. Differences in repository structures and query formats, for example, have worsened the interoperability and the reusability of management applications. To resolve these problems, it is important to divide data models, which represent a particular type of repository, from an information model that is independent of repositories. The latter is desired to be vender-neutral [3,4]. CIM is one of the industry-common conceptual views of the management environment. And Web-Based Enterprise Management (WBEM) is an implementation of management middleware that utilizes CIM. The dependency resolution facility described in this paper makes use of application programming interfaces (APIs) of WBEM.

2.2   Meta-level

The concept of Meta-level, which is discussed in the Object Management Group (OMG), is applied for a comprehensive discussion about an information model. The Meta-level is composed of four layers: the instance layer (short M0), the model layer (M1), the metamodel layer (M2), and the meta-metamodel layer (M3). Elements at lower layers are defined by upper layers. The element at M0 is a so-called *instance* which maintains state (e.g., ComputerSystem.Name = "host0"), and the element at M1 is a type of *instance*, that is, a *so-called class* (e.g., ComputerSystem class). M2 defines how to represent M1 elements. For example, the M1 element of CIM is defined by *class*, *property*, and *association*, which are the M2 elements. In this layer, CIM differs from other models such as Shared Information and Data (SID) [3,6], which is promoted by the TeleManagement Forum (TMF). For example, CIM defines that *association* is derived from a *class*, whereas SID defines that an *association* is not derived from a *class* and an *association-class* is derived from both *association* and *class*. Such relationships between the M2 elements are defined by M3. In this paper, CIM Metaschema is regarded as a metamodel (M2), CIM Core Model and Common Model are regarded as a model (M1), and CIM instance is regarded as an instance (M0).

2.3 WQL

Our proposal provides CIM with a query facility. As regards the query facility, WBEM Query Language (WQL) is a possible query language, which is a subset of SQL, and its basic structure is described below.

Select <Property> From <Class>   [Where <Condition>]

Conditions on properties of CIM are inputted into the *Where* clause, and the *Select* clause indicates properties which are to be retrieved as output. This means that there is a static relationship between input and output and the query is thereby "one-way". Although the WQL is advantageous in terms of its well-known syntax, the M2 elements of RDB (e.g., *table* and *column*) do not correspond to those of CIM (e.g., *class*, *property*, *association*, and *qualifier*). This fact may make it difficult to retrieve *qualifier* or *property* of an *association instance*, even if the semantics of clauses are transformed.

2.4 XML, XPath, and RDF

An approach for managing dependencies with XML, XML Path Language (XPath), and the Resource Description Framework (RDF) has been proposed. Dependencies are defined using *class* and *property* of an RDF Schema (RDFS), which is a vocabulary definition language, and the model element might be one of CIM [7]. And actual dependency data is retrieved as an XML document from managed resources with instrumentations such as WBEM. The query is realized by an XPath Query Language, which does not have any reverse query mechanisms. The reverse query should hence be described, if it is required. This approach is, nevertheless, promising because it may utilize several advanced Semantic Web technologies.

3   Management System Using the Rule-Based CIM Query Facility

This section addresses the architecture of the management system using our CIM query facility. Section 3.1 describes the basic concept of the facility and overview of the architecture. Section 3.2 describes the basis of the query description. We discuss the sufficient capability to query CIM in Section 3.3 and the enhancement of the query usability in Section 3.4. Section 3.5 describes the interaction with external management applications and shows the capability to query bi-directionally.

3.1 Overview

In the following, M0 elements such as CIM *instances* and *association instances* are regarded as query targets. An *instance* represents the existence of a particular type of system component in a managed system, and *association instance* represents an existence of a particular type of relationship between system components. The types of *instance* and *association instance*, which are the M1 elements, therefore can be regarded as predicates that may become true or false depending on variables representing the state of system components. The basic concept of our approach is that CIM model (M1) elements can be treated as predicates and such M1 predicates can be defined by M2 predicates, because M1 elements are defined by M2 elements. The definition is realized by a rule-based language. The details of M2 predicates are described in Section 3.3.

It is easy for system administrators to describe a query based on the rule-based predicate definition, because the concept is similar to one's way of thinking about a dependency in an actual management environment. For example, an interesting dependency such as *Bookstore-Switch*, as described in Section 1, can be regarded as a combination of the dependencies *hosted* and *having-connection*. This predicate definition is shown in Section 3.5.

The proposed CIM query facility, which deals with above-mentioned predicates, is similar to a Prolog processor. One predicate is replaced with a combination of other predicates recursively, unless it is a built-in predicate. If a built-in predicate is called, WBEM API is utilized to obtain M0 elements instead of unifying facts within the processor. This unification process including a backtracking-algorithm makes it possible to retrieve the M0 elements, which makes the interesting predicate true.

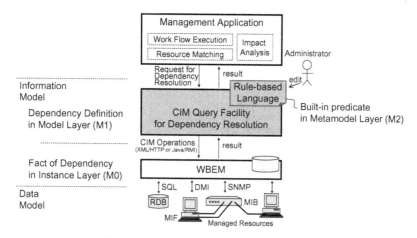

Fig. 1. Architecture of Management System

Fig. 1 shows the whole architecture of a management system using developed dependency resolution facility. Management applications are components with some specific management functions such as work flow execution, impact analysis, and resource matching. These management applications request the confirmation of dependency existence or query resources with some dependencies. The dependency resolution facility retrieves information one after another from WBEM in accordance with dependencies described by administrators. The actual dependency information is stored in WBEM as CIM *instances* and *association instances* (M0). These instances might be dynamic data or static data. Dynamic data might be retrieved from managed resources via WBEM on demand, while static data is stored in the repository of WBEM. The model in the managed resource can be thought as a data model, because it might depend on some repository formats. The correspondences with the Meta-level are listed in Table 1.

Table 1. Correspondances to Meta-level

Meta-level		Example	This System
Instance Layer	M0	CIM_ComputerSystem.Name="host0"	Query Target (e.g. WBEM)
Model Layer	M1	CIM_ComputerSystem	Definition of Dependency
Metamodel Layer	M2	CIM::Class, Association, Property	Built-in Predicate
Meta-metamodel Layer	M3	MOF::Class	

3.2   Basis of Query Description

The way to describe dependencies is syntactically similar to Prolog. Fig. 2 shows samples of the description. As for the definition of a new predicate using a rule, the variable should be selected from a free variable or a bound variable. A free variable, which is shown by a question mark, is able to become a variable whose value is not yet decided. And a bound variable, which is shown by an exclamation mark must be a variable which value must be determined. In Fig. 2(c), the predicate is defined using a bound variable, so the term should be filled with a concrete variable as an input. The predicate with some bound variables has some restrictions on the direction of the query.

(a) computerSystem(*?compSys*):-
     class("ComputerSystem", *?compSys*).

(b) fileServer(*?fServer*):-
     computerSystem(*?fServer*),
     property("Dedicated", *?fServer*, 16).

(c) linuxFileServer(*!LFServer*):-
     fileServer(*!LFServer*),
     association("InstalledOS", *!LFServer*, *?opSys*),
     class("OperatingSystem", *?opSys*),
     property("OSType", *?opSys*, 36).

Fig. 2. Examples of Query Description

3.3   Built-in Predicate

The examples of the built-in predicates, which are key-components of this query facility, are shown in Fig. 2. There are three built-in predicates: class predicate (Fig. 2(a)), property predicate (Fig. 2(b)), and association predicate (Fig. 2(c)). Furthermore, these predicates correspond to CIM operations: enumerateInstances, getProperty, and associator. This means that these predicates have restrictions on variables. The first term of each predicate should specify a model (M1) element, because each predicate represents the metamodel (M2) element. The second terms of a property predicate and an association predicate should be a bound variable, because these are input parameters of CIM operations. The second term of the class predicate and the third terms of the property predicate and association predicate should be free variables, because these are dealt with the outputs of the operations. These correspondences are listed in Table 2.

Table 2. Built-in Predicates Corresponding to CIM Metamodel Elements

Predicates (M2)	Terms			Corresponding CIM Operations
	1st (M1)	2nd (M0)	3rd (M0)	
class	bound variable (name of a class)	free variable (instance)		enumerateInstance( )
property	bound variable (name of a property)	bound variable (belonging instance)	free variable (value of the property)	getProperty( )
association	bound variable (name of an association)	bound variable (associating instance)	free variable (associated instance)	associator( )

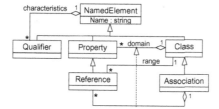

Fig. 3. CIM Metamodel (extracted from CIM Metaschema)

The reason these predicates are prepared is as follows. As described in Section 2.2, the M1 element is defined by the M2 elements. A predicate corresponding to a CIM model (M1) element is thus defined by the CIM metamodel (M2). The design of our predicates is as follows. Fig. 3 shows an extracted CIM metamodel. Since all M2 elements have a *name* property, all built-in predicates have a *name* term, which can specify an M1 element. A *Property* is aggregated by a *Class* and an *Association* aggregate multiple *References*, each of which is associated with a *Class*. These relationships are reflected on the 2nd terms and 3rd terms of the predicates. Though we list only three predicates in Table 2, another predicate can be mentioned as long as it reflects the relationship in Fig. 3. An example of the relationship is as follows: a *Qualifier* can be aggregated by any element and an *Association* can aggregate *Properties*. Usage of the *Qualifier* predicate may enable M0 elements of particular version of CIM to be queried. This design concept of built-in predicates is applicable to SID, which has a different metamodel from CIM.

3.4   Enhancement of Usability

This section describes a macro of the query for the enhancement of the usability. The macro described here means that pre-described predicates are combined into more readable predicates. This facility is important because CIM is designed on the basis of the concept that reusability among the industry is more important than the usability and readability. To enhance the reusability, managed resources are modeled in functional aspects. For example, a router is not modeled as a Router class, but as a combination of functional classes such as ComputerSystem and IPProtocolEndpoint. It is true that such a *divide-and-conquer* strategy is useful for reusability, but it is not so readable. It is therefore useful to re-organize these functional predicates into a more usable and readable predicate. For example, predicate *fileserver* shown in Fig.2(b) is quite readable, while it is not so readable that a value of the *Dedicated* property of *ComputerSystem* class means the type of server.

Table 3. Predicate Stack

Predicate Stack		Example	Feature
Dependency Predicate		ActiveConnectionBetweenRouterAndFileServer(?a, ?b).	Usability
Component Predicate	Definable	Router(?a). FileServer(?b).	↑
Model Predicate (M1)		ComputerSystem(?a). ActiveConnection(!a, ?b).	↓
Metamodel Predicate (M2)	Built-In	Class("ComputerSystem", ?a). Association("ActiveConnection", !a, ?b).	Reusability

Since our rule-based language enables a new predicate to be defined by using pre-defined multiple predicates, it is easy to define the macro of the query naturally. Table 3 indicates a predicate stack as the guideline of macro definition. The predicates in the upper layer are defined by the predicates at the lower layer. Fig. 2(a) shows an example that a model predicate is defined by a metamodel predicate, and Fig. 2(b) shows an example that component predicate is defined by a model predicate. Predicates at the lower two layers depend on CIM, while predicates at the upper two layers are independent of CIM and are suitable for management applications and system administrators. We thereby suppose that the predicates at the lower layer are defined by those who are familiar with CIM and predicates at the upper layer are defined by those who describe a query for some management applications.

3.5 Usage of the CIM Query Facility

The interaction between this rule-based CIM query facility and management applications is as follows. There are two patterns in a dependency resolution. One is the pattern that resources are queried in accordance with defined dependencies (Pattern 1), and the other is the pattern that the existence of the dependency is checked (Pattern 2). These patterns have the same semantics as a Prolog.

Pattern 1: The input to CIM query facility is a predicate and its list of parameters (Fig. 4). If some parameters are filled with data and the others are filled with *null*, the filled data act as a key to a query, and the parameters filled with *null* can be retrieved from WBEM. It is therefore possible to execute a reverse query using a same query description, which is impossible using WQL. In the example of bookstore service discussed in Section 1, Fig. 4(c) shows the query for impact analysis, while Fig. 4(b) shows the query for root cause analysis.

(a) BookstoreSwitch(?bookstore, ?switch) :-
        Bookstore(?bookstore),
        hosted(?bookstore, ?server),
        Server(?server),
        HavingConnectivity(?server, ?switch),
        Switch(?switch).

(b) Input   : BookstoreSwitch(Bookstore_1, **null**)
     Output : { (Bookstore_1, **switch_1**),
               (Bookstore_1, **switch_2**),
               (Bookstore_1, **switch_3**) }

(c) Input   : BookstoreSwitch(**null** , switch_1)
     Output : { (**Bookstore_1**, switch_1),
               (**Bookstore_2**, switch_1)}

Fig. 4. Examples of Input and Output

Pattern 2: Filling all terms with some values makes it possible to check if given dependencies exist or not. If there is a given dependency in WBEM, the value *true* is returned.

4   Prototype Implementation

This section describes the use case of utility computing for an illustration. In Section 4.1, a service model is described and a required sequence are described. In Section 4.2, we show an example of the query description, and an evaluation of query performance is shown in Section 4.3.

4.1   Service Model

We utilize our dependency resolution facility for utility computing. We suppose that servers in a data center (DC) are shared by several service providers. When workloads on allocated servers increase, the service provider may request an additional server with some requirements on resources such as the type of operating system and IP address range. It is regarded that the service provider is a virtual organization (VO) as defined in [8]. In addition, it is assumed that whether the administrators of a VO can monitor resource information such as servers and network devices depends on the access control policy of a DC. For example, Fig. 5 shows the context that the monitor of the identifications of network devices such as firewalls are restricted to a VO, and what can be monitored is the assigned servers and their locations such as DMZ or internal-LAN. Therefore, when the DC receives a request for an additional server, it needs to retrieve detail information about pool servers and network devices in order to realize a resource matching [9] and filling parameters of workflow templates. The CIM query facility is applied to this information retrieval. To put it more concretely, among the following steps that consists an overall sequence of our implementation, the facility is used in Step 2 and Step 5.

Step 1: VO requests an additional server with some requirements on resources.
Step 2: DC collects servers which match the request among the pool servers.
Step 3: DC selects the most suitable server among the collected servers.
Step 4: DC prepares a workflow template required for the configuration change.
Step 5: DC fills the workflow with parameters.
Step 6: DC executes the completed workflow.

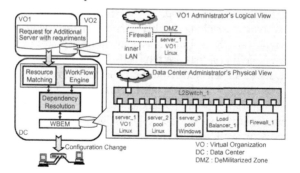

Fig. 5. Architecture of the Prototype System

The configuration change is realized by the control of servers and network devices such as a layer 2 switch (L2SW), a firewall, and a load balancers. In the prototype system, we use an NEC ES8000 L2SW, a Cisco PIX 515E firewall, and an Alteon

ACEDirector3 load balancer as managed resources. And we use WBEMServices as a WBEM server, and its runtime environment is as follows: Linux RedHat 7.3, Celron 1.7 GHz CPU, and 512 MB Memory.

4.2   Predicate Definition for Resource Collection

This section describes the outline of the experimental implementation according to the above-mentioned sequence. In particular, we introduce a sample query and an object diagram which represents objects existing in a WBEM server.

In Step 1, a VO generates the request for a server with following requirements.

Requirement 1: Linux OS is required.

Requirement 2: The domain at which the server is to be allocated is DMZ.

Requirement 3: The server's IP address should be within the subnet 192.168.10.0.

In Step 2, the resource matching facility collects pool servers which have Linux OS. In our prototype, pool servers are represented as the servers belonging to the *pool* organization. The collection is thereby realized by the query shown in Fig. 6, and the object diagram which represents the target of query is shown in Fig. 7.

```
CompSysInVLANofOpSysOrg( ?compSys, ?vlanid, ?osType, ?org):-
    Organization              ( ?orginst),
    property                  ( "Organization",        ?orginst,        ?org),
    OrganizationDependency ( ?orginst,                 ?vlan),
    property                  ( "VLANId",               ?vlan,          ?vlanid),
    EndstationInVLAN          ( ?vlan,                  ?vlan_endstation_endpoint),
    EndpointIdentity          ( ?vlan_endstation_endpoint, ?ip_protocol_endpoint),
    EndpointIdentity          ( ?ip_protocol_endpoint,  ?lan_endpoint),
    PortImplementsEndpoint ( ?lan_endpoint,            ?ether_port),
    SystemDevice              ( ?ether_port,            ?compSys),
    OperatingSystem           ( ?os),
    property                  ( "OSType",               ?os,            ?osType),
    RunningOS                 ( ?os,                    ?compSys).
```

Fig. 6. Query Description

If the CIM query facility receives the predicate *CompSysInVLANofOpSysOrg* and its parameters (*null, null, 36, "pool"*), the list (*"server_2", 5, 36, "pool"*) is returned to the resource matching facility. The fact that dedicated property is 36 means that the type of OS is Linux, as shown in Fig.2(c). If there are plural appropriate servers, the plural lists are returned. The resources are thereby collected.

In Step 3, one server is selected from the collected servers on the basis of a first-match strategy. In Step 4, a hard-coded workflow template is retrieved. This workflow is filled with appropriate parameters in Step 5. The retrievals are realized by the CIM query facility, that is, specifying of network device such as a switch, a load balancer, and a firewall, and the retrieval of required configuration data such as administrative IP addresses, port numbers, and VLAN numbers. In Step 6, the completed workflow is executed and the result of the execution is reflected on WBEM.

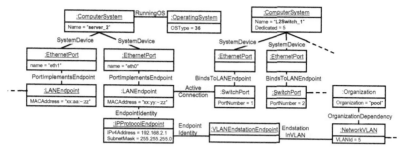

Fig. 7. Object Diagram of Query Target

4.3 Performance Evaluation

The execution time used in the all steps was 59.6 seconds. This performance was observed under an experimental condition that a CIM query facility was connected with WBEM using XML/HTTP. After the protocol of the connection was changed to Java/RMI, the execution time improved 45.2 seconds. This implies that our approach, which can exclude an XML parser, has an advantage in terms of the execution time. Furthermore, we provided a cache and connection-pooling with a CIM Query Facility and we obtained the execution time of 32.5 seconds. Under this condition, the execution time from Step 1 to Step 5 is about 16 seconds, while the method enumerateInstances, getProperty, and associators was called 12 times, 114 times and 114 times respectively. We have confirmed much time was consumed by the responses from WBEM and the overhead of the query facility was negligible.

The scalability issue was investigated by changing the total number of instances and association instances existing in the CIM repository of WBEM. Fig. 8 shows the execution time of a similar query. The figures in the graph indicate the number of pool servers. This result indicates the scalability problem, though the cause is supposed to stem from the usage of the WBEM API of the enumerateInstances method.

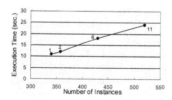

Fig. 8. Result of Scalability Investigation

5 Conclusion

We focus on the dependency resolution facility among the important issues in autonomic computing and utility computing. The discovery of system components which have particular dependencies is realized by an association traversal, and therefore we enhance a query facility of CIM. The required features of the facility are ease of query description, bi-directional query execution, and sufficient capability to query CIM. This CIM query facility is based on a predicate logic and a rule-based language. The ease of query description is realized by the rule-based language that can combine multiple predicates into a new predicate representing a query, because it is similar to the system administrator's concept that an interesting dependency is combined with pre-known dependencies. The capability to define a macro also contributes to the ease of description, because the model element of CIM is based on the design concept that a reusability takes priority over an usability and readability. Bi-direction query execution can be realized by the unification process. Sufficient capability to query CIM can be realized by the preparation of the built-in predicates corresponding to CIM metamodel elements. The discussion based on a Meta-level indicates that our approach is independent of CIM. The proposed CIM query facility was validated by implementing it in a utility computing application. The basic behavior of the query facility and the dynamic server allocation was illustrated.

References

[1]   A. Keller, U. Blumenthal, and G. Kar, "Classification and Computation of Dependencies for Distributed Management," 5th IEEE Symposium on Computers and Communications (ISCC), July 2000.
[2]   A. Keller, and G. Kar, "Determining Service Dependencies in Distributed Systems," IEEE International Conference on Communications (ICC), June 2001.
[3]   J. Strassner, "Policy Based Network Management : Solutions for the Next Generation," Morgan Kaufmann, Aug. 2003.
[4]   A. Westerinen, et al., "Terminology for Policy-Based Management," IETF RFC3198, Nov. 2001.
[5]   CIM standards. http://www.dmtf.org/standards/standard_cim.php
[6]   TMF, "GB922: Shared Information/Data (SID) Model: Concepts, Principles, and Business Entities," July 2003.
[7]   C. Ensel, and A. Keller, "Managing Application Service Dependencies with XML and the Resource Description Framework," IFIP/IEEE International Symposium on Integrated Management (IM2001), May 2001.
[8]   I. Foster, C. Kesselman, and S. Tuecke, "The Anatomy of the Grid," International J. Supercomputer Applications, 2001.
[9]   H. Tangmunarunkit, S. Decker, and C. Kesselman, "Ontology-based Resource Matching in the Grid - The Grid meets the Semantic Web," 1st Workshop On Semantics in P2P and Grid Computing at the 12th International World Wide Web Conference, May 2003.

Work in Progress: Availability-Aware Self-Configuration in Autonomic Systems

David M. Chess, Vibhore Kumar, Alla Segal, and Ian Whalley

IBM Thomas J. Watson Research Center, P.O. Box 704,
Yorktown Heights, NY 10598, USA
{chess,vibhore,segal,inw}@us.ibm.com

Abstract. The Unity project is a prototype autonomic system demonstrating and validating a number of ideas about self-managing computing systems. We are currently working to enhance the self-configuring and self-optimizing aspects of the system by incorporating the notion of component availability into the system's policies, and into its models of itself.

1 Introduction

The vision of autonomic computing is of a world where complex distributed systems manage themselves to a far greater extent than they do today [1]. The Unity project [2] is a prototype autonomic system, designed to develop and validate various ideas about how this self-management can be achieved in practice. The aspects of self-management that we explore in Unity include self-configuration and self-optimization; the system initially configures parts of itself with a minimal amount of explicit human input, and during operation it reallocates and reconfigures certain of its resources to optimize its behavior according to human-specified policies.

In our current research, we are investigating ways to enhance the self-configuration and self-optimization aspects of Unity by incorporating the concept of availability into the system's policies and models of itself. The notions of availability and related concepts that we employ here are essentially those of [3]; availability is the condition of readiness for correct service.

(Space does not allow a significant list of previous work relevant to this project; the reader is invited to consult references such as [4].)

1.1 Availability in the Present System

In the current Unity system, availability is implicitly supported in one way: one component of the system (the policy repository) is implemented as a self-healing cluster of synchronized services; other components of the system ensure that if one member of the cluster goes down, another service instance is brought up and enters the cluster to take its place.

A. Sahai and F. Wu (Eds.): DSOM 2004, LNCS 3278, pp. 257-258, 2004.
© IFIP International Federation for Information Processing 2004

2 Stages of Availability Awareness

The first and simplest enhancement we plan to make will involve moving the constant representing the number of clustered copies of the repository to create, from its current location in a configuration file into a simple policy in the system's policy infrastructure. While this still does not involve the system in any availability-related calculations, it will at least leverage the commonality and deployment abilities of the policy subsystem.

In the second stage, we will replace the constant number with a desired availability target, representing a required percentage of uptime. We will then do a straightforward calculation based on MTBF and MTTR estimates for the repository component, to determine the initial size of the repository cluster. (Estimating the proper MTBF and MTTR figures from logs and other data will be addressed in a related project.)

In the third stage, we will replace the static required availability target with a service-level utility function as defined in [5], representing the business value of various levels of repository availability. Together with a similar representation of the cost impact of running additional repositories (including the impact on the rest of the system of devoting resources to those repositories), this will allow the system to calculate the optimum number of repositories for the given utility and cost functions.

The third stage requires obtaining the utility and cost functions from outside the system. In the fourth and final stage of this design, we will enrich the system's model of itself sufficiently to derive those functions from the model (and from the higher-level utility functions describing the business value of the system's overall behavior). The system (or more accurately, the solution manager component which determines and maintains the composition of the system) will use its model of the system's behaviors to estimate the value of repository availability (in terms of the impact of having the repository unavailable on the overall value produced) and the cost of running multiple repositories, and use these functions to do the calculations as in the third stage.

We solicit communication from others investigating similar problems or related technologies in this area.

References

1. Kephart, J., Chess, D.: "The Vision of Autonomic Computing", IEEE Computer 36(1): 41-50, 2003.
2. Chess, D., Segal, A., Whalley, I., White, S.: "Unity: Experiences with a Prototype Autonomic Computing System", International Conference on Autonomic Computing (ICAC-04), 2004.
3. Avizienis, A., Laprie, J-C., Randell, B.: "Fundamental Concepts of Dependability," Research Report N01145, LAAS-CNRS, April 2001.
4. Marcus, E., Stern, H.: "Blueprints for High Availability: Designing Resilient Distributed Systems", John Wiley & Sons, 1st Edition, January 31, 2000.
5. Walsh, W., Tesauro, G., Kephart, J., Das, R.: "Utility Functions in Autonomic Systems," International Conference on Autonomic Computing (ICAC-04), 2004.

ABHA: A Framework for Autonomic Job Recovery

Charles Earl[1], Emilio Remolina[1], Jim Ong[1], John Brown[2], Chris Kuszmaul[3], and
Brad Stone[4]

[1] Stottler Henke Associates
{earl,remolina,ong}@shai.com
[2]Pentum Group,Inc.
johnbrown@pentum.com
[3]chris_kuszmaul@hotmail.com
[4]bstone@aspirinsoftware.com

Abstract. Key issues to address in autonomic job recovery for cluster
computing are recognizing job failure; understanding the failure sufficiently to
know if and how to restart the job; and rapidly integrating this information into
the cluster architecture so that the failure is better mitigated in the future. The
Agent Based High Availability (ABHA) system provides an API and a
collection of services for building autonomic batch job recovery into cluster
computing environments. An agent API allows users to define agents for failure
diagnosis and recovery. It is currently being evaluated in the U.S. Department of
Energy's STAR project.

1 Introduction

In production high-performance cluster computing environments, batch jobs can fail
for many reasons: transient and permanent hardware failures; software configuration
errors; insufficient computing, storage, or network resources; incorrectly specified
application inputs or buggy application code. Simplistic job recovery policies (e.g.
blind restart) can lead to low quality of service and inefficient use of cluster resources.
To provide high throughput and high reliability, it is necessary to determine the cause
of task failure in enough detail to select and execute the appropriate job recovery.

While many job failures require human intervention for proper troubleshooting and
repair, a significant number can be delegated to autonomic [1] software.

We are developing a platform called the Agent Based High Availability (ABHA)
that provides autonomic recovery for batch jobs running on cluster and grid computing
environments. ABHA is being tested in the context of the U.S. Department of Energy's
STAR project [2] at Lawrence Berkeley National Laboratory (LBNL). We are now
evaluating it on production facilities there.

2 Architecture

A complete model for autonomic job recovery has to address four problems: 1)
recognition of job failure; 2) determination of appropriate failure recovery, which may

A. Sahai and F. Wu (Eds.): DSOM 2004, LNCS 3278, pp. 259–262, 2004.
© IFIP International Federation for Information Processing 2004

require diagnosis to select between alternatives; 3) the ability to initiate recovery actions; and 4) using that knowledge to avoid or mitigate the failure in the future.

ABHA uses a collection of distributed agents to address these problems. Agents provide robustness, local monitoring and recovery with global communication, and separation of concerns for creating new error management details.

Figure 1 depicts the core components of the system in a typical configuration. Agents collect information about the system and jobs running on it and share that information with other agents by producing events that are distributed by a centralized *Facilitator*. Agents use this shared information to predict and diagnose job failures, make job recovery recommendations, and autonomously perform job recovery.

Agents can be deployed on various nodes throughout the cluster as dictated by the configuration of the site. For example, agents can gather information from and issue commands to distributed resource managers (e.g. Condor [3] or LSF [4]), filter and interpret information collected from other system monitors (e.g. Ganglia [5]), provide detailed information from specific jobs, or collect information from services deployed through the system (e.g. NFS).

ABHA deploys a centralized Reasoner (based on the Java Expert System Shell [6]) that interprets rules that are run against the events sent to the Facilitator. The behavior of remote agents can also be specified using rules. ABHA provides C++, Java, and Perl APIs for developing agents. The Facilitator is implemented using the Java Message Service (JMS) API and can be configured to provide fail-over and persistent event storage. A graphical user interface allows inspection of events and control of agents.

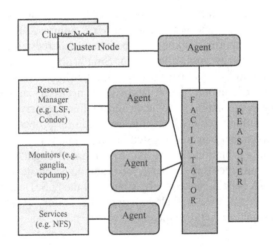

Fig. 1. ABHA Architecture

3   An Example

One example provides an illustration of the functionality of ABHA and the kinds of recovery issues that it can address. The STAR production cluster at LBNL [7] maintains a clustered file system for storage of experimental data. Each node is referred to as a disk vault. The typical STAR batch job will be assigned to run on one of 344 compute nodes and will access data that is remotely mounted on one of the 65 disk vaults. If too many jobs try to read data at the same time, the disk vault goes into a thrashing mode and only reboot can bring it back. A reboot can be avoided by intervening when disk vault I/O reaches a critical value. An administrator can suspend jobs accessing the overloaded vault, adjust their resource requirements, and shepherd each job them the queue until the load on the vault reaches acceptable levels.

We developed and tested a solution to this problem on our local cluster. Rules loaded by the Reasoner agent direct diagnosis and recovery. The main rule is paraphrased below.

```
IF(high_diskvault_load ON ?dv AT ?T1)
  AND(max_dvio_consumer ?dv ?node ?T1)
  AND (lsf_job ?node ?job ?T1)
  AND (job_mounts ?job ?dv)
THEN
  (lsf_suspend (jobs_using_vault ?dv))
  (restart ?job)
  (UNTIL(normal_diskvault_load ON ?dv)

    (lsf_restart (pick ?jobs)))
```

A ganglia agent filters information from the ganglia monitor, sending high_ diskvault_load when the load on one of the disk vault machines exceeds a threshold.

The Reasoner agent then requests the tcpdump agent to determine which machine consumes the most I/O bandwidth with respect to the vault. The tcpdump agent posts this information as a max_dvio_consumer event.

The Reasoner then requests the lsf agent to determine the jobs running on the offending host, and returns these in an lsf_job event. The rule then requests mount information from local_node_monitor agent on the node on which the job is running. The local_node_monitor agent returns this information in a job_mounts event. The Reasoner then follows the THEN part of the rule: it suspends jobs running against the disk vault, adjusts the priority of the offending job, and once the offending job has finished, restarts remaining jobs, until the load on the disk vault returns to normal.

4   Remaining Work

We are evaluating on the PDSF production cluster. A Grid service implementation of ABHA is also being developed for the STAR Grid project [7].

References

1. Chess, D., Kephart, J.: The Vision of Autonomic Computing. IEEE Computer Magazine 1 (2003) 41-50.
2. STAR experiment website http://www.star.bnl.gov/.
3. Condor project website http://www.cs.wisc.edu/condor/.
4. Platform Computing LSF http://www.platform.com
5. Ganglia project website http://ganglia.sourceforge.net/.
6. JESS website at http://herzberg.ca.sandia.gov/jess
7. Parallel Distributed Systems Facility website http://www.nersc.gov/nusers/resources/PDSF/

Can ISPs and Overlay Networks Form a Synergistic Co-existence?

Ram Keralapura[1,2], Nina Taft[2], Gianluca Iannaccone[2], and Chen-Nee Chuah[1]*

[1] Univ. of California, Davis
[2] Intel Research

1 Introduction

Overlay networks are becoming increasingly popular for their ability to provide effective and reliable service catered to specific applications [1][2][3]. For instance, this concept has been used in peer-to-peer services like SplitStream, content delivery networks like Akamai, resilient networks like RON and so on.

Overlay networks consist of a number of nodes (spanning one or many domains) that collaborate in a distributed application. One of the underlying paradigms of overlay networks is to give applications more control over routing decisions, that would otherwise be carried out solely at the IP layer. Overlay networks typically monitor multiple paths between pairs of nodes, and select the one based on its own requirements (e.g., delay, bandwidth, etc.). Allowing routing control to take place at both the application layer and the IP layer, could have profound implications on how ISPs design, maintain and run their networks. The architecture and protocols that carriers use to run their networks are based on assumptions about how their customers and traffic behave. It is possible that the approach used by overlay networks could call into question some of carriers' assumptions thus rendering it more difficult for them to achieve their goals.

In this paper, we identify some potentially problematic interactions between overlay and layer-3 networks. We raise a key question: *Can overlay networks and underlying IP networks form a synergistic co-existence?* Given the recent rise in popularity of overlay networks, we believe that now is the time to address these issues. We hypothesize that it could be problematic to have routing control in two layers, when each of the layers is unaware of key things happening in the other layer. ISPs may be unaware of which nodes are participating in an overlay and their routing strategy. Overlay networks are unaware of an ISP's topology, load balancing schemes, routing protocol timer values, etc. We believe that ISPs need to clearly understand the implications of overlay network behavior.

2 Sample Interaction Issues

Traffic Matrix (TM) Estimation: A traffic matrix specifies the traffic demand from origin nodes to destination nodes for a single domain. A TM is a

---

* This work was partly supported by the NSF CAREER Grant No. 0238348.

A. Sahai and F. Wu (Eds.): DSOM 2004, LNCS 3278, pp. 263–265, 2004.
© IFIP International Federation for Information Processing 2004

critical input for many traffic engineering tasks (e.g, capacity planning, failure provisioning, etc.) and hence ISPs undergo considerable effort to estimate TMs. Many flows whose ultimate destination lies outside an ISP's domain still appear inside the TM which specifies an exit router in the domain. If this traffic belongs to an overlay network that uses its own path selection mechanism and spans multiple domains, the overlay can alter the egress router for that flow from a particular domain. For example, consider two domains with two peering links between them. Suppose the layer-3 path from a node in the first domain to a destination node in the second domain uses the first peering link. An overlay network can decide to route to the destination node via an intermediate overlay node that causes the path taken to traverse the second peering link, thereby changing the exit node from the first domain and subsequently the TM of that domain. If this were to happen for large flows, it could affect a significant portion of the TM. If this were to happen often, it would increase the dynamic nature of the TM which might then require more frequent updates to remain accurate.

Failure Reaction: It has been shown recently [4] that there are a large range of failure types in the Internet, some intermittent and some long-lasting, and that overall failures happen surprisingly often. As overlay networks use frequent active probing to assess the quality of their paths, they could react to failure events at a time scale either faster or similar to ISPs. If multiple overlay networks that have their nodes in a domain experiencing a failure, react to the failure closely in time, then it is easy to see that all of them might choose the same next best path, causing congestion on that path. If two overlays have similar values for their probe timeouts, they could become synchronized in their search for a new path, thereby leading to load thrashing (or traffic oscillations). All of this is due to the relationship between the failure reaction timers of a carrier's routing protocol, and the path probing timeouts of each of the multiple overlays. We believe that careful guidelines should be developed for the selection of such timeouts. Traffic oscillations in the network due to such race conditions are undesirable for ISPs that are held accountable for performance degradation.

Load Balancing: ISPs usually have a target for the distribution of load across their network; for example, they want a low average and variance of link loads network-wide. Failures trigger overlay networks to redistribute their traffic by probing a limited set of alternate paths (constrained by where other overlay nodes reside). As overlay networks lack the global knowledge of the ISP's domain, the resulting distribution of load across all links could differ significantly from what would happen if an ISP handles the load shift all by itself. In this way overlays can undermine an ISP's load balancing strategy.

3   Summary

We have identified a few critical problems that ISPs may face due to overlay networks. Using simple examples, we show that it is important to address these issues before the impact of overlay networks is detrimental to the Internet. The co-existence of multiple overlays is likely to exacerbate these problems.

References

[1] D. Anderson, H. Balakrishna, M. Kaashoek and R. Morris: "Resilient Overlay Networks", *SOSP*, Oct 2001.
[2] Akamai: http://www.akamai.com
[3] B. Zhao, L. Huang, J. Stribling, A. Joseph and J. Kubiatowicz: "Exploiting Routing Redundancy via Structured Peer-to-Peer Overlays", *ICNP*, Nov 2003.
[4] A. Markopoulou, G. Iannaccone, S. Bhattacharrya, C. N. Chuah and C. Diot: "Characterization of Failures in an IP Backbone Network", *INFOCOM*, Mar 2004

Simplifying Correlation Rule Creation for Effective Systems Monitoring

C. Araujo[1], A. Biazetti[1], A. Bussani[2], J. Dinger[1], M. Feridun[2], and A. Tanner[2]

[1] IBM Software Group, Tivoli Raleigh Development Lab, Raleigh, NC 12345, USA
{caraujo, abiazett, jd}@us.ibm.com
[2] IBM Research, Zurich Research Laboratory, 8803 Rueschlikon, Switzerland
{bus, fer, axs}@zurich.ibm.com

Abstract. Event correlation is a necessary component of systems management but is perceived as a difficult function to set up and maintain. We report on our work to develop a set of tools and techniques to simplify event correlation and thereby reduce overall operating costs. The tools prototyped are described and our current plans for future tool development outlined.

Event correlation is a key component of systems management. Events from multiple resources, e.g., network elements, servers, applications, are collected and analyzed to detect problems such as component failures, security breeches and failed business processes. Management solutions require correlation for filtering and analyzing massive numbers of events, for example by removing duplicate events, or for detecting event sequences that signal a significant occurrence in the managed systems. Relevant event patterns need to be identified and formulated as rules, and mechanisms provided to map observed events into the defined patterns. Many systems allow correlation of events where the patterns are expressed as rules [1]. The difficulty lies in identifying the different and relevant patterns of events, as patterns change and new ones are introduced. Our goal is to develop tools to help operators and systems management architects to identify event patterns, to create rules to implement the patterns, test their validity, and to monitor and manage the rules during their lifecycle.

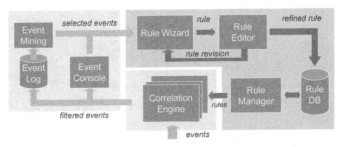

Fig. 1. Tools for automated correlation rule generation

The tool collection is shown in Figure 1. The *correlation engines* use installed rules to filter incoming events, which are logged (*Event Log*) and displayed on the *event console*. By *event mining* [2, 3] or operator intervention, patterns of events that need to be filtered or in sum indicate a situation are selected. In the *rule wizard* and the *rule*

A. Sahai and F. Wu (Eds.): DSOM 2004, LNCS 3278, pp. 266–268, 2004.

editor, the patterns are used as input to create rules, possibly through several refinements, stored in the *rule database*, and distributed for deployment to the relevant correlation engines.

Here, we describe the first stage of our work focusing on the prototype developed to create rules based on events selected by an operator from an event console. The automation of the rule-generation process begins with the operator selecting a number of related events from the event console, for example false positives that should be filtered out. First, the operator invokes the rule wizard which allows him to select a pre-defined rule pattern to apply to the selected events. The prototype offers six patterns: *filter* to match an event against a predicate; *collection* to gather matching events within a time interval; *duplicates* to suppress duplicate events by forwarding the first matching event and blocking similar events until the end of the time interval; *threshold* to look for a sequence of similar events crossing a threshold value within a time interval; and *sequence* to detect the presence/absence of a sequence of events (in order or random) within a time interval. Second, the operator can select the parameters relevant to the selected pattern, e.g. the time interval during which the pattern should occur. The third step generates the predicates used in selecting pattern-relevant events. The operator is presented with the attributes available in each event and selects the one to be used in the predicate to filter the incoming events. With this information, the wizard automatically generates a predicate expression for the rule. Finally, the operator specifies actions to be executed when the rule triggers, i.e., detects the defined pattern. Actions can include updates to the events (e.g. relating to another event, changing attributes of an event, closing/acknowledging an event) or sending notifications (paging, email) to interested parties among others.

An example application of the rule wizard for a fax server demonstrates the usefulness of the approach. In the case of a failure, a number of related events, such as *rfboard_down* and *rfqueue_down* are observed by the operator at the console. From experience the operator knows that these are related to a defective fax server and decides to create a rule to collect and summarize them into one event. He selects the related events at the console and invokes the rule wizard, which shows the selected events and the rule pattern options. The operator chooses the sequence pattern, configures rule parameters, e.g., the time window, selection attributes, e.g., event type, and selects an action to summarize all selected events into a single *nt_rfserver_down* event. The rule is automatically created, and once deployed will result in just one summary event displayed on the event console, instead of the multiple original ones.

We have developed and demonstrated a prototype rule wizard and rule editor, and integrated it with the IBM Tivoli Event Console (TEC). The prototype enables automatic creation of rules, which greatly helps operators by providing a simple way to create rules based on observed events. Our follow-on work and areas of investigation focus on the development and integration of tools for testing and debugging newly created rules–for example checking how new rules interact with the existing deployed rule sets—using the current event stream, historical event logs or simulated event flows as an additional refinement step prior to rule deployment in the real environment. The rule wizard can be extended to define frequently occurring and typical high-level tasks of an operator, such as 'filter these events out' or 'page administrator when these events occur together' as templates for use by less skilled operators. We also address instrumentation of the correlation engine to collect real-time data on rule behavior and performance as feedback into rule design and improvement, and for the management of the lifecycle of the rules.

References

[1] IBM Tivoli Event Console,
    http://www.ibm.com/software/tivoli/products/enterprise-console/.
[2] J. L. Hellerstein, S. Ma and C. Perng, "Discovering actionable patterns from event data", IBM Systems Journal, vol. 41, issue 3, pp. 475-493, 2002.
[3] K. Julisch, "Clustering Intrusion Detection Alarms to Support Root Cause Analysis", ACM Transactions on Information and System Security, 6(4):1-29, 2003

Author Index

Agarwal, Manoj K.   171
Al-Shaer, Ehab   28
Appleby, Karen   171
Araujo, C.   266

Badonnel, Remi   15
Bartolini, Claudio   64
Beller, André   40
Beyer, Dirk   100
Bhaskaran, Kumar   52
Biazetti, A.   266
Boutaba, Raouf   208
Brasileiro, Francisco V.   220
Brown, John   259
Burchard, Lars-Olof   112
Bussani, A.   266

Chang, Henry   52
Cherkaoui, Omar   147
Chess, David M.   257
Choi, Eunmi   135
Chuah, Chen-Nee   263
Cirne, Walfredo   220
Cridlig, V.   183

Deca, Rudy   147
Dillenburg, Fabiane   196
Dinger, J.   266

Earl, Charles   259

Feridun, M.   266
Festor, O.   183

Garschhammer, Markus   1
Gaspary, Luciano Paschoal   196
Gupta, Manish   171

Hallé, Sylvain   147
Hinrich, Tim   159
Horiuchi, Hiroki   232

Iannaccone, Gianluca   263
Iraqi, Youssef   208

Jamhour, Edgard   40

Jeng, Jun-Jang   52

Kar, Gautam   171
Karmouch, Ahmed   76
Keller, Alexander   15
Keralapura, Ram   263
Konishi, Koichi   245
Kouyama, Takeshi   232
Kudo, Masato   245
Kumar, Vibhore   257
Kuszmaul, Chris   259

Lee, Chul   124
Lim, Sang Soek   124
Lim, Seung Ho   124
Linnert, Barry   112
Locatelli, Fábio Elias   196
Lohmann, Samir   196
Lopes, Raquel V.   220
Love, Nathaniel   159

Machiraju, Vijay   100
Maeda, Naoto   88
Mekouar, Loubna   208
Melchiors, Cristina   196
Min, Dugki   135

Nakadai, Shinji   245
Neogi, Anindya   171
Nishikawa, Masayuki   232

Ong, Jim   259

Park, Kyu Ho   124
Pellenz, Marcelo   40
Petrie, Charles   159
Puche, Daniel   147

Ramshaw, Lyle   159
Remolina, Emilio   259
Roelle, Harald   1

Sahai, Akhil   100, 159
Sailer, Anca   171
Sallé, Mathias   64
Samaan, Nancy   76
Santos, Cipriano A.   100

Segal, Alla   257
Singhal, Sharad   100, 159
State, R.   183
Stone, Brad   259

Taft, Nina   263
Tanner, A.   266
Tonouchi, Toshio   88

Villemaire, Roger   147

Whalley, Ian   257

Yoshihara, Kiyohito   232

Zhang, Bin   28
Zhu, Xiaoyun   100

Lecture Notes in Computer Science

For information about Vols. 1–3193

please contact your bookseller or Springer

Vol. 3305: P.M.A. Sloot, B. Chopard, A.G. Hoekstra (Eds.), Cellular Automata. XV, 883 pages. 2004.

Vol. 3302: W.-N. Chin (Ed.), Programming Languages and Systems. XIII, 453 pages. 2004.

Vol. 3299: F. Wang (Ed.), Automated Technology for Verification and Analysis. XII, 506 pages. 2004.

Vol. 3293: C.-H. Chi, M. van Steen, C. Wills (Eds.), Web Content Caching and Distribution. IX, 283 pages. 2004.

Vol. 3292: R. Meersman, Z. Tari, A. Corsaro (Eds.), On the Move to Meaningful Internet Systems 2004: OTM 2004 Workshops. XXIII, 885 pages. 2004.

Vol. 3291: R. Meersman, Z. Tari (Eds.), On the Move to Meaningful Internet Systems 2004: CoopIS, DOA, and ODBASE. XXV, 824 pages. 2004.

Vol. 3290: R. Meersman, Z. Tari (Eds.), On the Move to Meaningful Internet Systems 2004: CoopIS, DOA, and ODBASE. XXV, 823 pages. 2004.

Vol. 3287: A. Sanfeliu, J.F.M. Trinidad, J.A. Carrasco Ochoa (Eds.), Progress in Pattern Recognition, Image Analysis and Applications. XVII, 703 pages. 2004.

Vol. 3286: G. Karsai, E. Visser (Eds.), Generative Programming and Component Engineering. XIII, 491 pages. 2004.

Vol. 3284: A. Karmouch, L. Korba, E.R.M. Madeira (Eds.), Mobility Aware Technologies and Applications. XII, 382 pages. 2004.

Vol. 3281: T. Dingsøyr (Ed.), Software Process Improvement. X, 207 pages. 2004.

Vol. 3280: C. Aykanat, T. Dayar, İ. Körpeoğlu (Eds.), Computer and Information Sciences - ISCIS 2004. XVIII, 1009 pages. 2004.

Vol. 3278: A. Sahai, F. Wu (Eds.), Utility Computing. XI, 270 pages. 2004.

Vol. 3274: R. Guerraoui (Ed.), Distributed Computing. XIII, 465 pages. 2004.

Vol. 3273: T. Baar, A. Strohmeier, A. Moreira, S.J. Mellor (Eds.), <<UML>> 2004 - The Unified Modelling Language. XIII, 454 pages. 2004.

Vol. 3271: J. Vicente, D. Hutchison (Eds.), Management of Multimedia Networks and Services. XIII, 335 pages. 2004.

Vol. 3270: M. Jeckle, R. Kowalczyk, P. Braun (Eds.), Grid Services Engineering and Management. X, 165 pages. 2004.

Vol. 3269: J. Lopez, S. Qing, E. Okamoto (Eds.), Information and Communications Security. XI, 564 pages. 2004.

Vol. 3266: J. Solé-Pareta, M. Smirnov, P.V. Mieghem, J. Domingo-Pascual, E. Monteiro, P. Reichl, B. Stiller, R.J. Gibbens (Eds.), Quality of Service in the Emerging Networking Panorama. XVI, 390 pages. 2004.

Vol. 3265: R.E. Frederking, K.B. Taylor (Eds.), Machine Translation: From Real Users to Research. XI, 392 pages. 2004. (Subseries LNAI).

Vol. 3264: G. Paliouras, Y. Sakakibara (Eds.), Grammatical Inference: Algorithms and Applications. XI, 291 pages. 2004. (Subseries LNAI).

Vol. 3263: M. Weske, P. Liggesmeyer (Eds.), Object-Oriented and Internet-Based Technologies. XII, 239 pages. 2004.

Vol. 3262: M.M. Freire, P. Chemouil, P. Lorenz, A. Gravey (Eds.), Universal Multiservice Networks. XIII, 556 pages. 2004.

Vol. 3261: T. Yakhno (Ed.), Advances in Information Systems. XIV, 617 pages. 2004.

Vol. 3260: I.G.M.M. Niemegeers, S.H. de Groot (Eds.), Personal Wireless Communications. XIV, 478 pages. 2004.

Vol. 3258: M. Wallace (Ed.), Principles and Practice of Constraint Programming – CP 2004. XVII, 822 pages. 2004.

Vol. 3257: E. Motta, N.R. Shadbolt, A. Stutt, N. Gibbins (Eds.), Engineering Knowledge in the Age of the Semantic Web. XVII, 517 pages. 2004. (Subseries LNAI).

Vol. 3256: H. Ehrig, G. Engels, F. Parisi-Presicce, G. Rozenberg (Eds.), Graph Transformations. XII, 451 pages. 2004.

Vol. 3255: A. Benczúr, J. Demetrovics, G. Gottlob (Eds.), Advances in Databases and Information Systems. XI, 423 pages. 2004.

Vol. 3254: E. Macii, V. Paliouras, O. Koufopavlou (Eds.), Integrated Circuit and System Design. XVI, 910 pages. 2004.

Vol. 3253: Y. Lakhnech, S. Yovine (Eds.), Formal Techniques, Modelling and Analysis of Timed and Fault-Tolerant Systems. X, 397 pages. 2004.

Vol. 3252: H. Jin, Y. Pan, N. Xiao, J. Sun (Eds.), Grid and Cooperative Computing - GCC 2004 Workshops. XVIII, 785 pages. 2004.

Vol. 3251: H. Jin, Y. Pan, N. Xiao, J. Sun (Eds.), Grid and Cooperative Computing - GCC 2004. XXII, 1025 pages. 2004.

Vol. 3250: L.-J. (LJ) Zhang, M. Jeckle (Eds.), Web Services. X, 301 pages. 2004.

Vol. 3249: B. Buchberger, J.A. Campbell (Eds.), Artificial Intelligence and Symbolic Computation. X, 285 pages. 2004. (Subseries LNAI).

Vol. 3246: A. Apostolico, M. Melucci (Eds.), String Processing and Information Retrieval. XIV, 332 pages. 2004.

Vol. 3245: E. Suzuki, S. Arikawa (Eds.), Discovery Science. XIV, 430 pages. 2004. (Subseries LNAI).

Vol. 3244: S. Ben-David, J. Case, A. Maruoka (Eds.), Algorithmic Learning Theory. XIV, 505 pages. 2004. (Subseries LNAI).

Vol. 3243: S. Leonardi (Ed.), Algorithms and Models for the Web-Graph. VIII, 189 pages. 2004.

Vol. 3242: X. Yao, E. Burke, J.A. Lozano, J. Smith, J.J. Merelo-Guervós, J.A. Bullinaria, J. Rowe, P. Tiño, A. Kabán, H.-P. Schwefel (Eds.), Parallel Problem Solving from Nature - PPSN VIII. XX, 1185 pages. 2004.

Vol. 3241: D. Kranzlmüller, P. Kacsuk, J.J. Dongarra (Eds.), Recent Advances in Parallel Virtual Machine and Message Passing Interface. XIII, 452 pages. 2004.

Vol. 3240: I. Jonassen, J. Kim (Eds.), Algorithms in Bioinformatics. IX, 476 pages. 2004. (Subseries LNBI).

Vol. 3239: G. Nicosia, V. Cutello, P.J. Bentley, J. Timmis (Eds.), Artificial Immune Systems. XII, 444 pages. 2004.

Vol. 3238: S. Biundo, T. Frühwirth, G. Palm (Eds.), KI 2004: Advances in Artificial Intelligence. XI, 467 pages. 2004. (Subseries LNAI).

Vol. 3236: M. Núñez, Z. Maamar, F.L. Pelayo, K. Pousttchi, F. Rubio (Eds.), Applying Formal Methods: Testing, Performance, and M/E-Commerce. XI, 381 pages. 2004.

Vol. 3235: D. de Frutos-Escrig, M. Nunez (Eds.), Formal Techniques for Networked and Distributed Systems – FORTE 2004. X, 377 pages. 2004.

Vol. 3232: R. Heery, L. Lyon (Eds.), Research and Advanced Technology for Digital Libraries. XV, 528 pages. 2004.

Vol. 3231: H.-A. Jacobsen (Ed.), Middleware 2004. XV, 514 pages. 2004.

Vol. 3230: J.L. Vicedo, P. Martínez-Barco, R. Muñoz, M. Saiz Noeda (Eds.), Advances in Natural Language Processing. XII, 488 pages. 2004. (Subseries LNAI).

Vol. 3229: J.J. Alferes, J. Leite (Eds.), Logics in Artificial Intelligence. XIV, 744 pages. 2004. (Subseries LNAI).

Vol. 3226: M. Bouzeghoub, C. Goble, V. Kashyap, S. Spaccapietra (Eds.), Semantics of a Networked World. XIII, 326 pages. 2004.

Vol. 3225: K. Zhang, Y. Zheng (Eds.), Information Security. XII, 442 pages. 2004.

Vol. 3224: E. Jonsson, A. Valdes, M. Almgren (Eds.), Recent Advances in Intrusion Detection. XII, 315 pages. 2004.

Vol. 3223: K. Slind, A. Bunker, G. Gopalakrishnan (Eds.), Theorem Proving in Higher Order Logics. VIII, 337 pages. 2004.

Vol. 3222: H. Jin, G.R. Gao, Z. Xu, H. Chen (Eds.), Network and Parallel Computing. XX, 694 pages. 2004.

Vol. 3221: S. Albers, T. Radzik (Eds.), Algorithms – ESA 2004. XVIII, 836 pages. 2004.

Vol. 3220: J.C. Lester, R.M. Vicari, F. Paraguaçu (Eds.), Intelligent Tutoring Systems. XXI, 920 pages. 2004.

Vol. 3219: M. Heisel, P. Liggesmeyer, S. Wittmann (Eds.), Computer Safety, Reliability, and Security. XI, 339 pages. 2004.

Vol. 3217: C. Barillot, D.R. Haynor, P. Hellier (Eds.), Medical Image Computing and Computer-Assisted Intervention – MICCAI 2004. XXXVIII, 1114 pages. 2004.

Vol. 3216: C. Barillot, D.R. Haynor, P. Hellier (Eds.), Medical Image Computing and Computer-Assisted Intervention – MICCAI 2004. XXXVIII, 930 pages. 2004.

Vol. 3215: M.G.. Negoita, R.J. Howlett, L.C. Jain (Eds.), Knowledge-Based Intelligent Information and Engineering Systems. LVII, 906 pages. 2004. (Subseries LNAI).

Vol. 3214: M.G.. Negoita, R.J. Howlett, L.C. Jain (Eds.), Knowledge-Based Intelligent Information and Engineering Systems. LVIII, 1302 pages. 2004. (Subseries LNAI).

Vol. 3213: M.G.. Negoita, R.J. Howlett, L.C. Jain (Eds.), Knowledge-Based Intelligent Information and Engineering Systems. LVIII, 1280 pages. 2004. (Subseries LNAI).

Vol. 3212: A. Campilho, M. Kamel (Eds.), Image Analysis and Recognition. XXIX, 862 pages. 2004.

Vol. 3211: A. Campilho, M. Kamel (Eds.), Image Analysis and Recognition. XXIX, 880 pages. 2004.

Vol. 3210: J. Marcinkowski, A. Tarlecki (Eds.), Computer Science Logic. XI, 520 pages. 2004.

Vol. 3209: B. Berendt, A. Hotho, D. Mladenic, M. van Someren, M. Spiliopoulou, G. Stumme (Eds.), Web Mining: From Web to Semantic Web. IX, 201 pages. 2004. (Subseries LNAI).

Vol. 3208: H.J. Ohlbach, S. Schaffert (Eds.), Principles and Practice of Semantic Web Reasoning. VII, 165 pages. 2004.

Vol. 3207: L.T. Yang, M. Guo, G.R. Gao, N.K. Jha (Eds.), Embedded and Ubiquitous Computing. XX, 1116 pages. 2004.

Vol. 3206: P. Sojka, I. Kopecek, K. Pala (Eds.), Text, Speech and Dialogue. XIII, 667 pages. 2004. (Subseries LNAI).

Vol. 3205: N. Davies, E. Mynatt, I. Siio (Eds.), UbiComp 2004: Ubiquitous Computing. XVI, 452 pages. 2004.

Vol. 3204: C.A. Peña Reyes, Coevolutionary Fuzzy Modeling. XIII, 129 pages. 2004.

Vol. 3203: J. Becker, M. Platzner, S. Vernalde (Eds.), Field Programmable Logic and Application. XXX, 1198 pages. 2004.

Vol. 3202: J.-F. Boulicaut, F. Esposito, F. Giannotti, D. Pedreschi (Eds.), Knowledge Discovery in Databases: PKDD 2004. XIX, 560 pages. 2004. (Subseries LNAI).

Vol. 3201: J.-F. Boulicaut, F. Esposito, F. Giannotti, D. Pedreschi (Eds.), Machine Learning: ECML 2004. XVIII, 580 pages. 2004. (Subseries LNAI).

Vol. 3199: H. Schepers (Ed.), Software and Compilers for Embedded Systems. X, 259 pages. 2004.

Vol. 3198: G.-J. de Vreede, L.A. Guerrero, G. Marín Raventós (Eds.), Groupware: Design, Implementation and Use. XI, 378 pages. 2004.

Vol. 3196: C. Stary, C. Stephanidis (Eds.), User-Centered Interaction Paradigms for Universal Access in the Information Society. XII, 488 pages. 2004.

Vol. 3195: C.G. Puntonet, A. Prieto (Eds.), Independent Component Analysis and Blind Signal Separation. XXIII, 1266 pages. 2004.

Vol. 3194: R. Camacho, R. King, A. Srinivasan (Eds.), Inductive Logic Programming. XI, 361 pages. 2004. (Subseries LNAI).